"Why be a Christian in this religiously pluralistic world? This book answers that question. Netland has deep knowledge of both the various religions of the world and of recent scholarly discussions of pluralism. His arguments are careful, incisive, and sensible. In addition, the book is faithfully Christian and helpful to the Christian community. I recommend the book highly to all who are interested in the problems of religious pluralism and Christian mission."

—**Stephen T. Davis**, Claremont McKenna College

"Not many thinkers are equally at home in John Hick, Alvin Plantinga, and the history of Buddhism, and fewer still are able to combine these interests with much else, as Harold Netland has, in a persuasive proposal about Christianity and the plural global scene. Clear but not simplistic, balanced but not anemic, gentle but not compromising, this volume demonstrates that an informed faith is well able to ground mission in today's world."

—**Stephen Williams**, Union Theological College, Ireland

"For several decades now, Netland's work has illuminated the path toward an evangelical theology of religions. In *Christianity and Religious Diversity*, Netland extends his analysis of religion and its intersection with culture, modernization, and globalization. With philosophical clarity, theological nuance, and interreligious sensitivity, Netland serves once again as a wise and faithful guide for followers of Jesus seeking to understand our religiously diverse world."

—**Paul Rhodes Eddy**, Bethel University

CHRISTIANITY
and RELIGIOUS
DIVERSITY

CLARIFYING CHRISTIAN COMMITMENTS
in a GLOBALIZING AGE

· · · · · · ● ● ⬤ ● ● · · · · ·

HAROLD A. NETLAND

B
Baker Academic
a division of Baker Publishing Group
Grand Rapids, Michigan

© 2015 by Harold A. Netland

Published by Baker Academic
a division of Baker Publishing Group
P.O. Box 6287, Grand Rapids, MI 49516-6287
www.bakeracademic.com

Printed in the United States of America

Library of Congress Cataloging-in-Publication Data
Netland, Harold A., 1955–
    Christianity and religious diversity : clarifying Christian commitments in a globalizing age
/ Harold A. Netland.
        pages cm
    Includes bibliographical references and index.
    ISBN 978-0-8010-3857-0 (pbk. : alk. paper)
    1. Christianity and other religions. I. Title. II. Title: Christianity and religious diversity.
BR127.N376 2015
261.2—dc23   2014049295

15   16   17   18   19   20   21   7   6   5   4   3   2   1

For Tite Tiénou

Friend
Colleague
Global Christian Statesman

Contents

Introduction

In his haunting 1971 classic song "Imagine," John Lennon invites us to consider a world without religion. Although Lennon assures us that imagining such a world is "easy if you try," this is not so easily done in the early twenty-first century. Religion, in one form or another, is inescapable in much of the world today, and it is difficult indeed to conceptualize our present world without the influences—positive and negative—of religion.

One cannot appreciate current events without having some understanding of the role of religious institutions, beliefs, and practices in societies throughout the world. The significance of religion today is acknowledged not only by religious studies specialists but also by political scientists, economists, military strategists, marketing specialists, the media, and business leaders. Although the numbers of atheists, agnostics, and the nonreligious are increasing, much of the world remains highly religious.[1]

Christian leaders in Asia and Africa have been aware of the importance of understanding other religious traditions for a long time, and Western missionaries generally have understood that effective ministry requires some grasp of the surrounding religious worldviews. Debates over contextualization of the gospel inevitably involve grappling with local religious concepts, institutions, and practices.[2] But the religious landscape of Europe and North America is rapidly changing, and among Western Christian leaders there also is growing

1. See Monica Duffy Toft, Daniel Pilpott, and Timothy Samuel Shah, *God's Century: Resurgent Religion and Global Politics* (New York: Norton, 2011); Todd M. Johnson and Brian J. Grim, *The World's Religions in Figures: An Introduction to International Religious Demography* (Oxford: Wiley-Blackwell, 2013).

2. Until relatively recently, many Western Christians have assumed that contextualization of the gospel is something that occurs only when Western missionaries take the gospel to non-Western

appreciation of the need for understanding other religious traditions. Christian theologians are increasingly addressing issues in the theology of religions as a regular part of their discipline. Given globalization, ordinary lay Christians find themselves interacting with religious others within their own neighborhoods, schools, and workplaces. Pastors and chaplains are finding that some understanding of other religions is essential for their ministries. Whereas it used to be possible for European or American Christians to leave questions about other religions to missionaries or religious studies specialists, this is no longer the case. Western societies are becoming more religiously diverse; with increasing globalization, questions about the relation between the Christian faith and other religious ways can no longer be ignored.

Despite the growing awareness of the importance of religion, however, there is often confusion over just what we mean by "religion" and how religious beliefs, values, and practices relate to other aspects of individual and communal life. Misunderstandings also arise concerning particular religions, such as Islam, and their relation to Christianity. Christian theologians, pastors, missiologists, and laypeople struggle with how they should think about and respond to other religious traditions. European and American societies are undergoing massive social, cultural, and religious changes, and many Christians are perplexed about how to make sense of the new realities.

In the chapters that follow, I explore some of the issues emerging from the increased awareness of religious diversity in the West. This is not a book on the theology of religions; elsewhere I have written on theological issues in the encounter with religious others.[3] But although not strictly an exercise in theology of religions, the discussion in these chapters is very relevant to theological debates about the religions. Current discussions in theology of religions are sometimes problematic because they are based on flawed understandings of the concept of religion itself, the relation between religion and culture, or the nature of particular religions such as Hinduism, Buddhism, or Islam. Responsible theology of religions requires more than simply sound biblical exegesis; it also demands proper understanding of the phenomena that go under the category of religion. In this sense, this book is an attempt to clarify certain basic concepts, to show how religions have been shaped by modernization and in turn adapted to it, and to explore some of the epistemological issues arising from Christians' new awareness of religious diversity.

---

cultures. Thankfully, there is growing appreciation of the fact that all cultures, including Western cultures, need appropriate contextualization of the gospel of Jesus Christ.

3. Harold A. Netland, *Encountering Religious Pluralism* (Downers Grove, IL: InterVarsity, 2001), chap. 10; Gerald R. McDermott and Harold A. Netland, *A Trinitarian Theology of Religions: An Evangelical Proposal* (New York: Oxford University Press, 2014).

This is not a comprehensive introduction to the subject of religion in the modern world. What follows is a highly selective treatment of some issues, especially as they relate to the theme of religious diversity in the modern world and the implications for Christian commitments. For many people in Europe and North America, the growing awareness of religious diversity and disagreement has made it more difficult to believe that there is one true religion and that Christianity is in fact the true religion. This is not the case with everyone: many Christians remain untroubled by religious diversity and experience few doubts about the truth of their beliefs. But many people, Christians and non-Christians alike, find the new realities deeply disturbing and question whether it makes any sense to claim that Jesus Christ is the one Lord and Savior for all peoples in all cultures at all times. One response to such questions is to become agnostic about all religious claims: how could we possibly know which religious tradition, if any, is true? Another popular response is to embrace some form of religious pluralism and maintain that, in spite of the obvious differences among the religions, they can all (or at least the "good" ones) be regarded as more or less equally true and effective ways of responding to the religious ultimate. This book is primarily addressing the cluster of issues associated with these responses.

The chapters in part 1 examine the concept of religion itself, as well as the idea of world religions such as Buddhism or Hinduism, and consider some ways in which our understanding of religion and the religions have been shaped by the processes of modernization and globalization. There is a complex but fascinating story to be told here, and understanding these developments can help us to avoid some problematic assumptions about religion today. Chapter 1 considers some recent debates over the concept of religion, issues in the definition of religion, and the relation of religion to culture. This sets out the conceptual framework for understanding religion that is adopted through succeeding chapters.

Ways in which the religions have been shaped by modernization and globalization are explored in chapter 2, with special attention being given to the much-debated notion of secularization. While classical secularization theory is now largely discredited, there are important ways in which societies and religions change with modernization and globalization. One effect of these transformations is that religious commitments are made with the awareness of other available options, resulting in epistemological uncertainty about one's own beliefs.

Today many think of the great world religions as unchanging, static entities simply passed on from ancient times to the present. Chapter 3 looks at Buddhism in the modern world, reporting ways in which it has adapted to modern, global realities. One of the by-products of the modern missionary movement and globalization is the fact that Jesus is now a global figure, adopted by many different religious traditions. Chapter 4 traces the theme of Jesus as one among many great religious leaders, showing how this is developed by Indian leaders in the Hindu Renaissance such as Mahatma Gandhi, the Western religious pluralist John Hick, and the Japanese novelist Shusaku Endo.

The chapters in part 2 are concerned with implications from the preceding discussion for Christian commitments. Chapters 5 through 7 pursue some of the philosophical issues stemming from our awareness of religious diversity while justifying our religious beliefs. The popular idea that all the major religions can somehow be accepted as true is shown to be untenable in chapter 5. What does it really mean to say that Christianity is the true religion? Some of the issues involved in such a claim are explored in chapter 6. Although I do not argue for its truth here, I clarify in what sense one might make such a claim and what might be involved in justifying it. Does awareness of religious disagreement and diversity require Christians to provide sufficient evidence for their own beliefs in order to be rational in so believing? This question takes us to the heart of some of the more controversial issues in religious epistemology. Various responses to the question are explored, and I offer my own conclusions about the place of reasons and evidence for belief in light of religious diversity. The final chapter briefly discusses how disciples of Jesus Christ should live and witness amid religiously diverse and pluralistic societies.

The issues addressed in this book have been with me for a long time. As a child of missionary parents in northern Japan, I was quite aware of religious differences between the small number of Japanese Christians in church with us on Sunday and the many other Japanese who frequented local Buddhist temples and Shinto shrines. Much later, as an adult living in Japan and teaching at a theological college, I had to address questions about the relation of Christianity to Japanese religious and cultural traditions. During my doctoral studies in philosophy, I had the privilege of studying under John Hick, who at the time was working on what later became *An Interpretation of Religion*, his version of religious pluralism.[4] My first book, *Dissonant Voices*, was an early attempt to respond to the issues raised by Hick.[5] Although I reject his model of religious pluralism, I have always felt that Hick had an unusually keen understanding of the epistemological issues raised by religious diversity.

4. John Hick, *An Interpretation of Religion: Human Responses to the Transcendent* (New Haven: Yale University Press, 1989; 2nd ed., 2004).
5. Harold A. Netland, *Dissonant Voices: Religious Pluralism and the Question of Truth* (Grand Rapids: Eerdmans, 1991).

Since 1993 I have been teaching at Trinity Evangelical Divinity School in Deerfield, Illinois, in two very different areas: philosophy of religion and missions / intercultural studies. While working with very different bodies of literature and keeping current in the debates in two distinct academic disciplines is certainly challenging, I have found the rewards of such interdisciplinary study to be very significant. The subject of this book in particular demands an interdisciplinary approach that draws upon history, intercultural studies, philosophy, and religious studies in addition to theology. I am grateful to Trinity for the opportunity to teach courses that encourage such interdisciplinary research and reflection. It is a privilege to be able to teach bright and thoughtful students, and the material in the following chapters has been discussed and debated in many classes at Trinity over the years.

I am indebted to many people who have helped me in my understanding of these issues. While I cannot mention everyone by name, a few should definitely be credited. I am grateful to the late John Hick for the privilege of studying with him and through his influence being forced to grapple with the epistemological questions prompted by religious diversity. In the past few years I have participated in some public discussions with Paul Knitter on religious pluralism. He has helped me to better understand the diversity among pluralists and also to think more carefully about some of my own positions.[6] I have also benefited from conversations on these issues with Tim Tennent, Richard Mouw, Gerald McDermott, Terry Muck, and many others. I am especially grateful to my colleagues Keith Yandell, Bob Priest, Tom McCall, Peter Cha, and my brother John Netland for carefully reading and commenting on earlier drafts of these chapters. Their advice has strengthened the argument throughout and prevented even greater deficiencies in the text than what remain.

Special thanks are also due to Jim Kinney of Baker Academic. Jim has been supportive of this project and patient in spite of numerous delays, and this book would not have been completed without his persistent encouragement.

Finally, portions of chapter 7 appeared in earlier form in my article "Natural Theology and Religious Diversity"[7] and are included here with permission of the journal editors.

---

6. The product of one such public discussion is *Can Only One Religion Be True? Paul Knitter and Harold Netland in Dialogue*, ed. Robert B. Stewart (Minneapolis: Fortress, 2013).

7. *Faith and Philosophy* 21.4 (October 2004): 501–18.

PART 1

Religion(s) in a Modern, Globalizing World

$=\!=$ 1 $=\!=$

Rethinking Religion(s)

Talk about religion in general or particular religions such as Islam or Hinduism is so common today that it is easy to assume we know just what we mean by these terms. But this is not necessarily the case. Although we do have a general sense of the meaning of "religion," trying to clarify just what religion is and how it differs from what is not religious can be perplexing. Confusion over meaning can result in problematic judgments in a variety of areas, from public policy debates to theological conclusions about other religions or even missiological experiments in contextualizing the gospel in diverse cultural settings. In this chapter we will try to clarify the concept of religion by examining issues in definition, the modern construction of the concept of religion, and the relation between the concepts of religion, worldview, and culture. We begin by considering two different ways of understanding religion: the theological and the phenomenological approaches.

Theological and Phenomenological Understandings of Religion

It is not unusual for Christians to make a distinction between religion and the Christian faith: while the beliefs and practices of Buddhists, Hindus, Muslims, and Daoists might exemplify religion, those of genuine Christians do not. After all, the Christian faith is not about religion at all; it is a relationship with the living God through Jesus Christ. Religion is about empty, meaningless rituals, whereas genuine Christian faith involves the gift of new life by God's grace.

But Christians are not the only ones to exempt their own commitments from the category of religion. Buddhists typically insist that Buddhism is not a religion, that it is a philosophy. Hindus deny that their practices and beliefs constitute religion; they are simply following a way of life rooted in the eternal dharma (Truth), or *sanatana*-dharma. Similarly, Daoists say they are simply living in accordance with the Dao (Way). And so on. It is not unusual for religious believers to regard their own beliefs and practices as exceptional.

It is true that being a disciple of Jesus Christ cannot be equated simply with joining the religion of Christianity. But acknowledging this does not settle the question whether being a follower of Jesus involves participating in religion. What we need is a clear understanding of the concept of religion and how being a disciple of Jesus is related to this concept. One approach to the issue is to characterize religion in explicitly Christian theological categories and themes. Religion in general, as well as particular religions, are then understood in terms of Christian values and teachings. This is often the approach taken by Christian theologians and missiologists, and it serves an important function. Thoughtful Christians trying to make sense of the world we live in need to develop a genuinely Christian perspective on the religions, and doing so requires use of Christian categories and themes.

Perhaps the most well-known Christian characterization of religion is that given by the great Swiss theologian Karl Barth: "The Revelation of God as the Abolition of Religion."[1] Based on a particular interpretation of this lengthy section in his *Church Dogmatics*, many readers have understood Barth as being very negative on the religions. In the English translation of the *Dogmatics*, Barth is presented as claiming that God's revelation in Jesus Christ results in the abolition of religion and that religion is to be rejected as unbelief. But recent studies have shown that Barth's views were actually more subtle and complex than initially presumed.[2]

1. Karl Barth, *The Doctrine of the Word of God*, vol. I/2 of *Church Dogmatics*, ed. G. W. Bromiley and T. F. Torrance (New York: Charles Scribner's Sons, 1956), 280–361 (see esp. paragraph 17). An earlier version of this section appeared in Gerald R. McDermott and Harold A. Netland, *A Trinitarian Theology of Religions: An Evangelical Proposal* (New York: Oxford University Press, 2014), 227–33.
2. See Peter Harrison, "Karl Barth and the Non-Christian Religions," *Journal of Ecumenical Studies* 23.2 (Spring 1986): 207–24; Garrett Green, "Challenging the Religious Studies Canon: Karl Barth's Theory of Religion," *Journal of Religion* 75 (1995): 473–86; J. A. Di Noia, "Religion and the Religions," in *The Cambridge Companion to Karl Barth*, ed. John Webster (Cambridge: Cambridge University Press, 2000), 243–57.

The English translation of Barth's *Dogmatics* rendered *Aufhebung der Religion* as "abolition of religion," but this has been criticized for missing the subtlety of Barth's position. Garrett Green suggests the term "sublation" instead of "abolition" as a more accurate rendering of Barth's position.[3] Barth's discussion actually contains a tension between God's revelation as the dissolution and the elevation of religion, something captured better in "sublation" than "abolition." Moreover, Barth also characterizes religion as *Unglaube*, a term usually translated as "unbelief." But Green argues that a better translation is "faithlessness" or "unfaith."[4] When seen in light of God's revelation, human religiosity is thus characterized by the lack of faith, or "an unwillingness to yield to the saving power of divine grace and revelation, and to surrender all those purely human attempts to know and satisfy God which together comprise human religion and religiosity."[5]

Barth's comments on religion are located within his broader discussion of the possibility of revelation in light of the work of the Holy Spirit. Barth begins this extensive section with a critique of the manner in which nineteenth- and early twentieth-century liberal theology placed the notion of religion—rather than God's revelation—at the center of theological inquiry. According to Barth, the result was an unhealthy "reversal of revelation and religion." Instead of interpreting religious expression in light of God's self-revelation in Jesus Christ, theologians interpret revelation in terms of religion.[6] Barth staunchly opposes any attempt to identify God's revelation with even the best in human civilization, as he believes that classical liberalism did. Di Noia states, "It is this reversal of revelation and religion that Barth laments and, in paragraph 17, endeavors to correct."[7] Barth declares,

> Revelation is God's self-offering and self-manifestation. Revelation encounters man on the presupposition and in confirmation of the fact that man's attempts to know God from his own standpoint are wholly and entirely futile; not because of any necessity in principle, but because of a practical necessity of fact. In revelation God tells man that He is God, and that as such He is his Lord. In telling him this, revelation tells him something utterly new, something which apart from revelation he does not know and cannot tell either himself or others.[8]

3. Green, "Challenging the Religious Studies Canon," 477. Peter Harrison proposes "superseding" as a better translation. Harrison, "Karl Barth and the Non-Christian Religions," 208n3.

4. Green, "Challenging the Religious Studies Canon," 480.

5. Di Noia, "Religion and the Religions," 250.

6. Barth, *Word of God*, 284.

7. Di Noia, "Religion and the Religions," 248.

8. Barth, *Word of God*, 301.

Thus, when religion—including empirical Christianity as manifest throughout history—is viewed in light of divine revelation, it is revealed as *Unglaube*, or faithlessness. But this is a judgment that can only be made in light of God's self-disclosure in Jesus Christ. "It is only by the revelation of God in Jesus Christ that we can characterize religion as idolatry and self-righteousness, and in this way show it to be unbelief [*Unglaube*]."[9]

Yet even as divine revelation negates religion, it also elevates or exalts religion. The term *Aufhebung* includes both poles of this dialectic. God's self-revelation does not totally eliminate or destroy religion. Barth states, "We do not need to delete or retract anything from the admission that in His revelation God is present in the world of human religion. But what we have to discern is that this means that *God* is present."[10] God's elevation of religion comes as God's gracious activity in Jesus Christ results in the Christian religion becoming the true religion. Barth was willing to speak of Christianity as the true religion, but not because of any inherent virtue in Christianity itself. We can only speak of Christianity as the true religion in the sense in which we speak of a "justified sinner."[11] Like a sinner justified by God's grace, the empirical religion of Christianity can become the true religion insofar as it is taken up by divine grace.

Barth's rich and provocative discussion deserves more extensive treatment than can be given here. For our purposes, the critical point is that methodologically he begins from the perspective of God's self-revelation in Jesus Christ, and in light of this all religions—including Christianity—are deficient.

This presents an important methodological issue for how we approach the study of religion: Should our understanding of religion come from careful observation of religious phenomena in the world around us? Or from God's authoritative self-revelation in Jesus Christ and Scripture? Or some combination of both? The Indian theologian D. T. Niles tells of a conversation with

9. Ibid., 314.
10. Ibid., 197.
11. Ibid., 325. In spite of Barth's strong Christocentrist understanding of revelation, he does acknowledge vestiges of divine revelation outside of Scripture, speaking of "other words" and "other lights":

> We recognize that the fact that Jesus Christ is the one Word of God does not mean that in the Bible, the Church and the world there are not other words which are quite notable in their way, other lights which are quite clear and other revelations which are quite real. . . . Nor does it follow from our statement that every word spoken outside the circle of the Bible and the Church is a word of false prophecy and therefore value-less, empty and corrupt, that all the lights which rise and shine in this outer sphere are misleading and all the revelations are necessarily untrue. (Karl Barth, *The Doctrine of Reconciliation*, vol. IV/3 of *Church Dogmatics*, trans. G. W. Bromiley [Edinburgh: T&T Clark, 1961], 97)

Karl Barth that illustrates the issue. In light of Barth's depiction of religion as *Unglaube*, Niles once asked Barth how many Hindus he had actually met. "None," Barth responded. "How then," asked Niles, "do you know that Hinduism is unbelief?" Barth replied, "A priori!"[12] The implication seems to be that a theological assessment of religions does not require empirical observation of actual religious beliefs and practices but can be deduced solely from God's revelation.[13]

One need not agree with Barth on all points to appreciate his insistence that, as Christians, we must understand human religiosity in light of God's definitive self-revelation in Jesus Christ. A Christian theology of religions must be shaped by biblical themes. But is Scripture *all* we need for understanding religion? Or, along with Scripture, do we also need skills enabling us to understand the religious dimension of people? It depends, once again, upon what we mean by "religion," and this can be illustrated by considering the definition of religion offered by another theologian, Paul Tillich.

Tillich famously defines religion as "the state of being grasped by an ultimate concern, a concern which qualifies all other concerns as preliminary and which itself contains the answer to the question of the meaning of life."[14] Tillich's definition has been used widely by both theologians and religious studies scholars. He captures nicely something important about religion, for religions do address matters of ultimate concern.

But Tillich's definition is so broad that it excludes very little from the religious domain, for virtually *everyone* has an ultimate concern of some kind; thus on this view everyone is religious. This has certain theological advantages, since many theologians insist that all people, even explicit atheists, are really inherently religious whether they acknowledge this or not. In other words, no one is neutral with respect to God; each person stands in some relation to God the Creator, even if it is a relation of rebellion or denial. Even those who deny God's reality are religious in their rebellion. As Johannes Blauw says, "A man without 'religion' is a contradiction in itself. . . . Man is 'uncurably [*sic*] religious' because his relation to God belongs to the very essence of

12. D. T. Niles, "Karl Barth—A Personal Memory," *South East Asia Journal of Theology* 11 (Autumn 1969): 10–11.

13. Although Barth's reply might suggest that he had no interest in actual religious practices, Barth was in fact well aware of other religions. In "The Revelation of God as the Abolition of Religion," Barth offers a perceptive discussion of the Pure Land tradition of Japanese Buddhism, pointing out clear parallels between aspects of Pure Land teachings and Protestant Christianity and even referring to Pure Land Buddhism as a "providential disposition." See *Word of God*, 340–44.

14. Paul Tillich, *Christianity and the Encounter of World Religions* (New York: Columbia University Press, 1963), 4.

man himself. Man is only man as man-before-God."[15] Similarly, J. H. Bavinck characterizes religion as a kind of response to God's revelation: "It is possible to believe that religion by its very nature is a response. . . . In his religion man feels that he is addressed by a supernatural power, that a god reveals and manifests himself to him. Religion is the human answer to divine, or at least allegedly divine, revelation. . . . Religion is by its very nature a communion, in which man answers and reacts to God's revelation."[16] As Bavinck himself acknowledges, this perspective presupposes that God exists and has revealed himself to humankind. As a response to God's self-revelation, then, religion can be either positive or negative. "Religion can be a profound and sincere seeking of God; it can also be a flight from God, an endeavor to escape from His presence, under the guise of love and obedient service. At the bottom of it lies a relationship, an encounter."[17]

As a Christian theological perspective about human beings being created by God and living in some kind of response to their Creator and Judge, this is undoubtedly correct, though incomplete. A more comprehensive theological explanation of religion would include, in addition to revelation, the biblical themes of creation, common grace, human sin and rebellion, and the influence of the demonic realm.[18] But notice two things about this perspective. First, in providing an explicitly Christian account of human religiosity, it presupposes the truth of Christian theism. Second, on Bavinck's view religion is something that applies to *all* human beings as creatures of God. Everyone, even a person who rejects religious affiliation, is inherently religious and manifests a basic orientation toward God, either of worship or rebellion. There is an important insight here, and any theology of religions that reflects the thrust of Scripture will need to incorporate this theme.

But is this sufficient for an understanding of religions? Definitions serve particular purposes, so it is important to clarify the purpose of a proposed definition of religion. As used in ordinary discourse, the word "religion" is a term of classification; it is intended to apply to certain things but not to others. Demographers distinguish those who are religious from those who are not; the Internal Revenue Service recognizes some organizations as religious for tax purposes but not others; and we might describe Aunt Maggie as

15. Johannes Blauw, "The Biblical View of Man in His Religion," in *The Theology of the Christian Mission*, ed. Gerald H. Anderson (New York: McGraw-Hill, 1961), 32.
16. J. H. Bavinck, *The Church between Temple and Mosque: A Study of the Relationship between the Christian Faith and Other Religions* (Grand Rapids: Eerdmans, 1966), 18–19.
17. Ibid., 19.
18. These themes are incorporated into a theological account of religion in Harold A. Netland, *Encountering Religious Pluralism* (Downers Grove, IL: InterVarsity, 2001), chap. 10; and McDermott and Netland, *Trinitarian Theology of Religions*.

"devoutly religious," while we say Cousin Jimmy is "agnostic." If "religion" is being used descriptively to pick out certain realities but not others, or to refer to some ways of living as opposed to others, then Tillich's definition is not helpful, for it includes too much. Is religion a category that applies to all human beings or just to a subset of humankind?

Even if we adopt the theological point that all people—even those who explicitly deny God's reality—stand in some relation to God, there is still the empirical question of whether "religious" is a useful category for identifying some groups but not others. As we observe how people live, there is an important distinction to be made, for example, between (1) those who believe in an eternal Creator who has revealed himself to us, whether in the Bible or in the Qur'an, and who try to live in accordance with this conviction, and (2) those who believe that this life is all there is and that there is nothing beyond the physical world to which we are accountable. These are two very different ways of living and understanding reality, and we need some way to distinguish these groups. The word "religious" is useful in referring to the former group but not the latter. Here "religion" is being used in a descriptive or phenomenological sense, not in a theological sense.

Whether we should adopt a theological or a phenomenological definition of religion will depend upon the purposes of the definition. If the intent is to provide an explanation or account of religious phenomena from an explicitly Christian perspective, then a theological understanding of religion derived from Scripture and Christian theological resources is necessary. But notice that even an explicitly theological explanation presupposes the logically more basic phenomenological understanding of religion. Since a theological account provides a Christian understanding of what we observe in the religions, it is crucial that the theological definition accurately reflects actual religious beliefs and practices. An adequate theological perspective on religion requires not only faithfulness to the biblical witness but also an accurate description of the institutions, beliefs, and practices of religious people. Otherwise the theological account is misapplied. If, for example, we are to have an adequate theological account of Chinese ancestral practices, then we need not only an understanding of the relevant biblical and theological teachings but also an accurate portrayal of the practices themselves—what they are and their significance for the participants. So a theological definition of religion actually presupposes a phenomenological understanding of religion. One obtains a reliable descriptive or phenomenological perspective from careful observation of the lived realities of actual religious communities. In what follows we will be concerned primarily not with a theological account of religion but rather with an empirical, phenomenological, or descriptive understanding of religion as we encounter it among diverse human communities.

"Religion" and "World Religions"

When people in the West think about religion, it is usually in terms of the so-called world religions—Christianity, Judaism, Islam, Hinduism, Buddhism, and perhaps Daoism and Confucianism. Some of the more popular courses in universities are those that introduce the world religions. We are so accustomed to the designation "world religions" that it might come as a surprise to learn that this is a modern category.

The first use of the English term "world religions" was in C. P. Tiele's article "Religions" in the 1885 (9th) edition of the *Encyclopedia Britannica*.[19] We commonly think of Buddhism as a world religion today, but the idea of Buddhism as a particular religion found throughout Asia developed in the early nineteenth century. Philip Almond argues that it was only in the 1820s and 1830s, with the British encounter with Asian Buddhists scattered throughout the British Empire, that Europeans came to think of the distinctive rituals, institutions, beliefs, and narratives among followers of the Buddha in various parts of Asia as comprising a single religion: Buddhism.[20] Islam was already recognized by some as a world religion, although others still thought of it simply as the religion of the Arabs. But by the early decades of the twentieth century, the idea of a half-dozen major world religions was taking hold, so that theologian Ernst Troeltsch's 1923 essay "The Place of Christianity among the World Religions" identifies Christianity, Judaism, Islam, Buddhism, Zoroastrianism, and Confucianism as "the great world religions."[21]

Tomoko Masuzawa observes that the designation "world religions" presupposes that there is something identifiable as religion, "a genus comprising many species, and that Christianity, for example, is but one of them."[22] Both the idea of world religions and the notion of a general category of religion, with many particular varieties identified as the religions of the world, are modern developments. Kim Knott states, "Scholars are generally in agreement that 'religion' is a historical and scholarly construct."[23]

19. Tomoko Masuzawa, "World Religions," *Encyclopedia of Religion*, ed. Lindsay Jones, 2nd ed. (New York: Thomson Gale, 2005), 14:9800, 9802.

20. Philip C. Almond, *The British Discovery of Buddhism* (Cambridge: Cambridge University Press, 1988), 8–12.

21. Ernst Troeltsch, "The Place of Christianity among the World Religions," in *Christianity and Other Religions: Selected Readings*, ed. John Hick and Brian Hebblethwaite (Philadelphia: Fortress, 1980), 19.

22. Masuzawa, "World Religions," 9800.

23. Kim Knott, "How to Study Religion in the Modern World," in *Religions in the Modern World: Traditions and Transformations*, ed. Linda Woodhead, Hiroko Kawanami, and Christopher Partridge, 2nd ed. (London: Routledge, 2009), 16. See, e.g., Tomoko Masuzawa, *The Invention of World Religions: Or, How European Universalism Was Preserved in the Language*

This might strike many as strange. After all, it is not as though recent schol-ars invented the idea that people pray, worship in churches or temples, or offer sacrifices to the spirits of ancestors. People throughout history have expressed beliefs in God or gods, have prayed and meditated, and have regarded various texts as sacred or divinely inspired. Kevin Schilbrack has helpfully delineated the "religion as a modern construct" discourse into three distinct claims. The first is that the term "religion" is a modern, social construct. "Whether or not religion has always existed, critics say, the concept *religion* is a relatively recent invention. According to them, the concept of 'a' religion as a particular system of beliefs embodied in a bounded community was largely unknown prior to the seventeenth century, and the concept of 'religion' as a generic something which different cultures (or all cultures) share was not thought until the nineteenth century."[24] The second claim is that the term "religion" distorts the cultural phenomena on which it is imposed. The term is problematic because "it is not and cannot be culturally neutral but rather carries with it connotations derived from its modern, Western, Christian origins." Rather than a category that reflects accurately the patterns found among peoples outside European Christendom, the modern concept of religion carries with it meanings derived from Christian history. And the third claim follows upon the second: the mod-ern construction of "religion" is not an innocent activity but is ideologically motivated and "serves the purposes of modern western power."[25] The impli-cation of the claims taken together is "that if religion is socially constructed, then religion is not a thing in the world but rather a product of the Western

---

of Pluralism (Chicago: University of Chicago Press, 2005); Talal Asad, *Genealogies of Religion: Discipline and Reasons of Power in Christianity and Islam* (Baltimore: Johns Hopkins University Press, 1993); Brent Nongbri, *Before Religion: A History of a Modern Concept* (New Haven: Yale University Press, 2013); Jason Ananda Josephson, *The Invention of Religion in Japan* (Chicago: University of Chicago Press, 2012); Guy G. Stroumsa, *A New Science: The Discovery of Religion in the Age of Reason* (Cambridge, MA: Harvard University Press, 2010); S. N. Balagangadhara, *"The Heathen in His Blindness . . .": Asia, the West and the Dynamic of Religion* (Leiden: Brill, 1994); Timothy Fitzgerald, *The Ideology of Religious Studies* (New York: Oxford University Press, 2000); Daniel Dubuisson, *The Western Construction of Religion: Myths, Knowledge, and Reality* (Baltimore: Johns Hopkins University Press, 2003).

24. Kevin Schilbrack, "Religions: Are There Any?," *Journal of the American Academy of Religion* 78.4 (December 2010): 1113–14.

25. Ibid., 1115. This criticism is part of the larger critique of Orientalism and its depiction of non-Western peoples and cultures. The seminal work here is Edward Said, *Orientalism* (New York: Vintage, 1978). For Said, Orientalism signifies "the complicity between Western academic accounts of the nature of 'the Orient' and the hegemonic political agendas of West-ern imperialism" (83). Said's thesis was that the depiction of "the East" by modern European scholars is not the strictly objective, scientific, and factual portrayal that Western scholars presume it to be; rather, it is both inaccurate in its portrayal and serves colonialist agendas by controlling, marginalizing, and subjugating Eastern realities to the supposedly superior Western realities.

imagination. This use of language distorts what it describes and is ideologically motivated to be pejorative towards nonwestern cultures."[26]

Properly qualified, there is truth in this critique. In thinking about religion
globally, we need especially to be careful about imposing meanings from
European and American experiences with Christianity onto other ways
of thinking and behaving. Having a sacred, authoritative text (the Bible)
is central to Christianity but is not so important in some other religious
traditions. Doctrines and beliefs are crucial to Christian faith but not so
significant in Shinto. And it is true that some Europeans and Americans used
the notion of religion, with Christianity as the highest form of religion, as
a way of contrasting the supposed virtues of Christian/Western civilization
with the vices of people in Asia, Africa, and Latin America. But the issues
here are complex, and the critique needs to be carefully qualified. We will
focus upon the first claim about the social construction of the modern notion of religion, and I will argue that although there is an important sense
in which this claim is true, it does not necessarily follow that the idea of
religion is inapplicable or should be abandoned. Properly qualified, it is an
important and useful category for helping us understand aspects of collective human behavior.[27]

Growing Awareness of Religious Others

The modern understanding of religion and the religions developed within the
context of the emerging European awareness of two sets of binary oppositions: first, the growing distinction between Christianity (or Christendom)
in Europe and "secular" domains of intellectual and social life; and second,
the distinction between Christianity and what increasingly became known
as "other religions." Increased awareness of difference in both cases is, of
course, part of the historical narrative of the modern era, a period emerging
about the sixteenth century in Europe and coinciding with the subsequent

26. Schilbrack, "Religions: Are There Any?," 1116.
27. "Religion" is not the only concept in the field of religious studies that is a modern construct.
Peter van der Veer claims that "spirituality" also is "a modern Western concept, like 'religion,'
'magic,' and 'secularity.'" He notes that there is no equivalent term in either Sanskrit or Chinese
and that "despite the ubiquitous reference to India and China (and indeed Asia) as 'spiritual,'
spirituality is a modern, Western term." Like "religion," the term "spirituality" is notoriously
difficult to define. Van der Veer argues that "the spiritual and the secular are produced simultaneously as two connected alternatives to institutionalized religion in Euro-American modernity."
Peter van der Veer, *The Modern Spirit of Asia: The Spiritual and the Secular in China and India*
(Princeton: Princeton University Press, 2014), 35–36.

global expansion of European and American interests.[28] Thus, Brent Nongbri observes, "What is modern about the ideas of 'religions' and 'being religious' is the isolation and naming of some things as 'religious' and others as 'not religious.'"[29] The idea of religion as a distinctive sphere of collective human life is thus related to that of secularization, which will be considered in chapter 2.

The development of the concept of religion, and of particular religions such as Hinduism or Buddhism, was part of the European (and later, American) effort to come to grips with the diverse ways of living for peoples in Asia, Africa, and the Americas. But given the ongoing interactions between Western colonizers and colonized peoples, the concept cannot be restricted to Western discourse since it also becomes part of the intellectual currency of Asians, Africans, and Latin Americans in their efforts at self-definition. In this way the modern concept of religion is globalized. José Casanova points out the links between the modern understandings of religion with the notion of the secular and the processes of globalization. He observes that "one of the most important global trends is the globalization of the category of 'religion' itself and of the binary classification of reality, 'religious/secular,' that it entails." In other words, "'religion' as a discursive reality, indeed, as an abstract category and as a system of classifications of reality, used by modern individuals as well as by modern societies across the world, by religious as well as by secular authorities, has become an undisputable global social fact."[30]

To appreciate the modern developments, we must remind ourselves of the situation in premodern Europe. The relation between Christians and "religious others" changed from the fourth century onward, as Christianity was transformed from a small, minority sect into the dominant religion of

28. Although the modern concept of religion is primarily a product of changes within Europe and the Western encounter with Asian religious traditions, it was also shaped by developments in India, China, and Japan as these nations reacted against the challenges posed by modernization, colonialism, and Christian missions. A particularly fascinating example is found in the ways in which early modern Japan, during the Meiji Era (1867–1912), struggled with the place of religion in the new social order. Emerging from over two centuries of self-imposed isolation from the rest of the world in the 1860s, Japan launched an ambitious program of modernization, including attempts to adopt European and American patterns of distinguishing religion from civil authorities. Although by the turn of the century there was a clear alignment between the Japanese state and Shinto, there were vigorous debates in the preceding decades over the nature of religion (*shukyo*) and whether the state should be secular and kept distinct from religious traditions. See Trent E. Maxey, *The "Greatest Problem": Religion and State Formation in Meiji Japan* (Cambridge, MA: Harvard University Press, 2014); Helen Hardacre, *Shinto and the State: 1868–1988* (Princeton: Princeton University Press, 1989).

29. Nongbri, *Before Religion*, 4.

30. José Casanova, "The Secular, Secularizations, Secularisms," in *Rethinking Secularism*, ed. Craig Calhoun, Mark Juergensmeyer, and Jonathan VanAntwerpen (New York: Oxford University Press, 2011), 62.

the empire. As institutional Christianity became increasingly identified with the social, political, and intellectual centers of power, other religious beliefs and practices were marginalized and condemned as heretical. Western European society became religiously more homogenized, and throughout the Middle Ages there was little knowledge of the enormous religious diversity in the rest the world. Medieval Europeans thought in terms of four basic religious categories—Christians, Jews, Muslims, and pagans—with the latter category covering everyone not included in the first three.[31] In some areas in the Middle East, there was extensive interaction between Christians and Muslims, as Muslims conquered land occupied by Christians.[32] Most European Christians, however, lived without direct acquaintance with adherents of other religions.

But everything changed for Europeans after 1492 and the ensuing voyages of discovery, as the bewildering diversity of human cultures became evident. Traditional ways of thinking were challenged as explorers, diplomats, and missionaries sent back a steady stream of reports detailing the strange habits of newly encountered peoples. With the increase of new information, efforts were made to understand and explain the ways of living of those in Africa, the Americas, India, China, and the islands of the Pacific. Early understandings of culture and religion developed out of these explanations. The idea of religion as a distinct domain of social life, and that there are significant differences among peoples' religious beliefs and practices, became widely accepted. The notion of religion developed in parallel with the idea of culture, another modern concept intended to help us understand differences among various peoples.

It is common to locate the beginning of the academic or "scientific" study of religion in the late nineteenth and early twentieth centuries. Guy Stroumsa, however, argues persuasively that the modern study of religion actually originated in the sixteenth century and that at least three major historical events were necessary for this development. "The first was the Great Discoveries, initially of the Americas and then South and East Asia, which provided the laboratories where new categories were invented by Spanish and Italian missionaries to describe and analyze hitherto unknown phenomena." The second major event was the Renaissance, with its renewed interest in antiquity and the development of modern philology. The third "impetus for the new science" was the devastating wars of religion in Western Europe following the Reformation.

31. Eric J. Sharpe, "The Study of Religion in Historical Perspective," in *The Routledge Companion to the Study of Religion*, ed. John R. Hinnells (London: Routledge, 2005), 25.
32. See esp. Sidney H. Griffith, *The Church in the Shadow of the Mosque: Christians and Muslims in the World of Islam* (Princeton: Princeton University Press, 2008).

For many scholars, Catholic and Protestant, the claim of their own faith to express divine truth had lost much of its persuasive force. The violent and painful divisions of Christendom had cast doubt on the validity of Christianity itself. As anyone could see, the Turks, those followers of the "false prophet" Muhammad, showed a much more tolerant attitude toward Christian, Jewish, and sectarian "outsiders" than did Christian authorities toward "outsiders" throughout Europe. This questioning of one's own Christian faith, with its universal pretensions, was a major incentive toward the new understanding of religions as reflecting, rather than perennial truth, the values of the specific society in which they blossomed.[33]

Beginning in the sixteenth century, reports from explorers, merchants, and missionaries stimulated widespread interest in the cultural and religious practices of peoples around the world. Books and pamphlets describing the new lands were devoured by curious readers in Europe. Stroumsa states, "The newly discovered continents and cultures were slowly becoming part of the 'cultural landscape,' or what the French call the *imaginaire*, of European intellectuals. . . . This new knowledge of the diverse religions practiced around the world entailed the urgent need to redefine religion as a universal phenomenon, with a strong emphasis on ritual, rather than on beliefs."[34]

One of the more remarkable publications of this time is *Cérémonies et coutumes religieuses de tous les peuples du monde* [Religious ceremonies and customs of the peoples of the world], by Bernard Picart and Jean Frederic Bernard, published between 1723 and 1737 in seven volumes of over 3,000 pages. The book provides a sweeping survey of the religious traditions known to Europeans in the early 1700s, combining careful descriptions of practices among Jews, various Christian groups, Africans, Hindus in India, the Incas, the Japanese, Native Americans, Muslims, and others, with detailed engravings depicting such rituals by the famed engraver Bernard Picart. The book "marked a major turning point in European attitudes toward religious belief." For it

> sowed the radical idea that religions could be compared on equal terms, and therefore that all religions were equally worthy of respect—and criticism. It turned belief in one unique, absolute, and God-given truth into "religion," that is, into individualized ceremonies and customs that reflected the truths relative to each people and culture. This global survey of religious practices effectively disaggregated and delimited the sacred, making it specific to time, place, and institutions. Once labeled in time and place, religion became not an

33. Stroumsa, *A New Science*, 5–6.
34. Ibid., 3.

unchanging system of beliefs but a discrete entity concerned everywhere with the gods or the heavenly.[35]

Religious Ceremonies and Customs was widely read not only by intellectuals but also by ordinary citizens curious about the new worlds.

There is some irony in the fact that religious studies as an academic discipline developed in part on the basis of the extensive reports by Christian missionaries—as well as travelers and administrators in the expanding colonialist empires—in Asia, Latin America, and Africa.[36] Early missionaries were often careful ethnographers, recording rich descriptions of the people among whom they lived and ministered. They also served as brokers between the old and new worlds, not only translating the Bible into local languages but also making available the sacred texts of other religions in European languages. But as modern religious studies became an established academic discipline within the university, the relation between it and theologians or missiologists became strained as each group regarded the other with suspicion. Religious studies scholars, as they pursued the allegedly "objective" study of religion, were especially critical of theological judgments about religious beliefs and practices made by theologians. Theologians and missiologists, in turn, rejected the reductionistic naturalism that seemed to govern religious studies. Our contemporary concept of religion is thus to some extent an innovation that emerged with the dissolution of Christendom in Europe, the growing secularization of European societies, the growing awareness of religious diversity worldwide, and the repercussions from European colonialism and Christian missionary activity in Asia.

Hinduism as a Modern Construct

The idea that religion is a modern construct is perhaps most apparent in the case of Hinduism and India. Hinduism is typically treated in textbooks as one of the major world religions. But the idea of Hinduism as a distinct religion is a modern notion that developed within the context of the encounter between India and the West during the eighteenth and nineteenth centuries. Scholars typically point to the role of British Orientalist scholars and administrators, missionary interest in Indian religious texts, and use of the census

35. Lynn Hunt, Margaret C. Jacob, and Wijnand Mijnhardt, *The Book That Changed Europe: Picart and Bernard's "Religious Ceremonies of the World"* (Cambridge, MA: Harvard University Press, 2010), 1–2.
36. Eric J. Sharpe, *Comparative Religion: A History* (LaSalle, IL: Open Court, 1986), 144–45.

to identify as Hindu all Indians who were not Muslim, Christian, Sikh, or Zoroastrian as encouraging the idea that Hindus comprise a distinct and cohesive religious group. Geoffrey Oddie reports, "It is now well established that the terms 'Hindu' and 'Hinduism' were categories invented by outsiders in an attempt to interpret and explain the complexities they found in Indian religious and social life."[37] The word "Hindu" was originally the Persian variant of the Sanskrit *sindhu*, referring to the Indus River. The early use of the term was primarily as a geographical concept, designating everything native to India, and it carried no particular religious significance. Thus, in the early nineteenth century, long after the arrival of the British East India Company, "it was still not uncommon for references to be made to 'Hindoo Christians' and 'Hindoo Muslims' as distinct from those who were not native-born or culturally indigenous to the subcontinent."[38]

But in the nineteenth century the term "Hindu" took on distinctively religious meanings, and "Hinduism" was introduced as a term designating India's native religion (singular). Perhaps the earliest use of "Hindoo" and "Hindooism" by a Westerner as designating a religious system was by Charles Grant in a letter in 1787.[39] The Baptist missionary William Ward in Serampore similarly spoke of "Hindooism," "the Hindoo system," and "the Hindoo superstition" in 1801.[40] Oddie suggests that the first person to use "Hinduism" to denote some kind of coherent religious system was the Indian social and religious reformer Rammohan Roy (1772–1833), who used the term in English publications in 1816.[41] The term "Hinduism" became increasingly adopted in English publications by missionaries and Indians in the 1820s and 1830s, with the former using it as a negative contrast to Christianity whereas the latter held it up as a positive alternative to the religion of British colonialists.[42]

37. See Geoffrey A. Oddie, "Constructing 'Hinduism': The Impact of the Protestant Missionary Movement on Hindu Self-Understanding," in *Christians and Missionaries in India: Cross-Cultural Communication Since 1500*, ed. Robert Eric Frykenberg (Grand Rapids: Eerdmans, 2003), 156.

38. Robert Eric Frykenberg, "Constructions of Hinduism at the Nexus of History and Religion," *Journal of Interdisciplinary History* 23.3 (Winter 1993): 525.

39. Will Sweetman, "Unity and Plurality: Hinduism and the Religions of India in Early European Scholarship," *Religion* 31 (2001): 209. I am grateful to Professor Peter Vethanayagamony for calling my attention to this essay.

40. Oddie, "Constructing 'Hinduism,'" 156–57.

41. Ibid., 162.

42. The modern construction of the concept of religion or of Hinduism as a religion was not simply a matter of Europeans and Americans imposing a concept from the outside upon Indians, Chinese, or Japanese. As van der Veer observes, "It is not possible to see the transformation of concepts like religion as the passive reception of Western categories in the rest of the world. Indians and Chinese are actively involved in this transformation, as are Europeans and Americans" (*Modern Spirit of Asia*, 29–30).

The story of this term's transformation in meaning is as fascinating as it is complex and includes the contributions of at least four distinct groups, each with its own agenda in shaping India's social, cultural, and religious identity: the British colonial administrators, some of whom were also accomplished linguists and scholars of Indian history; the Indian elite who assisted the British in administering India; Western missionaries; and Indian intellectuals who were both active in the anti-British movement for Indian independence and reformers of the ancient Brahmanic religious traditions.[43] "Hinduism" became a general category for the religious traditions of India that were not Islamic, Christian, Sikh, Zoroastrian, Jain, or Buddhist. Despite the bewildering variety of popular religious and philosophical traditions in this category, it became common to use "Hinduism" in speaking of an allegedly indigenous, "coherent, comprehensive, and unified religious system that could be compared to other systems such as Christianity and Islam."[44] Hinduism was characterized in terms of India's ancient Brahmanic traditions rooted in the Vedic scriptures and, under the influence of modern Indian intellectuals such as Swami Vivekananda (1863–1902) and Sarvepalli Radhakrishnan (1888–1975) as well as those in the West captivated by images of the "exotic East," it became especially identified with the esoteric mysticism and monism of the Advaita Vedanta tradition.[45] More recently, radical nationalists associated with the *Hindutva* movement have tried to define Hinduism in terms of ancient indigenous religious traditions inextricably linked to the land of India, so that to be authentically Indian is to be Hindu. Christians and Muslims are by definition, then, not authentically Indian.[46]

Reification of Religion and the Religions

The criticism that our concept of religion is a modern social construct takes several forms, but a common theme throughout is the charge that to speak

43. See Frykenberg, "Constructions of Hinduism at the Nexus of History and Religion"; Peter van der Veer, *Imperial Encounters: Religion and Modernity in India and Britain* (Princeton: Princeton University Press, 2001); Brian K. Pennington, *Was Hinduism Invented? Britons, Indians, and the Colonial Construction of Religion* (New York: Oxford University Press, 2005).
44. Geoffrey A. Oddie, "Constructing 'Hinduism,'" 155.
45. See Richard King, *Orientalism and Religion: Postcolonial Theory, India and "The Mystic East"* (London: Routledge, 1999), chap. 6; Jyotirmaya Sharma, *A Restatement of Religion: Swami Vivekananda and the Making of Hindu Nationalism* (New Haven: Yale University Press, 2013).
46. See "Hindutva: Vinayak Damodar Savarkar and the Rise of Hindu Nationalism," in *Hinduism: A Reader*, ed. Deepak Sarma (Oxford: Blackwell, 2008), 373–90; C. Ram-Prasad, "Contemporary Political Hinduism," in *The Blackwell Companion to Hinduism*, ed. Gavin Flood (Oxford: Blackwell, 2003), 526–50.

of religion in general or about religions such as Hinduism or Buddhism is to engage in the reification of religion. "Religion" and "Hinduism" are said to be reified concepts in that they give the impression of categories with neat, clear boundaries that refer to concrete realities in the world when in fact no such entities exist. Critics claim that reification is found in the tendency to think of religion as a clearly defined, transhistorical, and transcultural category, a genus of which there are many species—such as Islam, Hinduism, Christianity, and Buddhism. What is especially objectionable is the idea that there is a common "essence" that defines religion, so that all particular religions partake of this essence of religion.

One of the major reasons given for maintaining that our modern notion of religion is a modern construct comes from etymology. Scholars point out that the languages of the ancient world did not have terms corresponding to the meaning of "religion" today, nor did they have terms denoting distinct religions such as Hinduism or Judaism or Buddhism.[47] For example, ancient Greek and Latin did not have single terms that carried the same meanings as the English word "religion" does today. "Religion" is often said to be derived from the Latin *religio* or *religari*, but neither word carried the same meaning as "religion" does today. There was no Greek equivalent for the Latin *religio*.[48]

Until the modern era, moreover, non-Western languages generally have not had equivalent words for the English term "religion." Eric Sharpe states, "In recent years, where non-western traditions have thought in 'religious' terms, they have done so through the medium of some European language. A Hindu writing in English may be happy enough to speak of 'religion': in Sanskrit, Hindi, or Tamil he must use words having a different connotation."[49] The Sanskrit term normally used in these contexts is "dharma," which can be translated into English as "truth," "duty," "law," "order," or "right." Similarly, the Japanese term for "religion" today is *shukyo*, but it was only around 1873 that it was adopted as the Japanese translation for "religion."[50] *Shukyo* is a modern term, influenced by late nineteenth-century debates over the "scientific" study of religion in Europe and America, and it carries connotations somewhat foreign to traditional Japanese approaches to religious practices.

47. See esp. Nongbri, *Before Religion*, chaps. 2–4.
48. On developments in meaning of *religio*, see Peter Henrici, "The Concept of Religion from Cicero to Schleiermacher," in *Catholic Engagement with World Religions: A Comprehensive Study*, ed. Karl J. Becker and Ilaria Morali (Maryknoll, NY: Orbis Books, 2010), 1–20.
49. Eric J. Sharpe, *Understanding Religion* (New York: St. Martin's Press, 1983), 39.
50. Robert Kisala, "Japanese Religions," *Nanzan Guide to Japanese Religions*, ed. Paul L. Swanson and Clark Chilson (Honolulu: University of Hawaii Press, 2006), 4.

[*Shukyo*] is a derived word that came into prominence in the nineteenth century as a result of Japanese encounters with the West and particularly with Christian missionaries, to denote a concept and view of religion commonplace in the realm of nineteenth-century Christian theology but at that time not found in Japan, of religion as a specific, belief-framed entity. The term *shukyo*, thus, in origin at least, implies a separation of that which is religious from other aspects of society and culture, and contains implications of belief and commitment to one order or movement—something that has not been traditionally a common factor in Japanese religious behaviour and something that tends to exclude many of the phenomena involved in the Japanese religious process.[51]

According to Jason Josephson, the Japanese term *shukyo* was then exported to China and Korea and translated into Chinese and Korean, with the result that "Japanese interpretations of 'religion' influenced the conceptual reorganization of national traditions across the region."[52] Anna Sun notes that "the [Chinese] term *jiao* did not acquire its current usage as 'religion' until the turn of the twentieth century."[53] The term had been used as early as the ninth century in *sanjiao* (three teachings) to refer to Buddhist, Confucian, and Daoist teachings, but there it has the meaning of teachings and not of religion as we use the term today.

One of the most significant early works calling for rethinking our modern understanding of "religion" and "the religions" is Wilfred Cantwell Smith's *The Meaning and End of Religion* (1962).[54] Smith, a historian and Islamicist, argues that the notion of "religion" as a distinct entity—and especially of "the religions" (plural)—is a modern confusion that ought to be abandoned. He states, for example, "There are Hindus but there is no Hinduism."[55] Smith was especially concerned to refute the notion that specific religions are distinct, abstract entities with unchanging essences that somehow exist apart from the internal faith commitments of religious individuals. "Neither religion in general nor any one of the religions, I will contend, is in itself an intelligible entity, a valid object of inquiry or of concern either for the scholar or for the man of faith."[56] Smith is not denying that there are identifiable religious rituals and beliefs characterizing particular communities and that there are important differences among religious groups. But what he does reject is the idea that

51. Ian Reader, *Religion in Contemporary Japan* (London: Macmillan, 1991), 13–14.
52. Josephson, *Invention of Religion in Japan*, x (see also 7). See also Jun'ichi Isomae, "Deconstructing 'Japanese Religion,'" *Japanese Journal of Religious Studies* 32.2 (2005): 235–48.
53. Anna Sun, *Confucianism as a World Religion: Contested Histories and Contemporary Realities* (Princeton: Princeton University Press, 2013), 23.
54. Wilfred Cantwell Smith, *The Meaning and End of Religion* (New York: Harper & Row, 1962).
55. Ibid., 65.
56. Ibid., 12.

there is an unchanging essence of Hinduism as a religion and especially that this consists in certain beliefs or doctrines.

Smith makes an important distinction between what he calls the external "cumulative tradition" of particular religious communities and the inner faith of individual adherents.[57] The cumulative tradition is formed over time and includes religious buildings, sacred scriptures, doctrines, moral codes, rituals, legal and social institutions, in short, "anything that can be and is transmitted from one person, one generation, to another, and that an historian can observe."[58] It is significant that Smith includes religious beliefs as part of the cumulative tradition.

Although most people emphasize the cumulative tradition, Smith argues that far more important is the inner faith of religious individuals. Faith, for Smith, is logically prior to beliefs and is an intensely personal disposition to follow God that finds expression within the broader life of a religious community. Thus Smith speaks of faith as "that propensity of man that across the centuries and across the world has given rise to and has been nurtured by a prodigious variety of religious forms, and yet has remained elusive and personal, prior to and beyond the forms."[59] Smith contends that when most people think about religion in general or about a particular religion, what they have in mind is the external cumulative tradition rather than the inner faith of religious persons. To speak of religion as a generic category, or of Hinduism or Christianity as species of this general concept, is to reify or essentialize what is really an intensely personal faith experience of individuals.

Smith's call for us to observe carefully the actual commitments of religious believers and not to be misled by abstract systems is an important reminder. There are no religions apart from actual religious communities. But in emphasizing this, Smith draws too sharp a distinction between the inner faith of religious believers and the external cumulative tradition, which has only secondary status. What Smith calls the cumulative tradition (including beliefs) is integral to a religious community's self-understanding and cannot so easily be divorced from the believers' inner "faith disposition."

Social Construction of What?

How should we respond to the claim that our understanding of religion is a modern construct and therefore is misleading or inappropriate? There is

57. Ibid., 194.
58. Ibid., 156–57.
59. Wilfred Cantwell Smith, *Faith and Belief* (Princeton: Princeton University Press, 1979), 3.

no question that the notion of religion, as the term is used today, is to some extent a modern intellectual construct that has developed through the interactions between Europeans and Americans with diverse peoples of Asia, Latin America, and Africa. Furthermore, critics correctly point out that the concept can be used in misleading and unhelpful ways. But it hardly follows from this that the concept of religion itself is mistaken and should be abandoned. The academic landscape is full of concepts that were developed in modern times but help us better understand basic features of the world. As Schilbrack observes, "Despite social constructionist arguments about the invention of the concept of religion, one can legitimately use the term 'religions' to refer to certain kinds of social patterns that exist in the world."[60]

The concept of religion is socially constructed in the sense that its meaning is derived from and dependent upon human behavior and social interactions. The referent of the term is what Schilbrack calls "socially dependent facts," or states of affairs whose existence depends upon human behavior. "The existence of religion is clearly a socially dependent fact: it would not exist if there were no people."[61] What the concept of religion refers to—particular beliefs, practices, and social institutions—are socially constructed in the sense that they develop as human beings interact with each other and try to make sense of human experience and the world. But they are objective realities in that they are not *simply* the products of religious studies scholars' imaginations; they are also "out there" in the world, part of the "stuff" of reality, as are other socially dependent facts (e.g., baseball games, political elections, national holidays, free-market capitalism).

> To show that a concept is a social construction says nothing about whether or not that concept identifies something real. The concept of "molecule" and "magnetic field" are socially constructed, but this alone does not show that the entities so labeled are chimerical. Or, to take cultural examples, "gender" and "sexism" and even "colonialism" and "imperialism" are social constructions, but nevertheless indicate social realities that exist in the world.[62]

Critics charge that use of "religion" or "Hinduism" is reification, that is, treating something as an abstraction, or a bounded, static reality existing apart from the diverse, changing particularities in the actual world. Similarly, use of "religion" is said to be essentialist in that it assumes the existence of a common core or essence to religion that is shared by every particular religion.

60. Kevin Schilbrack, "What *Isn't* Religion?," *Journal of Religion* 93.3 (July 2013): 292.
61. Schilbrack, "Religions: Are There Any?," 1118.
62. Ibid., 1121.

While one must be careful not to impose greater homogeneity on the religious phenomena than is warranted, there is nothing in the concept of religion itself that requires such distortion. Later I will suggest a way of characterizing religion without resorting to an essentialist definition.

Moreover, we should not read too much into the fact that, before the modern era, many languages did not have a particular term corresponding to the English word "religion." Brent Nongbri makes a crucial distinction between having a word in a given language and users of that language having a particular concept: "Does the absence of a word or phrase equivalent to 'religion' in a given language mean that the speakers of the language also lack the *concept* of religion?"[63] Similarly, lack of single terms in two languages that have the same meanings does not entail that speakers of these languages do not share similar understandings on a particular subject. There is no single term in Hebrew or Greek that is identical in meaning to the English word "sin." The word "sin" is used to translate a variety of terms in Hebrew and Greek, but we should not conclude from this that the concept of sin is (merely) a construct of the English-speaking world or that those in biblical times could not understand what speakers of English mean by the word "sin."[64]

Similarly, people who did not have special terms in their languages equivalent to the English word "religion" nevertheless were able to participate in activities and to hold beliefs and values that today are included in the category of religion. The lack of a particular word equivalent to the English term "religion" does not necessarily indicate that what we mean by "religion" was absent in a given society or that people of that society could not comprehend what we mean today by the term. The absence of single terms for "religion" or "Hinduism" in fourteenth-century India, for example, does not mean that there were no particular rituals, institutions, or beliefs of the time that we today would identify as religious—or that people at that time were unable to distinguish what we today call Hindus from other groups. Those who worshiped Vishnu, believed in reincarnation, and maintained strict caste distinctions were different—and were treated differently—from those who prayed to Allah and regarded Muhammad as the final and greatest prophet. This is not simply a matter of modern outsiders making certain anachronistic judgments about

63. Nongbri, *Before Religion*, 23.
64. See the incisive essay by Robert Priest, "'Experience-Near Theologizing' in Diverse Human Contexts," in *Globalizing Theology: Belief and Practice in an Era of World Christianity*, ed. Craig Ott and Harold A. Netland (Grand Rapids: Baker Academic, 2006), 180–95. Through an analysis of the moral discourse of the Aguaruna of Peru, Priest illustrates how even though a particular language may not have a single term that corresponds precisely in meaning to the English word "sin," it can have a rich vocabulary for depicting moral failure and thus be fully adequate in capturing the range of biblical meanings brought together in the English word "sin."

earlier Indian communities. These differences were acknowledged by insiders of what we today call Hinduism and Islam.

Insiders to particular religious communities regularly make judgments about other groups, carefully distinguishing their own community and tradition from those that are alien. It is true that the religious and intellectual landscape of India has been remarkably eclectic and syncretistic, so that diverse traditions have coexisted over centuries. Yet, even in ancient times, the boundaries between those who today are known as Hindus and the early Buddhists and Jains were clear. The former regarded the latter two groups as sufficiently different that, in spite of certain similarities, the followers of the Buddha and of Mahavira (the founder of Jainism) were rejected by the Brahmins. In ancient India there was a clear distinction between those who accepted the authority of the Vedas and those who did not, with the latter being rejected as heretics by the Brahmins.[65] Accordingly, Hinduism, Buddhism, and Jainism developed over time as three distinct religions.

The fact that "Hinduism" and "Buddhism" are to some extent modern constructs does not necessarily mean that such concepts are *merely* constructions. The issue here is whether the concepts of Hinduism, Buddhism, Islam, Christianity, and so forth are helpful categories for understanding and sorting out the lived realities of particular communities. Properly understood, I think they are. While not without problems, the concept of religion is important for making sense of significant aspects of collective human life. If we reject "religion" or "Hinduism" or "Christianity" as inappropriate, we will simply need to come up with new words to denote the distinct communities and religious traditions to which these terms have customarily referred.

On Defining "Religion"

What, then, do we mean when we speak of religion? Our concern here is not primarily with a theological explanation of religion but rather with a phenomenological definition that depicts the religious realities in our world. The difficulty with definitions of religion is one of inclusion and exclusion: just what is to be included and what excluded by the concept? Coming up with the necessary and sufficient conditions for something being identified as "religion" is notoriously challenging, but we should not be misled by this. As Joshua Thurow reminds us, "Lots of important concepts are very difficult to

---

65. Wendy Doniger O'Flaherty, "The Origin of Heresy in Hindu Mythology," *History of Religions* 10.4 (1971): 272.

define, but nevertheless we manage to get on quite well conversing with them and studying their referents."[66] Consider, for starters, the difficulty of defining the terms "meaning," "knowledge," "justice," or "beauty."

Scholars typically distinguish functional definitions from substantive definitions of religion. Functional definitions define religion in terms of what religious beliefs, practices, or institutions do for participants (provide social cohesion or sense of identity), whereas substantive definitions focus on things that all religions are said to have in common (belief in gods/spirits, sacred rituals). Functional definitions tend to be so broad that they exclude little from the religious domain, whereas the difficulty with substantive definitions is identifying a set of characteristics that all examples of religion share. Each approach has important insights, and Kevin Schilbrack helpfully observes that a satisfactory definition should include both functional and substantive elements.[67]

It is best not to expect that an acceptable definition will identify essential qualities found in all instances of religion. In his influential work *An Interpretation of Religion*, John Hick suggests that we draw upon the philosopher Ludwig Wittgenstein's insights regarding "family-resemblance" concepts in determining the meaning of "religion."[68] In a now-classic discussion of the word "game," Wittgenstein pointed out that there is no single feature shared by all games and no one definition that captures all meanings of "game" in its many uses.[69] Yet the diverse meanings of "game" do bear some resemblance to each other. Despite some differences in meaning, there is a network of similarities among the many uses of "game," not unlike the resemblances among members of a natural family, so that we can recognize some relationships among the denotations of the term in various contexts. Similarly, although there may not be one property shared by all religions, there are sufficient similarities among particular cases such that it makes sense to speak of Theravada Buddhism, Protestant Christianity, Mormonism, Vedanta Hinduism, and Shia Islam—to name just a few examples—as religions. There are certain overlapping patterns and sufficiently common features so that applying the term "religion" to them makes sense.

William Cavanaugh objects to Hick's family-resemblance characterization of religion because he claims that it still includes the idea of identifying

66. Joshua C. Thurow, "Religion, 'Religion,' and Tolerance," in *Religion, Intolerance, and Conflict*, ed. Steve Clarke, Russell Powell, and Julian Savulescu (New York: Oxford University Press, 2013), 155.

67. Schilbrack, "What *Isn't* Religion?," 295–98.

68. John Hick, *An Interpretation of Religion: Human Responses to the Transcendent*, 2nd ed. (New Haven: Yale University Press, 2004), 3–5.

69. See Ludwig Wittgenstein, *Philosophical Investigations*, trans. G. E. M. Anscombe, 3rd ed. (New York: Macmillan, 1958), 31, sec. 66.

essential features of religion and thus "would be to return to the essentialism that the family-resemblance theory is meant to escape."[70] But Thurow correctly points out that the family-resemblance characterization does not rely on there being necessary properties defining the essence of religion that all religions must have. The idea is rather that there is "a set of core features" that collectively differentiate religion; while not all religions will manifest all of the features, the presence of a sufficient number or degree of these features identifies something as a religion.[71]

What might some of these core features be? Keith Yandell draws attention to the fact that one feature of the world religions is their analysis of our current state in terms of diagnosis and cure: "A religion proposes a *diagnosis* (an account of what it takes the basic problem facing human beings to be) and a *cure* (a way of permanently and desirably solving that problem)."[72] While this clearly fits world religions such as Hinduism, Buddhism, Christianity, and Islam, it is less clear that it fits a religion such as Shinto.

Based on common characteristics of what we typically regard as religions, Ninian Smart, one of the most influential figures in twentieth-century religious studies, argues that religions include seven distinct dimensions.[73] (1) The *ritual* dimension involves ordered actions (prayer, meditation, almsgiving, funerals, marriage ceremonies) that carry significant meaning within the religious community. Another is (2) the *mythological* or *narrative* dimension. Religions typically include rich narratives about significant figures who model appropriate behavior, or stories about the origin of the cosmos or how the current state of affairs came to be. Most religions also supply (3) the *doctrinal* or *philosophical* dimension. Doctrines can be thought of as systematic attempts to clarify and integrate the central beliefs of a religious tradition.

Religions characteristically have much to say about moral values and principles, resulting in (4) the *ethical* dimension. (5) The *social* and *institutional dimension* reflects patterns and mores dictating desirable relationships among believers in the religious community, as well as the institutions that provide necessary structure to the tradition. (6) The *experiential dimension* involves

70. William T. Cavanaugh, *The Myth of Religious Violence* (New York: Oxford University Press, 2009), 20.

71. Thurow, "Religion, 'Religion,' and Tolerance," 156.

72. Keith Yandell, *Philosophy of Religion: A Contemporary Introduction* (London: Routledge, 1999), 17, with original emphasis. Our focus in this chapter is on the major religions such as Hinduism, Buddhism, Christianity, and Islam. A somewhat different set of issues concerns indigenous or tribal religious traditions, or religious traditions among nonliterate communities.

73. See Ninian Smart, *The World's Religions*, 2nd ed. (Cambridge: Cambridge University Press, 1998), 11–22; idem, *Worldviews: Crosscultural Explorations of Human Beliefs*, 2nd ed. (Englewood Cliffs, NJ: Prentice-Hall, 1995).

participation of the religious believer in the patterns of the religious tradition through worship, prayer, meditation, pilgrimage, and so forth. Finally, (7) the *material dimension* refers to the many visible or material objects—religious art, icons, buildings, gardens, instruments to help in worship, and the like—important for the practice of religion. Smart's multidimensional approach to the study of religions helps us to appreciate the complex, integrated nature of religions.

Not all religions place the same significance on each of the dimensions. Doctrines, for example, are very important in Christianity and Islam but relatively insignificant in Shinto, which emphasizes ritual. The seven dimensions should not be regarded as exhaustive. In *Dimensions of the Sacred*, Smart adds the political and economic dimensions to the seven earlier dimensions of religion.[74] For not only do the major religions have internal mechanisms for determining legitimate exercise of power or authority, but they also have political implications globally for those outside the religion. Moreover, any understanding of religion in the past three centuries must include the complex relation between religion and nationalism, for often modern nationalism has a religious component.[75] What Yandell and Smart have identified serve as core features of religion: when these are present in sufficient measure, we identify something as a religion.

We will briefly consider two definitions of religion that build upon the core features identified above. Roger Schmidt defines religions as "systems of meaning embodied in a pattern of life, a community of faith, and a worldview that articulate a view of the sacred and of what ultimately matters."[76] Religions thus involve complex, integrative systems of meaning that are rooted in particular understandings of what is ultimately real and significant. For theistic religions, what is of ultimate significance is God, and everything else derives its significance in relation to God. Nontheistic religions ascribe ultimate significance to a particular state (nirvana or sunyata [emptiness] in Buddhism) or cosmic principle or reality (the Dao in Daoism).

According to the sociologist of religion Fenggang Yang, "A religion is a unified system of beliefs and practices about life and the world relative to the supernatural that unite the believers or followers into a social organization or moral community."[77] Yang maintains that there are four essential elements

74. Ninian Smart, *Dimensions of the Sacred: An Anatomy of the World's Beliefs* (London: HarperCollins, 1996), 10.

75. A related subject is what Robert Bellah terms civil religion. See Robert Bellah, "Civil Religion in America," *Daedalus* 96 (1967): 1–21.

76. Roger Schmidt et al., *Patterns of Religion* (Belmont, CA: Wadsworth, 1999), 10.

77. Fenggang Yang, *Religion in China: Survival and Revival under Communist Rule* (New York: Oxford University Press, 2012), 36.

of a religion: "(1) a belief in the supernatural; (2) a set of beliefs regarding life and the world; (3) a set of ritual practices manifesting the beliefs; and (4) a distinct social organization or moral community of the believers and practitioners."[78] What especially sets a religion apart from other systems of social organization is the first element, belief in the supernatural. This need not be belief in God, in many gods, or even belief in supernatural beings as such. The supernatural can include special powers or forces that transcend the space-time world accessible to the five senses. Religions typically include belief that reality includes more than simply the world of the senses and that our existence involves more than simply life in this world.

The understanding of religion being developed here is one that emphasizes the social and communal component of religious life.[79] Religions are not abstract systems; they find concrete expression in specific communities of people who try to live out the values and ideals of the religion. A religion calls for a distinctive way of life, and adherents in good standing within the religion are expected to conform to the established ideals. Religion thus provides an interpretive matrix within which particular groups of people understand themselves and what they regard as truly ultimate, and order their lives accordingly.

The notion of "boundaries" is critical to religious communities. Christians are considered distinct from Hindus, Buddhists, and Muslims, and Protestant Pentecostals are regarded as different from Russian Orthodox Christians. Although it is common to treat religious boundaries as fixed and inviolable, David Vishanoff reminds us that religious boundaries are in part "imagined constructs" that serve particular purposes and that distinguish religious communities in terms of their perceived differences by obscuring other ways in which the communities are alike.[80] Ethnicity, nationality, language, practices (dietary restrictions, prayer rituals, clothing, marriage expectations), beliefs, sacred texts, and sacred space can all contribute to constructing boundaries between communities and establishing or reinforcing religious identities. But differences between communities occur within a broader context of shared beliefs and practices, so that what are regarded as distinct religions often have a great deal in common (Hindu, Jain, and Buddhist communities in India, for

78. Ibid.

79. This contrasts sharply with William James's highly individualistic view of religion as "the feelings, acts, and experiences of individual men in their solitude, so far as they apprehend themselves to stand in relation to whatever they may consider the divine." William James, *The Varieties of Religious Experience* (New York: Random House, 1936 [1902]), 31–32.

80. David R. Vishanoff, "Boundaries and Encounters," in *Understanding Interreligious Relations*, ed. David Cheetham, Douglas Pratt, and David Thomas (New York: Oxford University Press, 2013), 341–64.

example, share certain beliefs and practices). Moreover, boundaries can be fluid and change, as both individuals and communities negotiate boundaries, so that what once were markers of difference between religious groups can later be signs of commonality.

In what follows we will adopt the characteristics and definitions of Yandell, Smart, Schmidt, and Yang as capturing what we mean by "religion."

This way of thinking about religion is helpful in considering world religions such as Christianity and Islam, as well as smaller and newer religions such as Baha'i and Rissho Kosei-kai in Japan. But some cases are less clear. In the mid-twentieth century there was considerable debate over whether Marxism or Communism should be understood as a religion. Ninian Smart is well aware that if one adopts the seven dimensions of religion he proposes, then a seemingly good case could be made for including Marxism, secular humanism, or even forms of nationalism as religions.[81] There have been ongoing disputes over whether Confucianism is a religion or a social or ethical philosophy. Anna Sun discusses four distinct periods since the sixteenth century, including 2000–2004, when Chinese scholars and others engaged in vigorous debate over whether Confucianism is a religion.[82] Disputes over what is to be included as religious continue today. Is Scientology a religion? How about Transcendental Meditation? Secular humanism?

The family-resemblance view of religion and the core features identified above allow for some messiness and disagreement on boundary cases. It is helpful to think of a continuum along which we have possible instances of religion, with clear paradigm cases of religions at one end and clear cases of what are not religions at the other. In between there can be cases that are less clear. Along these lines, Yang has proposed a classification of religions depending upon the extent to which a particular case exemplifies all four elements that he regards as central to religion.[83] The cases that clearly have all four are full religions. Those with significantly less of one or more of the elements are called semireligions. Quasi religions are cases such as civil religion or ancestral practices, in which the four elements are diffused and the beliefs and practices are embedded in other institutions so that they do not exist as part of a stand-alone organization or system. Cases that lack belief in the supernatural, yet share with religions the other elements, are called pseudoreligions. One need

81. Ninian Smart, *The World's Religions*, 10–26; idem, *Beyond Ideology: Religion and the Future of Western Civilization* (San Francisco: Harper & Row, 1981), 208–37; idem, *Concept and Empathy: Essays in the Study of Religion*, ed. Donald Wiebe (New York: New York University Press, 1986), 143–53.

82. Sun, *Confucianism as a World Religion*, 17–93.

83. Yang, *Religion in China*, 36–43.

not agree completely with Yang's classification in order to see that there are ways in which ambiguous boundary cases can be handled.

Worldviews

As cited above, Schmidt defines religions as "systems of meaning embodied in a pattern of life, a community of faith, and a *worldview* that articulate a view of the sacred and of what ultimately matters."[84] He seems to suggest that each religion has a worldview, and this reflects much common discourse about religions. We often speak, for example, of the Christian worldview as compared with the Buddhist worldview, and in doing so we usually are contrasting Christian beliefs with Buddhist beliefs. This makes sense, for beliefs or doctrines are important to religions. As Ninian Smart observes, "The world religions owe some of their living power to their success in presenting a total picture of reality, through a coherent system of doctrines."[85] Thus one of Smart's dimensions of religions is the philosophical or doctrinal dimension. Religious practices grow out of implicit or explicit truth claims about reality; as Schilbrack puts it, "Religious communities understand their practices and the values they teach as in accord with the nature of things."[86] Yang also gives prominence to the place of belief in his definition of religion. Focus upon beliefs naturally leads to the idea of a comprehensive perspective or worldview, and comparing religions can include assessing the worldviews embedded within the religions. It is tempting, then, to think of a worldview as simply a comprehensive set of beliefs, or, as Ronald Nash puts it, "a conceptual scheme by which we consciously or unconsciously place or fit everything we believe and by which we interpret and judge reality."[87] The title of Nash's book—*Worldviews in Conflict: Choosing Christianity in a World of Ideas*—reflects a popular way of thinking about religions: they are collections of beliefs or doctrines, and comparing Christianity and Buddhism is just a matter of examining their respective doctrines.

The notion of worldview is important for the study of religion, but it is a messy and contested concept and needs to be treated carefully.[88] Beliefs or

84. Schmidt et al., *Patterns of Religion*, 10, with emphasis added.
85. Ninian Smart, *The Religious Experience*, 5th ed. (Upper Saddle River, NJ: Prentice-Hall, 1996), 5.
86. Schilbrack, "What *Isn't* Religion?," 304.
87. Ronald H. Nash, *Worldviews in Conflict: Choosing Christianity in a World of Ideas* (Grand Rapids: Zondervan, 1992), 16.
88. For a helpful overview of ways in which the concept of worldview has been used in the West in the modern era, especially among theologians and some philosophers, see David K. Naugle, *Worldview: The History of a Concept* (Grand Rapids: Eerdmans, 2002).

doctrines are important in Christianity, and so Christians often give priority to religious teachings or doctrines when thinking about religions. But, as we have seen, doctrines comprise just one aspect of religions. Thus we should not think of worldviews as merely sets of beliefs, nor should we give undue emphasis to worldviews in understanding religions.

In the late twentieth century, Christian missiologists looked to the concept of worldview to help explain cultural differences, so that diverse cultures were distinguished in terms of their respective worldviews. But worldviews include more than merely beliefs. Cultural anthropologist Paul Hiebert thus developed a sophisticated understanding of worldview that includes more than just the cognitive dimensions of culture. While acknowledging the importance of beliefs, Hiebert also emphasizes the affective or moral dimensions such that worldviews include values and basic commitments about proper conduct. For Hiebert, a worldview is "the foundational cognitive, affective, and evaluative assumptions and frameworks a group of people makes about the nature of reality which they use to order their lives." A worldview "encompasses people's images or maps of the reality of all things that they use for living their lives."[89]

Ninian Smart also makes use of the concept of worldview and, like Hiebert, he insists that worldview be thought of not simply in terms of beliefs but also in relation to the seven dimensions that he outlines for understanding religions. Smart's use of worldview helps him to address the problem of ambiguous cases in determining the boundaries for religion. Earlier we observed that it can be difficult to determine whether something like Confucianism or Marxism is a religion. Smart uses the concept of worldview to set that question aside and to broaden the discussion, so that regardless of whether we call Marxism a religion, we can compare Marxism with religions such as Christianity or Buddhism by analyzing their respective worldviews. Smart argues that religions should be regarded as a subset of a broader category of worldviews, ideologies, or world philosophies. The study of religions should be part of a broader comparative inquiry, which Smart calls "worldview analysis."[90]

This has two advantages. First, without necessarily resolving the question of whether Marxism or Confucianism is a religion, it enables us to compare such systems with religions such as Christianity or Islam, noticing similarities and differences. Second, worldview analysis facilitates discussion of Indian, Chinese, and Japanese intellectual traditions that defy neat classification as

89. Paul Hiebert, *Transforming Worldviews: An Anthropological Understanding of How People Change* (Grand Rapids: Baker Academic, 2008), 25–26.
90. See, e.g., Ninian Smart, *Worldviews*; idem, *World Philosophies*, ed. Oliver Leaman, 2nd ed. (London: Routledge, 2008 [2000]); idem, *Beyond Ideology*.

either religious or philosophical. In Western universities one typically studies Buddhism in the religious studies department rather than the philosophy department, whereas many Buddhist intellectuals insist that Buddhism is a philosophy and not a religion. Focus upon worldview analysis, rather than trying to determine whether Buddhist teachings are "really" religious or philosophical, allows for inclusion of the views of Buddhist thinkers such as Nagarjuna or Dogen along with other philosophers such as Wittgenstein or Hume in comparative analysis.

Although the notion of worldview is important for understanding religions, we should not expect worldviews to be unrealistically tidy, coherent, or systematic. If we are considering the worldviews of actual religious communities, we should not be surprised to find them imprecise, often unclear, and not completely consistent. Moreover, worldviews can apply either to individuals or to larger groups, resulting again in some messiness and ambiguity. Each individual can be said to have a worldview, and in most cases these are implicit and not carefully thought through. So each Buddhist, for example, can be said to have a particular worldview. While we would expect some significant similarities among the worldviews of a group of Buddhists (such as Theravada Buddhists in Bangkok in 2010), we should also not be surprised by clear differences as well. People are different: even among those who profess the same religious affiliation, there can be pronounced differences and even inconsistencies. This is especially the case when we are considering people who may be from the same religious group but have different ethnic, class, or cultural locations.

Culture(s)

From our discussion to this point, it is clear that religions are closely related to cultures. But although they are related concepts, religion and culture are distinct: neither can be reduced to the other. Failure to appreciate both the close relation and the differences between religion and culture can result in confusion.

What do we mean by "culture"? The concept of culture, like that of religion, is modern. This does not mean that what the term "culture" denotes did not exist before the modern era. As far back as history takes us, people have lived together in communities in patterned, ordered ways characterized by different languages, beliefs, institutions, and customs. Although they may not have had our modern understanding of culture, ancient peoples were very much aware of differences among peoples in these areas. Within the nineteenth and twentieth centuries, the notion of culture became widely adopted as a way of explaining these differences.

Tomoko Masuzawa distinguishes two ways of understanding culture in the modern West. On the one hand, there has been the tendency to think in terms of "high culture," viewing "culture as edification." In this sense, culture is something that a select, elite supergroup manifests, that is, "the sum total of superior, morally and spiritually edifying human accomplishments."[91] Especially during the nineteenth century, culture (*Kultur* in German) was thought of in terms of sophisticated or refined habits of living reflected in an appreciation for proper education (notably in literature and the arts) and carefully crafted expectations for social interaction. On this understanding, not all people have culture; it is a quality that must be cultivated through proper training and is available only to the privileged.

But there is another way of understanding culture, one that became widely accepted in the twentieth century. Due to the influence of anthropology, there developed an understanding of culture that was ethnographically informed and was based upon the lived realities of ordinary people in actual communities. The early anthropologist Edward Burnett Tylor (1832–1917), for example, began his 1877 work *Primitive Culture* with this statement: "Culture or Civilization, taken in its wide ethnographic sense, is that complex whole which includes knowledge, belief, art, morals, law, custom, and any other capabilities and habits acquired by man as a member of society."[92] Although Tylor used "culture" and "civilization" interchangeably, he clearly was advancing a different perspective than the culture-as-edification model.

Masuzawa refers to this new understanding as viewing "culture as a complex whole." It presents culture as "expressly holistic, rather than narrowly discriminating, descriptive rather than evaluative, and . . . [it] presupposes the multiplicity of cultures and does not imply obvious 'standards of excellence.'"[93] With the adoption of this view, there was a twofold shift in popular thinking about culture. First, culture was no longer the possession of just the elite; all communities were now understood as manifesting culture. Furthermore, culture was no longer thought of in the singular as a general cumulative human construction. The idea of a particular culture as something observable within a specific, local community emerged. As awareness of the differences among peoples increased, it became common to speak in terms of many cultures (plural).

Significantly, Christian missionaries were instrumental in developing the modern understanding of culture. The careful collection of ethnographic data

91. Tomoko Masuzawa, "Culture," in *Critical Terms for Religious Studies*, ed. Mark C. Taylor (Chicago: University of Chicago Press, 1998), 73–74.

92. Edward Burnett Tylor, *The Origins of Culture*, vol. 1 of *Primitive Culture* (1877; repr., New York: Harper Torchbooks, 1958), 1.

93. Masuzawa, "Culture," 77.

by missionaries around the world provided the material out of which our current understanding of culture was formed.[94] John Beattie observes, "It was the reports of eighteenth- and nineteenth-century missionaries and travelers in Africa, North America, the Pacific and elsewhere that provided the raw material upon which the first anthropological works, written in the second half of the [nineteenth century], were based."[95]

The concept of "culture," like that of religion, is notoriously difficult to define. In their exhaustive survey published in 1952, A. L. Kroeber and Clyde Kluckhohn identify 164 distinct definitions of culture.[96] But the following definitions capture nicely what we generally mean by "culture" today. According to Roger Lohmann, "In its most basic sense, culture is that portion or aspect of thought and behavior that is learned and capable of being taught to others. . . . Culture includes customs and worldviews that provide a mental model of reality and a guide for appropriate and moral action."[97] Similarly, Paul Hiebert speaks of culture as "the integrated system of learned patterns of behavior, ideas, and products characteristic of a society."[98] Anthropologists developed an understanding of culture as a "semiotic system." Thus Clifford Geertz defines culture as "an historically transmitted pattern of meanings embodied in symbols, a system of inherited conceptions expressed in symbolic forms by means of which men communicate, perpetuate, and develop their knowledge about and attitudes toward life."[99]

People often think of cultures as discrete, homogenous, self-contained entities, which each stand on their own, with little connection with other cultures. Moreover, it is sometimes assumed that each culture manifests an internally coherent and systematic order: from the outside a culture might make little sense, but from within there is an internal "logic" and coherence. But this can be misleading. While it is true that cultures must be understood on their own terms and that their patterns can often seem strange to outsiders, we must not

---

94. See Robert J. Priest, "Anthropology and Missiology: Reflections on the Relationship," in *Paradigm Shifts in Christian Witness*, ed. Charles E. Van Engen, Darrell Whiteman, and J. Dudley Woodberry (Maryknoll, NY: Orbis Books, 2008), 23–28; Charles R. Taber, *The World Is Too Much with Us: "Culture" in Modern Protestant Missions* (Macon, GA: Mercer University Press, 1991), chaps. 2–4; Patrick Harries, "Anthropology," in *Missions and Empire*, ed. Norman Etherington (New York: Oxford University Press, 2005), 239–60; Masuzawa, "Culture," 84–87.

95. John Beattie, *Other Cultures: Aims, Methods, and Achievements in Social Anthropology* (New York: Free Press, 1964), 5.

96. A. L. Kroeber and Clyde Kluckhohn, *Culture: A Critical Review of Concepts and Definitions* (New York: Vintage Books, 1952), 291.

97. Roger Ivar Lohmann, "Culture," in *Encyclopedia of Religion*, ed. Lindsay Jones, 2nd ed. (New York: Thomson Gale, 2005), 3:2086.

98. Paul Hiebert, *Cultural Anthropology*, 2nd ed. (Grand Rapids: Baker, 1983), 25.

99. Clifford Geertz, *The Interpretation of Cultures* (New York: Random House, 1973), 89.

overly systematize them. Cultures typically contain within them a measure of internal tension and fragmentation, as aspects of the culture are contested by various parties. (This is also the case with religions.) Moreover, most cultures do not operate as entirely discrete, self-contained systems; peoples are continually coming into contact with other groups, sharing ideas, or borrowing words and practices. In other words, cultures—like religions—are continually undergoing change as they encounter other peoples and ways of living.

Furthermore, since the notion of culture is somewhat vague, we can think of a culture in a broad or a narrow sense. We can, for example, speak broadly of American culture or Mexican culture. While rather vague, there are identifiable characteristics distinguishing the two. But we can also think in terms of a much more narrow understanding of culture, so that second-generation Korean Americans in Chicago, for example, manifest a distinctive culture. Moreover, an individual can simultaneously be a part of several different cultures: one can be part of American culture, second-generation Chicago Korean American culture, and Midwestern evangelical Christian culture. Because the boundaries separating one culture from another are fluid and imprecise, it is not always clear where one culture ends and another begins (consider the boundaries between the following: American culture and Canadian culture, first-generation Korean American culture and second-generation Korean American culture, the culture of Japanese Buddhists and the culture of Japanese Christians).

Finally, cultures involve symbolic meanings that help to define a group of people, establish boundaries, and provide normative expectations for behavior. In times of significant change, these symbolic meanings can be contested, with competing subgroups trying to define the meanings in ways that advance their own objectives. Thus, while culture provides cohesion and identity for a group, it can also include within it deep tensions and conflict. This, too, is characteristic of many religions.

Religions, Cultures, and Worldviews

In concluding this chapter, we will make several observations about the relationships between religions, cultures, and worldviews. First, we cannot assume a simple, direct link between a religion, a worldview, and a culture, so that a given religion has a particular worldview and this in turn is reflected in a distinctive culture. In some cases it might be possible to trace such alignments; perhaps Japanese Shinto, which is so closely tied to the Japanese people and culture, might be an example. But in general, this way of thinking is misleading, as can be seen by considering the case of Christianity.

Although we might speak in very general terms of *the* worldview of Christianity, in actuality there are multiple Christian worldviews. The issue is how broadly or narrowly we wish to understand "worldview." Thus in one sense we can speak of the worldview of the Bible, while also acknowledging that in some ways the worldview of Abram in Genesis 12 is somewhat different from that of the apostle Paul in the Letter to the Romans. This is not to suggest that the two are incompatible but merely to recognize that each is to some extent the product of different times and places. Similarly, we might speak of the different worldviews of Christians in third-century Damascus, fourteenth-century Paris, nineteenth-century Tokyo, and twenty-first-century Nairobi: all might be basically faithful to Scripture, but to some extent each will also reflect the influences of their particular context.

Furthermore, given globalization, it is very difficult to identify a particular religion with a particular culture since the major religions have become embedded within many different cultures. Buddhism, as we shall see in chapter 3, originated in northern India but then spread throughout the south and east of Asia, becoming an integral part of the cultures of Sri Lanka, Thailand, Tibet, Burma, China, Korea, Vietnam, Japan, and now North America and Europe. Christianity has spread from its birthplace in Jerusalem to all parts of the world, and Islam has become part of diverse cultures not only in the Middle East but throughout North Africa, Asia, Europe, and North America. We cannot identify the major religions with a particular culture nor predict someone's religious affiliation simply by knowing their nationality or homeland.

Second, the concepts of religion and culture are not coextensive, and neither can be reduced to the other. Using our earlier definitions of culture and religion, although all religions include a cultural component, it is not clear that all cultures include a religious element. If we think of religions in terms of the seven dimensions suggested by Ninian Smart, then any particular religion will include cultural expression. But there seem to be societies and cultures today that are nonreligious, or at least ones in which religious commitments, institutions, and practices have little social significance. So although we can conceive of cultures that have no obvious religious component, we cannot think of religions without some cultural manifestations.

And yet a given religion cannot be reduced simply to culture. For although religions are always culturally embedded, they also transcend particular cultures so that "religion" and "culture" are not interchangeable terms. As we saw above, Buddhism can find expression in many different societies and cultures, so that we have Thai Buddhism, Chinese Buddhism, Japanese Buddhism, and American Buddhism. Similarly, although there are various cultural expressions of Christianity—American Christianity, Kenyan Christianity, Korean

Christianity—there is an important sense in which Christianity as a religion is distinct from any of these particular cultural expressions.

Third, religions and cultures are fluid and change over time. As empirical realities, the major religions have always been flexible and adaptable to fresh contexts. Neither cultures nor religions are completely self-contained, discrete, hermetically sealed systems that remain intact throughout time. Both cultures and religions contain internal variation and fluid boundaries; they are continually undergoing change as they encounter and are influenced by other traditions.

Furthermore, the meanings of rituals, special terms, or institutions also can change over time. In some cases what once clearly had religious meanings can come to have meanings that are not obviously religious. A good example is the tea ceremony (*cha-no-yu*) in Japan, which originally was strongly influenced by the principles and values of Zen Buddhism and was initially performed in Buddhist monasteries.[100] But today the tea ceremony is no longer thought of as Buddhist so much as simply a Japanese cultural ceremony, and some Japanese Christian pastors have become masters of the ceremony, using it to establish a bond between the Christian community and non-Christian Japanese.

Fourth, religions and cultures seem to be different: although we can readily think in terms of a person having multiple cultural identities simultaneously, the idea of someone having multiple religious identities simultaneously seems more problematic. Earlier we noted that a person can be part of several distinct cultures. A Pakistani Muslim immigrant to the United States might at the same time be part of American culture, second-generation Pakistani immigrant culture, Islamic culture, and the culture of doctoral students at the University of Chicago. Each of these cultural contexts is somewhat distinctive, but there is no difficulty in saying that the same person participates in each of them.

But can we say the same about religion? Can one, for example, simultaneously be Christian, Hindu, and Muslim as these religions have traditionally been understood? On the one hand, there are religious and social contexts in which an individual identifies with several religious traditions at the same time. Studies of Japanese religions, for example, regularly record numbers of religious adherents of Shinto, Buddhism, and the various new religious movements that far exceed the total Japanese population: many Japanese will self-identify with two or more religious traditions.[101] Most Japanese do not think it

---

100. See G. B. Sansom, *Japan: A Short Cultural History* (Stanford, CA: Stanford University Press, 1952), 345, 400–401; D. T. Suzuki, *Zen and Japanese Culture* (Princeton: Princeton University Press, 1959), 272–73.

101. See Ian Reader, *Religion in Contemporary Japan*, 6; Jan Van Bragt, "Multiple Religious Belonging of the Japanese People," in *Many Mansions? Multiple Religious Belonging and Christian Identity*, ed. Catherine Cornille (Maryknoll, NY: Orbis Books, 2002), 7–19.

strange to participate in two or more religious traditions simultaneously. This raises obvious difficulties for Christians, who traditionally have not regarded multiple religious belonging as an option.

But multiple religious belonging also is a growing phenomenon among Christians, especially in the West, who choose to identify with more than one religious tradition. Interfaith marriages are on the rise. And growing numbers of people claim more than one religious tradition.[102] Alan Watts, for example, became disillusioned with the Church of England, turned to the East, and became a popular promoter of Zen in the West in the 1960s and '70s and characterizes his own hybrid spirituality as "between Mahayana Buddhism and Taoism, with a certain leaning towards Vedanta and Catholicism, or rather the Orthodox Church of Eastern Europe."[103] Spiritual eclecticism is increasingly accepted in the West. The prominent Roman Catholic theologian Paul Knitter has identified himself as both a Christian and a Buddhist. Baptized as a Christian in 1939, in 2008 Knitter publicly identified himself also as a Buddhist.[104]

There seems to be a difference here in how we think of cultures and religions. In some contexts it makes sense to think of someone participating in several distinct cultural contexts simultaneously because we do not normally think of cultures as being mutually incompatible. But the difficulty with multiple religious identification, at least in many cases, is the fact that some of the central beliefs of the major religions are mutually incompatible. Are the worldviews of Buddhism, Hinduism, Islam, and Christianity really compatible, so that one could be an adherent of two or more simultaneously? Beliefs in the form of truth claims play a role and have significance in many religions, especially in monotheistic religions, that they do not in cultures. Can one be a genuine follower of Theravada Buddhism, which denies the reality of both the soul and Brahman, while also fully embracing Vedanta Hinduism, which affirms the reality of both? Can one really be a traditional Christian, affirming the Trinity and the incarnation in Jesus of Nazareth, while also fully accepting the Islamic insistence that Jesus was merely a human prophet? On the other hand, to the extent that truth claims are minimized and other aspects of religion become significant (such as rituals or moral values), it may make sense to speak of belonging to two religious traditions simultaneously.

This leads to a final difference between religions and cultures. Whereas it does not make sense to speak of one culture being true or normative for all

102. See Amy Frykhom, "Double Belonging: One Person, Two Faiths," *Christian Century* 128.2 (January 25, 2011): 20–23.

103. As cited in Thomas A. Tweed and Stephen Prothero, eds., *Asian Religions in America: A Documentary History* (New York: Oxford University Press, 1999), 229.

104. Paul F. Knitter, *Without Buddha I Could Not Be a Christian* (Oxford: Oneworld, 2009).

people at all times, there is an important sense in which we can speak of one religious tradition being true and normative for all. A very legitimate criticism of nineteenth-century Western missionaries is their tendency not to distinguish the gospel from European or American cultures and to assume that becoming a disciple of Jesus Christ involves adopting Western culture as well. Few today would wish to maintain that just one culture is somehow normative for all people in all places and times.

But it is not so easy to dismiss the idea of there being one true religion for all people. Properly understood, this is how Christians, Buddhists, and Muslims, for example, have traditionally thought about their own religion. Religions make claims about the nature of reality that are accepted by their adherents as true, and this puts religions and worldviews in a different category than cultures. In chapter 6 we will further explore what is involved in asserting that a particular religion is true, applying this specifically to the claim that Christianity is the true religion.

2

Secularization, Globalization, and the Religions

We have seen some of the ambiguities in the concept of religion, noticing in particular the significant overlap between the concepts of culture and religion. But another feature of religions makes them difficult to characterize in simple and clear terms. Religions, as we encounter them in actual historical and social settings, are not static entities, frozen in time: they change in certain ways as they respond to fresh circumstances. In a sense religions are continually redefining themselves as they struggle to hold on to what is normative from the past even as they adapt to fresh challenges and opportunities.

This is true of Christianity as an empirical religion. On one level, of course, Jesus Christ remains "the same yesterday and today and forever" (Heb. 13:8), and the gospel of Jesus Christ is unchanging (Gal. 1:9). The ideals of the Christian faith—what it means to live as a community of Christ's disciples, transformed by the supernatural work of the Holy Spirit—do not vary with time and place. But the particular ways in which Christians throughout history and around the world have understood the implications of the gospel and the significance of Jesus do change somewhat, resulting in different expressions of the Christian faith. For example, although they may all accept the gospel and be equally committed to the lordship of Jesus Christ, communities of

41

Christians in Damascus in the second century, in Uppsala in the twelfth century, in London in the eighteenth century, and in Nairobi in the twenty-first
century are different in important respects.[1] Similarly, we can trace significant
changes within other religions such as Buddhism, Islam, and Hinduism, as
each is forced to come to grips with new social and cultural contexts.

In this chapter we will examine some ways in which religions have changed as
they encountered the effects of modernization and globalization. Few subjects
are as complex or controversial as religion in the modern world; in discussing this, one must beware of simplistic generalizations that ignore the messy
and complicated realities of the past four hundred years. What follows is
hardly a comprehensive discussion. I will focus on certain patterns emerging
in Europe and North America associated with the much-contested notion of
secularization, identifying how they have encouraged an environment in which,
for many people, claims about exclusive religious truth appear increasingly
implausible and more pluralistic perspectives seem reasonable.

Modernization and Globalization

One of the most significant challenges to established religions in the past
five centuries comes from the massive social and intellectual transformations
associated with modernization. As modernity has introduced new ways of
understanding the cosmos and humankind's place in it, traditional religions
have been forced to come to grips with these new ways of thinking and living.
Since modernization emerged in Europe when Christendom was dominant,
Christianity was the first religion to struggle with modernity. The past four
or five centuries of Christian history can be understood, in part, as Christianity's ongoing engagement with both the positive and negative features of
modernity. During the nineteenth and twentieth centuries, Hinduism and Buddhism embarked upon their own encounters with modernization and Western
colonialism; in the process each religion was also modified in important ways.
The tensions evident today within Islam worldwide, including the radicaliza-
tion of some Muslim groups, are due in part to its much more recent struggle
with modernity and globalization.

Modernization refers to the process of social and intellectual transformations, beginning around the fifteenth century in Europe, which were brought
about by industrialization and the growing dominance of technology in all

---

1. See the classic essay by Andrew F. Walls, "The Gospel as Prisoner and Liberator of Culture," in his *The Missionary Movement in Christian History: Studies in the Transmission of
Faith* (Maryknoll, NY: Orbis Books, 1996), 3–15.

of life. These transformations include urbanization; the proliferation of institutions and practices associated with market capitalism; the new scientific understandings of the cosmos and the human body, radically altering our views about natural phenomena; liberal democratic forms of government based upon the rights of citizens; and the power of critical inquiry in all domains, resulting in a check upon religious authoritarianism. Modernization does not merely produce greater efficiency in accomplishing tasks or more conveniences for our consumption; it also affects how we understand ourselves and relate to the world around us. Sociologist Max Weber was one of the first social theorists to consider carefully the impact of modernization on ordinary living, and he identified the increasing rationalization of all areas of life, which accompanies the emergence of free-market capitalism and the institutions associated with it, as a major effect of modernization.[2] Modernization thus results in the increased bureaucratization of social life, the increasingly pervasive application of scientific methodology and assumptions to public and private domains, the separation of one's private or family life from the workplace due to the rise of autonomous business institutions, and the proliferation of new institutions to handle increasingly specialized tasks. Modernity, the way of thinking and living associated with modernization, has also been shaped by some powerful intellectual forces over the past four centuries, and we will consider the impact of the European Enlightenment below.

But before looking at the historical Enlightenment, we should observe that modernization has been accompanied by continually deepening interconnections among peoples worldwide, a process now commonly referred to as globalization. Since the mid-twentieth century, we have entered a new phase in world history as geographically distant parts of the earth have become linked together in unprecedented ways. As Frank Lechner and John Boli observe, "After World War II, the infrastructure for communication and transportation improved dramatically, connecting groups, institutions, and countries in new ways. More people can travel, or migrate, more easily to distant parts of the globe; satellite broadcasts bring world events to an increasingly global audience; the Internet begins to knit together world-spanning interest groups of educated users."[3]

On one level, global connections are not new. Trade, war, and migrations linked diverse people throughout the ancient world, and ever since the European

2. See Max Weber, *The Protestant Ethic and the Spirit of Capitalism* (London: Allen & Unwin, 1930); idem, *The Sociology of Religion* (London: Methuen, 1966); idem, *Economy and Society: An Outline of Interpretive Sociology* (New York: Badminster, 1968).

3. Frank Lechner and John Boli, *The Globalization Reader*, 2nd ed. (Oxford: Blackwell, 2004), xvii.

voyages of discovery in the sixteenth and seventeenth centuries, cultures around the globe have become increasingly interconnected. But the late twentieth century introduced something new. Nayan Chanda states, "The big differences that mark the globalization of the early years with that of the present are in the *velocity* with which products and ideas are transferred, the ever-growing *volume* of consumers and products and their *variety*, and the resultant increase in the *visibility* of the process."[4] The break with the past has been brought about by the staggering technological innovations of the twentieth century, exemplified in the computer and telecommunications industries. "In fact, information processed by the microchip is the single most important factor that distinguishes today's globalization from the slowly growing interconnection and interdependence of the past."[5]

At the heart of globalization is the reality that local patterns are shaped in significant ways by developments elsewhere. Thus Anthony Giddens defines globalization as "the intensification of worldwide social relations which link distant localities in such a way that local happenings are shaped by events occurring many miles away and vice versa."[6] For Malcolm Waters, globalization is "a social process in which the constraints of geography on economic, political, social and cultural arrangements recede, in which people become increasingly aware that they are receding, and in which people act accordingly."[7] Globalization is thus a process involving increased interrelatedness across traditional boundaries in multiple dimensions, including politics, economics, culture, and religion.

To some extent, religions have always been affected by contact with different intellectual and cultural forces. Mark Juergensmeyer reminds us that "religious communities and traditions have always maintained permeable boundaries. They have moved, shifted, and interacted with one another around the globe. . . . Religion is global in that it is related to the global transportation of peoples, and of ideas."[8] Some religions in particular have intentionally moved across boundaries, becoming part of new cultural settings. Religions such as Christianity, Islam, and Buddhism are what Juergensmeyer calls

4. Nayan Chanda, *Bound Together: How Traders, Preachers, Adventurers, and Warriors Shaped Globalization* (New Haven: Yale University Press, 2007), xiii, with original emphasis. For a historical perspective on globalization, see the essays in A. G. Hopkins, ed., *Globalization in World History* (New York: Norton, 2002).

5. Chanda, *Bound Together*, 103.

6. Anthony Giddens, *The Consequences of Modernity* (Stanford, CA: Stanford University Press, 1990), 64.

7. Malcolm Waters, *Globalization*, 2nd ed. (New York: Routledge, 2001), 5.

8. Mark Juergensmeyer, "Thinking Globally about Religion," *The Oxford Handbook of Global Religions*, ed. Mark Juergensmeyer (New York: Oxford University Press, 2006), 4–5.

transnational religions, "religious traditions with universal pretensions and global ambitions." In these religions, "at the core of their faith is the notion that their religion is greater than any local group and cannot be confined to the cultural boundaries of any particular region."[9] But the globalization of the past two centuries has affected religious traditions in profound ways. For example, European and American colonialism and the modern missionary movements have been instrumental in the revitalization of Hindu, Buddhist, and Islamic movements as well as helping to shape the particular forms these religions have taken. Religious traditions have influenced each other, resulting in the hybridization of traditions and the emergence of new religious movements.

Nayan Chanda points out that one of the formative influences upon globalization has been missionary activity, as devout adherents of Buddhism, Christianity, and Islam crossed geographic, linguistic, and cultural boundaries to spread their faith.

> For all the horror it visited upon people over the long span of history, missionary activity had the effect of shrinking the world. The spread of these proselytizing faiths brought dispersed communities into contact, both peaceful and violent. Preachers enriched languages of their converts, introduced printing technology, and transformed cultures for better or for worse. If the world today looks more homogenous than at any time in the past it is because a vast number of people have come to embrace the great religions that streamed out of the foothills of the Himalayas and deserts of the Middle East. In the remotest corner of the planet you will find a mosque, a church, or a temple. To appreciate the significance of preachers and missionaries in making the world smaller, you have to imagine a world in which Buddhism is practiced in just a little corner of India, and Christianity and Islam remain the faiths of the Arabian Desert.[10]

Christianity can thus be seen as both an agent in globalization and a product of it. Through the modern missionary movements of the nineteenth and twentieth centuries, Christianity served as a significant instrument of globalization. That is, by carrying the gospel worldwide and establishing Christian churches in linguistic, religious, and cultural contexts in which they did not previously exist, Christianity was instrumental in developing interconnections between local communities of believers and Christians elsewhere. As Christians emerged among diverse local groups, a new sense of identity developed that transcended and relativized prior indigenous markers of identity, thereby connecting as fellow Christians what would otherwise have remained disparate groups.

9. Ibid., 7.
10. Chanda, *Bound Together*, 112–13.

One way in which to think about the effects of modernization and globalization upon religion is to observe that, with modernity, being religious in a traditional sense is not as easy as it used to be. Religious beliefs and practices that in premodern times were largely unquestioned are no longer taken for granted. This does not necessarily mean that modern people stop being religious, but it does suggest that they are religious in different ways. In many modern, globalizing societies, for example, the proliferation of available options ensures that those who express religious commitments do so with the awareness that others adopt quite different beliefs and practices. These alternative paths in turn become live options for many today. To be sure, there are many modern believers who remain deeply committed to their own faith and for whom other religious traditions do not present realistic options. But for many others, it becomes more difficult to retain confidence in the unique truth of their own position as they encounter intelligent and morally respectable followers of other traditions. In Europe and North America, the cumulative effects of the disestablishment of Christianity and freedom of religious expression, the marginalization of traditional Christian institutions and practices, a deepening skepticism about the claims of orthodox Christianity, and the existential awareness of cultural and religious diversity due to globalization make it more difficult for many to confidently embrace the truth of orthodox Christianity. Thus in the West we find not only growing numbers of those who explicitly reject religion altogether but also the proliferation of nontraditional and theologically unorthodox versions of Christianity as well as alternative spiritualities.

There is no single paradigm or model that includes and explains the many very diverse religious patterns of the past four centuries. A decline in religious affiliation occurs in some places, but religious vitality and growth appear elsewhere. There are humanistic and progressive forms of religion, which try to combine religious commitment with whatever the wisdom of the age might be, and there are antimodernizing and antiglobalizing forms of religion as well. Religion can be a force for enormous good in promoting human welfare, but it can also be a source of bigotry, abuse, and horrifying violence.

As religions come to grips with modernity, they confront the values and ideals often associated with the Enlightenment. Although it is easy to exaggerate the impact of the Enlightenment upon modern societies—contrary to some observers, modernity is much more than simply "the Enlightenment mentality"—there is no question that the intellectual and cultural patterns of the past three centuries have been powerfully shaped by Enlightenment ideals and developments. This is true not only of Europe and North America but of much of the rest of the world as well.

The Enlightenment

Beginning in Europe during the eighteenth century, the Enlightenment was an intellectual and cultural movement—or better, a series of such movements—that subjected traditional ways of thinking to rigorous critique. Enlightenment thinkers were disillusioned with traditional religious, social, and intellectual patterns and looked to reason, science, and social reform for guidance in constructing a better world.

Although somewhat arbitrary, the English (1688) and French (1789) Revolutions provide convenient historical markers for the Enlightenment. The Enlightenment was a diverse, international movement centered primarily in England, Scotland, and France, which then spread throughout Europe and the American colonies. Enlightenment thinkers included academics, journalists, and government officials active in public life who were eager to apply reason to the many practical problems of the day, calling for reform in the legal and penal systems, education, politics, and economics.

Enlightenment thinkers are frequently depicted as being obsessed with reason and universal truths. On this view, the seventeenth-century philosopher and scientist René Descartes (1596–1650), with his agenda for a comprehensive system for knowledge producing certainty in all areas of inquiry through rigorous deduction from indubitable premises, is sometimes said to epitomize Enlightenment assumptions. Theologian and missiologist Lesslie Newbigin, for example, frequently uses Descartes to characterize what he regards as an Enlightenment rationalism that has dominated subsequent Western thought.[11] But this is misleading. Historians typically locate the Enlightenment in the eighteenth century, whereas Descartes lived in the seventeenth century, during what is often call the Age of Reason. Although Descartes's influence upon subsequent European thinkers was significant, his rationalism was largely abandoned by eighteenth-century thinkers who favored more empiricist approaches stemming from Francis Bacon and John Locke. Contrary to Newbigin's characterization, many Enlightenment thinkers were actually quite skeptical about reason.

The Enlightenment was not a monolithic movement: it took different forms in England, Scotland, Germany, France, Italy, the Netherlands, Russia, and the American colonies. Nevertheless, certain common themes can be noted. Luis Dupré, for example, identifies the emphasis upon reason and emancipation

---

11. See Lesslie Newbigin, *Truth to Tell: The Gospel as Public Truth* (Grand Rapids: Eerdmans, 1991), 25–27, 35–36; idem, *The Gospel in a Pluralist Society* (Grand Rapids: Eerdmans, 1989), 17–18, 28–29, 32–33; idem, "Truth and Authority in Modernity," in *Faith and Modernity*, ed. Philip Sampson, Vinay Samuel, and Chris Sugden (Oxford: Regnum, 1994), 62, 72.

as especially characteristic of Enlightenment thought.[12] These themes are expressed in the classic essay "What Is Enlightenment?" by Immanuel Kant (1724–1804), one of the last Enlightenment thinkers. "Enlightenment is man's emergence from his self-imposed nonage. Nonage is the inability to use one's own understanding without another's guidance." Enlightenment thinkers refused to simply accept things on authority, especially religious authority. "Dare to know! (*Sapere aude!*) 'Have the courage to use your own understanding' is therefore the motto of the Enlightenment."[13] For Kant, the enlightened use of reason leads to freedom and autonomy: "This enlightenment requires nothing but *freedom*—and the most innocent of all that may be called 'freedom': freedom to make public use of one's reason in all matters."[14] Previously the critical use of reason had been restricted by religious and political authoritarianism, superstition, and ignorance, but humankind could now cast off these impediments and take control of its own destiny.

Although the critical use of reason was central to Enlightenment thinkers, not all agreed on the capacity of reason to uncover truth. Skepticism has a long history in Western thought. The Sophists, influential itinerant teachers of rhetoric in fifth-century BC Athens, appealed to human fallibility in judgments and the rich diversity in beliefs and customs in the Mediterranean world to undermine confidence in one's ability to know what is true. Sophists were especially critical of claims to religious knowledge or universal moral truths. Plato's philosophical writings, which emphasize the unchanging nature of truth and our ability to know some truths, must be understood in light of the pervasive relativism and skepticism during his time. But in spite of the impressive work of Plato and his student Aristotle, skepticism continued to be popular in the ancient world.

Pyrrhonian skepticism is associated with Pyrrho of Elis (d. 270 BC), who is said to have advocated withholding judgments of any kind on all matters concerning which there are conflicting opinions. The only surviving texts of Pyrrhonian skepticism are those included in Sextus Empiricus's (ca. AD 200) *Outlines of Pyrrhonism* and *Against the Dogmatists*. The skepticism of Sextus Empiricus was introduced to Renaissance Europe in the mid-sixteenth century; this, along with the growing awareness of religious and cultural diversity in the New World, encouraged a pervasive skepticism and relativism. Julia Annas and Jonathan Barnes observe, "It was the rediscovery of Sextus

12. Luis Dupré, *The Enlightenment and the Intellectual Foundations of Modern Culture* (New Haven: Yale University Press, 2004), 7.
13. Immanuel Kant, "What Is Enlightenment?," in *The Enlightenment: A Comprehensive Anthology*, ed. Peter Gay (New York: Simon & Schuster, 1973), 384.
14. Ibid., 385.

and of Greek skepticism which shaped the course of philosophy for the next three hundred years."[15]

The influence of Sextus is clearly evident in Michel de Montaigne's (1533–92) *In Defense of Raymond Sebond* (1580), a sustained attack upon the powers of reason. "There is a plague on man: his opinion that he knows something. That is why ignorance is so strongly advocated by our religion [Christianity] as a quality appropriate to belief and obedience." Echoing an ancient theme, Montaigne declares, "A wise man can be mistaken; a hundred men can; indeed, according to us, the whole human race has gone wrong for centuries at a time over this or that: so how can we be sure that human nature ever stops getting things wrong, and that she is not wrong now, in our own period?"[16] Montaigne not only uses the classical skeptical arguments from earlier times; he also appeals repeatedly to the growing awareness of diversity of beliefs and customs to undermine confidence in reason.[17]

Eighteenth-century Enlightenment thinkers were deeply ambivalent about the powers of reason. The idea that nature was rational and governed by orderly, lawlike principles was widely accepted. But many intellectuals, especially in the British Isles, rejected the rationalism inherent in Descartes's vision of an epistemological system modeled after the geometric method, which produces complete certainty about disputed matters. The eighteenth century saw a clear shift away from earlier rationalism toward empiricism and human experience as the source of knowledge.

Many Enlightenment thinkers, such as Denis Diderot (1713–84) and Baron P. d'Holbach (1723–89), were remarkably optimistic about the powers of reason to uncover truth. Others, such as Voltaire (1694–1778), were less positive, acknowledging reason's limitations but regarding it as the only reliable guide for understanding that humans have. However, the Scottish philosopher David Hume (1711–76), one of the most influential Enlightenment figures, was deeply skeptical about reason. Hume famously declared, "Reason is, and ought only to be, the slave of the passions, and can never pretend to any other office than to serve and obey them."[18] Thus historian Peter Gay argues that the Enlightenment should not be construed as an age of reason so much as an age of criticism. "The claim for the omnicompetence of criticism was in no way a claim for

15. Julia Annas and Jonathan Barnes, *The Modes of Skepticism: Ancient Texts and Modern Interpretations* (Cambridge: Cambridge University Press, 1985), 5.

16. Montaigne, *An Apology for Raymond Sebond*, trans. and ed. M. A. Screech (London: Penguin Books, 1987), 53, 156.

17. For a helpful discussion of Montaigne's skepticism in the context of the early modern search for certainty, see Susan E. Schreiner's *Are You Alone Wise? The Search for Certainty in the Early Modern Era* (New York: Oxford University Press, 2011), 333–57.

18. David Hume, *A Treatise of Human Nature* (New York: Doubleday, 1961), 2.3.3, p. 375.

the omnipotence of reason. It was a political demand for the right to question everything, rather than the assertion that all could be known or mastered by rationality."[19] Enlightenment views on religion were shaped by developments in the sixteenth and seventeenth centuries, including religious skepticism; the growing awareness of other religions and cultures; the crisis in religious authority prompted by the Protestant Reformation and the proliferation of new religious movements; the bitter wars of religion, which mixed intra-Christian sectarianism with political rivalries; and the impact of a mechanistic view of the universe derived from Newton and the emerging sciences.

Many thinkers advocated a kind of natural religion, which held that the natural order provides the basis for belief in a deity and for moral obligation, which were said to be common to all human beings.[20] Most Enlightenment figures did not reject religion as such but advocated a natural, nonsectarian, "reasonable" religion as the foundation of morality. An early example of such natural religion is found in Lord Herbert of Cherbury (1583–1648). In his *De veritate* (1624), or *On Truth as It Is Distinguished from Revelation, Probability, Possibility, and Falsehood*, Herbert claims that there are some "common notions" among the religions that mark "true religion."[21] These include belief that (1) there is a supreme God; (2) this deity ought to be worshiped; (3) the connection between virtue and piety is the most important part of religious practice; (4) wickedness must be expiated by repentance; and (5) there is reward or punishment in the afterlife. Most Enlightenment thinkers were theists or deists of some kind: explicit atheism was rare. Deists believed in a God who created the world but who does not intervene in the operations of the universe or in human affairs. They believed in moral obligations and immortality, but they rejected supernatural phenomena such as miracles and divine special revelation.

But Enlightenment thinkers were relentless in their attack upon traditional, orthodox Christianity as irrational. The institutional church, especially the Roman Catholic Church, was vehemently criticized for rampant corruption, clergy sexual abuse, intolerance, superstition, and ignorance. Belief in supernatural miracles, special revelation, and the incarnation was dismissed as irrational. The Bible, accepted by orthodox Christians as the inspired special

19. Peter Gay, *The Enlightenment: An Interpretation; The Rise of Modern Paganism* (New York: Norton, 1966), 141.
20. See Peter Harrison, *"Religion" and the Religions in the English Enlightenment* (Cambridge: Cambridge University Press, 1990).
21. See Herbert of Cherbury, "Common Notions concerning Religion," in *Christianity and Plurality: Classical and Contemporary Readings*, ed. Richard J. Plantinga (Oxford: Blackwell, 1999), 171–81. See also J. Samuel Preus, *Explaining Religion* (New Haven: Yale University Press, 1987), 23–39.

revelation of God, came under unprecedented criticism.[22] The unity, internal consistency, and historical reliability of the Bible were questioned, and the uniqueness of the Bible was undermined by comparing it with newly acquired information about sacred texts of Chinese and Indian religions.

The most trenchant critique of orthodox Christianity came from philosophers David Hume and Immanuel Kant. Hume presented a threefold critique of religion, each aspect of which was directed against a popular way of defending orthodoxy in the eighteenth century.[23] In the notorious essay "Of Miracles," Hume argues that even if a miracle were in principle possible, one can never be justified in believing that a particular phenomenon is in fact a miracle rather than simply an anomaly. Hume's *Dialogues concerning Natural Religion*, published posthumously in 1779, provides a penetrating critique of the teleological argument, widely used by deists as well as orthodox theologians to support belief in the existence of God. His *Natural History of Religion* (1757) is an early attempt to explain religion in strictly naturalistic terms as rooted in fear, thereby subverting the contemporary attempt to ground religion in a special human sentiment or natural dispositions. Although he insisted that he was not an atheist, Hume's writings were understood as removing grounds for rational belief in God. With respect to God's existence, Hume concludes, "The whole is a riddle, an enigma, an inexplicable mystery. Doubt, uncertainty, suspense of judgment appear the only result of our most accurate scrutiny concerning this subject."[24]

Although Immanuel Kant was not hostile to religion as such, his philosophical system entails a radical reinterpretation of how we understand religious claims.[25] The critical epistemology of the *Critique of Pure Reason* (1781)

---

22. See Colin Brown, *Jesus in European Protestant Thought, 1778–1860* (Durham, NC: Labyrinth, 1985).

23. For an analysis of Hume's views on religion, see Keith Yandell, *Hume's "Inexplicable Mystery": His Views on Religion* (Philadelphia: Temple University Press, 1990).

24. David Hume, *The Natural History of Religion*, ed. H. E. Root (Stanford, CA: Stanford University Press, 1956), 76. Here Hume echoes the ancient philosopher Cicero (d. 43 BC), who concludes his *De natura deorum* (*On the nature of the gods*) with "This more or less is what I have to say about the nature of the gods: it is not my design to disprove [belief in the gods], but to bring you to understand how obscure it is and how difficult to explain." Cicero, *De natura deorum*, trans. H. Rackham (Cambridge, MA: Harvard University Press, 1951), 381.

25. Helpful introductions to Kant's views on epistemology, metaphysics, and religion can be found in Allen Wood, *Kant's Moral Religion* (Ithaca, NY: Cornell University Press, 1970); Paul Guyer, ed., *The Cambridge Companion to Kant* (Cambridge: Cambridge University Press, 1992); Philip J. Rossi and Michael Wreen, eds., *Kant's Philosophy of Religion Reconsidered* (Bloomington: Indiana University Press, 1991). A different reading of Kant's views on religion is offered in Chris L. Firestone and Stephen R. Palmquist, eds., *Kant and the New Philosophy of Religion* (Bloomington: Indiana University Press, 2006), which in turn is the subject of a symposium discussion in *Philosophia Christi* 9.1 (2007): 8–97.

removes the possibility of any genuine knowledge about God. One of the consequences of Kant's epistemology is the limitation of knowledge to the realm of possible sense experience, thus ruling out any knowledge about a transcendent God. Kant argues, however, that we can be entitled to believe in God's existence on the basis of "practical reason." The implications of moral obligation are such that we are justified in believing, on practical or moral grounds, that God exists although we cannot claim this as an item of knowledge.

Kant's *Religion within the Limits of Reason Alone* (1793) gives eloquent expression to a common Enlightenment theme also widely accepted today, that a genuinely "true religion" must be universally accessible and thus cannot be based upon the contingencies of a special revelation to a particular group at a particular time. Enlightenment thinkers rejected the "scandal of particularity" of orthodox Christianity's teachings on divine special revelation in the Bible and the incarnation in Jesus of Nazareth. Kant, for example, claims that "rational religion" requires universality and cannot be based upon particular events or truths to which only some people have access. "A church dispenses with the most important mark of truth, namely, a rightful claim to universality, when it bases itself upon a revealed faith. For such a faith, being historical (even though it be far more widely disseminated and more completely secured for remotest posterity through the agency of scripture) can never be universally communicated so as to produce conviction."[26] Gotthold Ephraim Lessing (1729–81), another Enlightenment figure, speaks of the "ugly, broad ditch" separating universal truths of religion from the particular contingencies of history. Historical evidence cannot substantiate theological claims because "accidental truths of history can never become the proof of necessary truths of reason."[27] Similarly, Voltaire claims, "If God had wished to make his cult known to me, it would be because this cult was necessary to our species. If it were necessary, he would have bestowed it on all alike, just as he has given everyone two eyes and a mouth. . . . The principles of universal reason are common to all civilized peoples, all recognize a God; they can then flatter themselves that such knowledge is truth. Yet each of them has a different religion."[28] And Jean-Jacques Rousseau (1712–78), who advocates a

26. Immanuel Kant, *Religion within the Limits of Reason Alone*, trans. Theodore M. Greene and Hoyt H. Hudson (New York: Harper Torchbooks, 1934), 3.6.100; see also 3.6.105, 110–11, 175–77.

27. See Gotthold Ephraim Lessing, "On the Proof of the Spirit and of Power," in *Lessing's Theological Writings*, trans. and ed. Henry Chadwick (Stanford, CA: Stanford University Press, 1957), 53, 55.

28. Voltaire, as cited in Dupré, *The Enlightenment*, 236.

form of natural religion based not on reason but on a special feeling common to all people, rejects the idea of one true religion that can legitimately claim a special divine revelation.[29]

In the nineteenth and twentieth centuries, the ideas that the "principles of universal reason are common to all civilized peoples" and that "all recognize a God" were increasingly rejected, as Europeans and Americans became impressed with the enormous diversity in beliefs and practices found worldwide. Confidence in one's ability to discern a rational universal religion was replaced by religious skepticism and relativism. But what remains influential is the Enlightenment conviction that there cannot be a true religion that is normative for all peoples and based upon a special revelation to a particular people or a particular historical event.

The call for religious toleration, another enduring contribution of the Enlightenment, was in part a response to the brutal religious wars of the sixteenth and seventeenth centuries.[30] The classic case for religious tolerance is found in John Locke's *A Letter concerning Toleration* (1685) and *Two Treatises on Government* (1690).[31] Locke's justification for tolerance is based on a distinction between a civil jurisdiction that is not responsible for the "care of souls" and an ecclesiastical one that maintains such responsibility but is not to interfere in civic matters. Locke argues that religious beliefs cannot be coerced but must be voluntarily accepted. Other thinkers such as Spinoza, Bayle, Voltaire, Rousseau, Diderot, and Lessing also advocated tolerance but did so in part because of religious skepticism. Since we are unable to determine which, if any, religion is true, prudence demands that we allow for diversity of religious belief so long as the public welfare is not threatened.[32]

By the early 1800s the Enlightenment was already being eclipsed by other movements, especially Romanticism. Yet the Enlightenment has had enormous impact upon modern societies, not only in the West but also worldwide. Dupré sees its legacy in a pervasive "critical consciousness" in modern societies, so that traditional authority is no longer accepted uncritically.[33] Although chastened by over two centuries of devastating warfare, genocide, and exposure to the

29. See "The Creed of a Savoyard Vicar" in book 4 of Rousseau, *Émile, or, On Education*, trans. Allan Bloom (New York: Basic Books, 1979), esp. 295–99.

30. Perez Zagorin, *How the Idea of Religious Toleration Came to the West* (Princeton: Princeton University Press, 2003).

31. John Locke, *Epistola de Tolerantia: A Letter on Toleration*, ed. Raymond Klibansky, trans. J. W. Gough (Oxford: Clarendon, 1968); idem, *Two Treatises of Government*, with introduction by Peter Laslett (Cambridge: Cambridge University Press, 1966).

32. See Alan Levine, ed., *Early Modern Skepticism and the Origins of Toleration* (New York: Lexington, 1999).

33. Dupré, *The Enlightenment*, xiii.

darker side of science, Enlightenment influence can be seen in the continued confidence modern people have in education, science, and technology to improve life. Enlightenment ideals are reflected also in the political disestablishment of religion and in the freedom of religious expression, which are increasingly adopted throughout the world, and in the international recognition of the importance of individual human rights, as codified in the United Nations' Universal Declaration of Human Rights (1945).[34] "Religious tolerance; the separation between cult and public life; the protection of the individual conscience against religious compulsion, social pressure, or cultural prejudice—all of these have become nonnegotiable positions for Western believers."[35] The Enlightenment legacy is also linked to the secularization of European and American societies. Perez Zagorin observes, "The ultimate importance of the Enlightenment lay in its long-run contribution to the gradual secularization and liberalization of Western society. Secularization in the eighteenth and nineteenth centuries chiefly meant the declining dominance of the Christian religion and churches over individual minds and in political and social life."[36]

Secularization

We should begin our discussion of secularization by making the conceptual distinctions between the secular, secularization, and secularism.[37] Although clearly related, these are different concepts. As I use these terms, "secularization" refers to a supposedly empirically observable, historical process of social, intellectual, cultural, and political change such that traditional religious patterns are modified, resulting in the increased fragmentation, differentiation, and pluralization of society and the decline, in some sense, of religious influence. Whether secularization is occurring is an empirical question that can be answered in principle by careful historical, social, and cultural observation. (Whether one welcomes or bemoans such changes is an entirely separate issue.)

34. The Enlightenment was not the only force behind such concerns. Nayan Chanda (*Bound Together*, 137) observes that one of the positive effects of Christian missionary activity in the nineteenth and twentieth centuries was the concern with the human rights of all people, the "globalization of values." He states, "The awareness about the rights of a fellow human being from a totally different culture and the search for common ethical principles and international social objectives have led to the rise of new 'missionary' organizations such as Amnesty International and Human Rights Watch."

35. Dupré, *The Enlightenment*, 338.

36. Zagorin, *How the Idea of Religious Toleration Came to the West*, 291.

37. José Casanova, "The Secular, Secularizations, Secularisms," in *Rethinking Secularism*, ed. Craig Calhoun, Mark Juergensmeyer, and Jonathan VanAntwerpen (New York: Oxford University Press, 2011), 54.

Secularism, by contrast, is a way of thinking and living, an ideology or worldview: it maintains that religious claims are either simply false (there is no transcendent spiritual reality) or at least that we can and should live as if they are false. This world is all that there is, period. Secularism as a worldview does not necessarily follow from the sociohistorical fact (if it is a fact) of secularization. Whether secularism does in fact result from secularization—and if so, whether this is a necessary consequence—is a contested issue in the ongoing secularization debate.

The meaning of the term "secular" is more contested than "secularization" or "secularism." At a basic level, the secular is simply that which is distinguished from the sacred or the religious. But there are many ways in which this distinction can be made, and it need not be taken as implying opposition between the secular and the religious. For example, a secular government does not derive its public legitimacy from any particular religious authority and does not in principle favor any particular religious (or nonreligious) tradition. A secular government is not necessarily neutral with respect to religion. Neutrality in policy decisions is an impossible ideal since every policy decision has implications—positive for some, but negative for others. But a secular government can strive to be impartial in its treatment of religious and nonreligious perspectives, not favoring any particular religious or nonreligious tradition. Similarly, a secular education need not be antireligious or anti-Christian. An appropriately secular education is one that tries to be impartial in its treatment of religious issues and perspectives. Nevertheless, in common use "secular" is often understood as implying a certain tension with what is religious, and although secularization may not entail secularism, there does seem to be a significant change in how religion is regarded and practiced in more secular societies.

The most powerful impetus for classical secularization theory came from the early giants of sociology, Émile Durkheim (1858–1917) and Max Weber (1864–1920). Rob Warner gives a good, concise overview of classical secularization theory:

> Both Durkheim and Weber recognized that Western modernity appeared increasingly inhospitable to religion. Grounded in the deteriorating condition of Christianity in Western Europe and building upon these scholars' insights, classical secularization theory argued that the demise of religion was sociologically determined and culturally inevitable. Secularization was understood therefore to be both a process of social change, closely intertwined with the evolution of the modern world, and also a theory of increasing religious marginalization not only descriptive of present and past transitions but predictive of a future

society where religion would have little or no public influence, social utility or plausible claim to a revelatory authority that in any way transcended reason.[38]

In the early twentieth century, there was general acceptance of the idea that modernization results in the decline of religion. Advocates did not necessarily insist that religion will be eliminated but felt that, with modernization, religious belief and practice eventually decline, and religion becomes increasingly socially marginalized. Peter Berger, an influential early proponent of the thesis, defines secularization in a seminal 1967 work, *The Sacred Canopy*, as "the process by which sectors of society and culture are removed from the domination of religious institutions and symbols." Secularization, he claims, manifests itself in Europe by "the evacuation by the Christian churches of areas previously under their control or influence—as in the separation of church and state, or in the expropriation of church lands, or in the emancipation of education from ecclesiastical authority."[39] On the individual level, there is a "secularization of consciousness" so that increasing numbers of people simply no longer accept religious teachings. Consequently, "the modern West has produced an increasing number of individuals who look upon the world and their own lives without the benefit of religious interpretations."[40] In other words, "secularization has resulted in a widespread collapse of the plausibility of traditional religious definitions of reality."[41]

Similarly, Bryan Wilson defines secularization as "the process in which religious consciousness, activities, and institutions lose social significance. It indicates that religion becomes marginal to the operation of the social system, and that the essential functions for the operation of society become rationalized, passing out of the control of agencies devoted to the supernatural."[42] Scientific ways of thinking, resulting in the "disenchantment [*Entzauberung*] of the world"; the differentiation of modern institutions; the disestablishment of religion in modern democracies; the massive changes brought about by migration and urbanization; and the information explosion accompanying the telecommunications revolutions have all contributed to undermining traditional religious ways of life.

38. Rob Warner, *Secularization and Its Discontents* (New York: Continuum, 2010), 2.
39. Peter Berger, *The Sacred Canopy: The Social Construction of Reality* (New York: Anchor Books, 1967), 107.
40. Ibid., 108.
41. Ibid., 127.
42. Bryan Wilson, "Secularization," *The Encyclopedia of Religion*, ed. Mircea Eliade (New York: Macmillan, 1987), 12:160. See also idem, *Religion in Secular Society: A Sociological Comment* (Harmondsworth, UK: Penguin, 1966); idem, *Religion in Sociological Perspective* (Oxford: Oxford University Press, 1982).

Perhaps the most vigorous advocate of the classical secularization thesis today is Steve Bruce. According to Bruce, secularization includes three inter-related changes: the decline of popular involvement with the churches, the decline in scope and influence of religious institutions, and the decline in the popularity and influence of religious beliefs.[43] Drawing upon data from societies in Western Europe, Bruce argues that the evidence clearly shows dramatic decline for Christianity in all three areas. The result is "that the plausibility of any single overarching moral and religious system declined, to be displaced by competing conceptions that, while they may have had much to say to priva-tized, individual experience, could have little connection to the performance of social roles or the operation of social systems."[44] Bruce contends that "three things—the social power of religion, the number of people who take it seri-ously, and how seriously anyone takes it—are causally related." The causal factors are associated with modernization, producing a situation in which "the declining power of religion causes a decline in the number of religious people and the extent to which people are religious."[45] Contrary to what some might expect, however, Bruce maintains that the end point of secularization is not atheism but simply religious indifference.[46]

There is no question that certain areas of Europe—Great Britain, Scandi-navia, Germany, France, the Czech Republic—are showing a marked decline in participation in religious activities. Secularization theory is most plausible when considering societies such as that in Great Britain.[47] In 2010 Rob Warner surveyed data on church attendance in England and concluded, "The English church attendance surveys (1979–2005) have provided a quarter of a century narrative of sustained church decline. . . . The trajectory appears unremitting: the Christian churches have become ever more marginalized, with less and less people attending on Sundays. The scale and speed of decline are stagger-ing: English congregations have on average halved in size in the last quarter century."[48] Similar patterns are found in other parts of Europe.

> Europe has for centuries been the heartland of Christianity, not only in terms of demographics, but also in global influence in theology and mission. In 1910, 66% of the world's Christians lived in Europe, but this had fallen substantially to around 25% a century later. In 1910 Europe was nearly 95% Christian and

43. Steve Bruce, *Religion in the Modern World: From Cathedrals to Cults* (Oxford: Oxford University Press, 1996), 26.

44. Ibid., 14.

45. Steve Bruce, *Secularization* (New York: Oxford University Press, 2011), 2.

46. Steve Bruce, *God Is Dead: Secularization in the West* (Oxford: Blackwell, 2002), 42.

47. See, e.g., the data provided by Bruce in ibid., 63–74.

48. Rob Warner, *Secularization and Its Discontents*, 7.

the religiously unaffiliated represented only 0.5% of the population. By 2010 the Christian percentage had fallen to 78.6%; Christian switching to atheism and agnosticism had raised the religiously unaffiliated combined share of the European population to 14.7%.[49]

Thus the classical secularization theory became widely influential, especially when considering Europe, so that religion was regarded as being in steady decline as societies modernize.

This understanding of secularization, however, has been subjected to withering criticism since the 1980s. In an influential 1993 essay, Stephen Warner declares, "That the reigning theory does not seem to work has become an open secret."[50] Peter Berger, an architect of the earlier perspective, later abandoned the classical theory. Writing in 2002, he observes, "It is fair to say that the majority of sociologists dealing with religion today no longer adhere to the equation of modernity and secularization."[51] Critics not only call into question the evidence alleged to support the traditional thesis but also produce impressive counterevidence from around the world indicating that, far from being the norm, secularization in Western Europe might itself be an anomaly. Advocates of the classical thesis generally consider only developments concerning Christianity and the West, giving priority to evidence from some parts of Western Europe and ignoring data on modernization and other religions in Asia, Latin America, and Africa.

Contrary to what the classical thesis would lead us to expect, religion continues to flourish around the world—including in many highly modernized societies. Berger points out that "the world today is massively religious, is *anything but* the secularized world that has been predicted (whether joyfully or despondently) by so many analysts of modernity."[52] The authors of *God's Century: Resurgent Religion and Global Politics* state,

The secularization thesis has proven a poor guide to global historical reality. Contrary to its predictions, the portion of the world population adhering to Catholic Christianity, Protestant Christianity, Islam, and Hinduism jumped from

49. Todd M. Johnson and Brian J. Grim, *The World's Religions in Figures* (Oxford: Wiley-Blackwell, 2013), 83.

50. R. Stephen Warner, "Work in Progress toward a New Paradigm for the Sociological Study of Religion in the United States," *American Journal of Sociology* 98.5 (March 1993): 1048.

51. Peter Berger, "Secularization and De-secularization," in *Religions in the Modern World*, ed. Linda Woodhead, Paul Fletcher, Hiroko Kawanami, and David Smith (London: Routledge, 2002), 291.

52. Peter Berger, *The Desecularization of the World* (Grand Rapids: Eerdmans, 1999), 9. Further critiques are summarized in Alan Aldridge, *Religion in the Contemporary World* (Cambridge: Polity, 2000), chap. 5; and Rob Warner, *Secularization and Its Discontents*, chaps. 1–3.

50 percent in 1900 to 64 percent in 2000. . . . Thus, over the past four decades, religion's influence on politics has reversed its decline and become more powerful on every continent and across every major religion.

The authors argue that "a dramatic and worldwide increase in the political influence of religion has occurred in roughly the past forty years."[53]

In particular, the classical thesis cannot account for the continuing social significance of religion in the United States and the rise of fundamentalist religious movements worldwide. As Berger observes, "Most of the world today is certainly not secular. It's very religious. So is the US. The one exception to this is Western Europe. One of the most interesting questions in the sociology of religion today is not, How do you explain the fundamentalism in Iran? but, Why is Western Europe different?"[54]

Social theorists unhappy with classical secularization theory have responded in various ways. Some simply reject the notion of secularization as no longer useful. As early as 1965, David Martin, for example, suggested that the term "secularization" be abandoned.[55] Martin did not heed his own advice, however, and went on to develop a sophisticated and nuanced alternative view of secularization.[56] Martin takes into account a much more diverse set of social contexts than was the case with traditional secularization theory. Not only does he examine the diverse social, religious, and political influences in societies throughout Europe, but he also looks carefully at developments in Latin America and elsewhere.[57] The comparative studies enabled him to move away from a model that regards secularization as a unified and homogenous process taking much the same form wherever it occurs. Although secularization in some sense can be found in many societies around the globe, its forms and trajectories vary, depending upon variables concerning the past history of the particular society's relation to monopolistic religious power. Moreover,

53. Monica Duffy Toft, Daniel Philpott, and Timothy Samuel Shah, *God's Century: Resurgent Religion and Global Politics* (New York: Norton, 2011), 2, 9.

54. Peter Berger, "Epistemological Modesty: An Interview with Peter Berger," *Christian Century* 114.30 (October 29, 1997): 974. See also Peter Berger, Grace Davie, and Effie Fokas, *Religious America, Secular Europe? A Theme and Variations* (Burlington, VT: Ashgate, 2008).

55. David Martin, "Towards Eliminating the Concept of Secularization," in *Penguin Survey of the Social Sciences*, ed. J. Gould (Harmondsworth, UK: Penguin Books, 1965), 169–82.

56. See David Martin, *A General Theory of Secularization* (Oxford: Blackwell, 1978); idem, *On Secularization: Towards a Revised General Theory* (Burlington, VT: Ashgate, 2005); idem, *The Future of Christianity: Reflections on Violence and Democracy, Religion and Secularization* (Burlington, VT: Ashgate, 2011).

57. Martin published groundbreaking studies on Pentecostalism in Latin America and around the world. See David Martin, *Tongues of Fire: The Explosion of Protestantism in Latin America* (Oxford: Blackwell, 1990); idem, *Pentecostalism: The World Their Parish* (Oxford: Blackwell, 2002).

according to Martin, patterns of secularization do not move unilaterally in a linear direction; they can be cyclical, reflected in an ebb and flow in religion's relation to social change.

Sociologist Grace Davie has also developed a complex view of secularization, comparing patterns in Europe with those in the United States, Latin America, and portions of Africa that reflect continuing religious vitality.[58] Davie made an important distinction between two aspects of secularization: institutional religious participation, such as church attendance, and personal beliefs. While there are clear indicators of declining participation in institutional religion in Great Britain, the data on religious beliefs are more ambiguous. Davie suggested that declining levels of church attendance seem to be accompanied by continuing assent to many religious beliefs, so that what we have is a case of "believing without belonging."[59] Giving undue attention to quantifiable metrics such as church attendance can distort the religious landscape.

In his seminal work, *Public Religions in the Modern World* (1994), José Casanova maintains that secularization includes three distinct components: "Secularization as differentiation of the secular spheres from religious institutions and norms, secularization as decline of religious beliefs and practices, and secularization as marginalization of religion to a privatized sphere."[60] Casanova argues that although the classical thesis tied all three together in one general theory of secularization, the three components should be distinguished and treated separately. When evidence for the three independent components is evaluated, only the first can be substantiated. The heart of secularization, then, is in the increasing differentiation of social institutions and their emancipation from religious authority.[61] Casanova concludes,

> While the two minor subtheses of the theory of secularization, namely, "the decline of religion" and "the privatization of religion," have undergone numerous critiques and revisions in the last fifteen years, the core of the thesis, namely, the understanding of secularization as a single process of functional differentiation of the various secular institutional spheres of modern societies from religion, remains relatively uncontested.[62]

58. Grace Davie, *Europe: The Exceptional Case; Parameters of Faith in the Modern World* (London: Darton, Longman & Todd, 2002).

59. Grace Davie, *Religion in Britain since 1945: Believing without Belonging* (Oxford: Blackwell, 2004). Warner observes that some social observers have reversed Davie's formula, noticing that some societies manifest the opposite pattern, namely, belonging without believing. Rob Warner, *Secularization and Its Discontents*, 50.

60. José Casanova, *Public Religions in the Modern World* (Chicago: University of Chicago Press, 1994), 211.

61. Ibid., 212.

62. Casanova, "The Secular, Secularizations, Secularisms," 61.

A host of scholars have analyzed the changing religious patterns in the United States and provide explanations for the continued flourishing of religion in America despite its being one of the most modernized and technologically advanced societies on earth.[63] Some point to the religious vitality introduced by the large number of immigrants since the 1960s. But, contrary to popular perception, which sees immigration as contributing to the growing diversity of religions in America, "the great majority of the newcomers are Christian." Although some immigrants are Buddhist, Hindu, Muslim, or Sikh, Stephen Warner states that "at least two-thirds or more of post-1965 immigrants are Christian. . . . One consequence of the new, post-1965 immigration will surely be that white Americans will come to see that Christianity is neither theirs nor their European ancestors' alone. New immigrants of myriad races and national origins are now practicing their Christianities on these shores."[64]

Rodney Stark and others have developed a fresh model for explaining the resiliency of religion in America. Rational choice theory adapts economic principles of supply, demand, and regulation and applies them to the "marketplace of religions."[65] Rational choice theory maintains that the religious demand is more or less constant across societies, but the vitality of religious expression within societies depends upon the degree to which the supply side of the equation is free from state-sponsored religious monopolies. Religion continues to flourish in America because, contrary to many European societies, there is no legacy of a state-sponsored church. Religious denominations are forced to compete with each other for religious "market share," and this encourages religious entrepreneurial creativity. Contrary to classical secularization theory, the religious pluralization of society does not erode religious commitment:

63. See, e.g., Robert Wuthnow, *The Restructuring of American Religion: Society and Faith since World War II* (Princeton: Princeton University Press, 1988); idem, *After Heaven: Spirituality in America since the 1950s* (Berkeley: University of California Press, 1998); idem, *The God Problem: Expressing Faith and Being Reasonable* (Berkeley: University of California Press, 2012); Christian Smith, *American Evangelicalism: Embattled and Thriving* (Chicago: University of Chicago Press, 1998); Wade Clark Roof, *Spiritual Marketplace: Baby Boomers and the Remaking of American Religion* (Princeton: Princeton University Press, 1999); Robert D. Putnam and David E. Campbell, *American Grace: How Religion Divides and Unites Us* (New York: Simon & Schuster, 2010).

64. R. Stephen Warner, "The De-Europeanization of American Christianity," in *A Nation of Religions: The Politics of Pluralism in Multireligious America*, ed. Stephen Prothero (Chapel Hill: University of North Carolina Press, 2006), 234.

65. See Rodney Stark and William Sims Bainbridge, *The Future of Religion* (Berkeley: University of California Press, 1985); idem, *A Theory of Religion* (New York: Peter Lang, 1987); Rodney Stark and Roger Finke, *Acts of Faith: Explaining the Human Side of Religion* (Berkeley: University of California Press, 2000).

it enhances religious vitality. "It is when the religious market is free enough to offer several brands of religion, at several levels of tension with the socio-cultural environment, that the greatest proportion of the population receives appropriate compensators and responds with firm religious commitment."[66] But rational choice theory has strong critics who argue that even if it were plausible with respect to the United States, it has little explanatory force in other contexts.[67]

Religious Belief in a Secular Age

One of the more perceptive observers of intellectual and social changes in Europe and North America in modern times is the Canadian philosopher and social theorist Charles Taylor. In his magisterial study, *A Secular Age* (2007), Taylor turns his attention to the changes in religious commitment or belief in Europe during the past four centuries. Although he is critical of the classical secularization thesis, he acknowledges that religious commitment today is both different from what it used to be and more difficult to sustain. According to Taylor, the heart of the issue is captured in the following question: "Why was it virtually impossible not to believe in God in, say, 1500 in our Western society, while in 2000 many of us find this not only easy, but even inescapable?"[68] In framing his study around this question, Taylor is examining the set of personal and public conditions that influence the plausibility of belief in God. He argues that in Europe, and to some extent in North America, modernization has brought about a profound change in these conditions so that what was once taken for granted now is contested. Taylor's analysis—extended over eight hundred dense pages—is rich and multifaceted, and we cannot begin to summarize it adequately here. But I will briefly mention a dominant theme

---

66. Stark and Bainbridge, *A Theory of Religion*, 149.

67. See Rob Warner, *Secularization and Its Discontents*, 78–82; Lawrence A. Young, ed., *Rational Choice Theory and Religion* (London: Routledge, 1997); William Swatos and Daniel Olson, *The Secularization Debate* (Lanham, MD: Rowman & Littlefield, 2000); Steve Bruce, *Choice and Religion* (Oxford: Oxford University Press, 1999). Interestingly, Fenggang Yang adopts a version of rational choice theory in his analysis of the resurgence of religions in China today. See Fenggang Yang, *Religion in China: Survival and Revival under Communist Rule* (New York: Oxford University Press, 2012), 14–23.

68. Charles Taylor, *A Secular Age* (Cambridge, MA: Harvard University Press, 2007), 26. The book has stimulated extensive debate, with at least two collections of essays by noted historians, philosophers, and sociologists addressing his work. See the essays in Calhoun, Juergensmeyer, and VanAntwerpen, *Rethinking Secularism*; Michael Warner, Jonathan VanAntwerpen, and Craig Calhoun, eds., *Varieties of Secularism in a Secular Age* (Cambridge, MA: Harvard University Press, 2010).

in his model that has implications for the plausibility of the idea that there is one true religion for everyone.

Taylor suggests that we think of secularization in the West in terms of three fundamental changes resulting in three distinct senses of secularity.[69] First, there are changes in public institutions and practices, so that "whereas the political organization of all pre-modern societies was in some way connected to, based on, guaranteed by some faith in, or adherence to God, or some notion of ultimate reality, the modern Western state is free from this connection." This is similar to what others speak of as the differentiation of society, or the division of life into increasingly specialized domains, most of which have no direct religious connection. The second transformation consists in the declining numbers of those who continue to embrace traditional religious beliefs and practices. In this sense secularity "consists in the falling off of religious belief and practice, in people turning away from God, and no longer going to Church." These two transformations correspond to the changes highlighted in the traditional secularization thesis and are especially evident in some parts of Europe.

But the third transformation concerns the ways in which modern people "are religious." Taylor states, "It is obvious that a decline in belief and practice has occurred, and beyond this, that the unchallengeable status that belief enjoyed in earlier centuries has been lost. This is the major phenomenon of 'secularization.'"[70] And yet, despite decline in religious commitment in the West, many people continue to embrace religion or spirituality, although the ways in which they do so are markedly different from premodern times. The shift here "consists, among other things, of a move from a society where belief in God is unchallenged and indeed unproblematic, to one in which it is understood to be one option among others, and frequently not the easiest to embrace." In this sense secularization involves the change that "takes us from a society in which it was virtually impossible not to believe in God, to one in which faith, even for the staunchest believer, is one human possibility among others. . . . Belief in God is no longer axiomatic. There are alternatives."[71] Even when one continues to affirm Christian teachings, the nature of belief—the conditions within which one continues in belief—are different than they were before.

What do we mean when we speak of Western modernity as "secular"? There are all sorts of ways of describing it: the separation of religion from public life,

69. Charles Taylor, *Secular Age*, 1–3.
70. Ibid., 530.
71. Ibid., 3.

the decline of religious belief and practice. But while one cannot avoid touching on these, my main interest here lies in another facet of our age: belief in God, or in the transcendent in any form, is contested; it is an option among many; it is therefore fragile; for some people in some milieus, it is very difficult, even "weird." Five hundred years ago in Western civilization, this wasn't so.[72]

One of the factors that affects the conditions of belief and makes traditional Christian teachings more problematic is loss of a sense of transcendence. The modern, secular age is one in which people—including many religious people—make sense of things in terms of this-worldly causality. Previously one thought of events as directly related to the causal activity of God (or angels or demons); today people assume natural causal explanations for illness, storms, earthquakes, or wars from within the human or physical realms. Picking up on Weber's notion of disenchantment (*Entzauberung*), Taylor states, "Everyone can agree that one of the big differences between us and our ancestors of 500 years ago is that they lived in an 'enchanted' world and we do not."[73] In the modern era, people do not experience the world as an enchanted place with supernatural spirits and forces. Modern people think and act within what Taylor calls "the immanent frame," that is, an idea of the natural order that can be understood without reference to anything beyond itself. "The sense of the immanent frame is that of living in impersonal orders, cosmic, social, and ethical orders that can be fully explained in their own terms and don't need to be conceived as dependent on anything outside, on the 'supernatural' or the 'transcendent.'"[74] Within the immanent frame, three critical orders—the cosmic (universe), the social, and the moral—are understood strictly in natural, "this-worldly," or immanent terms, devoid of reference to the supernatural or transcendent realm. It is not so much that people are explicitly atheistic (most are not) but that they live their lives as if God were absent. It is difficult for modern people to live consciously in and really imagine a world in which God is an ever-present reality. Modernity has brought about a radically different "social imaginary,"[75] or way in which people imagine their social existence,

72. Charles Taylor, "Western Secularity," in Calhoun, Juergensmeyer, and VanAntwerpen, *Rethinking Secularism*, 49.

73. Ibid., 38.

74. Charles Taylor, "Afterword," in Warner, VanAntwerpen, and Calhoun, *Varieties of Secularism*, 306–7.

75. For Taylor, a social imaginary is "the way we collectively imagine, even pretheoretically, our social life in the contemporary western world." A social imaginary is not a formal theory but rather "the way ordinary people 'imagine' their social surroundings"; it is "that common understanding which makes possible common practices, and a widely shared sense of legitimacy" (Taylor, *Secular Age*, 146, 171–72).

so that modern people in the West live "within a purely immanent order, that is, the possibility of really conceiving of, of imagining, ourselves within such an order, one that could be accounted for on its own terms, which thus leaves belief in the transcendent as a kind of 'optional extra'—something it had never been before in any human society."[76]

Another way to put this is to say that modernization and globalization have brought about fragmentation of our social framework so that there is no religious or moral monopoly of the sources of legitimacy. We live with the awareness that our commitments and way of life portray merely one among many possible options, some of which seem just as plausible as ours. Our religious beliefs and practices are fragile in that they cannot simply be taken for granted.

> It is a pluralist world, in which many forms of belief and unbelief jostle, and hence fragilize each other. It is a world in which belief has lost many of the social matrices which made it seem "obvious" and unchallengeable. . . . The salient feature of Western societies is not so much a decline of religious faith and practice, though there has been lots of that, more in some societies than in others, but rather a mutual fragilization of different religious positions, as well as of the outlooks both of belief and unbelief.[77]

Secularization in this sense echoes a prominent theme in the later writings of Peter Berger, who maintains that "modernity pluralizes the lifeworlds of individuals and consequently undermines all taken-for-granted certainties."[78] The awareness of a range of possible options for belief and lifestyle can be disconcerting.

> Cultural plurality is experienced by the individual, not just as something external—all those people he bumps into—but as an internal reality, a set of options present in his mind. In other words, the different cultures he encounters in his social environment are transformed into alternative scenarios, options, for his own life. The very phrase "religious preference" (another American contribution to the language of modernity!) perfectly catches this fact: The individual's religion is not something irrevocably given, a *datum* that he can change no more than he can change his genetic inheritance; rather, religion becomes a choice, a product of the individual's ongoing project of world and self-construction. . . . We do have a problem of belief, and it not only raises the question of why we

76. Taylor, "Western Secularity," 50–51.
77. Taylor, *Secular Age*, 531, 595.
78. Peter Berger, "Reflections on the Sociology of Religion Today," in *Sociology of Religion* 62 (2001): 449.

should believe in God but why we should believe in *this* God. There are others, after all, and today they are made available in an unprecedented way through the religious supermarket of modern pluralism.[79]

Christians thus confront a basic question: "If our situation forces us to choose between the gods, since no god can any longer be taken for granted, why should we choose the biblical God?"[80]

Despite its many deserved accolades, *A Secular Age* has also come in for some criticism. One criticism—which Taylor himself acknowledges—is that in his focus on the West, Taylor has "neglected the way in which Western understandings of religion were informed through the precolonial and then the colonial encounter with other parts of the world."[81] Peter van der Veer in particular has argued that secularization cannot be understood apart from appreciating how the Western colonial encounter with Asia impacted European developments.[82] Van der Veer contends that modernity and European secularization must be understood within the context of what he calls "interactional history." That is,

> the project of modernity, with all its revolutionary ideas of nations, equality, citizenship, democracy, and rights, is developed not only in Atlantic interactions between the United States and Europe but also in interactions with Asian and African societies that are coming within the orbit of imperial expansion. Instead of the oft-assumed *universalism* of the Enlightenment, I would propose to look at the *universalization* of ideas that emerge from a history of interactions. Enlightened notions of rationality and progress are not simply invented in Europe and accepted elsewhere but are both produced and universally spread in the expansion of European power.[83]

A second criticism concerns the extent to which Taylor's analysis can be extended to other modern societies outside the West. Taylor restricts his focus to the West, and especially to Europe, and he acknowledges the need for careful study of many non-Western contexts to see whether the patterns he identifies

79. Peter Berger, *A Far Glory: The Quest for Faith in an Age of Credulity* (New York: Anchor Books, 1992), 67, 146–47, with original emphasis.

80. Peter Berger, *Questions of Faith: A Skeptical Affirmation of Christianity* (Oxford: Blackwell, 2004), 20.

81. Taylor, "Afterword," 301.

82. Peter van der Veer, *Imperial Encounters* (Princeton: Princeton University Press, 2007); idem, *The Modern Spirit of Asia: The Spiritual and the Secular in China and India* (Princeton: Princeton University Press, 2014).

83. Peter van der Veer, "Smash Temples, Burn Books: Comparing Secularist Projects in India and China," in Calhoun, Juergensmeyer, and VanAntwerpen, *Rethinking Secularism*, 270–71.

in the West are present elsewhere. "We are more and more living in a world of 'multiple modernities.' These crucial changes need to be studied in their different civilizational sites before we rush to global generalization."[84]

Can models of secularization, devised to explain developments in the West, be extended to societies in Asia, Latin America, and Africa that are also undergoing modernization and globalization? We cannot simply assume that patterns of secularization in the West will necessarily appear in modernizing societies elsewhere. José Casanova, for example, states,

> The very category of secularization becomes deeply problematic once it is conceptualized in a Eurocentric way as a universal process of progressive human societal development from "belief" to "unbelief" and from traditional "religion" to modern "secularity" and once it is then transferred to other world religions and other civilizational areas with very different dynamics of structuration of the relations and tensions between religion and world or between cosmological transcendence and worldly immanence. Moreover, in the same way as Western secular modernity is fundamentally and inevitably post-Christian, the emerging multiple modernities in the different postaxial civilizational areas are likely to be post-Hindu, or post-Confucian, or post-Muslim; that is, they will also be particular and contingent refashionings and transformations of existing civilizational patterns and social imaginaries mixed with modern secular ones.[85]

Casanova's comments are important, and we need many careful studies of the impact of modernization and globalization upon societies elsewhere before global generalizations can be made.

Richard Madsen applies Taylor's discussion to modern Asian societies and concludes that while there are some senses in which China, Indonesia, and Taiwan can be regarded as secular, these societies also manifest important differences from the West.[86] Madsen acknowledges evidence there of political secularism, so that the state is regarded as (somewhat) neutral with regard to religious belief and practice. But it is less clear that there is a marked decline in religious belief, and Taylor's third sense of secularism—the changing conditions of belief so that belief in God is one option among many—does not seem to fit many Asian societies. In part this is because belief plays a different role in Asian religious traditions than it does in Christianity, so there is less evidence of a crisis in belief.

84. Taylor, *Secular Age*, 21. See also Taylor, "Western Secularity," 36.
85. Casanova, "The Secular, Secularizations, Secularisms," 63–64.
86. Richard Madsen, "Secularism, Religious Change, and Social Conflict in Asia," in Calhoun, Juergensmeyer, and VanAntwerpen, *Rethinking Secularism*, 248–69.

Although many people in these and most other Asian societies continue to practice religion, it is a different kind of religion from that in most Western societies—more a matter of ritual and myth than belief and deeply embedded in the social, economic, and political life of local communities. It is part of the public life of local communities. Religion has not undergone the transition from public practice to private belief that Taylor discerns in the West.[87]

At the same time, it would be wrong to conclude that secularization is simply a Western phenomenon and thereby ignore apparent similarities among modernizing societies worldwide.[88] Peter van der Veer describes the developing idea of the secular in Europe and helpfully compares that with the secular in India and China, especially in relation to the concepts of spirituality and nationalism in the latter countries. He argues for a fresh understanding of spirituality that is not in opposition to secular modernity "but instead shows its centrality to the modern project."[89] Debates over secularization should consider not only institutional forms of religion but also the more amorphous modern notion of spirituality, comparing the relation between secularity and spirituality as this develops in somewhat different ways in Europe, India, and China.

Japan also serves as an interesting focal point for assessing the global relevance of models of secularization. The Japanese live in one of the most technologically advanced, highly educated, and modernized societies on earth today. Japan also has a long and rich set of religious traditions and institutions. In one sense, the Japanese seem highly religious: temples and shrines are ubiquitous, and participation in religious activities seems to be high. But assessing the significance of religion in Japan is difficult, and we cannot assume that religion functions in Japan the same as in Europe or North America. Part of the difficulty is due to the fact that standard markers of religious vitality in the West—clear professions of belief in religious teachings, regular attendance in worship services, baptism—do not have the same significance in Japanese society. Robert Kisala observes, "In contrast to the situation in many European countries and some other areas of the West, where we see relatively high levels of at least nominal religious affiliation and low levels of participation in religious rites, religion in Japan is marked by almost universal participation in certain rites and customs but low levels of self-acknowledged affiliation to a religious group."[90]

87. Ibid., 266.
88. See, e.g., Yang, *Religion in China*; Rajeev Bhargava, ed., *Secularism and Its Critics* (Delhi: Oxford University Press, 1998), which includes essays examining secularism in India.
89. Van der Veer, *Modern Spirit of Asia*, 7.
90. Robert Kisala, "Japanese Religions," in *Nanzan Guide to Japanese Religions*, ed. Paul L. Swanson and Clark Chilson (Honolulu: University of Hawaii Press, 2006), 3.

In spite of the prevalence of religious symbols, however, Japanese society also appears to be highly secular. Ian Reader states,

> As a highly developed non-Western country with increasingly high levels of urbanization and education, [Japan] can serve as a test case of whether claims underlying the notion of secularization are viable. In particular, Japan can provide a valid test case for examining whether modernization, advanced educational systems, increasing urbanization and a shift from a rural/agricultural economy towards urban and technological modes of production may lead to a decline in religious faith, engagement and belonging.[91]

Some, such as Rodney Stark, appealed to the apparent vitality of Japanese religious traditions as counterevidence to the secularization thesis.[92] In response, Reader examines a wide variety of evidence—such as multiple surveys of religious beliefs; the numbers of temples, shrines, and Buddhist and Shinto priests; and participation in popular folk rituals and Buddhist funerals or observance of the Buddhist or Shinto family altars—and concludes that all indicators show a clear decline in religious affiliation and participation.

> I contend that Japan, rather than providing comfort for the opponents of secularization theory, shows almost the exact opposite and that secularization (in terms of the idea of a "decline of religion" and a public withdrawal from engagement with the religious sphere) is a growing force to be reckoned with in Japan today. Moreover, there are clear correlations between modernisation, urbanisation and higher levels of education (factors often cited as formative forces in the secularisation process), and declining levels of religious belief and practice, whether individually or institutionally.[93]

We cannot summarize the substantial evidence Reader draws upon here, but given the significance of funerals, the ancestral cult, and beliefs about the afterlife for traditional Japanese religious practices, the decline in these areas is highly significant. Reader reports results from one survey indicating that less than 50 percent of Japanese profess belief in an afterlife.[94] In 1999 only 14.9 percent of young people reported firmly believing in the existence of life

91. Ian Reader, "Secularisation, R.I.P.? Nonsense! The 'Rush Hour away from the Gods' and the Decline of Religion in Contemporary Japan," *Journal of Religion in Japan* 1 (2012): 9–10. See also idem, "Buddhism in Crisis? Institutional Decline in Modern Japan," *Buddhist Studies Review* 28.2 (2011): 233–63.

92. Reader's "Secularisation, R.I.P.? Nonsense!" is a response to claims made in Rodney Stark, "Secularization, R.I.P.," in *Sociology of Religion* 60.3 (1999): 249–73.

93. Reader, "Secularisation, R.I.P.?," 10–11.

94. Ibid., 18.

after death, with 36.0 percent saying they believe in it to some degree, down from 29.9 percent and 40.2 percent respectively in 1992. Although funerals in Japan have traditionally been Buddhist, in the past two decades there has been a significant increase in nonreligious funerals; as a result, 26 percent of all funerals in Tokyo in 2006 were nonreligious and had no Buddhist elements at all. Surveys also indicate a steady decline in Japanese households that maintain the traditional Buddhist altar (*butsudan*) or Shinto altar (*kamidana*). Reader observes that public dissatisfaction with religion, including Buddhism, is so pervasive that new phrases have been adopted: *shukyobanare* (estrangement from religion) and *bukkyobanare* (estrangement from Buddhism).[95]

> The Japanese avoid religious organisations and declare repeatedly in surveys that they do not have faith and that religion is not important; they are turning in increasing numbers to ways of dealing with death that repudiate their Buddhist traditions and that are overtly secular and non-religious. They no longer get Shinto and Buddhist altars for their houses—and people in the households that have them appear to be becoming increasingly lax about performing acts of worship before them.[96]

Reader concludes that far from being irrelevant or providing counterevidence to secularization, evidence from Japan shows that secularization theory should not be dismissed prematurely. "The Japanese case informs us that secularisation is a force to be reckoned with in the modern world rather than an idea to be consigned to the grave."[97] Clearly the debate over the relation between modernization and religions is far from over.

95. Ibid., 16.
96. Ibid., 33.
97. Ibid., 34.

3

Buddhism in the Modern World

In the first two chapters we saw that religions are not static, unchanging entities that are simply passed on intact from one age to another. Religions such as Hinduism, Buddhism, and Christianity, as we encounter them today, are in part the products of changing social, cultural, and political realities brought about by modernization. In some cases the actual beliefs and practices of religious communities have changed. The ways in which we think about Hinduism, Buddhism, and Christianity have also changed. This is certainly the case with Buddhism, a religion that has undergone remarkable transformations as it moved from its initial home in India onward throughout Asia and then into North America and Europe. Buddhism, as we know it today, has been shaped through its encounter with modernization, Western colonialism, and the Christian missionary movement.

In this chapter we will examine how Europeans came to think about Buddhism as a religion and some of the ways in which Buddhism has been affected by modernization and the West. Although it is easy to assume that the Buddhism we see in Asia today is simply the ancient dharma of the Buddha transmitted faithfully for over two millennia, the reality is more complex. Not only have the teachings and practices of Buddhism changed as it adapted to the diverse cultures and religious traditions of Asia, but also the various Asian forms of Buddhism were transformed to some extent by their encounters with modernization and the West. Buddhism is now a global religion, with significant numbers of adherents in North America, Europe, and parts of Latin America. But in most locations, Buddhism today reflects the results of the complex and fascinating encounter between ancient traditions and modern ways.

Buddhism: A Short Overview

What we call Buddhism is a broad family of religious and philosophical traditions that appeared initially in India but have developed over the past 2,500 years in various cultures.[1] Buddhism quickly spread from its homeland into south, central, and east Asia. As Buddhist teaching was embraced by people in very different cultural and religious settings, Buddhism itself changed, resulting in an enormous variety in teachings and practices among contemporary Buddhists. But all Buddhist traditions claim to trace their beliefs and practices in some sense back to the Enlightenment of Gautama the Buddha.

Texts on world religions generally introduce Buddhism by telling the story of Siddhartha Gautama, who was born into a life of luxury and pleasure. Upon being confronted with disease, old age, and death, however, young Gautama rejected his palace life and embarked upon a quest to discover the causes of suffering and its cure. After experimenting with various ascetic meditative disciplines, Gautama became fully enlightened, or awakened. The Buddha (literally, the Awakened One), as he was now called, is said to have grasped the fundamental causes of suffering and how to make them cease. The Buddha's insights were expressed in the Four Noble Truths, which became the core principles for Buddhist teaching. Those who embraced these teachings and practiced the Noble Eightfold Path successfully could, like the Buddha, break the causal chain driving rebirth and suffering, thus gaining the bliss of nirvana. Over the next forty-five years, the Buddha traveled widely, teaching these truths and attracting many disciples.

The popular story of the Buddha's enlightenment, summarized above, comes from the Buddhacarita by Asvaghosa, which is usually dated in the late first or second century AD.[2] Questions about Gautama's life are complicated by the fact that written accounts of his life do not appear until 300–400 years after

1. Helpful introductions to Buddhism include Donald S. Lopez Jr., *The Story of Buddhism: A Concise Guide to Its History and Teachings* (New York: HarperCollins, 2001); Donald W. Mitchell, *Buddhism: Introducing the Buddhist Experience*, 2nd ed. (New York: Oxford University Press, 2008); Richard H. Robinson and Willard L. Johnson, *The Buddhist Religion*, 4th ed. (Belmont, CA: Wadsworth, 1997).

2. Buddhacarita 4 in *Buddhist Scriptures*, ed. and trans. by Edward Conze (New York: Penguin Books, 1959), 4–5. See Donald S. Lopez Jr., *From Stone to Flesh: A Short History of the Buddha* (Chicago: University of Chicago Press, 2013), 10–11.

his death. There is uncertainty about the century in which Gautama lived, with Western scholars generally accepting the dates 563–483 BC for his life, whereas Chinese and Japanese scholars often place him in the fifth century BC. The Japanese scholar Hajime Nakamura, for example, argues for 466–386 BC.[3]

Nevertheless, the heart of the Buddha's teaching is said to be the Four Noble Truths, preached during his first sermon.[4] The First Truth states that all existence is characterized by dukkha, which is usually translated as suffering, pain, or discontent. Even the most intense pleasures are temporary, and all of existence involves unsatisfactoriness. The Second Truth teaches that the fundamental cause of suffering is tanha, which is thirst, craving, or desire. It is desire itself, not simply wrong desires, that causes suffering. According to the Third Truth, when desire or craving ceases, then suffering ceases as well. The Fourth Truth sets out the Noble Eightfold Path, which provides the way to eliminate desire and suffering through a combination of correct understanding and moral action.

The Four Noble Truths reflect simplicity and a clear logical structure. An initial diagnosis of the cause of suffering is followed by a prescription for the cure. Both diagnosis and cure are based upon a sophisticated metaphysic that presupposes multiple rebirths regulated by the principle of karma and the teachings of anatta (absence of self) and anicca (impermanence). Like most Indian religious and philosophical systems, the Buddha accepted the idea of multiple rebirths regulated by karma. Unlike the Brahmins and Jains, however, he based his teachings on the radical notion of the impermanence of everything apart from nirvana. Everything that exists is in continual flux, and beings are continually being reborn, with the conditions of one's rebirth determined by previous dispositions and actions.

A consequence of the teaching on impermanence is anatta, or denying the reality of a substantial, enduring soul or person. This innovation set the Buddha's teachings apart from that of the Brahmins and Jains. But if there is no soul or enduring person, what then is reborn? What is passed on from one life to another is the cumulative karmic effects of actions and dispositions, which in the next life combine under appropriate conditions to form again the illusion of an enduring self. Clinging to and acting upon the false idea of an

3. See Hajime Nakamura, *Gotama Buddha: A Biography Based upon the Most Reliable Texts*, vol. 1, trans. Gaynor Sekimori (Tokyo: Kosei, 2000); David Edward Shaner, "Biographies of the Buddha," *Philosophy East and West* 37.3 (July 1987): 306–22; Peter Harvey, "Buddha, Story of," in *Encyclopedia of Buddhism*, ed. Damien Keown and Charles S. Prebish (London: Routledge, 2010), 137–49.
4. From the Samyutta-Nikaya, in *A Source Book in Indian Philosophy*, ed. Sarvepalli Radhakrishnan and Charles A. Moore (Princeton: Princeton University Press, 1957), 65.

enduring soul feeds desire, thereby perpetuating rebirths and suffering. When the fires of desire and the conditions producing rebirth are eliminated, there is no more birth, resulting in nirvana, the only permanent and unconditioned reality. The soteriological goal of early Buddhism was attaining nirvana by eliminating the causal conditions for rebirth.

In time, Buddhists developed sophisticated elaborations of these basic teachings, involving highly technical discussions of epistemology and ontology. Many schools developed, with Buddhism eventually evolving into three very broad traditions: the Theravada, Mahayana, and Vajrayana (or Tibetan) traditions. Furthermore, running across all three traditions is the important distinction between "high" or philosophical Buddhism and "folk" Buddhism. The former refers to the intellectually sophisticated philosophical Buddhism practiced by scholars and monks; the latter is the Buddhism of the laity, the ordinary men and women who often cared little about the doctrinal subtleties. Folk Buddhism typically combines Buddhist teachings with an assortment of local folk religious beliefs and practices, including an enchanted world of spirits, gods, ghosts, demons, and magical forces that would be frowned upon by philosophical Buddhism.

Buddhism has always been a missionary religion, moving beyond India first into what is today Sri Lanka and Southeast Asia, then throughout northern and eastern Asia. Nakamura observes, "Soon after the founding of the Order, the Buddha sent out his followers on missionary journeys to spread the Dharma with the command, 'Fare ye forth, brethren, on the mission that is for the good of the many, for the happiness of the many; to take compassion to the world; to work for the profit and good and happiness of gods and men. Go singly; go not in pairs.'"[5] Buddhist teachings and practices were transmitted by merchants who came to India for business, converted to Buddhism, and then returned to their homes with the new teaching.[6] According to tradition, King Asoka, the great third-century BC Mauryan ruler of many peoples of south Asia who converted to Buddhism, sent Buddhist emissaries to rulers in Syria, Egypt, and Macedonia in the west, and to Sri Lanka and Southeast Asia to the south.[7] Buddhism moved north into China sometime during the first

5. Hajime Nakamura, "Unity and Diversity in Buddhism," in *The Path of the Buddha: Buddhism Interpreted by Buddhists*, ed. Kenneth W. Morgan (New York: Ronald, 1956), 367. For a helpful study of the missionary nature of twentieth-century Buddhism, see *Buddhist Missionaries in the Era of Globalization*, ed. Linda Learman (Honolulu: University of Hawaii Press, 2005).

6. Akira Hirakawa, *A History of Indian Buddhism: From Sakyamuni to Early Mahayana*, trans. and ed. Paul Groner (Honolulu: University of Hawaii Press, 1990), 76–77.

7. D. W. Mitchell, *Buddhism*, 70–72.

century AD and then into Korea in the fourth century. It was introduced into Japan in the sixth century and Tibet in the seventh century. Although for over two millennia it was found exclusively in Asia, in the nineteenth and twentieth centuries Buddhism became established in North America and Europe, and today it is a genuinely global religion.

Theravada Buddhism

Although no current Buddhist school can trace its origin directly back to Gautama, Theravada Buddhism is generally accepted as reflecting more closely the teachings of the early Buddhist community than do other forms of Buddhism. It is found today in Sri Lanka, Myanmar (Burma), Thailand, Laos, and Kampuchea (Cambodia) as well as in immigrant communities in the West.

Theravada Buddhism tends to be more conservative and less doctrinally innovative than other forms of Buddhism. For example, Theravada Buddhists accept the Pali Canon as faithfully conveying the teachings of Gautama and thus as fully authoritative. By contrast, Mahayana Buddhists acknowledge the authority of the Pali Canon yet also recognize many other sutras and commentaries as equally, and sometimes more, authoritative than the Pali texts. While generally discouraging metaphysical speculation, the Theravada tradition emphasizes the Four Noble Truths and the Path of Purification (as outlined in the Noble Eightfold Path) as the way to enlightenment and nirvana. The one who follows the Path of Purification successfully is an arahat (arhat), or "worthy one," free from all defilements, and will not be reborn. Buddhists give special reverence to the Three Refuges, or the Three Jewels—the Buddha, the dharma, and the sangha. One formally identifies oneself as a Buddhist with the public profession of the following formula:

> I go to the Buddha for refuge.
> I go to the dharma for refuge.
> I go to the sangha for refuge.

The term "Buddha" is not a proper name but rather a descriptive title meaning Awakened One or Enlightened One. Buddhism has always maintained that there were other buddhas prior to Gautama and there will be others to come in the future. "The key role of a perfect Buddha is, by his own efforts to rediscover the timeless truths and practices of the *Dharma* . . . at a time when they have been lost to society."[8] Theravada Buddhism emphasizes

---

8. Harvey, "Buddha," in *Encyclopedia of Buddhism*, 93.

the humanity of Gautama the Buddha, discouraging speculation about his metaphysical status after attaining Enlightenment. Gautama was a man, but because of the perfections developed through his many previous lives, he was a man with extraordinary abilities. Once enlightened, however, the Buddha was no longer merely a human since "he had perfected and transcended his humanness" and was thus beyond humans and the gods.[9]

The term "dharma" has various meanings in Indian religious and philosophical thought, but in Buddhism it refers to the teachings of the Buddha. The dharma includes but also transcends the teachings of the historical Gautama. "The *Dharma* itself, however, is transhistorical and exists whether or not it has been perceived by anyone or disseminated as a body of teachings over time by the Sangha."[10] The sangha is the monastic community comprising the disciples of the Buddha who have committed themselves to living out the teachings of the Buddha. So the Three Refuges reflect the interrelationship between the eternal truth; the Buddha, who discovers and passes on this truth; and the monastic community that maintains and practices this truth.

Theravada Buddhism insists that individuals are responsible for their own liberation from rebirth. Although the Buddha proclaimed the dharma and thus can be said to assist all sentient beings, it is up to each individual to grasp the truth, to appropriate it, and thereby to attain nirvana. Only those in a monastic community who have properly mastered the necessary disciplines under a qualified mentor can hope to realize enlightenment in this life. The rest must be content with trying to improve their place in the next life, eventually positioning themselves for possibly attaining nirvana.

Traditional Buddhist cosmology includes many levels of heavens and hells, inhabited by gods, demigods, humans, animals, ghosts, and hell beings.[11] Rebirth is determined by the relative weight of good karma or meritorious actions over bad karma. It is not surprising, then, that hope for a good rebirth has resulted in the importance of *punyu*, or merit, in Theravada Buddhism. Giving alms to monks, practicing morality, respecting elders, listening to preaching, or even having one's son undergo ordination as a monk can all produce merit. An elaborate system for attaining and transferring merit (what Richard Gombrich

9. Ibid. Buddhism does not deny the reality of gods and other supernatural beings, but it includes them within the causal nexus determining all existents and regards them as irrelevant to attaining enlightenment. See U. Thittila, "The Fundamental Principles of Theravada Buddhism," in Morgan, *The Path of the Buddha*, 71. What it does deny is the reality of an almighty Creator who creates everything that is apart from God and exists.

10. Damien Keown, "Dharma," *Encyclopedia of Buddhism*, 271.

11. See Lopez, *Story of Buddhism*, 19–24.

calls "spiritual cash") has developed, so that merit can even be transferred from the living to those who have died.[12]

Mahayana Buddhism

A distinct Buddhist movement known as the Mahayana, or Great Vehicle—in contrast with what is somewhat pejoratively referred to as the Hinayana, or Lesser Vehicle—developed roughly from 100 BC to AD 100. Mahayana is today the dominant form of Buddhism in China, Korea, Vietnam, and Japan and is also found in the West. Like Theravada, Mahayana Buddhism claims to represent the original teaching of the Buddha.

Whereas Theravada restricted the path toward enlightenment to the few, Mahayana traditions opened the path toward liberation to the many. Mahayana provides a vast multitude of spiritual guides and saviors—especially the bodhisattvas—to assist the common people in deliverance from suffering. Bodhisattvas are benevolent supernatural beings who, out of compassion, come to the aid of sentient beings caught up in the cycle of rebirth.[13] The bodhisattva came to represent the ideal of compassion and became the object of meditation, supplication, and even worship by the masses.

As Buddhism spread throughout Asia it encountered cultures quite different from those of the Indian subcontinent, some of which had rich intellectual and religious traditions of their own. Buddhism in northern Asia has been remarkably flexible in adapting to new environments in China, Tibet, Korea, and Japan.[14] The Chinese social and cultural context, for example, was different from that of India. The notions of rebirth and karma, so central to Indian religious and philosophical thought, were lacking among the Chinese. Release from rebirth was thus not the critical issue for Chinese, who had a much more positive view of life, nature, and society. Consequently, one finds in the Mahayana tradition as it developed in China, Korea, and Japan a decreasing emphasis on nirvana as release from rebirth and greater focus on the idea of enlightenment in this life.

Unlike the Theravada tradition, Mahayana Buddhism developed elaborate metaphysical teachings, including that of the Three Bodies of Buddha, three distinguishable but closely related levels or dimensions of the "Buddha

12. Richard Gombrich, *Theravada Buddhism: A Social History from Ancient Benares to Modern Colombo* (London: Routledge & Kegan Paul, 1988), 124–27.

13. See Paul Williams, *Mahayana Buddhism: The Doctrinal Foundations*, 2nd ed. (New York: Routledge, 2009), 55–62; D. W. Mitchell, *Buddhism*, 119–32.

14. See Kenneth K. S. Ch'en, *The Chinese Transformation of Buddhism* (Princeton: Princeton University Press, 1973).

essence."[15] The historical Gautama Buddha was said to be a human manifestation of an underlying, all-inclusive Buddha essence, the dharmakaya, or law body. The dharmakaya, synonymous with tathata, or "thusness/suchness," is the nondual, formless reality underlying the phenomenal world and includes all the perfections of the eternal dharma. On a second level, the Buddha essence is manifest as the Body of Bliss, or sambhogakaya, and it is here that bodhisattvas and Buddhas apprehend and enjoy the Buddha essence. Finally, there is the Transformation Body, or the nirmanakaya, in accord with which Buddhas appear at select moments in time to teach the dharma to sentient beings. In this sense the historical Gautama can be regarded as a historical, human manifestation of the dharmakaya.

The doctrine of the Buddha's Bodies is also related to another prominent Mahayana theme, the tathagatagarbha, or "womb or embryo of the Buddha." All living beings are said to possess or participate in the tathagatagarbha, or the universal Buddha nature. The idea that all living beings are potential Buddhas because of their participation in the universal Buddha nature has been a prominent and controversial theme in Chinese and Japanese Mahayana schools. In the late twentieth century there emerged a vigorous debate among Japanese Buddhist scholars over whether the tathagatagarbha doctrine is authentically Buddhist.[16]

As it spread throughout East Asia, Buddhism was influenced by indigenous religious beliefs and practices. What became known as Zen Buddhism, for example, is in part the product of the encounter between Buddhist teachings and practices introduced from India and Chinese Daoist traditions.[17] Zen maintains that the core of what the Buddha realized in his enlightenment was communicated directly and nonverbally from Gautama to one of his disciples and has been passed on successively from master to disciple ever since. A famous Zen tradition declares,

> Once when the World Honored One [Gautama the Buddha] was staying on the Mount of the Vulture, he held up a flower before the assembled ones. All fell silent. Only the venerable Kasyapa broke into a smile. The Honored One then spoke: "The eye of the true Dharma, the wonderful Mind of Nirvana, the

15. See Paul Williams, *Mahayana Buddhism*, chap. 8; Paul J. Griffiths, *On Being Buddha: The Classical Doctrine of Buddhahood* (Albany: State University of New York Press, 1994).
16. See the essays in Jamie Hubbard and Paul L. Swanson, eds., *Pruning the Buddha Tree: The Storm over Critical Buddhism* (Honolulu: University of Hawaii Press, 1997).
17. For the historical development of Zen, see Heinrich Dumoulin, *India and China*, vol. 1 of *Zen Buddhism: A History*, trans. James W. Heisig and Paul Knitter (New York: Macmillan, 1988); idem, *Japan*, vol. 2 of *Zen Buddhism: A History*, trans. James W. Heisig and Paul Knitter (New York: Macmillan, 1990).

true formless Form, the mysterious Gate of the Dharma, which rests not upon words and letters, and a special transmission . . . outside the scriptures; this I hand over to the great Kasyapa."[18]

In other words, the mature and complete teaching of the Buddha is not what has been taught traditionally within the Theravada school but is actually something far deeper, something inexpressible in human words.

The tradition claims that the "wonderful Mind of Nirvana" was then transmitted nonverbally through twenty-eight Indian patriarchs, the last of whom was the legendary Bodhidharma (ca. AD 470–543), said to have brought the "lamp of enlightenment" to China. Tradition attributes to Bodhidharma the formulation of the famous four-line stanza said to express the heart of Zen:

> A special transmission outside the scriptures,
> Not founded upon words and letters;
> By pointing directly to [one's] mind
> It lets one see into [one's own true] nature and [thus] attain
> Buddhahood.[19]

In China this tradition became known as Ch'an Buddhism.[20] In Zen, enlightenment (*wu* in Chinese; *satori* or *kensho* in Japanese) is said to be a direct, intuitive insight into the true nature of reality, an understanding that transcends conceptualization and verbalization.

Although Theravada Buddhism teaches enlightenment through one's own efforts, some of the most popular forms of Mahayana Buddhism are the Pure Land schools, which teach that salvation, understood as rebirth in the Pure Land, cannot be attained through self-effort but is available only through the merit of the Buddha Amitabha (Amida in Japan). The Pure Land traditions have theistic elements and differ from Theravada Buddhism in their teaching that salvation comes only through the "other power" of Amida and not one's own efforts.[21]

18. From the Mumonkan, as cited in Heinrich Dumoulin, *Zen Enlightenment: Origin and Meaning* (New York: Weatherhill, 1979), 16.

19. As cited in Dumoulin, *Zen Buddhism*, 1:85. Most scholars think this formulation actually came much later than the time of Bodhidharma. See Kenneth K. S. Ch'en, *Buddhism in China: A Historical Survey* (Princeton: Princeton University Press, 1964), 350–53.

20. "Ch'an" is a Chinese rendering of the Sanskrit term "Dhyana" (meditation); "Zen" is the Japanese adaptation of "Ch'an."

21. On Pure Land Buddhism, see Alfred Bloom, *Shinran's Gospel of Pure Grace* (Tucson: University of Arizona Press, 1965); Esben Andreasen, *Popular Buddhism in Japan: Shin Buddhist Religion and Culture* (Honolulu: University of Hawaii Press, 1998); Jan Van Bragt, "Buddhism—Jodo Shinshu—Christianity: Does Jodo Shinshu Form a Bridge between Buddhism and Christianity?," *Japanese Religions* 18 (January 1993): 47–75.

Vajrayana/Tibetan Buddhism

Roughly five centuries after the emergence of Mahayana, Vajrayana (Thunderbolt, or Diamond Vehicle) Buddhism, or Buddhist Tantra, developed in India. The term "tantra" refers to Buddhist texts concerned with rituals or instructions that open the mind to esoteric teachings and practices.[22] Indian Tantrism provided Buddhists with a way in which the long and arduous path to liberation could be shortened by learning to harness supernormal or magical powers. Esoteric tantric practices—including special physical postures of body and hands, visualization of deities, breathing exercises, manipulation of subtle forms of energy in the body, and even certain sexual rituals—were said not only to provide special powers in this life but also to aid in attaining nirvana.[23] Buddhist traditions that adopted the tantra texts became known as Vajrayana Buddhism and have been especially influential in Tibetan Buddhism.

Buddhism was introduced into Tibet in the seventh century AD. The indigenous Tibetan Bon religion had been shamanistic and animistic, involving sacrificial rituals, magicians/diviners, and worship of various deities.[24] Over time, Tibetan Buddhism became distinguished by its commitment to rigorous scholarship of Buddhist texts, philosophical acumen, discipline, and tantric practices. The Geluk tradition is best known in the West because of its association with the Dalai Lama. Tibetan Buddhism is well known for its teaching of tulku reincarnation, according to which some lamas who have already attained lamahood in a previous life are said to reincarnate. The current Dalai Lama, Tenzin Gyatso (b. 1935), is the fourteenth Dalai Lama and is regarded in Tibetan Buddhism as not only a reincarnation of previous Dalai Lamas but also an incarnation of the Buddha Avalokitesvara.

The Western "Discovery" of Buddhism

The earliest direct reference to Buddhists among Christians is in the *Stromata* of the second-century church father Clement of Alexandria, who speaks of Indians who "follow the precepts of Boutta."[25] The ninth-century Nestorian Christians in China had some contact with Buddhists, as evidenced by the

22. Lopez, *Story of Buddhism*, 213.
23. D. W. Mitchell, *Buddhism*, 154–56.
24. See Per Kvaerne, "The Religions of Tibet," in *The Religious Traditions of Asia*, ed. Joseph Kitagawa (New York: Macmillan, 1989), 196–98.
25. As cited in Lopez, *From Stone to Flesh*, 7.

twentieth-century discovery of the "Jesus sutras," writings that express Christian teachings in direct reference to Buddhist concepts.[26] According to Donald Lopez, the first European to tell the story of Gautama's rejection of a life of luxury and subsequent enlightenment was the explorer Marco Polo, who spent 1271–95 in Asia.[27]

One of the earliest accounts of a Christian engagement with Buddhism is found in the diaries of William of Rubruck, a Franciscan friar who participated in a debate with a Buddhist in 1254 before Möngke Khan, the grandson of the notorious Mongol ruler Genghis Khan. The Buddhist pressed William hard on the problem of evil, an issue that Buddhists regard as devastating for monotheism: "If your God is as you say, why does he make the half of things evil?" When William insisted that all that proceeds from God is good, the Buddhist demanded, "Whence then comes evil?"[28]

Ippolito Desideri (d. 1733), an Italian Jesuit missionary to Tibet, made a careful study of Tibetan Buddhism and wrote a major work in Tibetan titled *Inquiry into the Doctrines of Previous Lives and of Emptiness, Offered to Scholars of Tibet by the White Lama Called Ippolito*. He treated Buddhist teachings as serious philosophical claims and employed forms of argumentation accepted by the Buddhist community in raising questions about the truth of two central doctrines of Buddhism: teachings on rebirth and emptiness (sunyata). Lopez calls this "the most sophisticated work ever written in the Tibetan language by a European," a book that "reveals a deep and nuanced understanding of Tibetan Buddhist doctrine and philosophy."[29] Desideri addressed Buddhist scholars respectfully "in their own language and on their own terms," for he saw in Tibetan Buddhism "a commitment both to rational philosophy and to ethical practice."[30]

Despite these early contacts, Europeans at the time did not have a concept of Buddhism as a distinct religion practiced throughout Asia. Marco Polo, for example, did not speak of Buddhism as such but rather referred to Buddhists simply as idolaters. Dr. Engelbert Kaempfer (1651–1716), physician to the Dutch Embassy in Japan, was one of the first to realize that, despite differences in language and some beliefs and practices, the same religion of

---

26. Ibid., 64–65. See also Lawrence Sutin, *All Is Change: The Two-Thousand-Year Journey of Buddhism to the West* (New York: Little, Brown, 2006), 36–37.

27. Lopez, *From Stone to Flesh*, 12.

28. Richard Fox Young, "*Deus Unus* or *Dei Plures Sunt*? The Function of Inclusivism in the Buddhist Defense of Mongol Folk Religion against William of Rubruck (1254)," *Journal of Ecumenical Studies* 26.1 (1989): 115.

29. Lopez, *From Stone to Flesh*, 108. See also Trent Pomplun, *Jesuit on the Top of the World: Ippolito Desideri's Mission to Tibet* (New York: Oxford University Press, 2010).

30. Lopez, *From Stone to Flesh*, 110.

Buddhism was being practiced across Asia.[31] Before the eighteenth century there were scattered reports from travelers and missionaries in Ceylon, Burma, Siam, Tibet, China, and Japan about followers of the Buddha—who was variously identified as Baoda, Bedou, Budam, Chakya, Fo, Gaudma, Saman, or Si Tsun[32]—although it was not clear that these all referred to the same individual. The idea of Buddhism as a religion that is practiced across Asia could only develop once it was recognized that these many names were all denoting Siddhartha Gautama, the founder of Buddhism. Philip Almond observes that, during the first half of the nineteenth century, Europeans "discovered" Buddhism as a religion, and a crucial part of this "was the recognition that there were various culturally diffuse religious phenomena, which had apparent relationship with each other."[33]

The story of the European discovery of Buddhism in the nineteenth century; the formation of an idealized image of Gautama the Buddha and philosophical, textual Buddhism; and the subsequent adaptation of this image by Buddhist intellectuals in Asia together illustrate what Peter van der Veer calls interactional history.[34] British colonialism involved a reciprocal relationship between the colonizer and the colonies, so that both the colonies and Great Britain itself were transformed through the encounter. British intellectuals became fascinated with Buddhism, or better, a particular image of Buddhism, incorporating Buddhist themes into literature and philosophy and often playing off positive aspects of their image of Buddhism against the perceived liabilities of institutional Christianity.[35] In turn, Asian intellectuals adopted aspects of this idealized image of Buddhism, incorporating them into a modernized form of Buddhism that was held up as a positive alternative to Western colonialist cultures and Christian missions.

Almond sees the process of the British "creation" of Buddhism passing through two phases. During the first phase, roughly the first four decades of the nineteenth century, "Buddhism was an object which was instanced and manifested 'out there' in the Orient, in a spatial location geographically, culturally, and therefore imaginatively *other*."[36] This was the view of

31. Ibid., 137.
32. Lopez lists over 200 different names for the Buddha in various Asian languages. See Lopez, *From Stone to Flesh*, 235–37.
33. Philip C. Almond, *The British Discovery of Buddhism* (Cambridge: Cambridge University Press, 1988), 7–8.
34. Peter van der Veer, *Imperial Encounters: Religion and Modernity in India and Britain* (Princeton: Princeton University Press, 2001), 8–11.
35. See J. Jeffrey Franklin, *The Lotus and the Lion: Buddhism and the British Empire* (Ithaca, NY: Cornell University Press, 2008).
36. Almond, *British Discovery of Buddhism*, 12, with original emphasis.

Buddhism constructed through reports from travelers to Asia, missionaries, traders, and soldiers, and it reflected a perception of the "Oriental present." But by the 1850s there was a massive effort to collect and translate Buddhist texts, especially from Pali; what emerged from this was an idealized vision of Buddhism in its "pristine" past, a textual Buddhism devoid of the superstitions and corruptions evident among Asian Buddhists in the present. "Buddhism, by 1860, had come to exist, not in the Orient, but in the Oriental libraries and institutes of the West, in its texts and manuscripts, at the desks of the Western savants who interpreted it."[37] This idealized view of Buddhism not only shaped European and American perspectives but also became a part of the self-understanding of Asian Buddhists as they came to grips with the many challenges of modernity and the West.

Buddhist Modernism

What is known today as Buddhism, not only in the West but also in modernizing Asian societies, is not simply a faithful transmission of the ancient teachings and practices of the early Buddhist community in India but rather a form of Buddhism that has been shaped through encounters with Western colonialism, Christian missions, and modernization. David McMahan observes, "What many Americans and Europeans often understand by the term 'Buddhism,' however, is actually a modern hybrid tradition with roots in the European Enlightenment no less than the Buddha's enlightenment, in Romanticism and transcendentalism as much as the Pali canon, and in the clash of Asian cultures and colonial powers as much as in mindfulness and meditation."[38] This hybrid tradition is referred to by McMahan as Buddhist modernism.

McMahan identifies three developments defining Buddhist modernism: detraditionalization, demythologization, and psychologization.[39] Detraditionalization involves the modern tendencies to elevate reason, experience, and intuition over traditional practices and authority structures, so that Buddhist practice becomes individualized and privatized, a matter of personal choice. With demythologization, traditional Buddhist beliefs regarded as problematic under modernity—belief in the many levels of hell, meritorious actions, rebirth not only as humans but also as animals or hungry ghosts, the existence of an array of demons, spirits, and gods—are ignored or reinterpreted in nonliteral

37. Ibid., 13.
38. David L. McMahan, *The Making of Buddhist Modernism* (New York: Oxford University Press, 2008), 5. See also idem, ed., *Buddhism in the Modern World* (London: Routledge, 2012).
39. McMahan, *Making of Buddhist Modernism*, 42–59.

terms. Similarly, during the past century Buddhism has become especially linked to Western psychology, with Buddhist metaphysical claims being translated into psychoanalytic language and the interior life of the mind. Buddhism becomes a form of spiritual therapy that can be practiced quite apart from accepting the traditional doctrines it advances.[40]

One area in which European influences have changed Buddhism is in the Western emphasis upon written texts as defining Buddhist thought and practice. There was a remarkable interest in the early texts of Buddhism during the later nineteenth century as European scholars developed the ability to read these texts in their original languages and translated them into European languages. In 1881 T. W. Rhys Davids (1843–1922), together with his wife, Caroline, founded the Pali Text Society, which was devoted to translating texts from the ancient Pali language. At his death, ninety-four volumes (constituting more than 26,000 pages) had been translated and published by the society.[41] Translation of Buddhist texts was also promoted by Friedrich Max Müller (1823–1900), professor at Oxford University, who edited *The Sacred Books of the East*. But arguably the most influential translator of Sanskrit texts and scholar of Buddhism in Europe at the time was Frenchman Eugène Burnouf (1801–52), whose *Introduction to the History of Indian Buddhism* (1844) would definitively shape modern images of Gautama the Buddha. Commenting on Burnouf's influence, Donald Lopez states,

> The Buddha that we know was not born in India in the fifth century BCE. He was born in Paris in 1844. . . . Burnouf described the Buddha and Buddhism for the first time in ways that would become so ingrained and natural that their origins in an 1844 French tome would eventually be forgotten. These would include that Buddhism is an Indian religion, that the Buddha is a historical figure, and, perhaps of particular consequence, that the Buddha was a human teacher of a religion, or perhaps a philosophy, that preaches ethics and morality without recourse to dogma, ritual, or metaphysics. The consequences of his portrayal of the Buddha and Buddhism would be profound.[42]

The emphasis upon Buddhist texts as defining Buddhist belief and practice was a European innovation that shaped modern understandings of Buddhism.

---

40. For an example of demythologized Buddhist modernism, see Stephen Batchelor, *Buddhism without Beliefs: A Contemporary Guide to Awakening* (New York: Riverhead Books, 1997); idem, "Life as a Question, Not a Fact," in *Why Buddhism? Westerners in Search of Wisdom*, ed. Vickie Mackenzie (London: Element, 2002), 142–62.

41. J. J. Clarke, *Oriental Enlightenment: The Encounter between Asian and Western Thought* (London: Routledge, 1997), 75.

42. Lopez, *From Stone to Flesh*, 3, 210–11.

To be sure, there is a long history of Buddhist interpretation and commentary on ancient texts, but for Buddhists the written text did not have the significance that the Bible, for example, has in Christianity. Some traditions, such as Zen, intentionally push beyond reliance upon the written or spoken word. In traditional Asian Buddhist communities, the written text was utilized only within certain contexts. As Lopez observes, "The vast majority of Buddhists across Asia have been illiterate," and this has implications for how Buddhists have regarded the written text.

> Thus, it is misleading to think of the Buddhist book solely as something to be read. Sutras were placed on altars and worshiped with offerings of flowers and incense, as the sutra itself often prescribed. Laypeople sought to accrue merit and avert misfortune by paying monks to come into their homes and chant sutras. Regardless of whether the audience (or the reader) could understand the content, the word of the Buddha was being heard, and this carried the power of a magic spell. . . . In China, some monasteries had halls devoted exclusively to the recitation of sutras. Laypeople could purchase certificates representing a given number of recitations of a sutra. Those certificates could then be offered (through burning) in services for deceased relatives. . . . Whether or not the text was comprehended, this was considered a meritorious act.[43]

Not even all monks were literate, and many monasteries had only a few written texts. Before the modern era, and even in many areas in Asia today, the written text was regarded as ancillary to oral tradition. Jay Garfield states, "One reads a text with a teacher: the text is an occasion for the transmission of an oral lineage, and most of what is important, what is to be learned, is in that oral transmission." The modern approach to Buddhist texts, by contrast, is "making it possible for students or practitioners of Buddhism to engage with its literary tradition independently of a teacher or an authority," and in so doing "we are creating, in the act of translation, a new Buddhism, both in the West and in traditionally Buddhist Asian cultures."[44]

The textual study of Buddhism also affected nineteenth-century European perceptions of Gautama the Buddha. With the exception of Christian theologians and missionaries, European intellectuals generally regarded the Buddha in very positive terms as a wise man of exemplary character who taught respectable moral principles, a reformer of morally questionable Hindu practices. Legends about the many previous lives of the Buddha and his miraculous

43. Lopez, *Story of Buddhism*, 188–89.
44. Jay L. Garfield, "Translation as Transmission and Transformation," in *TransBuddhism: Transmission, Translation, Transformation*, ed. Nalini Bhushan, Jay L. Garfield, and Abraham Zablocki (Amherst: University of Massachusetts Press, 2009), 97–99.

exploits were dismissed, and Gautama was firmly located in ancient Indian history. For Victorian intellectuals, "The Buddha is very much a human figure; one to be compared not with the gods, but with other historical personalities—with Jesus, Mohammed, or Luther."[45]

The humanization of Gautama coincided with an ongoing debate over whether Buddhism is a religion or a philosophy. Many scholars, including Max Müller, thought of Buddhism as a philosophy, not a religion.[46] This was due in part to the fact that they were not interested in the actual beliefs and practices of ordinary Buddhists in Asia but only in what they perceived as "original Buddhism" found in the Pali texts. Many scholars interpreted these texts as atheistic, and no atheistic system qualified as a religion. The Mahayana Sanskrit sutras tended to be more theistic than the Pali texts, but Orientalist scholars thought the Pali texts were earliest and thus more authoritative. Almond notes that it was only with Nathan Söderblom's and Rudolf Otto's definitions of religion in terms of "holiness" or "the Holy," and not in terms of belief in God or gods, that Buddhism was accepted as a religion. Thomas Huxley coined the term "agnosticism" in 1869, and some writers felt this was a better depiction of Buddhist thought than atheism.[47]

The Theosophical Society and Modern Buddhism

An especially interesting part of the story of modern Buddhism concerns the significant role of Theosophists in revitalizing Buddhism in Asia and stimulating interest in Buddhism in the West. Lawrence Sutin observes, "It is the central paradox of the Theosophical Society that its writings on Buddhism, by Blavatsky and others, were sometimes blatantly inaccurate as to matters of fact and even of basic doctrine—and yet there were many, in Europe, America, and even Asia, who were spurred by those writings to pursue a deeper understanding of Buddhist practice."[48]

Colonel Henry Steel Olcott (1832–1907), cofounder of the Theosophical Society, was instrumental in the revitalization and transformation of Buddhism in nineteenth-century Ceylon (now Sri Lanka), resulting in what has been called Protestant Buddhism. Although the Sinhalese Buddhist revival was already underway when Olcott arrived in Ceylon, he provided crucial leadership to the movement. Provoked by both British colonialist policies and

45. Almond, *British Discovery of Buddhism*, 56.
46. Ibid., 94.
47. Ibid., 99.
48. Sutin, *All Is Change*, 171–72.

Christian missionary practices, and guided by the virulently anti-Christian Olcott, Buddhism in Ceylon enjoyed a resurgence of popularity and redefined itself as a tradition of ancient wisdom that is fully compatible with modern science and tolerant of all faiths.[49] But even as Buddhism provided a protest movement against Western colonialism and Christian missions, it was itself heavily influenced by Protestant Christianity, especially in the increased significance given to the laity and the emphasis placed upon the written text.

The Theosophical Society was founded in 1875 in New York by Madame Helena Petrovna Blavatsky (1831–91) and Henry Steel Olcott. Blavatsky, born in Russia to an upper-class family, left an unhappy marriage at age eighteen and traveled the world. She claimed to have traveled throughout the Middle East and Asia, culminating in study in Tibet with mahatmas, "highly evolved teachers" of esoteric wisdom. In 1873 Blavatsky arrived in the United States, where she met Olcott, who was a lawyer, journalist, and student of spiritualism. Blavatsky and Olcott, along with a small group of other spiritualists, established the Theosophical Society as an organization devoted to seeking "knowledge of God and the higher spirits."[50] The stated goals of the society were "to form the nucleus of a Universal brotherhood of Humanity, without distinction of race, creed, sex, caste or color; to study the ancient and modern religions, philosophies and sciences . . . ; and to investigate the unexplained laws of Nature and the psychical powers latent in man."[51] Olcott served as the first president of the society (a post he held until his death); he provided the organizational skills necessary for the society while Blavatsky was the colorful and controversial inspiration behind the movement.

Although initially concerned with promoting a scientific perspective on spiritualism, Blavatsky and Olcott soon became more interested in Eastern religions. Their lectures and publications emphasized the esoteric ancient wisdom said to be common to all the great religions, but most evident in Hinduism and Buddhism. Blavatsky claimed that although this wisdom had been obscured by dogmatic and institutional religion (especially Christianity), certain spiritual adepts—mahatmas or masters—were communicating esoteric truths to her.

49. See Richard Gombrich and Gananath Obeyesekere, *Buddhism Transformed: Religious Change in Sri Lanka* (Princeton: Princeton University Press, 1988); Gombrich, *Theravada Buddhism*, chap. 7.
50. Stephen Prothero, *The White Buddhist: The Asian Odyssey of Henry Steel Olcott* (Bloomington: Indiana University Press, 1996), 49.
51. As cited in Harry Oldmeadow, *Journeys East: 20th Century Western Encounters with Eastern Religious Traditions* (Bloomington, IN: World Wisdom, 2004), 64.

Blavatsky's first major publication, *Isis Unveiled* (1877), asserts the essential unity and common origin of all great religions and that an esoteric truth behind all religions is preserved in the ancient Asian wisdom tradition.

In 1878 Blavatsky and Olcott went to India, establishing the Theosophical Society's headquarters outside of Madras (now Chennai). The Theosophical movement grew rapidly, both in India and in the West. In 1880 Olcott and Blavatsky formally converted to Buddhism, although their version of Buddhism was highly idiosyncratic. In 1887 Blavatsky moved to London, where she produced several more works before her death in 1891. In 1880 Olcott sailed to Ceylon, where he became active in the Buddhist revitalization movement and vigorously opposed Christian missions.

In 1881 Olcott, popularly known as the "White Buddhist," published in English *A Buddhist Catechism*. This was his attempt to combine elements from a variety of Buddhist traditions into one work that would set out the basic tenets all Buddhists in the world should be able to accept. *A Buddhist Catechism* would eventually go through more than forty editions, be translated into over twenty languages, and be used in Sri Lankan schools into the late twentieth century.[52] The *Catechism* reflects Olcott's view that what should unify all Asian Buddhists is a set of simple teachings that all modern Buddhists can affirm. Yet Olcott's proposal was hardly just a restatement of traditional Buddhist teachings. Stephen Prothero calls it "creole Buddhism" since it involved a "creolization" of liberal American Protestantism and traditional Theravada Buddhism. Contrary to Theravada teaching, for example, Olcott's Buddhism made room for both the notion of an enduring soul and a divinity of some sort.[53] "Long before he departed for Asia with the express intent of sitting as an ignorant disciple at the feet of monks and gurus there, Olcott had constructed for himself a relatively fixed image of 'Buddhism.' And this image bore at least as much resemblance to Blavatsky's theosophy and liberal Protestantism as it did to the Buddhism of Theravada monks."[54] In *Isis Unveiled* Blavatsky states: "When we use the term *Buddhists*, we do not mean to imply by it either the exoteric Buddhism instituted by the followers of Gautama-Buddha, nor the modern Buddhistic religion, but the secret philosophy of Sakyamuni, which in its essence is certainly

---

52. Prothero, *White Buddhist*, 101. Speaking of Olcott's *Catechism*, Gombrich notes, "This document . . . deserves to rank as a Theosophical rather than a Buddhist creed. But this is not widely realized, notably in Britain, where the connections between Theosophy and organized Buddhism have been intimate" (Gombrich, *Theravada Buddhism*, 186).

53. Prothero, *White Buddhist*, 7–9, 66–67.

54. Ibid., 66.

identical with the ancient wisdom-religion of the sanctuary, the pre-Vedic Brahmanism."[55]

Olcott established the Buddhist Theosophical Society, founded many Buddhist secondary schools modeled after Western-style education, initiated the Young Men's Buddhist Association, and engaged in vigorous polemics against Christian missions in Ceylon. He was popular among Sinhalese Buddhists because of his anti-Christian polemics, promotion of Buddhism as a modern scientific religion, and his efforts at social reform and education. Olcott sought to unify various Theravada schools into the Buddhist Ecclesiastical Council and launched the pan-Asian International Buddhist League. Buddhist scholars, however, were often ambivalent about Olcott, appreciating his attacks upon Christian missionaries but regarding his version of Buddhism as simplistic and misleading. In 1890, at an ecumenical Buddhist conference in India that included Theravada and Mahayana representatives from Ceylon, Bangladesh, Burma, and Japan, Olcott was able to get the delegates to accept a fourteen-point Buddhist Platform statement, which he believed contained the essence of the Buddhist dharma.[56]

While in Ceylon, Olcott befriended a Sinhalese Buddhist reformer, Don David Hewavitarne, better known as Anagarika Dharmapala (1864–1933). Dharmapala became a Theosophist, founded the Maha Bodhi Society (which was committed to the revitalization of Buddhism), and represented Buddhism at the 1893 World Parliament of Religions in Chicago. Although Dharmapala initially worked closely with Olcott, he eventually became disillusioned with Olcott's views, finding them to be insufficiently Buddhist and too influenced by Hindu teachings. He later renounced Olcott and Theosophy as incompatible with authentic Buddhism. Prothero contrasts the perspectives of the two men:

> Olcott and Dharmapala held two competing visions of the nature of religious commitment in a religiously pluralistic world. In Olcott's more liberal cosmos, his public theosophical vow to embrace all religions existed in a creative tension with his private Buddhist commitment to the Buddha, the Dharma, and the Sangha. For him, it was possible to be a Buddhist and a Hindu simultaneously. In Dharmapala's less irenic world, a "yes" to Buddhism implied a "no" to all other religious traditions. "Buddhism is absolutely opposed to the teachings of other existing religions," Dharmapala ultimately concluded, and "Theosophy is irreconcilable with Buddhism."[57]

55. Helena Petrovna Blavatsky, *Isis Unveiled: A Master-Key to the Mysteries of Ancient and Modern Science and Theology* (Pasadena, CA: Theosophical University Press, 1972), 2:142; as cited in Franklin, *Lotus and the Lion*, 76.

56. Sutin, *All Is Change*, 184.

57. Prothero, *White Buddhist*, 168.

Olcott also made two trips to Japan, in 1889 and 1891. His *Buddhist Cate-chism* had been translated into Japanese in 1886, and he was welcomed as one who forcefully argued for the superiority of Buddhism over Christianity. Japan at the time was undergoing rapid modernization, and Buddhism was being threatened by both Christian missions and an increasingly nationalistic government, which was trying to purge Shinto ideology of any Buddhist influences. Although Buddhist scholars rejected Olcott's version of Buddhism and were suspicious of his desire for an ecumenical transnational Asian Buddhist coalition, they were intrigued by the fact that an American Caucasian male was publicly promoting Buddhism.[58] The 1880s and '90s were a time of serious interest in the Theosophical Society among Buddhist reformers in Japan, even if Buddhist leaders were uncomfortable with some of Olcott's views.

The influence of the Theosophists upon Buddhism in Ceylon, and to some extent throughout Asia, can be seen in three areas in particular. First, through the publication and dissemination of *A Buddhist Catechism* and other manuals for understanding Buddhist teachings, they contributed to the modern emphasis upon the importance of texts for understanding Buddhism. Second, they elevated the place of the laity, encouraging them to read Buddhist texts for themselves and to engage in meditation. Gombrich points out that lay Buddhists traditionally did not meditate, since meditation was reserved for monks in a monastic community under strict supervision of superiors.[59] But Dharmapala and other Theosophists encouraged laypeople to practice meditation, learning about meditation from books, without recourse to a master. It is ironic that while meditation is often considered today to be the very heart of Buddhism, it is also the element that is "most detachable from the tradition itself," as many in Asia and the West now practice meditation without embracing the elaborate metaphysical framework that traditionally has given the practice its meaning.[60]

Third, Theosophists such as Olcott carefully crafted an image of Buddhism as modern, scientific, and fully compatible with the new world dawning at the turn of that century (1900). However, they did so by selectively adopting some teachings and abandoning others, by rejecting many of the actual practices and beliefs of ordinary Asian Buddhists as crass superstition, and by looking for an esoteric "hidden" meaning behind the explicit teachings. In portraying Buddhism as compatible with modern science, the Theosophists were both tapping into and shaping an emerging discourse in Western and Asian intellectual circles that contrasted Buddhism—supposedly a humanistic philosophy

---

58. Shin'ichi Yoshinaga, "Theosophy and Buddhist Reformers in the Middle of the Meiji Period," *Japanese Religions* 34.2 (July 2009): 126–27.
59. Gombrich, *Theravada Buddhism*, 191.
60. McMahan, *Making of Buddhist Modernism*, 185.

and not a religion—with Christianity. Donald Lopez states, "It is significant that claims for the compatibility of Buddhism and science began in Europe and America during the Victorian period, as Buddhism became fashionable in intellectual circles. Similar claims for the compatibility of Buddhism and science began in Asia at the same time, a time when Buddhist thinkers were defending themselves against the attacks of Christian missionaries." Efforts to depict Buddhism as a truly scientific religion "were directly precipitated by Christian attacks."[61] Lopez demonstrates, however, that the modern scientific Buddhism championed in the nineteenth and twentieth centuries has little in common with the earlier Buddhist teachings or the practices of Asian Buddhists. "It is clear that the Buddhism that is compatible with science must jettison much of what Buddhism has been, and is, in order to claim that compatibility."[62]

Buddhism Comes West

American awareness of Buddhism goes back at least to the Transcendentalists and other intellectuals in the 1840s. Buddhism came to Hawaii in the nineteenth century with Japanese and Chinese immigrants, and in the twentieth century it became established in North America and Europe.[63] Now Buddhism is a significant part of the religious landscape of the West. While the actual number of Buddhists in Europe and North America remains small—today about four million Buddhists are in the United States[64]—its religious and cultural impact has been far greater than numbers alone indicate.

61. Donald S. Lopez Jr., *The Scientific Buddha: His Short and Happy Life* (New Haven: Yale University Press, 2012), 10.

62. Ibid., 16. Scientific Buddhism ignores the cosmologies of classical Buddhist traditions, with their elaborate hierarchy of heavens and hells inhabited by gods, ghosts, and demons as well as humans and other sentient creatures. Lopez shows how, contrary to popular perception, Buddhist teaching on karma and rebirth actually is at odds with modern Darwinian notions of biological evolution and natural selection: "Far from teaching a dharma compatible with Darwin's theory of natural selection, it is perhaps more accurate to regard the Buddha as a counter-evolutionary, actively seeking the extinction of the human race, and indeed of all species, through the eradication of the selfish gene" (ibid., 80).

63. On Buddhism in the West, see James William Coleman, *The New Buddhism: The Western Transformation of an Ancient Tradition* (New York: Oxford University Press, 2001); Charles S. Prebish and Martin Baumann, eds., *Westward Dharma: Buddhism beyond Asia* (Berkeley: University of California Press, 2002); Charles S. Prebish and Kenneth K. Tanaka, eds., *The Faces of Buddhism in America* (Berkeley: University of California Press, 1998); Richard Hughes Seager, *Buddhism in America* (New York: Columbia University Press, 1999); Rick Fields, *How the Swans Came to the Lake: A Narrative History of Buddhism in America*, 3rd ed. (Boston: Shambhala, 1992).

64. See Richard Hughes Seager, *Buddhism in America*, 10–11; Robert Wuthnow and Wendy Cage, "Buddhists and Buddhism in the United States: The Scope and the Influence," *Journal for the Scientific Study of Religion* 43.3 (2004): 364.

David McMahan reminds us that European and American images of Buddhism have been filtered through modern cultural and intellectual lenses:

> Europeans encountering Buddhism in the late nineteenth century read many ideas in ancient Buddhist scriptures and philosophical texts that appeared to resonate with the modern, scientific attitude. They saw in textual Buddhism an experimental attitude, a de-emphasis on faith and belief, and a sophisticated philosophy—exquisitely rational, yet soaring beyond ordinary reason. Buddhism as practiced in Asian countries, however, seemed permeated by things quite counter to the modern, rationalistic attitude—practices and beliefs that appeared superstitious, magical, and ritualistic. A number of early Western admirers and modernizing Asians tried to extract the empirically minded philosophical and practical ingredients of Buddhism from what they considered its idolatrous and superstitious elements. This "demythologized" Buddhism—more accurately, "remythologized" in terms of the dominant European and American attitudes and beliefs—is what most Westerners still know of Buddhism.[65]

For many in the West, Buddhism seems to be a philosophically sophisticated and spiritually profound movement that can be detached from the crass, superstitious practices of the masses and that provides an attractive alternative to the Christendom with which they have become increasingly disillusioned.

In the twentieth century, at least until the prominence of the Dalai Lama and Tibetan Buddhism in the 1980s and '90s, the most widely known form of Buddhism was Zen. For many in the mid-twentieth century, the serene Zen monk in meditation came to symbolize the pristine ancient wisdom of the sage Gautama, and it was assumed that Japanese Zen is the authentic, pure dharma transmitted to a modern and materialistic world. But while Zen can claim to have roots in ancient Buddhist teachings and practices, its twentieth-century packaging includes many other elements. We will consider the role of D. T. Suzuki in shaping the image of Buddhism for the West, but before we do so, we should first note the context in which Suzuki lived and worked.

No single event was as significant for the public acceptance of Buddhism in America as the World's Parliament of Religions, held in Chicago in September 1893. Given extensive positive coverage by the press, the Parliament provided legitimation of Asian religions and presented a prominent platform from which Hindu and Buddhist spokesmen could address Western audiences.[66]

---

65. McMahan, "Repackaging Zen for the West," in *Westward Dharma*, 219.

66. On the 1893 World's Parliament of Religions, see Richard Hughes Seager, ed., *The Dawn of Religious Pluralism: Voices from the World's Parliament of Religions, 1893* (LaSalle, IL: Open Court, 1993); Eric J. Ziolkowski, ed., *A Museum of Faiths: Histories and Legacies of the 1893 World's Parliament of Religions* (Atlanta: Scholars, 1993); Joseph M. Kitagawa, "The 1893

Asian Buddhist participants included Anagarika Dharmapala from Ceylon and the Japanese Zen monk Shaku Soen. The Parliament of Religions took place at a critical time in Japan's emergence as a modern nation. While the United States was already a modern industrial nation and global power, Japan was just emerging from two centuries of self-imposed isolation from the rest of the world and embarking on an ambitious path of rapid modernization.

The attempt to combine modernization with traditional ways provoked social and political upheaval in Japan. The attractions of modernity were captured in the popular slogan *"Bunmei kaika!"* [Civilization and enlightenment!] while more cautious voices rallied around the slogan *"Toyo no dotoku, Seiyo no gakugei!"* [Eastern ethics, Western science!]. The tensions between modernity and tradition were overcome through a powerful form of religious nationalism which sought respect for Japan from Western powers. Militant nationalism, fueled by shrewd manipulation by militarists of Shinto ideology and the emperor cult, drove Japan to invade Manchuria and China in the 1930s and led eventually to World War II. The particular understanding of Zen that was introduced to the United States at the beginning of the twentieth century, and which has since then shaped American perceptions of Buddhism in general, was carefully cultivated during these tumultuous decades.

The Japanese delegation to the 1893 Parliament was deeply influenced by the efforts of progressives to produce a "new Buddhism" (*shin bukkyo*) that was thoroughly modern and fully equal to the intellectual and religious traditions of the West. Japanese cultural and religious leaders saw it as their mission "to convince intellectuals that Japanese Buddhism was the equal of Western philosophy, superior to Western religion and completely in accord with Western science."[67] It was important to the Japanese that the West acknowledge Buddhism as a legitimate world religion; just as Europeans and Americans had Christianity, so too Japan, as a modernizing nation, needed a modernized Buddhism recognized as a world religion. This vision of a kind of Buddhism compatible with modern science and equal if not superior to Christianity, while remaining rooted firmly in ancient, esoteric Japanese values, was to have an enormous effect upon how Buddhism was portrayed to the West.

The Parliament of Religions set in motion the first Buddhist missions to the United States. The Japanese delegation, led by Shaku Soen, returned to Japan convinced that the materialistic and hedonistic culture of America was hungering for Eastern spirituality. As Notto Thelle notes,

---

World's Parliament of Religions and Its Legacy," in *The History of Religions: Understanding Human Experience*, AAR Studies in Religion 47 (Atlanta: Scholars, 1987).

67. Judith Snodgrass, *Presenting Japanese Buddhism to the West: Orientalism, Occidentalism, and the Columbian Exposition* (Chapel Hill: University of North Carolina Press, 2003), 9.

The Japanese Buddhists did not hesitate to proclaim that the parliament was a unique breakthrough for Buddhist mission. The Buddhist presence was character-ized as "an epoch-making, unprecedented happening, unheard-of in history." It was felt that the situation was ripe for "Buddhism in Japan in the Far East to turn the wheel of Dharma in America in the Far West." At the dawn of the twentieth century Buddhism was appearing at the scene of world culture spreading the unfathomable light and compassion of the Buddha. A representative Buddhist journal concluded that the parliament was "the most brilliant fact in the history of Buddhism."[68]

Japanese Buddhists presented Buddhism as a dynamic spiritual and in-tellectual movement which is especially relevant to modern, educated West-ern audiences. Robert Sharf points out that Zen was introduced to the West "through the activities of an elite circle of internationally minded Japanese intellectuals and globe-trotting Zen priests, whose missionary zeal was often second only to their vexed fascination with Western culture."[69] The most effec-tive among them was D. T. Suzuki, whose reinterpretation of Buddhism was not only significant for Westerners but also for a Japan which was struggling to modernize and assert itself on the world stage.

D. T. Suzuki and Zen

Daisetzu Teitaro Suzuki (1870–1966) became interested in Zen while still in high school.[70] In the late 1880s Suzuki met Kitaro Nishida (1870–1945), later the founder of the Kyoto School of philosophy, and the two became lifelong friends. While a student at Tokyo Imperial University, Suzuki commuted to Kamakura, where he studied Buddhism under Shaku Soen.

While at the 1893 World's Parliament of Religions, Soen had met Dr. Paul Carus (1852–1919), head of the Open Court Publishing Company and editor

68. Notto Thelle, *Buddhism and Christianity in Japan: From Conflict to Dialogue, 1854–1899* (Honolulu: University of Hawaii Press, 1987), 221–22.

69. Robert H. Sharf, "The Zen of Japanese Nationalism," in *Curators of the Buddha: The Study of Buddhism under Colonialism*, ed. Donald S. Lopez Jr. (Chicago: University of Chicago Press, 1995), 108.

70. D. T. Suzuki provides two autobiographical accounts in his "Early Memories" and "An Autobiographical Account," both in *A Zen Life: D. T. Suzuki Remembered*, ed. Masao Abe (New York: Weatherhill, 1986), 3–26. This is a collection of largely sympathetic and appreciative essays. More critical assessments of Suzuki are found in Robert H. Sharf, "The Zen of Japanese Nationalism," 107–60; idem, "Whose Zen? Zen Nationalism Revisited," in *Rude Awakenings: Zen, the Kyoto School and the Question of Nationalism*, ed. James W. Heisig and John C. Maraldo (Honolulu: University of Hawaii Press, 1994), 40–51; McMahan, "Repackaging Zen for the West," 218–29; Bernard Faure, *Chan Insights and Oversights: An Epistemological Critique of the Chan Tradition* (Princeton: Princeton University Press, 1993), chap. 2.

of the journal *The Monist*. Carus was the son of a Protestant minister in Germany, but as an adult he rejected orthodox Christianity as incompatible with modern science and became a passionate advocate of "a religion of science."[71] Carus held that not only would such a religion be compatible with the latest insights of science, but it would also incorporate the central insights of all the world's great religions. Buddhism seemed to be particularly conducive to such a project. Carus found a sympathetic ally in Soen, who was eager to promote Buddhism in the West as a modern, universal religion. In an 1895 letter to Carus, Soen envisioned America as the birthplace of a new Buddhism: "Buddha who lived three thousand years ago being named Gautama, now lies bodily dead in India; but Buddhism in the twentieth century being named Truth, is just to be born in Chicago in the New World."[72] In 1894 Carus published *The Gospel of Buddha*, a highly sympathetic portrayal of Buddhism as a rational faith, fully compatible with science.[73] The book is an eclectic collection of passages from forty-five different Buddhist scriptures, combining Pali texts with Sanskrit texts. Carus freely reinterpreted key Buddhist notions such as no-self, nirvana, and emptiness, giving them a more theistic and morally positive sense. This undoubtedly made key Buddhist concepts seem less alien to an American audience still influenced by theism, but the book was also widely used in Ceylon and was translated into Japanese by D. T. Suzuki.[74]

In 1897, at Carus's invitation, Suzuki moved to LaSalle, Illinois, to work as a translator at Open Court Publishing. Returning to Japan in 1909, Suzuki taught at several universities, eventually taking a position in 1921 as professor of Buddhist philosophy at Otani University in Kyoto, where he launched the journal *Eastern Buddhist*. But it was only after reaching the age of fifty that Suzuki's career as an interpreter of Zen to the West really got under way. He published over a hundred books and articles on Buddhism and lectured at major American and European universities. Suzuki lived in Kamakura,

71. See Martin J. Verhoeven, "Americanizing the Buddha: Paul Carus and the Transformation of Asian Thought," in *Faces of Buddhism in America*, 207–27.

72. As quoted in Verhoeven, "Americanizing the Buddha," 216.

73. The claim that Buddhism is compatible with science was also made by many in the late twentieth and early twenty-first centuries. Donald Lopez points out the incongruity of this: "If Buddhism was compatible with the science of the nineteenth century, how can it also be compatible with the science of the twenty-first? If the Buddha long ago understood Newtonian physics, did he also understand quantum mechanics?" The content of the Buddha's enlightenment cannot change. "How can the same timeless truths be constantly reflected in discoveries that have changed, and continue to change, so drastically over time?" (Lopez, *Scientific Buddha*, 13).

74. Kayako Nagao, "Paul Carus' Involvement in the Modernization of Japanese Education and Buddhism," *Japanese Religions* 34.2 (July 2009): 172.

Japan, during World War II; in 1949, at the age of 79, he again traveled to the United States for an extended time of lecturing and writing. Suzuki returned to Japan in 1958, where he died in 1966 at the age of 95. As a result of his many writings, lectures, and extensive contacts with Western intellectuals, Suzuki had an enormous influence on American understandings of Buddhism in the twentieth century.[75]

Suzuki is often regarded by Westerners as a dispassionate, meticulous scholar of Buddhism, whose depiction of Zen is simply a restatement of classical Buddhism for Western audiences. In fact, however, Suzuki's views were controversial, and he was frequently criticized by Japanese Buddhists for his portrayal of Zen. Heinrich Dumoulin observes, "Japanese Zen Buddhists were often astounded at the transformations Zen was undergoing in the West, and they differentiated between the traditional form of Japanese Zen and that which they called 'Suzuki Zen.'"[76] Kayako Nagao states, "Suzuki often made mistakes in writing Buddhist terms, thereby exposing his lack of basic knowledge of Buddhist texts. He did not intend to understand Buddhist scriptures as they were, instead he read texts in a way that pleased him."[77]

Every scholar is to some extent the product of many different influences, and this was certainly the case with Suzuki. Recent scholarship highlights the diverse external influences on Suzuki and his formulation of Zen. In his teenage years, for example, Suzuki had contact with both Greek Orthodox and Protestant missionaries to Japan, and throughout his life he had ongoing conversations with Christian thinkers. Between 1903 and 1924, when his early writings on Zen were taking shape, Suzuki had strong interests in both Swedenborgianism and Theosophy.[78] Sutin notes that "in 1911 [Suzuki] married Beatrice Erskine Lane (1878–1938), an American who was a member of the Theosophical Society and ultimately wrote respected works on Zen and Shingon Buddhism. Husband and wife influenced each other's interests, for Suzuki became a member of the Order of the Eastern Star, an offshoot of the Theosophical movement led by Annie Besant."[79] In the 1920s Suzuki and his wife opened a Theosophical Lodge in Kyoto. Suzuki translated four of

---

75. See Larry A. Fader, "D. T. Suzuki's Contribution to the West," in Abe, *A Zen Life*, 95–108.
76. Dumoulin, *Zen Enlightenment*, 7.
77. Nagao, "Carus' Involvement in the Modernization of Japanese Education," 180.
78. See Thomas Tweed, "American Occultism and Japanese Buddhism: Albert J. Edmunds, D. T. Suzuki, and Translocative History," *Japanese Journal of Religious Studies* 32.2 (2005): 249–81. Many Japanese Buddhist intellectuals in the late nineteenth and early twentieth centuries, including Suzuki's mentor Shaku Soen, were also influenced by Unitarian missionaries to Japan. Suzuki himself had some contact with Unitarians. See Michel Mohr, *Buddhism, Unitarianism, and the Meiji Competition for Universality* (Cambridge, MA: Harvard University Press, 2014).
79. Sutin, *All Is Change*, 244.

the Swedish mystic Emanuel Swedenborg's works into Japanese, published a book-length study of Swedenborg in 1913, and helped to found the Japanese Swedenborg Society. Clearly more was at work in shaping Suzuki's views than simply ancient Buddhist teachings. Critics have pointed out three ways in particular that external influences as well as Suzuki's own agenda have affected his portrayal of Zen and Buddhism. In mentioning these, our purpose is not to denigrate Suzuki but simply to illustrate how the portrayal of a particular religion can be influenced by factors external to that tradition itself.

First, Suzuki's emphasis upon the paradoxical and irrational elements in Zen, treating these as defining characteristics of Buddhism at large, is said to be at odds with other traditional streams of Buddhism.[80] For example, in discussing characteristics of the satori (enlightenment) experience, Suzuki lists "irrationality" first. Suzuki states, "I mean that satori is not a conclusion to be reached by reasoning, and defies all intellectual determination. Those who have experienced it are always at a loss to explain it coherently or logically. . . . The *satori* experience is always characterized by irrationality, inexplicability, and incommunicability."[81] The experience of satori is said to be self-authenticating for the one experiencing it. "By this I mean that the knowledge realized by *satori* is final, that no amount of logical argument can refute it. Being direct and personal it is sufficient unto itself."[82] Suzuki emphasizes what he takes to be the "pure," immediate experience of enlightenment, an experience said to transcend all duality, concepts, doctrines, and rational reflection.[83]

But Suzuki has been criticized by Buddhist scholars for stressing the nonrational element in satori in a way that is not faithful to earlier Buddhist traditions. Buddhism has historically given careful attention to logic and epistemology, and Theravada Buddhists in particular emphasize the rationality of Buddhist principles. Many Buddhists emphasize that Buddhism is based solely upon reason and experience and, unlike Christianity, has no place for faith. Buddhist scholar Hajime Nakamura claims that "according to Buddhism, faith becomes superstition when it is not examined by reason. Theravada and

80. Dumoulin, *Zen Enlightenment*, 6.

81. Daisetz T. Suzuki, *The Essentials of Zen Buddhism: Selected from the Writings of Daisetz T. Suzuki*, ed. Bernard Phillips (Westport, CT: Greenwood, 1962), 163.

82. Ibid., 164.

83. Suzuki was echoing a theme prominent in the Kyoto School of Japanese philosophy, founded by his friend Kitaro Nishida. The Kyoto School was a creative intellectual movement that tried to develop a synthesis between traditional Western philosophical concerns and Zen Buddhism. Nishida's most significant work is *An Inquiry into the Good*, trans. Masao Abe and Christopher Ives (New Haven: Yale University Press, 1987 [1927]).

Mahayana Buddhism have accepted two standards for the truth of a statement: it must be in accord with the [Buddhist] scriptures and must be proved true by reasoning. No Buddhist is expected to believe anything which does not meet these two tests."[84] Similarly, K. N. Jayatilleke states, "In arguing with his opponents, the Buddha often shows that their theories lead to inconsistencies or contradictions, thereby demonstrating that they are false. . . . This means that truth must be consistent."[85] This is a very different understanding of the place of reason in Buddhism than that offered by Suzuki.

Second, critics charge that Suzuki ignores the great variety within Buddhism, to say nothing of other Asian philosophical and religious traditions, by identifying Japanese Zen with the "essence" not only of Buddhism but also of "Eastern spirituality" in general. Heinrich Dumoulin observes that in his writings Suzuki tends to "uproot" Zen from its "native Buddhist soil."[86] The "dehistoricizing" of Zen is evident in the priority Suzuki gives to the Rinzai School of Zen (of which he was a member) while ignoring Soto Zen; his minimizing of the Chinese Ch'an tradition; and his failure even to mention Son, the Korean version of Ch'an, although he undoubtedly knew about it from traveling to Korea during the Japanese occupation of Korea.[87] Furthermore, Suzuki disparaged the Theravada tradition as inadequately comprehending the core teaching of Gautama. The earlier Buddhists, we are told, were incapable of grasping the exalted teaching of the Buddha's Enlightenment, and thus early Buddhist literature focuses more on the Four Noble Truths rather than Enlightenment itself.[88]

One also finds in Suzuki a tension between two themes that are difficult to reconcile. On the one hand, Zen is said to have a universal status, transcending the particularities of culture and religion, since it is "the spirit of all religion and philosophy."[89] As David McMahan puts it, "Zen, as Suzuki presented it, is the pure experience of unmediated encounter with reality, and the spontaneous living in harmony with that reality." For Suzuki, Zen is not just a particular school of Buddhism but rather "an ahistorical essence of spirituality."[90] Furthermore, Suzuki, following Paul Carus, saw in Zen the

84. Nakamura, "Unity and Diversity in Buddhism," 372.
85. K. N. Jayatilleke, *The Message of the Buddha*, ed. Ninian Smart (New York: Free Press, 1974), 43–44.
86. Dumoulin, *Zen Enlightenment*, 6.
87. Faure, *Chan Insights and Oversights*, 57.
88. See, e.g., D. T. Suzuki, *Essays in Zen: First Series* (New York: Weidenfeld, 1961 [1949]), 164–66. For a contrasting Theravada perspective on Zen, see David Kalupahana, *Buddhist Philosophy: A Historical Analysis* (Honolulu: University of Hawaii Press, 1976), 163–77.
89. As quoted in Faure, *Chan Insights and Oversights*, 57.
90. McMahan, "Repackaging Zen for the West," 221.

potential for a unifying common ground for all the world religions. In an editorial comment in the *Eastern Buddhist*, Suzuki states, "Our standpoint is that the Mahayana ought to be considered one whole, individual thing and no sects, especially no sectarian prejudices, to be recognized in it, except as so many phases or aspects of one fundamental truth. In this respect Buddhism and Christianity and all other religious beliefs are not more than variations of one single original Faith, deeply embedded in the human soul."[91] As McMahan notes, "The essence of Zen, for Suzuki, was mysticism, which he believed was common to other religious traditions as well."[92]

Yet this universal emphasis is counterbalanced by a highly particularistic theme that locates the apex of "Eastern spirituality" and the essence of Buddhism in Japanese Zen. In a typical passage, Suzuki states, "In Zen are found systematized or rather crystallized, all the philosophy, religion, and life itself of the Far-Eastern people, especially the Japanese."[93] Robert Sharf observes that for Suzuki, "while Zen experience is the universal ground of religious truth, it is nonetheless an expression of a uniquely *Japanese* spirituality. . . . Zen is touted as the very heart of Asian spirituality, the essence of Japanese culture, and the key to the unique qualities of the Japanese race."[94] Commenting on Suzuki's influential book *Zen and Japanese Culture*, Sharf states:

> Virtually all of the major Japanese artistic traditions are reinterpreted as expressions of the "Zen experience," rendering Zen the metaphysical ground of Japanese culture itself. Given this exalted spiritual heritage, the Japanese are said to be culturally, if not racially, predisposed toward Zen insight; they have a deeper appreciation of the unity of man and nature, the oneness of life and death and so on. . . . The claim that Zen is the foundation of Japanese culture has the felicitous result of rendering the Japanese spiritual experience both unique and universal at the same time.[95]

Needless to say, not only other Asian Buddhists, but also Hindus, Sikhs, Jains, and Daoists would dispute the identification of "Eastern spirituality" with Japanese Zen.

91. As cited in Sharf, "Zen of Japanese Nationalism," 120–21.
92. McMahan, "Repackaging Zen for the West," 221.
93. Suzuki, *Essentials of Zen Buddhism*, 8.
94. Sharf, "Zen of Japanese Nationalism," 128, 111, with original emphasis.
95. Sharf, "Whose Zen?," 46. Sharf notes a certain irony in this discourse: "It was no coincidence that the notion of Zen as the foundation for Japanese moral, aesthetic, and spiritual superiority emerged full force in the 1930s, just as the Japanese were preparing for imperial expansion in East and Southeast Asia" (ibid.).

Finally, Suzuki's characterization of Zen draws upon the discourse of Orientalism, which shaped the encounters of early modern Japanese intellectuals with modernity and the West. Orientalist discourse,[96] which is usually associated with Western scholars, typically makes a sharp distinction between "the East" and "the West," with sweeping generalizations about "the East" that ignore the many differences within the diverse Asian societies, cultures, and religions. Orientalists are said to have depicted "the West" and "Western religion" (Christianity) in favorable terms whereas "the East" and "Eastern religion" are characterized in terms of negative contrasts with the West.

But some Asian intellectuals skillfully turned the tables by utilizing the discourse of Orientalism in order to construct fresh cultural and religious identities, thereby playing off the East against the West.[97] The West was then portrayed as crassly materialistic, crude, ethically insensitive, violent, spiritually bankrupt, and obsessed with a rationality and scientism that keeps it from recognizing genuine spiritual truth and insight. By contrast, the East was depicted as gentle and nonviolent, ethically sensitive, harmonious, wise, and guardian of an intuitive, mystical spirituality that transcends the superficial rationality of Western monotheism. While such sweeping generalizations are just as misleading as those of Western Orientalists, they can be highly effective in shaping perceptions about religions such as Hinduism or Buddhism in their encounter with modernity and the West. What was introduced by Suzuki to the West in the early twentieth century as the essence of Buddhism and Eastern spirituality was in part just such a construct of reverse Orientalism. The universality of Zen as the ground of all genuine religious truth, regardless of culture or religion, was thus juxtaposed against the esoteric particularities of "Eastern thought" exemplified in Japanese spirituality, thereby rendering Zen inaccessible to the "Western mind."

> Having lived through the military humiliation of Japan at the hands of the "culturally inferior" Occidental powers, Suzuki would devote a considerable portion of his prodigious energies tantalizing a legion of disenchanted Western intellectuals with the dream of an Oriental enlightenment. Yet all the while Suzuki held that the cultural and spiritual weaknesses of the Occident virtually precluded the possibility of Westerners ever coming to truly comprehend Zen. One is led to suspect that Suzuki's lifelong effort to bring Buddhist enlightenment

96. The seminal work here is Edward Said, *Orientalism* (New York: Vintage, 1978). See also Richard King, *Orientalism and Religion: Postcolonial Theory, India and the "Mystic East"* (New York: Routledge, 1999); and Philip A. Mellor, "Orientalism, Representation and Religion: The Reality behind the Myth," *Religion* 34 (2004): 99–112.

97. Ian Buruma and Avishai Margalit, *Occidentalism: The West in the Eyes of Its Enemies* (New York: Penguin, 2004).

to the Occident had become inextricably bound to a studied contempt for the West, a West whose own cultural arrogance and imperialist inclinations Suzuki had come to know all too well.[98]

In Suzuki's writings one can see an essentializing of both "the West" and "the East," with the one as the antithesis of the other. He skillfully promotes simplistic generalizations about "the West" and "the East" that are now widely accepted. For example, in one passage Suzuki states,

> The Western mind is: analytical, discriminative, differential, inductive, individualistic, intellectual, objective, scientific, generalizing, conceptual, schematic, impersonal, legalistic, organizing, power-wielding, self-assertive, disposed to impose its will upon others, etc. Against these Western traits, those of the East can be characterized as follows: synthetic, totalizing, integrative, nondiscriminative, deductive, nonsystematic, dogmatic, intuitive (rather, affective), nondiscursive, subjective, spiritually individualistic and socially group-minded, etc.[99]

Such sweeping generalizations bear little resemblance to the actual complexities within Asian, European, or North American cultures. Yet the attraction of Buddhism in the West is due in part to the skillful and effective use of such discourse to promote a profound and esoteric "Eastern spirituality" as the antidote to "Western rationalism and materialism."

> While Suzuki's Zen claimed a privileged perspective that transcended cultural difference, it was at the same time contrived as the antithesis of everything Suzuki found deplorable about the West. . . . We read repeatedly that the "West" is materialistic, the "East" spiritual, that the West is aggressive and imperialistic, while the East extols nonviolence and harmony, that the West values rationality, the East intuitive wisdom, that the West is dualistic, the East monistic, and that while the West is individualistic, setting man apart from nature, the East is communalistic, viewing man as one with nature. In short, his image of the East in general, and Japan in particular, is little more than a romantic inversion of Japanese negative stereotypes of the West.[100]

It is not surprising, then, that Suzuki's Zen was especially attractive to those who were growing disillusioned with Western culture and society.

All of this might invite a key question: Is Suzuki's Zen really authentic Buddhism? Significantly, there is an ongoing debate among Japanese scholars

98. Sharf, "Zen of Japanese Nationalism," 131.
99. As cited in Faure, *Chan Insights and Oversights*, 64–65n18.
100. Sharf, "Whose Zen?," 47–48.

today over whether Japanese Zen is really Buddhism at all.[101] But this is a matter for Buddhists themselves to decide. In recounting the critique of Suzuki, my purpose is not to suggest that he is not a "real" Buddhist or that his portrayal of Zen Buddhism is not authentically Buddhist. It is rather to illustrate how established religious traditions are continually undergoing some change as they encounter fresh challenges and opportunities and as ancient ways are adapted to new contexts.

101. See Paul L. Swanson, "Why They Say Zen Is Not Buddhism: Recent Japanese Critiques of Buddha-Nature," in *Pruning the Bodhi Tree*, 3–29.

4

Jesus in a Global, Postcolonial World

Today Jesus appears in some surprising places. Despite the small number of Christians in Japan, for example, there is a monument in northern Japan said to mark the burial place of Jesus.[1] Local legend maintains that after growing up in Galilee, Jesus lived in Japan before beginning his public ministry in Palestine. Facing opposition from Jewish leaders, Jesus returned to Japan, settling in a town near beautiful Lake Towada. Jesus's brother, Isukuri, was crucified in Jesus's place on the cross, and Jesus lived on in Japan until his death at age 106. How did this fascinating story become embedded in local narratives in a remote mountain area of northern Japan, far from known centers of Christianity? This seems to be a confused version of accounts about Jesus from the early Roman Catholic presence in Japan in the sixteenth and seventeenth centuries. Despite the fact that few Japanese today identify as Christian, Japan has had an ongoing fascination with Jesus. Several of the popular Japanese new religions have incorporated Jesus into their pantheon of deities and sages.[2]

1. John Koedyker, "Another Jesus," *Japan Christian Quarterly* 52.2 (1986): 167–69.
2. See Richard Fox Young, "The 'Christ' of the Japanese New Religions," *Japan Christian Quarterly* 57.1 (Winter, 1991): 18–28; Notto R. Thelle, "Jesus in Japanese Religions," *Japan Christian Quarterly* 49.1 (Winter 1983): 23–30.

Jesus has been adopted by many religions of the world.[3] Perhaps this is not so surprising, since Jesus is a towering figure in human history, and many traditions have found it necessary to accommodate him on their own terms. As Delbert Burkett observes, "Christianity has traditionally presented Jesus as the only way to the divine. As adherents of other religious traditions have encountered this claim, they have often found themselves compelled to respond. As part of their response, they have produced alternative visions of Jesus that are compatible with their own religious traditions."[4]

According to Islam, Jesus is a highly revered prophet—although he is in no way to be identified with God. The Dalai Lama states, "As a Buddhist, my attitude toward Jesus Christ is that he was either a fully enlightened being or a bodhisattva of a very high spiritual realization."[5] Jesus is also one of many divine manifestations or messengers of God in Baha'i. Jesus also has a prominent, if unorthodox, place in the remarkably successful new religion of Mormonism, or the Church of Jesus Christ of Latter-Day Saints. Portrayals of Jesus in non-Christian religions are generally positive—as a holy man, prophet, ethical teacher, mystic, miracle worker, even a bodhisattva—but none of them embrace the orthodox Christian teaching of Jesus as God incarnate, fully human and fully divine, the only Lord and Savior for all humankind. Jesus is reduced to something other than what Christian tradition has maintained.

Today it has become popular to think of Jesus as a great religious and moral leader but one who is not qualitatively different from other great religious figures. This is a distinctively modern view that has developed in parallel tracks in the West and in Asia, with each trajectory shaped to some extent by the other. The emergence of the "pluralistic Jesus" in the nineteenth and twentieth centuries is yet another example of what Peter van der Veer calls the interactional history of modernity.[6] In their perspectives on Jesus, European and American thinkers were influenced not only by higher critical views of the Bible but also by what they were learning about Hindus and Buddhists in Asia. Indian thinkers in turn were forced to come to grips with Jesus because of the challenge to traditional ways posed by colonialism and Christian

3. For a helpful source of texts from Judaism, Islam, Hinduism, and Buddhism on Jesus, see *Jesus beyond Christianity: The Classic Texts*, ed. Gregory A. Barker and Stephen E. Gregg (New York: Oxford University Press, 2010).

4. Delbert Burkett, "Images of Jesus: An Overview," in *The Blackwell Companion to Jesus*, ed. Delbert Burkett (Oxford: Blackwell, 2011), 4.

5. His Holiness the Dalai Lama, *The Good Heart: A Buddhist Perspective on the Teachings of Jesus*, ed. Robert Kiely (Boston: Wisdom, 1996), 83. See also Rita M. Gross and Terry Muck, eds., *Buddhists Talk about Jesus, Christians Talk about the Buddha* (New York: Continuum, 2000).

6. Peter van der Veer, *The Modern Spirit of Asia: The Spiritual and the Secular in China and India* (Princeton: Princeton University Press, 2014), 9, 24.

missions. Hindu practices such as suttee, caste, and child marriage were criticized as ethically deficient, and popular religious beliefs and practices were denounced as idolatry. Many on both sides (Hindu and Christian) thought of Christianity, because of its close ties with British culture and history, as associated with the colonialist enterprise. For many Christians, Jesus was a symbol both of what was wrong with Hinduism and the superiority of the West and Christianity. But, to the chagrin of many in the West, Indian social and religious reformers responded neither by converting to Christianity nor by rejecting Jesus outright. Instead, they selectively adopted elements of the Christian tradition but reinterpreted them to fit within reinvigorated Indian religious traditions. Jesus became a modern Hindu.

In turn, the Jesus of the Hindu Renaissance—moral and religious reformer, mystic—was welcomed as a familiar figure by liberal Western theologians, reinforcing a revisionist Christology gaining currency in Europe and North America that regarded Jesus as just one among many great moral and religious leaders. The rise of critical biblical scholarship in the West during the past three centuries has produced an astonishing variety of Jesuses, each supposedly embedded within the layers of the New Testament. The influence of higher critical perspectives is pervasive throughout the Western academy, and with globalization their impact is being felt worldwide. The global effect of secular universities should not be minimized, as bright international students take back to their homelands the revisionist views on Jesus acquired in the West. Peter Berger speaks of "a secular internationale," a "thin but very influential stratum of intellectuals, broadly defined as people with Western-style higher education, especially in the humanities and social sciences," who become carriers of secularism throughout the non-Western world.[7] This secularized international elite comprise a "faculty-club culture" in Asia, Latin America, and Africa, which spreads the values and ideologies of the Western intelligentsia "through the educational system, the legal system, various therapeutic institutions, think tanks, and at least some of the media of mass communication."[8] Higher critical views of Jesus and the New Testament are then taken for granted by academics in Tokyo, Mumbai, and Beijing as well as in Chicago or London.

In this chapter we will examine the idea that Jesus is one among many great moral and religious leaders as this has been expressed by some leading nineteenth- and twentieth-century thinkers. We will look briefly at the views of several leading Hindu thinkers and then conclude by examining the

7. Peter Berger, "Secularization and De-secularization," in *Religions in the Modern World*, ed. Linda Woodhead, Paul Fletcher, Hiroko Kawanami, and David Smith (London: Routledge, 2002), 293–94.
8. Peter Berger, "Four Faces of Global Culture," *National Interest* 49 (Fall 1997): 24–25.

perspectives of a Western pluralist theologian and a popular Japanese novelist. Although the particular context in which each lived is different, all regard
Jesus as a great religious and moral leader while rejecting the claim that he is
the unique incarnation of God, the only Lord and Savior for all.

British Colonialism, Christian Missions, and India

In the modern era, European interest in India begins with the 1498 voyage of
Vasco da Gama to the coast of southwestern India. During the eighteenth and
nineteenth centuries, European nations exerted increasing control over the
peoples of Asia, Africa, and the Americas. "In 1800 Western nations controlled
35 per cent of the world's land surface; by 1914 they were in charge of 84 per
cent. By the 1970s, the vast majority of these empires had been dismantled and
new independent nation states created in their wake."[9] The most extensive of
these empires was the British Empire. The English East India Company, which
had received a charter from Queen Elizabeth I in 1600, gradually extended
its control over India so that "by 1856 almost 70 per cent of the subcontinent
had fallen to the British."[10] After the tragic uprising or "mutiny" of 1857–58,
political authority for administering India was transferred from the East India
Company to the British Crown, and in 1877 Queen Victoria was proclaimed
Empress of India.

Westerners often regard Indian Christianity as little more than the religious
by-product of British colonialism, but in reality the Christian church has a
long history in India, quite possibly tracing its origin to the missionary work
of the apostle Thomas in the first century.[11] Regardless of whether Thomas
himself ever reached India, Christian communities were certainly present in
South India by the third century, if not earlier. Roman Catholic missionaries
arrived in the sixteenth and seventeenth centuries, with Protestants such as
William Carey following in the eighteenth century. The nineteenth century
witnessed a large influx of Western missionaries to India, so the missionary
presence in India coincided with the period of British colonial rule. Although

9. Linda Woodhead, "Modern Contexts of Religion," in *Religions in the Modern World:
Traditions and Transformations*, ed. Linda Woodhead, Hiroko Kawanami, and Christopher
Partridge, 2nd ed. (London: Routledge, 2009), 5.

10. Denis Judd, *The Lion and the Tiger: The Rise and Fall of the British Raj* (New York:
Oxford University Press, 2004), 47.

11. On the evidence for Thomas reaching India, see Samuel Hugh Moffett, *Beginnings to
1500*, vol. 1 of *A History of Christianity in Asia* (New York: HarperCollins, 1992), 25–36; Robert Eric Frykenberg, *Christianity in India: From Beginnings to the Present* (New York: Oxford
University Press, 2008), 91–115.

the missionary movement is sometimes dismissed as simply the religious side of British imperialism, the reality was far more complex. For example, the East India Company did not want Christian missionaries working in the territories under its control, and it successfully kept missionaries out of India until 1813. Even after missionaries were permitted, often the attitude of the colonial administrators was not sympathetic. Far from supporting Christian missions, the British Raj was committed to a policy of protecting all religious institutions in India, and in actual practice it was sometimes perceived by Christians as discriminating against Christian institutions. Robert Frykenberg concisely summarizes the ambivalent relationship between the administrators and missionaries:

> When missionaries finally gained access to Company territories, their efforts brought counter-currents of religious renewal, social reform, and the eventual rise of nationalisms. By the same token, the advent of modern forms of Christianity opened possibilities for communities long oppressed and overshadowed by Brahmanical dominance. The paradoxical result was that Christian missions often attracted their greatest followings where their connection to imperial authority was least in evidence. Moreover, dissenting and non-British missions flourished while missions too closely connected to the Anglican establishment faltered. Even as Christians struck deep roots among peoples on the social and territorial margins of India—the Dalit ("Untouchable") communities and *adivasi* ("aboriginal" or "tribal") communities—their influence hastened the construction (or invention) of modern, syndicated, Hinduism and Indian nationalism, as well as Islamic revivalisms.[12]

And yet, the perception among many Indians was that Christian missions and the colonial administration were intimately linked. Peter van der Veer reports, "Indians did not conceive the colonial state as neutral and secular but rather as fundamentally Christian. . . . A distinct feeling that the modernizing project of the colonial state was based on Western values and thus Christian in nature remained important. This feeling was further enhanced by the fact that many high ranking officials were self-conscious Christians who felt it their duty to support the missionizing effort."[13]

12. Robert Eric Frykenberg, "Christian Missions and the Raj," in *Missions and Empire*, ed. Norman Etherington (New York: Oxford University Press, 2005), 107.

13. Peter van der Veer, *Imperial Encounters: Religion and Modernity in India and Britain* (Princeton: Princeton University Press, 2001), 23. On Indian perceptions of the missionaries, see Richard Fox Young, "Some Hindu Perspectives on Christian Missionaries in the Indic World of the Mid-nineteenth Century," in *Christians, Cultural Interactions, and India's Religious Traditions*, ed. Judith M. Brown and Robert Eric Frykenberg (Grand Rapids: Eerdmans, 2002), 37–60.

In one of the ironies of imperial rule, British control of the subcontinent stimulated a common sense of identity among disparate groups of people who had long been divided by geography, language, religion, and ethnicity. In the 1880s, Indian nationalism emerged as many different kinds of Indians came together in common opposition against British rule. In 1885 the India National Congress was inaugurated, and the Muslim League was founded in 1906. In 1915, when Mohandas Gandhi returned to India from South Africa to engage in the struggle for swaraj (self-rule), he became a unifying figure for Indian nationalists and led nonviolent resistance to the British through a series of massive movements of civil disobedience in the 1920s and '30s. In 1947 British rule ended as the Indian Empire was divided into two separate independent nations, India and Pakistan. At this point, "80 per cent of the British Empire's subjects gained their independence at one stroke."[14]

The Hindu Renaissance

Stimulated by modern science, Western culture, and Christianity, several significant Hindu reform movements developed between 1875 and the outbreak of war in 1914. These movements tried to reconcile the best of traditional Indian culture and religion with Western ideals of democracy, humanism, moral activism, and science. The Hindu Renaissance, as the movements came to be known, had an ambivalent relationship with Christianity.[15] While many of the leaders had deep admiration for Jesus, they were generally sharply critical of traditional Christianity and missions.

Leading thinkers of the Hindu Renaissance tried to combine the best of Western science and the moral precepts of Christianity with a purified and modernized form of Hinduism. Although Christianity as such was rejected, Jesus as a moral and spiritual leader was readily embraced.[16] Eric Sharpe observes that these thinkers tended to draw "an abrupt distinction between

14. Judd, *Lion and the Tiger*, 2.

15. See *Neo-Hindu Views of Christianity*, ed. Arvind Sharma (Leiden: Brill, 1988); Torkel Brekke, *Makers of Modern Indian Religion in the Late Nineteenth Century* (New York: Oxford University Press, 2002); M. M. Thomas, *The Acknowledged Christ of the Indian Renaissance* (London: SCM, 1969).

16. Not all were so appreciative. Dayananda Sarasvati (1824–83) was a sharp critic of Christianity who called for a return to the Vedas as the source of all wisdom, including modern science. See J. T. F. Jordens, "Dayananda Sarasvati's Interpretation of Christianity," in Sharma, *Neo-Hindu Views of Christianity*, 120–42; Kenneth W. Jones, "Swami Dayananda Sarasvati's Critique of Christianity," in *Religious Controversy in British India: Dialogues in South Asian Languages*, ed. Kenneth Jones (Albany: State University of New York Press, 1992), 52–74.

Jesus as a moral teacher, accessible to all, and the Christian community which had come to carry his name, which was European in essence, whatever its pretensions to universality."[17] Ronald Neufeldt summarizes perspectives on Jesus within the Hindu Renaissance:

> Whether one looks at the issue of Christ as *avatara* or Christ as an ideal, there is a single thread that runs through Hindu views of Christ. This thread is the depiction of Christ as an Oriental or Asiatic. One might even be more specific and say that it is the depiction of Christ as the quintessential Hindu, the one who lives Hindu ideals as they ought to be lived and teaches the essence of Hindu truth as it ought to be taught. . . . The purpose of proposing Christ as Oriental is two-fold—to claim Christ and the teachings of Christ, however these may be interpreted, as indigenous to India, and to attack Eurocentric notions of Christ.[18]

Jesus became a Hindu yogi, one among many great religious leaders. In this, the Hindu Renaissance tapped into a powerful motif in Hindu thought, the idea that the divine reality can be understood and experienced in many different ways and that religious leaders from other traditions can be regarded as alternative voices echoing the one ultimate Truth.

Vivekananda

Narendranath Datta (1863–1902), whose religious name was Swami Vivekananda, was a leading spokesman for modern Hinduism and neo-Vedanta.[19] Educated at Scottish Church College, Vivekananda had a keen intellect and social conscience. For a time he belonged to the Brahmo Samaj, a reform movement promoting Hindu monotheism and rejecting the worship of images. But it was his encounter with Ramakrishna (1836–86), the charismatic Hindu mystic who taught that there is an essential unity to the great religions and claimed to have had mystical experiences of Jesus and Muhammad, that transformed Vivekananda's life.

17. Eric J. Sharpe, "Neo-Hindu Images of Christianity," in Sharma, *Neo-Hindu Views of Christianity*, 15.

18. Ronald Neufeldt, "Hindu Views of Christ," in *Hindu-Christian Dialogue: Perspectives and Encounters*, ed. Harold Coward (Maryknoll, NY: Orbis Books, 1989), 173.

19. Vedanta is a general category for philosophical and religious systems derived from the Upanishads, the later writings of the Vedas, which are the sacred texts of Hinduism. A particular focus of Vedanta is the nature of Brahman, the ultimate reality, and Brahman's relation to the created order. The two leading schools of Vedanta, Advaita Vedanta (Nondualist Vedanta) and Vishisht-Advaita Vedanta (Qualified Nondualist Vedanta), trace their teachings back to Shankara (788–820) and Ramanuja (1040?–1137) respectively.

Vivekananda was instrumental in the development of Hinduism as a world religion. He also was effective in cultivating the sense of a distinctive Indian spirituality at the heart of Hinduism, a perspective which, according to van der Veer, "had a major impact on Hindu nationalism of all forms, but also on global understandings of 'spirituality.'"[20] Torkel Brekke states that Vivekananda "sought to create a new basis for national unity and a religious ethic that would provide an initiative for charitable work among the poor in India," and a modernized version of ancient Vedanta teachings became the conceptual mechanism for this.[21] With Vivekananda, Hinduism became a rational and moral religion, purged of superstitious and immoral practices. There are some similarities between the rational moral religion of Hindu reformers such as Vivekananda and the perspectives of European Enlightenment thinkers. Superstitious practices and institutional religion were rejected in favor of a purified and rational religion. Modern Hindu spirituality was understood as having universal significance. Van der Veer points out that "whereas the European Christians tried to universalize their Christian tradition, Hindus did the same with their Hindu tradition. This reproduced the Hindu-Christian opposition, which was also the colonized-colonizer opposition. Colonialism provides the discursive frame in which Hindu rational religion emerges."[22]

Vivekananda regarded Hindu spirituality as universal: thus in his view Hinduism has a role to play on the global stage. As a Hindu delegate at the 1893 World's Parliament on Religions in Chicago, he electrified the crowd with his eloquent call for religious harmony and was hailed by the *New York Times* as "undoubtedly the greatest figure in the Parliament of Religions."[23] Vivekananda called for an end to proselytizing. "Do I wish that the Christian would become a Hindu? God forbid. Do I wish that the Hindu or Buddhist would become Christian? God forbid. . . . The Christian is not to become a Hindu or a Buddhist, nor a Buddhist to become a Christian. But each must assimilate the others and yet preserve its individuality and grow to its own law of growth."[24] Vivekananda sensed that the West was hungry for a different

---

20. Van der Veer, *Modern Spirit of Asia*, 48–49.

21. Brekke, *Makers of Modern Indian Religion*, 13. See also Jyotirmaya Sharma, *A Restatement of Religion: Swami Vivekananda and the Making of Hindu Nationalism* (New Haven: Yale University Press, 2013).

22. Peter van der Veer, "The Moral State: Religion, Nation, and Empire in Victorian Britain and British India," in *Nation and Religion: Perspectives on Europe and Asia*, ed. Peter van der Veer and Hartmut Lehman (Princeton: Princeton University Press, 1999), 31.

23. Marcus Baybrooke, *Inter-Faith Organizations, 1893–1979: An Historical Directory* (New York: Edwin Mellen, 1980), 6–7.

24. Vivekananda, "Impromptu Comments," in *Dawn of Religious Pluralism: Voices from the World's Parliament of Religions, 1893*, ed. Richard Hughes Seager (LaSalle, IL: Open Court, 1993), 336–37.

vision of spirituality, and he started the Vedanta Society in New York (1895) and the Ramakrishna Mission in India (1897).

Vivekananda's Hinduism combines the mystical experiences of Advaita Vedanta with a strong moral conscience and concern for social reform (he opposed discrimination based upon caste). He promoted a message of the essential unity of religions within a Vedanta framework, and he was a sharp critic of the claim that Christianity alone is the true religion.[25] Contrary to Christian claims, Vivekananda held that it is "the Vedanta, and the Vedanta alone, that can become the universal religion of man."[26] Only Vedanta is based upon an eternal principle, whereas other religions are based upon the lives and teachings of historical individuals. The Christian emphasis upon the historicity of the events in the New Testament was regarded by Vivekananda as a liability, not a strength. "If the Christian stands up and says, 'My religion is a historical religion and therefore yours is wrong and ours is true,' the [Hindu replies], 'Yours being historical, you confess that a man invented it nineteen hundred years ago. That which is true must be infinite and eternal. That is the one test of truth. It never decays, and it is always the same.'"[27] Vivekananda was especially critical of what he perceived as Christian exclusivism and intolerance.

> [Christianity] is the best for [Christians], but that is no sign that it is the best for others. . . . In Christianity, . . . when you speak of the Incarnation, of the Trinity, of salvation through Jesus Christ, I am with you. I say, "Very good, that I also hold true." But when you go on to say, "There is no other true religion, there is no other revelation of God," then I say, "Stop, I cannot go with you when you shut out, when you deny." Every religion has a message to deliver, something to teach man; but when it begins to protest, when it tries to disturb others, then it takes up a negative and therefore a dangerous position.[28]

Adopting a theme common to the Hindu Renaissance, Vivekananda understood Jesus as a moral and spiritual teacher whose insights were already anticipated—but in purer form—in the earlier Hindu mystics and even in

25. "The typical strategy of Vivekananda was to systematize a disparate set of traditions, make it intellectually available for a Westernized audience and defensible against Western critique, and incorporate it in the notion of Hindu spirituality carried by the Hindu nation, which was superior to Western materialism, brought to India by an aggressive and arrogant British nation" (van der Veer, "Moral State," 33).

26. As cited in M. M. Thomas, *The Acknowledged Christ of the Indian Renaissance* (London: SCM, 1969), 117.

27. As cited in Hal W. French, "Swami Vivekananda's Experiences and Interpretations of Christianity," in Sharma, *Neo-Hindu Views of Christianity*, 99.

28. Ibid., 94.

the Buddha. In an 1895 address he stated that "the very teachings of Christ (could) be traced back to those of Buddha," and he called the Buddha's teaching "the foreshadowing of that of Christ."[29] Vivekananda had respect not for the historical Jesus of first-century Palestine but rather for his conception of Jesus as an exemplification of eternal Hindu principles. Vivekananda's Jesus comes to realize his own essential identity with Brahman, and his teachings about a personal God are merely a concession to the masses, who are not yet ready for the highest truth of Vedanta.

Sarvepalli Radhakrishnan

Sarvepalli Radhakrishnan (1888–1975), one of the most influential modern spokesmen for Hinduism, was deeply impacted by the example of Vivekananda. Although Radhakrishnan was born into a Brahmin family, he attended Christian missionary schools, graduating from Madras Christian College with an MA in philosophy. Radhakrishnan taught philosophy at several universities in India, and he was the first Spalding Professor of Eastern Religions and Ethics at Oxford University. After Indian independence, he also served in a variety of diplomatic and political posts, including as Indian ambassador to the Soviet Union and then president of India. Radhakrishnan lectured throughout the world and was widely respected as a statesman and public intellectual who could bridge the cultures of East and West.[30]

At Madras Christian College, Radhakrishnan was bothered by the way Hinduism was dismissed as superstition and not granted equal status with Christianity. His master's thesis, "The Ethics of the Vedanta," was an attempt to defend Vedanta against Western philosophical criticisms. Reflecting back on his early encounters with Christian missionaries, Radhakrishnan said,

> At an impressionable period of my life, I became familiar not only with the teaching of the New Testament, but also with the criticisms levelled by Christian missionaries on Hindu beliefs and practices. My pride as a Hindu roused by the enterprise and eloquence of Swami Vivekananda was deeply hurt by the treatment accorded to Hinduism in missionary institutions. . . . The famous

29. Ibid., 96.
30. See Sarvepalli Radhakrishnan, *Indian Philosophy*, rev. ed., 2 vols. (London: Allen & Unwin, 1929–31); idem, *The Hindu View of Life* (London: Allen & Unwin, 1927); idem, *An Idealist View of Life* (London: Allen & Unwin, 1932); idem, *Eastern Religions and Western Thought*, rev. ed. (London: Oxford University Press, 1940). He was given the honor of a volume dedicated to his philosophy being included in the series Library of Living Philosophers. See *The Philosophy of Sarvepalli Radhakrishnan*, ed. Paul Arthur Schilpp (New York: Tudor, 1952).

Hindu scripture *Bhagavadgita* declares that if one has faith and devotion to the other gods, it is faith and devotion to the supreme One, though not in the prescribed way. . . . Doctrines about God are only guides to the seekers who have not reached the end. . . . They represent God under certain images, as possessing certain attributes and not as He is in Himself. . . . The different religions are not rival or competing forces, but fellow labourers in the same great task. . . . Bred in such beliefs, I was somewhat annoyed that truly religious people—as many Christian missionaries undoubtedly were—could treat as subjects for derision doctrines that others held in deepest reverence.[31]

Throughout his life, Radhakrishnan retained a negative attitude toward Christianity and was a strong critic of proselytizing and conversion.

Like Vivekananda, Radhakrishnan interpreted religions through the lenses of Advaita Vedanta nondualism. He distinguished the external forms of religion (doctrines, beliefs, and practices) from what these forms are trying to express—the intuitive insights grasped through mystical religious experience. The latter is at the heart of what he called the "religion of the Spirit."

Radhakrishnan was a sharp critic of religious claims to exclusive truth. "We cannot have religious unity and peace so long as we assert that we are in possession of the light and all others are groping in darkness. That very assertion is a challenge to a fight."[32] Many passages in Radhakrishnan's writings suggest that he regarded all religions as equally legitimate, alternative ways of responding to the divine mystery and that no single religion has privileged access to truth. For example, he states, "The name by which we call God and the rite by which we approach Him do not matter much. . . . Toleration is the homage which the finite mind pays to the inexhaustibility of the Infinite. . . . There are many possible roads from time to eternity and we need to choose one road. . . . The doctrine we adopt and the philosophy we profess do not matter anymore than the language we speak and the clothes we wear."[33] Radhakrishnan held up Hinduism as an example of the pluralistic and tolerant religion required in today's world, since it "seeks the unity of religion not in common creed but in a common quest."[34]

But it would be a mistake to regard Radhakrishnan as a genuine religious pluralist who does not privilege any particular religious tradition. Like Vivekananda before him, Radhakrishnan was a Hindu, and his pluralistic tendencies must be understood within the framework of his commitment to a

31. Sarvepalli Radhakrishnan, "My Search for Truth," in *Radhakrishnan: Selected Writings on Philosophy, Religion, and Culture*, ed. Robert A. McDermott (New York: Dutton, 1970), 37–39.
32. Radhakrishnan, *Hindu View of Life*, 42.
33. Radhakrishnan, *Eastern Religions and Western Thought*, 317–18.
34. Radhakrishnan, *Hindu View of Life*, 42.

rational, modernized version of Advaita Vedanta. Ninian Smart observes, "[Radhakrishnan's] neo-Hinduism . . . forms the basis of his attempt to reconcile the teachings of the different world religions. He interprets these as essentially affirming, or reaching toward, what is to be found in Vedanta, and is critical of dogmatic, and therefore divisive, attitudes in religion; they are a main cause of conflict between faiths."[35] Thus Radhakrishnan accepts the various religious traditions as fellow travelers on the search for truth, but he does so within a hierarchical framework that ranks religions according to the degree to which they approximate the vision of the Absolute in Vedanta. Paraphrasing the Bhagavad Gita, Radhakrishnan states, "The worshippers of the Absolute are the highest in rank; second to them are the worshippers of the personal God; then come the worshippers of the incarnations like Rama, Krsna [Krishna], Buddha; below them are those who worship ancestors, deities and sages, and lowest of all are the worshippers of the petty forces and spirits."[36] But this is hardly genuine pluralism. As Vinoth Ramachandra remarks, "This is simply religious imperialism masquerading as tolerance."[37] Not only theists such as Christians and Muslims, but also atheistic Buddhists and polytheistic Shintoists will reject Radhakrishnan's patronizing hierarchy.

Radhakrishnan has much to say about Jesus; like others in the Hindu Renaissance, he distinguishes the "religion of Jesus" from the "religion about Jesus." The latter is the religion of Christianity, shaped by the apostle Paul, Hellenistic culture, and centuries of subsequent European influence. By contrast, it is in the religion of Jesus that we find the universal significance of Jesus, which has much in common with Asian approaches to spirituality, according to Radhakrishnan.

He is willing to speak of Jesus as divine, but not in any exclusive or distinctive sense. Jesus's divinity and incarnation serve as models for the rest of us in our relationship with God. "The Incarnation of Christ is a supreme example of a universal truth. Jesus is given to us to become not merely Christians but Christs."[38] Radhakrishnan argues that Jesus's teachings were actually shaped by Indian religious and philosophical assumptions, which were allegedly influential in the environment in which Jesus grew up.[39] Jesus rejected the "exclusiveness"

35. Ninian Smart, "Radhakrishnan," in *The Encyclopedia of Religion*, ed. Paul Edwards (New York: Macmillan, 1967), 7:62.

36. Radhakrishnan, *Hindu View of Life*, 24.

37. Vinoth Ramachandra, *Faiths in Conflict? Christian Integrity in a Multicultural World* (Downers Grove, IL: InterVarsity, 1999), 74.

38. Sarvepalli Radhakrishnan, *East and West: Some Reflections* (London: Allen & Unwin, 1955), 75; as cited in Ishwar Harris, "S. Radhakrishnan's View of Christianity," in Sharma, *Neo-Hindu Views of Christianity*, 160.

39. Radhakrishnan, *Eastern Religions and Western Thought*, 174–75.

of Jewish thought. "In His teaching of the Kingdom of God, life eternal, ascetic emphasis, and even future life, He breaks away from the Jewish tradition and approximates to Hindu and Buddhist thought."[40] It turns out that Jesus and Gautama the Buddha are essentially the same in their teachings:

> There cannot be any difference of opinion regarding the view of life and the world of thought which seem common to Buddhism and Christianity in their early forms. Whether historically connected or not, they are the twin expressions of one great spiritual movement. . . . Buddha and Jesus are the earlier and later Hindu and Jewish representatives of the same upheaval of the human soul, whose typical expression we have in the Upanishads.[41]

There are, then, few things in Jesus's life or teachings that are distinctive or new, and what is of enduring value was actually borrowed from India.

The disregard for historical context is astonishing as Radhakrishnan cavalierly assimilates both Jesus and Gautama into a generic Hindu mystic. He combines rampant speculation with the flimsiest of evidence concerning Hindu or Buddhist influence in the first-century Mediterranean world, thereby to present a picture of Jesus of Nazareth utterly removed from his Jewish context. Radhakrishnan also ignores the historical context of Gautama, claiming that he was essentially a Hindu. For this, Radhakrishnan elicited sharp critiques from Buddhists for trying to ignore the clear differences between Gautama and contemporary Hindu teachings in order to see early Buddhism in continuity with Hinduism.[42]

Mohandas Gandhi

Mohandas Gandhi (1869–1948)—political leader, social reformer, religious visionary, and martyr—was one of the truly great men of the twentieth century. The man once dismissed by Winston Churchill as a "seditious fakir"[43] became the dominant figure in the struggle for independence for India, the jewel in the crown of the vast British Empire. But Gandhi is revered today not only for leading nonviolent resistance against the British but also as a moral leader who advocated for the oppressed and promoted peaceful coexistence

---

40. Ibid., 176.
41. Ibid., 186.
42. See T. R. V. Murti, "Radhakrishnan and Buddhism," in Schilpp, *Philosophy of Sarvepalli Radhakrishnan*, 567–605.
43. Homer Jack, "Introduction," *The Gandhi Reader*, ed. Homer A. Jack (New York: Grove, 1956), viii.

among different religious communities, especially Hindus and Muslims. As a result of his long life devoted to championing the cause of the powerless, his relentless pursuit of peaceful relations between religions, and his tragic assassination at the hands of a Hindu nationalist, Gandhi has become a globally recognized symbol of social justice and nonviolent resistance to evil.[44] David Hardiman claims that Gandhi's most significant legacy "has proved to be his technique of nonviolent civil resistance," which inspired and provided a model for social reform movements around the world.[45]

Gandhi was a complex man whose long and productive life must be understood in the context of the Indian subcontinent's encounter with modernization through the political and economic agency of British colonialism, Indian nationalism and the struggle for independence, religious tensions throughout the subcontinent (especially between Hindus and Muslims and compounded by the presence of large numbers of Western Christian missionaries), and ongoing movements of social reform.[46] In this brief discussion we will look at Gandhi's views on the relation among religions and his understanding of Jesus Christ. Gandhi embraced a pluralistic perspective on the religions, and it is often assumed that this pluralism is simply the product of his Hindu worldview. As we shall see, however, although Gandhi always claimed to be a Hindu, his views are eclectic and reflect many influences apart from ancient Hindu teachings.

Gandhi went to London in 1887 to study law, passed the bar exam in 1891, and then returned to India. After a brief stay in India, Gandhi moved to South Africa, where he practiced law from 1893 to 1914. While there he became active in the struggle against racism: Gandhi used his legal training to promote justice for nonwhites, especially Indian immigrants. In early 1915 Gandhi returned to India and became actively involved in the growing nationalist movement for Indian independence. Gandhi combined political activism with a struggle for social reform (he championed the cause of the untouchables, whom he referred to as harijans, or people of God) and religious harmony among Hindus, Muslims, and Christians. It was opposition to Gandhi's plea for religious tolerance between Hindus and Muslims that resulted in his assassination in 1948 at the hands of a Hindu.

44. Gandhi was certainly not perfect, and he has always had his critics. See, e.g., Richard Grenier, "The Gandhi Nobody Knows," *Commentary*, March 1983, 59–72.
45. David Hardiman, "Gandhi's Global Legacy," in *The Cambridge Companion to Gandhi*, ed. Judith M. Brown and Anthony Parel (Cambridge: Cambridge University Press, 2011), 239.
46. Among the more helpful works on Gandhi and his times are Brown and Parel, *Cambridge Companion to Gandhi*; Judith M. Brown, *Gandhi: Prisoner of Hope* (New Haven: Yale University Press, 1989); Louis Fischer, *The Life of Mahatma Gandhi* (New York: Harper & Row, 1950).

Gandhi grew up among adherents of different religions, and his father counted Jains and Muslims among his friends. Gandhi's mother became a follower of the popular Pranami religious movement, which had been influenced by Islam. Jains and Muslims were frequent visitors in the Gandhi home; Gandhi's closest childhood friend was a Muslim, and Raychand (Rajchandra Ravjibhai Mehta), his spiritual mentor as a young adult, was a Jain.[47] The eclectic nature of the influences upon Gandhi is nicely presented by Akeel Bilgrami:

> To this [the influence of Vaishnavism in the area], [Gandhi] added a great variety of elements—religious, moral, and philosophical. These included: Advaita-Vedantin ideas; Bhakti ideals of devotion (ideals through which he read his beloved Bhagavad Gita and made it, as he himself would say, his constant moral guide); the Jainism of his mentor Raychandbai; Buddhism and an admiration for the person of the Buddha that he acquired after being moved by Edwin Arnold's biography *The Light of Asia*; the theosophical notions (shorn of their occultism) that he got from exposure in England to Annie Besant, and Christianity—particularly the New Testament and what he took to be the moral instruction that comes from the very life and example of its founder—which he filtered through his admiring, though selective, reading of Tolstoy's writings, as well as what he took from his frequent encounter with missionaries both in South Africa and in India.[48]

Gandhi does not seem to have known any Christians as a child, but according to his later autobiography, his early impression of Christianity was negative. As an adult, Gandhi recalled the image of Christian missionaries and Christianity he had as a schoolboy in Rajkot.

> In those days Christian missionaries used to stand in a corner near the high school and hold forth, pouring abuse on Hindus and their gods. I could not endure this. I must have stood there to hear them only once, but that was enough to dissuade me from repeating the experiment. About the same time, I heard of a well-known Hindu having been converted to Christianity. It was the talk of the town that, when he was baptized, he had to eat beef and drink liquor, that he also had to change his clothes, and that thenceforth he began to go about in European costume including a hat. These things got on my nerves. Surely, thought I, a religion that compelled one to eat beef, drink liquor and change one's clothes did not deserve the name. I also heard that the new convert had

---

47. For the influence of Raychand on Gandhi, see Arvind Sharma, *Gandhi: A Spiritual Biography* (New Haven: Yale University Press, 2013), chap. 5.

48. Akeel Bilgrami, "Gandhi's Religion and Its Relation to His Politics," in Brown and Parel, *Cambridge Companion to Gandhi*, 93.

already begun abusing the religion of his ancestors, their customs and their country. All these things created in me a dislike for Christianity.[49]

In his writings, Gandhi referred to this incident several times, and it is instructive not only for what it says about his childhood but also because it illustrates how, when dealing with religion and culture, there can often be conflicting perceptions of an event. John C. B. Webster reports that the only missionary in Rajkot at the time was the Rev. H. R. Scott, and that upon reading Gandhi's account, Scott wrote to Gandhi, "denying most emphatically that he ever preached near the school, 'poured abuse on the Hindus and their gods,' or required converts to change their eating, drinking or clothing habits."[50] Scott suggested that these were simply rumors spread to keep young people from considering Christianity. According to Webster, "In reply Gandhi said he remembered the incident and the talk, but accepted Scott's repudiation. He also said that subsequent experience with missionaries and Indian converts confirmed the general truth to which the incident pointed."[51] Whatever the actual truth of the matter, it is clear that Gandhi's early impression of Christianity was negative.

During his time in London, Gandhi was exposed to a variety of religious influences. As a student of law, he became familiar with modern liberalism and its Enlightenment values, which were regarded as foundational to democracy.[52] Because of his vow to his mother to refrain from eating meat, he frequented a vegetarian restaurant, where he met an assortment of Theosophists, Fabian Socialists, and nontraditional Christian visionaries. But Gandhi also met devout Christians, through whom he secured a Bible. Although the Old Testament left him cold, he was attracted to the New Testament and was especially taken by the Sermon on the Mount.

The encounter with Theosophists had a lasting impact on Gandhi. In 1889 he was deeply impressed by a public lecture by Annie Besant, in which she emphasized her own "search for Truth," and he read Besant's *How I Became a Theosophist.*[53] Gandhi attended some of the meetings of the Theosophical Society, met Madame Blavatsky, and read Blavatsky's *Key to*

49. M. K. Gandhi, *An Autobiography: Or, The Story of My Experiments with Truth*, trans. Mahadev Desai (New York: Viking Penguin, 1982 [1927]), 47.

50. John C. B. Webster, "Gandhi and the Christians," in Coward, *Hindu-Christian Dialogue: Perspectives and Encounters*, 84.

51. Ibid. Gandhi's response to Scott is found in M. K. Gandhi, *Christian Missions: Their Place in India* (Ahmedabad: Navajivan Press, 1941).

52. Margaret Chatterjee, *Gandhi and the Challenge of Religious Diversity* (New Delhi: Promilla, 2005), 31.

53. Ibid., 71.

Theosophy.[54] Ironically, it was also through Theosophists in England that Gandhi was stimulated to learn more about his own Hindu tradition. Two Theosophists invited Gandhi to read with them Sir Edwin Arnold's English translation of the Hindu classic Bhagavad Gita, *The Song Celestial*, and thus began his lifelong fascination with the Gita. Gandhi was also introduced to *The Light of Asia*, Sir Edwin Arnold's epic poem on the life of Gautama the Buddha. It was his interaction with Europeans interested in Indian religious traditions that stimulated within himself a curiosity to learn more about his own Hindu heritage.

While in South Africa (1893–1914), Gandhi had extensive contact with evangelical Christians, and at one point it seemed that Gandhi might even become a Christian. He also had Muslim friends who were urging him to become Muslim. This was a confusing time. Gandhi turned for advice to his friend and mentor Raychand, back in India, writing him a list of questions about the religions, including whether any sacred text was really divinely inspired or any particular religion uniquely true.[55] This was unusual, for as Chatterjee observes, "Here we find a Hindu consulting a Jain about both Hinduism and Christianity."[56] Raychand responded by encouraging him to pursue his exploration of Hinduism while adopting a tolerant view of other religions. Gandhi also consulted a friend from England, Edward Maitland, founder of the Esoteric Union, about evangelical Christian claims concerning the Bible. Maitland had previously been president of the British Theosophical Society and held that the sacred texts of the many religions "were but the recurring historical revelations of a basic universal revelation" and that Jesus Christ "was the ideal of perfection, a perfection that was equally attainable by all men."[57] Maitland's response showed Gandhi that there were other ways of reading the Bible than that of the evangelicals.

In his autobiography, Gandhi uses an incident in South Africa with conservative Christians to explain his reasons for not accepting orthodox Christianity. A fellow lawyer and devout Christian, Mr. A. W. Baker, had an especially close relationship with Gandhi and encouraged him to commit his life to Jesus Christ. But Gandhi did not become a Christian.

> Mr. Baker was getting anxious about my future. He took me to the Wellington Convention. The Protestant Christians organize such gatherings every few years

54. Gandhi, *Autobiography*, 76–77.
55. Ibid., 135–36.
56. Chatterjee, *Gandhi and the Challenge of Religious Diversity*, 236.
57. J. F. T. Jordens, "Gandhi and Religious Pluralism," in *Modern Indian Responses to Religious Pluralism*, ed. Harold G. Coward (Albany: State University of New York Press, 1987), 6–7.

for religious enlightenment or, in other words, self-purification. . . . The chairman was the famous divine of the place, the Rev. Andrew Murray. Mr. Baker had hoped that the atmosphere of religious exaltation at the convention, and the enthusiasm and earnestness of the people attending it, would inevitably lead me to embrace Christianity.

But [Mr. Baker's] final hope was in the efficacy of prayer. He had an abiding faith in prayer. It was his firm conviction that God could not but listen to prayer fervently offered. He would cite the instances of men like George Müller of Bristol, who depended entirely on prayer even for his temporal needs. I listened to his discourses on the efficacy of prayer with unbiased attention, and assured him that nothing could prevent me from embracing Christianity, should I feel the call. . . .

This convention was an assemblage of devout Christians. I was delighted at their faith. I met the Rev. Murray. I saw that many were praying for me. I liked some of their hymns, they were very sweet.

The Convention lasted for three days. I could understand and appreciate the devoutness of those who attended it. But I saw no reason for changing my belief—my religion. It was impossible for me to believe that I could go to heaven or attain salvation only by becoming a Christian. When I frankly said so to some of the good Christian friends, they were shocked. But there was no help for it.

My difficulties lay deeper. It was more than I could believe that Jesus was the only incarnate son of God, and that only he who believed in him would have everlasting life. If God could have sons, all of us were His sons. If Jesus was like God, or God Himself, then all men were like God and could be God Himself. My reason was not ready to believe literally that Jesus by his death and by his blood redeemed the sins of the world. Metaphorically there might be some truth in it. Again, according to Christianity only human beings had souls, and not other living beings, for whom death meant complete extinction; while I held a contrary belief. I could accept Jesus as a martyr, an embodiment of sacrifice, and a divine teacher, but not as the most perfect man ever born. His death on the Cross was a great example to the world, but that there was anything like a mysterious or miraculous virtue in it, my heart could not accept. The pious lives of Christians did not give me anything that the lives of men of other faiths had failed to give. I had seen in other lives just the same reformation that I had heard of among Christians.

Philosophically there was nothing extraordinary in Christian principles. From the point of view of sacrifice, it seemed to me that the Hindus greatly surpassed the Christians. It was impossible for me to regard Christianity as the perfect religion or the greatest of all religions. . . . Though I took a path my Christian friends had not intended for me, I have remained forever indebted to them for the religious quest that they awakened in me. I shall always cherish the memory of their contact.[58]

58. Gandhi, *Autobiography*, 134–37.

Gandhi's reasons are thoughtful and reflect both influences from his Hindu background as well as themes found more broadly among critics of the Christian faith.

Gandhi did not offer a comprehensive philosophical or religious system. He was a Hindu, but a modern Hindu who combined ancient teachings with influences from other religious traditions and filtered them all through a strong moral conscience. Although Gandhi repeatedly used the word "God" in English, his views about the nature of God are somewhat unclear. Gandhi claimed to be a follower of the Hindu tradition of Vedanta, and thus he identified Truth with God. Vedantin thinkers disagreed over the question of whether Brahman, ultimately the sole reality, is a personal Being or nonpersonal Reality. But Gandhi refused to get involved in philosophical debates over the issue. He spoke of God or Brahman in both personal and nonpersonal terms, suggesting that both could be acceptable.[59] Moreover, following Vedanta, Gandhi held to an essential unity between one's inner self and Truth and Brahman. Thus Gandhi states, "I believe in the absolute oneness of God and therefore of humanity. What though we have many bodies? We have but one soul. The rays of the sun are many through refraction. But they have the same source."[60]

Given the Hindu framework, how did Gandhi respond to Christian teachings on Jesus Christ? From Gandhi's own statement quoted above, it is clear that he rejected orthodox Christian teachings about Jesus as the only incarnation of God and the only Savior for all humankind. Many factors are involved here, but I will briefly mention two things in particular that made the exclusiveness of orthodox Christology especially problematic. First, Gandhi was influenced by the Jain teaching of *anekantavada*, or the many-sidedness of reality and the perspectival nature of truth.[61] Jain epistemology stresses the fact that apart from those who are omniscient, any judgment we make about reality is necessarily limited and incomplete, and thus at best we can attain a partial glimpse of truth. A modest skepticism should lead to tolerance for opposing views, and thus Gandhi rejected dogmatic religious formulations that were presented as exclusively true.

Furthermore, there is in Hinduism a dominant theme that teaches the divinity of all creatures; thus if Jesus is the son of God, then we all are also children of God. Speaking to Lady Emily Kinnaird, a Christian, Gandhi stated, "With you, Jesus was the only begotten son of God. With me, He was a son

59. Margaret Chatterjee, *Gandhi's Religious Thought* (Notre Dame, IN: University of Notre Dame Press, 1983), 104; Glyn Richards, "Gandhi's Concept of Truth and the Advaita Tradition," *Religious Studies* 22 (1986): 2.

60. As cited in Glyn Richards, "Gandhi's Concept of Truth and the *Advaita* Tradition," 2.

61. Margaret Chatterjee, *Gandhi's Religious Thought*, 32–33.

of God, no matter how much purer than us all, but every one of us is a son of God and capable of doing what Jesus did, if we but endeavor to express the Divine within us."[62]

Gandhi had great respect for Jesus as a moral teacher; along with many leaders of the Hindu Renaissance, he made a clear distinction between Jesus and institutional Christianity—or perhaps we should say between Gandhi's interpretation of Jesus and European Christendom. "I regard Jesus as a great teacher of humanity, but I do not regard him as the only begotten son of God."[63] There is nothing about Jesus that sets him apart from other great leaders. "I therefore do not take as literally true the text that Jesus is the only begotten son of God. God cannot be the exclusive Father, and I cannot ascribe exclusive divinity to Jesus. He is as divine as Krishna or Rama or Mohammed or Zoroaster."[64] Gandhi did not see in Jesus much that was not also available in other religious traditions. "I have really not seen any fundamental distinction between Jesus and the other teachers I can understand, explain and appreciate. . . . I can pay equal homage to Jesus, Mohammed, Krishna, Buddha, Zoroaster, and others that may be named."[65] Speaking to Millie Polak, a close friend and Christian, Gandhi confided, "I was tremendously attracted to Christianity, but eventually, I came to the conclusion that there was nothing really in your Scriptures that we had not got in ours, and that to be a good Hindu also meant that I would be a good Christian. . . . There is only one God, but there are many paths to Him."[66]

For Gandhi, the heart of Jesus's teaching is contained in the Sermon on the Mount, the essence of which is "nonretaliation, or nonresistance to evil."[67] Yet he acknowledged that his own interpretation of the Sermon was at odds with classic Christian teaching.

> The message of Jesus, as I understand it, is contained in His Sermon on the Mount, unadulterated and taken as a whole, and even in connection with the Sermon on the Mount, my own humble interpretation of the message is in many respects different from the orthodox. The message, to my mind, has suffered distortion in the West. . . . If then I had to face only the Sermon on the Mount and my own interpretation of it, I should not hesitate to say, "Oh yes, I am a Christian."[68]

62. M. Gandhi, in *Gandhi on Christianity*, ed. Robert Ellsberg (Maryknoll, NY: Orbis Books, 1991), 15.
63. Ibid., 26.
64. Ibid., 66.
65. Ibid., 61.
66. Ibid., 12.
67. Ibid., 21.
68. Ibid., 19.

In the moral teaching of the Sermon and the cross of Christ, Gandhi saw the supreme example of his own principle of satyagraha, passive resistance or truth force, and thus he referred to Jesus as "the Prince of *satyagrahis*." Gandhi said, "It was the New Testament which really awakened me to the value of passive resistance. When I read in the Sermon on the Mount such passages as 'Resist not him that is evil; he who smiteth thee on thy right cheek turn to him the other also, and love your enemies, pray for them that persecute you, that ye may be the sons of your Father which is in heaven,' I was overjoyed."[69]

Like others in the Hindu Renaissance, Gandhi maintained that there is an essential unity to the religions. "Hindus, Mussalmans [Muslims], Christians, Parsis, Jews are convenient labels. But when I tear them down, I do not know which is which. We are all children of the same God."[70] Each religion can be regarded as true insofar as it promotes human well-being. "Personally, I do not regard any of the great religions of the world as false. All have served in enriching mankind and are even now serving their purpose."[71]

Not surprisingly, Gandhi was a sharp critic of Christian missions, and he repeatedly spoke of institutional Christianity, including Christian missions, as a European cultural distortion of the simple message of Jesus in the Sermon on the Mount. Institutional Christianity was condemned for its association with British colonialism. "Unfortunately, Christianity in India has been inextricably mixed up for the last one hundred and fifty years with British rule. It appears to us as synonymous with materialistic civilization and imperialistic exploitation by the stronger white races of the weaker races of the world."[72]

Many have commented that, despite his rejection of orthodox Christian teachings, Gandhi was in some ways more authentically Christian than professing Christians. E. Stanley Jones, Christian missionary and close friend of Gandhi, astutely observes,

> Mahatma Gandhi did not see in the Cross what the convinced Christian sees, namely, that God was in Christ reconciling the world unto himself and that he was bearing our sins in his body on a tree. Gandhi did not see that. But he did see that you can take on yourself suffering, and not give it, and thus conquer the heart of another. That he did see in the Cross, and that he put into practice, and put it into practice on a national scale. The difference then is this: we as Christians saw more in the Cross than Gandhi and put it into operation less;

69. As quoted in K. L. S. Rao, "Mahatma Gandhi and Christianity," in Sharma, *Neo-Hindu Views of Christianity*, 149.
70. M. Gandhi, in Ellsberg, *Gandhi on Christianity*, 25.
71. Ibid., 23.
72. Ibid., 44.

Gandhi saw less in the Cross than we and put it into practice more. We left the Cross a doctrine; Gandhi left it a deed.[73]

Vivekananda, Radhakrishnan, and Gandhi are fascinating figures who exemplify the tensions in India between the traditional and the modern; the encounter between Europe and India, between colonial power and the colonized; the eclectic mixing of religious traditions; and the simultaneous attraction and aversion to the New Testament portrait of Jesus. There is irony in the fact that although Gandhi grew up in India, he was not particularly knowledgeable about Hinduism until he traveled to England, where his interest in Indian traditions was stimulated through contact with Theosophists and Christians. Vivekananda, Radhakrishnan, and Gandhi were all products of the clash between traditional Hindu patterns and Western culture and Christianity. Each had significant exposure to Christianity and had positive views about Jesus, yet all three rejected orthodox Christian teachings on Jesus. Each in turn presented an alternative understanding of Jesus in line with Hindu assumptions, so that Jesus became the exemplification of mystical spirituality and moral conscience. For all three, Jesus is a great religious and ethical leader but not in principle any different from other great religious figures. And finally, all three had significant influence not only within India but also upon the West, and they have helped to shape the reinterpretation of Jesus along more pluralistic lines.

John Hick

John Hick (1922–2012) was born in England at a time when Gandhi was inspiring nonviolent resistance against the British Empire. Hick would eventually become one of the twentieth century's most influential theologians and philosophers, and he developed a model of religious pluralism that is a philosophically sophisticated version of themes espoused by Gandhi. His views on religious pluralism will be considered more fully in chapter 5. Here we are concerned with his perspective on Jesus Christ, and especially the similarities between his Christology and those of the modern Hindu thinkers examined above.

Although Hick's family was not particularly religious, as a young man he read widely and was briefly attracted by Theosophy. In his autobiography Hick states, "I was attracted by theosophy as the first coherent religious philosophy

---

73. E. Stanley Jones, *Mahatma Gandhi: An Interpretation* (New York: Abingdon-Cokesbury, 1948), 79–80.

that I had met—much more so than the Christianity I knew. But after a while I consciously dismissed it, with its precise levels of existence and invisible spheres and ranks of angelic beings, as too neat and tidy and professing to know too much. What I gained from it however was an interest, which continued until my evangelical Christian conversion and then hibernated for many years, in the eastern religions."[74]

While a student of law at University College, Hull, Hick experienced "a spiritual conversion in which the whole world of Christian belief and experience came vividly to life, and I became a Christian of a strongly evangelical and indeed fundamentalist kind."[75] Reflecting back on his early Christian life, Hick reports that he then "accepted as a whole and without question the entire evangelical package of theology—the verbal inspiration of the Bible; Creation and Fall; Jesus as God the Son incarnate, born of a virgin, conscious of his divine nature, and performing miracles of divine power; redemption by his blood from sin and guilt; Jesus's bodily resurrection, ascension, and future return in glory; heaven and hell."[76]

After World War II, Hick pursued doctoral studies in philosophy and theology at Oxford and Cambridge. During a long and productive career, Hick taught at Cornell University, Princeton Theological Seminary, Cambridge University, Birmingham University, and Claremont Graduate University, retiring in 1992. It was during his time at Birmingham in the 1960s and '70s that Hick experienced the growing ethnic and religious diversity of England and became active in the struggle against racial discrimination. His involvement in issues of social justice brought him into close contact with religious leaders of other faiths, which deepened his interest in other religions. In the 1970s Hick spent extended periods of time in both India and Sri Lanka, interacting with Hindu and Buddhist scholars.

During the 1960s Hick moved away from his earlier theological commitments, although he still remained broadly within the orthodox tradition. While at Princeton, he was embroiled in controversy over his views on the inspiration of the Bible and the virgin birth of Jesus, and by 1966 he had accepted soteriological universalism as a necessary part of a successful theodicy.[77] Hick also began to explore the relation between Christian faith and other religions,

74. John Hick, *John Hick: An Autobiography* (Oxford: Oneworld, 2002), 31.
75. John Hick, *God Has Many Names* (Philadelphia: Westminster, 1980), 14.
76. John Hick, "A Pluralist View," in *Four Views on Salvation in a Pluralistic World*, ed. Dennis L. Ockholm and Timothy R. Phillips (Grand Rapids: Zondervan, 1995), 30.
77. See John Hick, "Three Controversies," in *Problems of Religious Pluralism* (New York: St. Martin's Press, 1985), 1–15; idem, *Evil and the God of Love* (New York: HarperCollins, 1966; rev. ed., 1977).

speaking in 1973 of the need for a "Copernican revolution" in theology that involved "a shift from the dogma that Christianity is at the centre to the realization that it is *God* who is at the centre, and that all religions of mankind, including our own, serve and revolve around him."[78] During the next fifteen years, Hick published many articles and books in which he refined his views on religious pluralism, culminating in the publication of his 1986 Gifford lectures, *An Interpretation of Religion.*[79]

Although Hick had earlier been a staunch defender of orthodox two-nature Christology, in the 1960s he began to search for alternative ways of thinking about the significance of Jesus. In 1966 Hick observed that growing awareness of other religions was forcing fresh questions on the church. "In this new situation the old issue of the uniqueness of the Christian revelation, and of the Christian claim over against other religions, has become urgent and may become obsessive. At its heart lies the question of the uniqueness of Christ. It is on this central and most crucial issue that Christology stands today at the crossroads."[80] In 1973 Hick claimed that the doctrine of the incarnation should be reinterpreted in terms of a "myth," or a "story . . . which is not literally true . . . but which invites a particular attitude in its hearers."[81] The suggestion that the incarnation was a myth received extensive coverage by the Western media with the 1977 publication of *The Myth of God Incarnate*, edited by Hick.[82] In "Jesus and the World Religions," Hick argues that the incarnation should be understood not in terms of Jesus Christ literally being God and man but rather that, in a mythological or metaphorical sense, God was present and active in Jesus in a manner similar to ways in which he is present in other religious leaders. "I see the Nazarene, then, as intensely and overwhelmingly conscious of the divine reality of God. . . . Thus in Jesus's presence, we should have felt that we are in the presence of God—not in the sense that the man Jesus literally *is* God, but in the sense that he was so totally conscious of God that we could catch something of that consciousness by spiritual contagion."[83] In *The Metaphor of God Incarnate* (1993), Hick says, "We see in Jesus a human being extraordinarily open to God's influence and

78. John Hick, *God and the Universe of Faiths* (New York: St. Martin's Press, 1973), 131, with original emphasis.

79. John Hick, *An Interpretation of Religion* (New Haven: Yale University Press, 1989; 2nd ed., 2004).

80. John Hick, "Christology at the Crossroads," in *Prospect for Theology*, ed. F. G. Healey (London: Nisbett, 1966), 139.

81. John Hick, *God and the Universe of Faiths*, 166–67.

82. John Hick, ed., *The Myth of God Incarnate* (Philadelphia: Westminster, 1977).

83. John Hick, "Jesus and the World Religions," in *Myth of God Incarnate*, 172, with original emphasis.

thus living to an extraordinary extent as God's agent on earth, 'incarnating' the divine purpose for human life."[84] Given this reinterpretation of Jesus's significance, it is not surprising that Hick urges us to recognize that not only Jesus but also Moses, Gautama, Confucius, Zoroaster, Socrates, Muhammad, and Nanak "have in their different ways 'incarnated' the ideal of human life in response to the one divine Reality."[85] In other words, there is nothing in principle distinctive or unique about Jesus's relation to God; other great religious leaders can also be said to be "incarnations" of God in a similar metaphorical sense.[86]

Hick was not calling for Christians to abandon their commitments to Jesus as their Lord. But he argued that traditional claims about Jesus Christ as the only Lord and Savior for all humankind, as the utterly unique incarnation of God and thus fully God and fully man, should be rejected in favor of a metaphorical understanding of incarnation that sees Jesus as one among many great religious leaders with a special relationship with God. Jesus can be the Lord and Savior for Christians, so long as they acknowledge that adherents of other religions have their own, equally legitimate figures of ultimate commitment. Hick's rejection of the traditional, orthodox view was due primarily to his acceptance of the more radical conclusions of New Testament scholars and his conviction that traditional two-nature Christology is simply incoherent. But it could also well be that his increasing involvement in interreligious dialogue in the 1970s and '80s and growing appreciation for Hinduism and Buddhism had some effect on his move away from orthodox Christology.

There are some striking similarities between Hick's pluralistic understanding of Jesus and the views of Mahatma Gandhi. Hick has enormous appreciation for Gandhi and devotes three chapters of *The Fifth Dimension* to Gandhi's life and teachings.[87] He has acknowledged that his own model of religious pluralism is "along just the same lines as Gandhi's." Yet, despite having spent some time in India, Hick says that he is not aware of any direct influence from

84. John Hick, *The Metaphor of God Incarnate: Christology in a Pluralistic Age* (Louisville: Westminster/John Knox, 1993), 12.

85. Ibid., 96, 98.

86. An inconsistency in Hick's language should be noticed. In discussing the significance of Jesus, Hick speaks in terms of Jesus's relation to God, suggesting that Hick is a theist and understands Jesus in terms of theism. Yet, as will become clear in chapter 5, within Hick's model of religious pluralism, God, as understood within classical theism, is not the religious ultimate. "God" is simply a symbol through which theistic religious traditions understand and relate to what is truly ultimate—the Real.

87. John Hick, *The Fifth Dimension: An Exploration of the Spiritual Realm* (Oxford: Oneworld, 2004), chaps. 21–23.

Gandhi upon the development of his own views on pluralism.[88] Both Gandhi and Hick rejected exclusivist traditions, which insist that their particular doctrinal claims are uniquely true and normative for all people. Both regarded Jesus as a great moral and spiritual leader but not the definitive incarnation or revelation of God. Each in his own way reinterpreted religious doctrines in metaphorical terms, thereby deemphasizing metaphysical claims in favor of the practical effects of religious traditions upon the moral transformation of religious believers. And both Gandhi and Hick pointed beyond the particularities of various religions to a supposed common source that transcends religious labels and concepts.[89]

Shusaku Endo

In concluding this chapter, we will look at a major Japanese novelist whose writings probe issues of Christian faith and Japanese culture. Born in Tokyo, Shusaku Endo (1923–96) lived in Manchuria as a child. When he was ten years old, his parents divorced, and Endo lived with his mother, who converted to Roman Catholicism. At his mother's urging, Endo received baptism, and throughout his life he continued to identify himself as a Christian. Although Christians have been present in Japan since the sixteenth century, they compose about 1 or 2 percent of the Japanese population today, and Christianity is widely regarded as a foreign religion.

Japanese religions display a fascinating combination of modern and ancient patterns.[90] Today Japan is one of the world's most modernized, technologically advanced, and literate societies; yet despite recent decline in religious practice, ancient religious assumptions, values, and practices continue to flourish among many Japanese.[91] But religious expression in Japan is somewhat different from

---

88. Hick states, "I am not conscious of being directly influenced by Gandhi on this, but just delighted to find that so great a moral figure had thought the same" (personal communication, November 3, 2009).

89. See Sharada Sugirtharajah, "The Mahatma and the Philosopher: Mohandas Gandhi and John Hick and Their Search for Truth," in *Religious Pluralism and the Modern World: An Ongoing Engagement with John Hick*, ed. Sharada Sugirtharajah (New York: Palgrave Macmillan, 2012), 121–33.

90. Good introductions to Japanese religion include Ian Reader, *Religion in Contemporary Japan* (London: Macmillan, 1991); Ian Reader and George J. Tanabe Jr., *Practically Religious: Worldly Benefits and the Common Religion of Japan* (Honolulu: University of Hawaii Press, 1998); Susumu Shimazono, *From Salvation to Spirituality: Popular Religious Movements in Modern Japan* (Melbourne: Trans Pacific Press, 2004).

91. Ian Reader provides compelling evidence that religious belief and practice are declining, especially among younger Japanese. See Reader, "Secularisation, R.I.P.? Nonsense! The 'Rush

that of Europe and North America. Explicit religious beliefs or doctrines are relatively unimportant for most Japanese. Daoist and Buddhist influences have resulted in a general suspicion of words and precision in doctrines. Far more significant are ritual, experience, and the social dimensions of religion.

There is a kind of cultural or ethnic relativism in Japanese approaches to religion that connects religions with particular cultures and peoples.[92] Americans are Christians, Indians are Hindus, and Japanese are Buddhists; so long as each group maintains its proper boundaries and does not try to convert others, all religions can be accepted as legitimate. The Japanese have traditionally been suspicious of exclusivistic religious traditions. Although the Japanese have been remarkably accommodating of some foreign religious traditions (Buddhism entered Japan as a foreign religion), this openness has always been constrained within carefully defined parameters, including acceptance of the ancestral cult and a sense of common religious identity rooted in what it means to be "authentically Japanese." But with these constraints, many Japanese accept the idea that there can be different ways of responding to the divine.

Although explicit Christians in Japan are rare, many Japanese have had some contact with Christianity, and there is considerable interest in Jesus and Christian themes. Japan boasts a literacy rate of almost 100 percent, and Japanese are among the best educated people anywhere. Not surprisingly, literature and literary figures exert enormous cultural influence, and thus it is especially striking to see the fascination with Jesus demonstrated by some of Japan's leading literary figures. Many leading novelists in twentieth-century Japan incorporated Christian themes into their work, and some even wrote personal reflections on the person of Jesus.[93]

The writer who is best known for integrating Christian themes into his novels is Shusaku Endo. In his later years, Endo was probably the most recognized Christian in Japan: for many Japanese, he came to symbolize Japanese Christianity. In 1973 he published *A Life of Jesus*, a work that portrays the human Jesus as one who suffers with us, offering comfort and compassion to the weak and downtrodden. It quickly sold over 300,000 copies.[94] But Endo is

---

Hour away from the Gods' and the Decline of Religion in Contemporary Japan," *Journal of Religion in Japan* 1 (2012): 7–36.

92. See Hajime Nakamura, *Ways of Thinking of Eastern Peoples: India, China, Tibet, Japan*, ed. Philip P. Wiener (Honolulu: University of Hawaii Press, 1964), part 4.

93. See Noah S. Brannen, "Three Japanese Authors Look at Jesus: A Review," *Japan Christian Quarterly* 54.3 (Summer 1988): 132–41; Philip Williams, "Images of Jesus in Japanese Fiction," *Japan Christian Quarterly* 49.1 (Winter 1983): 12–22.

94. Shusaku Endo, *A Life of Jesus*, trans. Richard A. Schuchert (Tokyo: Tuttle, 1978 [1973]). Endo wrote two other works on Jesus, which have not been translated into English: *Watakushi no Iesu* [My Jesus] (1976) and *Kirisuto no Tanjo* [The birth of Christ] (1978), as well as other

best known for addressing the tension between Japanese culture and Christian faith in such novels as *Silence* and *The Samurai*.[95] In an oft-quoted statement, he says, "Christianity to me was like a Western suit my mother made me wear when I was growing up."[96] According to Chua, "A recurring theme in Endo's novels and non-fictional works is theological dissonance—between European Christianity and Japanese religiosity, Western monotheism and Asian pantheism, and between religious triumphalism and the inescapable reality of deep suffering."[97] Endo has been understood by many, Christians and non-Christians alike, as advancing the thesis that Japan is a "swamp" that is incompatible with Christianity: either Japan or Christianity must change if Christianity is to take root there. Endo's earlier works probe differences between Japanese culture and European cultures, and Japanese approaches to religion with European Christianity. Adrian Pennington observes that Endo's novels reflect the fascination by many postwar Japanese intellectuals with anthropologist Ruth Benedict's *The Chrysanthemum and the Sword* (1946) and its contrast of shame culture with sin culture.[98] The popularity of Endo's writings indicates that many Japanese not only have an interest in these issues but also some understanding of basic Christian themes.

Endo, however, also illustrates a further dimension of Japan's relationship with Jesus. Whereas Endo's earlier works grapple with questions of the relationship between Christianity and Japanese culture, by the 1970s Endo was moving away from more orthodox Christian views and exploring themes of religious diversity and pluralism. Pennington explains that in Endo's earlier novels, although the characters have no consciousness of sin, there is little doubt that what they are doing is evil. With *Silence*, however, the sense of evil recedes, and the picture of humans as weak is emphasized. According to the Japanese Lutheran theologian Kazo Kitamori, this is the point at which Endo leaves behind any orthodox understanding of Christianity.[99]

---

books and essays on theological themes. In what follows I am indebted to the excellent doctoral dissertation by How Chuang Chua, "Japanese Perspectives on the Death of Christ: A Study in Contextualized Christology" (PhD diss., Trinity Evangelical Divinity School, 2007), 201–83.

95. Shusaku Endo, *Silence*, trans. William Johnston (New York: Taplinger, 1969); idem, *The Samurai*, trans. Van C. Gessel (New York: Harper & Row, 1982).

96. As quoted in Noah S. Brannen, "Three Japanese Authors Look at Jesus," 139.

97. Chua, "Japanese Perspectives on the Death of Christ," 204–5.

98. Adrian Pennington, "Yoshimitsu, Benedict, Endō: Guilt, Shame and the Post-war Idea of Japan," *Japan Forum* 13.1 (2001): 98–99; Ruth Benedict, *The Chrysanthemum and the Sword: Patterns of Japanese Culture* (Tokyo: Tuttle, 1974 [1946]). I am grateful to John Netland not only for alerting me to Pennington's essay and other works on Endo but also for his helpful insights on Endo as a writer.

99. Pennington, "Yoshimitsu, Benedict, Endō," 100–101. Pennington is summarizing the observations of Kitamori, "Ashi no Itami no Bungaku: Endo Shusaku" [The literature of the pain

In *Watakushi no Iesu* (My Jesus), Endo states, "There are many ways to climb Mt. Fuji. You can approach the ascent from the north, south, east, or west. . . . In the same way, if one person lives sincerely as a Buddhist, and another lives sincerely as a Christian, in the end they will both arrive at the same truth."[100] Endo's move toward a more syncretistic and pluralistic faith was probably encouraged in part through his numerous visits to India in the late 1980s and early '90s. In a 1994 interview with William Johnston in which he discusses similarities and differences between Christianity and Buddhism, Endo raises what he regards as the central question concerning the two religions: How are we to think about "the Great Source of Life," which lies beyond both religions? "Do we call it the Christ or the Buddha"?[101] Endo's embrace of religious pluralism becomes clear in his final novel, *Deep River* (1994), published two years before his death. Although many regard the pluralism of *Deep River* as a departure from the stance of Endo's earlier novels, Mark Williams argues that it is "a logical extension to his spiritual questioning" in works such as *Silence*. Williams contends that *Deep River* is "a literary embodiment of the attitude of religious pluralism that Endo openly espoused during the latter half of his career but that can, in retrospect, be clearly seen germinating in his earlier works."[102]

Deep River, whose title refers to the Ganges, the sacred river of India, depicts the spiritual journey of Otsu, a young Japanese studying for the Catholic priesthood who is expelled from his order for his excessively positive views of other religions. Otsu eventually finds himself in India, serving the lower-caste peoples. Reflecting on his theological transformation, Otsu says,

> I now regret having spoken foolishly in front of the brethren of the Church. But it seems perfectly natural to me that many people select the god in whom they place their faith on the basis of the culture and traditions and climate of the land of their birth. I think that Europeans have chosen Christianity because it was the faith of their forefathers, and because Christian culture dominated their native lands. You can't say that the people of the Middle East chose to become Muslims and many Indians became Hindus after conducting rigorous comparisons of their religions with those of other peoples. . . . God has many

of the feet], in *Ureinaki Kami: Seisho to Bungaku* [God without cares: The Bible and literature] (Tokyo: Kodansha, 1991), 304–40.

100. As cited in Chua, "Japanese Perspectives on the Death of Christ," 265.

101. William Johnston, "Endo and Johnston Talk of Buddhism and Christianity," *America* 171.16 (November 19, 1994): 20. See also Chua, "Japanese Perspectives on the Death of Christ," 263–64.

102. Mark Williams, "Crossing the Deep River: Endo Shusaku and the Problem of Religious Pluralism," in *Xavier's Legacies: Catholicism in Modern Japanese Culture*, ed. Kevin M. Doak (Vancouver: UBC Press, 2011), 116.

different faces. I don't think God exists exclusively in the churches and chapels of Europe. I think he is also among the Jews and the Buddhists and the Hindus.[103]

Otsu is particularly fond of the following words ascribed to Gandhi: "There are many different religions, but they are merely different paths leading to the same place. What difference does it make which of those separate paths we walk, so long as they all arrive at the identical location?"[104]

Through the mouth of Otsu,[105] Endo gives expression to a theme deeply embedded within the Japanese religious consciousness. The idea that religion is culturally and historically conditioned and that various cultures have different although equally legitimate religious traditions has plausibility for many Japanese. Something like this view, dressed in Hindu garb, was advocated by thinkers in the Hindu Renaissance, and it is increasingly popular in much of the West. It has been given a sophisticated and persuasive defense in the writings of John Hick. Interestingly, many of Hick's works on religious pluralism have been translated into Japanese, several by Hiromasa Mase, for many years professor of philosophy at Keio University and himself a convert to Christian faith as a university student. Mase later became a close friend of Hick and subsequently adopted a pluralistic framework very similar to Hick's.

Although Endo never met John Hick, there is an interesting connection between the two men. In his personal journal, dated September 5, 1991, Endo includes his account of discovering a book by Hick.

A few days ago I was on the second floor of Taiseido Bookstore when I happened by chance to see [John Hick's] *Shukyo Tagen Shugi* [*Problems of Religious Pluralism*] at the corner of the bookshelf. It seemed to have been left there by a store clerk or a customer, and forgotten. But more than an accident, it was as if my subconscious had summoned it. Since my encounter with Jung, which was quite a while ago, I had not had the same feeling of being stirred in my heart until I read this book. Hick is a Christian theologian, but he believes that the different world religions are in fact seeking the same God, only through different paths, cultures, and symbols. He also criticizes Christianity for maintaining the tendency of subsuming the other religions within itself while at the same time claiming to dialogue with them following Vatican II. He also makes the daring claim that true religious pluralism has no place for a theology that proclaims

103. Shusaku Endo, *Deep River*, trans. Van C. Gessel (New York: New Directions, 1994), 121.
104. Ibid., 191.
105. John Netland points out that "whereas in previous novels the characters voicing similar thoughts [to Otsu in *Deep River*] are typically antagonists or morally compromised characters (like Ferreira or Inoue), Otsu is the first protagonist, and arguable Christ-figure, who arrives at this point of view" (personal communication, November 30, 2013).

Jesus as the Christ. In other words, the problems of Jesus' incarnation and the Trinity should be subject to the surgeon's knife. Since two days ago, I have been overwhelmed by this shocking book. And then so it happened that a staff member of Iwanami Publishing Company visited me and gave me the same author's *Kami Wa Oku No Na O Mostu* [*God Has Many Names*].[106]

Endo had been moving toward a perspective much like Hick's for some time, but as Chua observes, "Until his encounter with Hick, [Endo] apparently supposed that such a view was a distinctly non-Western view."[107] In a perceptive essay, theologian Anri Morimoto draws attention to the connections between popular Japanese religious commitments, John Hick's model of religious pluralism, and the later work of Shusaku Endo.

> The pluralistic understanding of religions represented by Hick has a peculiar charm to the Japanese. Japan is a "living museum of religions." Anyone who surveys the religious culture of Japan will be dismayed at the complexity and diversity of religions, both historical and contemporary. Religious pluralism is, as in other regions of Asia, not an ideological construction but a reality in which to live. A traditional Japanese poem captures the atmosphere: "Though there are many paths to climb atop a mountain, we all come to look at the same moon." Hick's pluralism offers an assurance of harmony among religions. It was this assurance that Endo found with great relief, especially since the idea came from a Western theologian.[108]

In Hick's pluralism, Endo clearly found something echoing his own convictions, and there is little question that to some extent *Deep River* reflects Hick's influence.[109]

There is considerable irony in all of this. John Hick was converted to Christianity while a university student in Scotland and was for a time, in his own

106. As quoted in Chua, "Japanese Perspectives on the Death of Christ," 264–65. Endo's journal was published after his death, first in 1997 and then again in 2000.

107. Ibid., 265. Concerning Hick's influence on Endo, see also Williams, "Crossing the Deep River."

108. Anri Morimoto, "The (More or Less) Same Light but from Different Lamps: The Post-pluralist Understanding of Religion from a Japanese Perspective," *International Journal for Philosophy of Religion* 53 (2003): 164. The reference to Japan as a "living museum of religions" is from H. Byron Earhart, *Japanese Religion: Unity and Diversity*, 2nd ed. (Belmont, CA: Dickenson, 1974), 1.

109. John Hick has also been influential among recent Chinese scholars. Many of his writings, including *An Interpretation of Religion*, have been translated into Chinese, with many Chinese philosophers and religious studies scholars interacting with his views. See Wang Zhicheng, "John Hick and Chinese Religious Studies," in Sugirtharajah, *Religious Pluralism and the Modern World*, 241–52.

words, a thoroughly orthodox and even fundamentalist Christian. He became an influential pluralist. Hiromasa Mase, who translated Hick's works into Japanese, was converted to Christianity when a student through the ministry of an evangelical Lutheran missionary in Japan. But in part through his contact with Hick, Mase became an outspoken advocate for pluralism in Japan.[110] Shusaku Endo became a Roman Catholic early on, yet the question of the relation of Christianity to Japanese culture and religions was something he struggled with throughout his life. All three, in their own ways, ended up rejecting orthodox Christianity in favor of pluralistic interpretations of Jesus. And all three adopted perspectives on Jesus and the religions remarkably similar to those of Vivekananda, Radhakrishnan, and Gandhi in India.

---

110. See Hiromasa Mase, "The Fall of Christian Imperialism," in *How Wide Is God's Mercy? Christian Perspectives on Religious Pluralism: Hayama Missionary Seminar, 1993*, ed. Dale W. Little (Tokyo: Hayama Seminar, 1993), 53–61; idem, "Religious Pluralism from a Japanese Perspective," *Theology and the Religions: A Dialogue*, ed. Viggo Mortensen (Grand Rapids: Eerdmans, 2003), 443–48.

PART 2

Christian Commitments in a Pluralistic World

$$= 5 =$$

Can All Religions Be True?

There is enormous diversity among religions in matters of dress, dietary restrictions, places of worship or meditation, festivals, social practices, and rite-of-passage rituals. This is what makes the study of religions so fascinating, and such differences are not particularly problematic. But when differences turn into disagreements, and especially when the controversies concern basic questions about the nature of the cosmos, our place in it, and how we are to live, then that is another matter. Religious disagreements seem to have the unfortunate consequence that some believers are correct and others mistaken about their beliefs.

Religions include teachings or doctrines that are to be accepted as true by a specific religion's believers. As Paul Griffiths puts it, "A religious claim . . . is a claim about the way things are, acceptance of or assent to which is required or strongly suggested by the fact of belonging to a particular form of religious life."[1] Although it is true that some religions give greater emphasis to doctrine than do others, beliefs do matter. Being a member of a religion in good standing includes accepting the basic teachings of that religion and ordering one's life accordingly, and religious disagreement over religious teachings produces the problem of conflicting truth claims.

1. Paul Griffiths, *Problems of Religious Diversity* (Oxford: Blackwell, 2001), 21.

The Problem of Conflicting Truth Claims

While there are undeniable similarities across religions on some issues, there are also sharp disagreements. If one takes the teachings of the religions seriously on their own terms, they certainly seem to be making radically different, and at times even incompatible, claims. The vexing problem of conflicting truth claims is acknowledged by Peter Byrne, who nevertheless advocates a version of religious pluralism:

> The fact of religious diversity means that different religions contain competing accounts of the nature of the metaphysically and axiologically ultimate reality and competing accounts of the character of the ultimate good human beings can attain through relation to this reality. . . . Even where there is considerable overlap in the accounts of the transcendent, sacred reality and of salvation offered by more than one religion (as with, for example, Christianity and Islam), there will be deep incompatibilities among the theories embedded in them.[2]

Religious disagreements are recognized also by the Dalai Lama, arguably the most prominent spokesman for religious unity and harmony today.

> There is no denying the fact that, although most religions are theistic—the belief in a Transcendent Being as creator—there are others, such as Buddhism, Jainism and one branch of ancient Indian religion known as Samkhya that are genuinely nontheistic. The differences between a belief in God and the absence of such a belief is a fundamental one; there is no point in pretending otherwise.
>
> Within the Abrahamic traditions, there is genuine doctrinal difference among the three about the status of Jesus Christ. For followers of Judaism, Jesus is not the Messiah promised in the Old Testament, while for Christians, Jesus is not only the promised Messiah or Christ but is, in fact, the Son of God. As the Gospel puts it, "I am the Way, the truth and the life" (John 14:6), so for Christians, Jesus Christ is the Way as well as the Truth—in fact, God himself. For Islam, Jesus is a prophet but not the culmination. That is Muhammad, who is God's last prophet, and the Qur'an represents the culmination of God's final message to his creatures.
>
> No benefit will come from denying that these are fundamental doctrinal differences among the three religions.[3]

2. Peter Byrne, "A Philosophical Approach to Questions about Religious Diversity," in *The Oxford Handbook of Religious Diversity*, ed. Chad V. Meister (New York: Oxford University Press, 2010), 30.

3. His Holiness the Dalai Lama, *Toward a True Kinship of Faiths: How the World's Religions Can Come Together* (New York: Doubleday, 2010), 133–34.

The Dalai Lama's comments are significant since he is often portrayed in the West as a pluralist who accepts all religions just as they are. But he acknowledges a fundamental disagreement between Buddhism and Christianity on the question of God's existence.

> Now from the philosophical point of view, the theory that God is the creator, is almighty and permanent, is in contradiction to the Buddhist teachings. From this point of view there is disagreement. For Buddhists, the universe has no first cause and hence no creator, nor can there be such a thing as a permanent, primordially pure being. So, of course, doctrinally there is conflict. The views are opposite to one another.[4]

Christians and Muslims believe that the universe was created by an eternal Creator; Buddhists deny this. Christians insist that Jesus Christ is the incarnate Word of God, fully God and fully man. Muslims reject this as blasphemous. While Hindus, Buddhists, and Jains all agree that there is rebirth, they disagree vigorously over whether there is an enduring, substantial person or soul that is reborn.

The major religions do share a certain formal structure. Each has a particular understanding of what constitutes the religious ultimate, or the ontologically highest reality; each claims that the cosmos at present is not as it should be and thus humankind suffers from some undesirable condition; and each offers a way to overcome the present predicament and to attain a superior state.

But the religions disagree when it comes to filling in this formal structure with specific, substantive teachings. Stephen Prothero observes, "What the world's religions share is not so much a finish line as a starting point. And where they begin is with this simple observation: something is wrong with the world. . . . Religious folk worldwide agree that something has gone awry. They part company, however, when it comes to stating just what has gone wrong, and they diverge sharply when they move from diagnosing the human problem to prescribing how to solve it."[5] All of the religions acknowledge that the present state of the world is not as it should be, but they disagree over the cause of this unsatisfactory state and its proper remedy. For Christians, the root cause is sin against a holy God, and the cure consists in repentance and reconciliation with God through the person and work of Jesus Christ on the cross. For many Buddhists, Hindus, and Jains the cause

4. The Dalai Lama, "Buddhism and Other Religions," in *Philosophy of Religion: Selected Readings*, ed. Michael Peterson et al., 4th ed. (New York: Oxford University Press, 2010), 578.
5. Stephen R. Prothero, *God Is Not One: The Eight Rival Religions That Run the World—and Why Their Differences Matter* (New York: HarperOne, 2010), 11.

lies in a fundamentally mistaken view of reality, and the remedy involves overcoming the limitations of such false views. But Hindus, Buddhists, and Jains disagree among themselves over the nature of the error and how it is to be overcome.

Such disagreements result in differences over how we are to live. Differences between Christianity and Theravada Buddhism—for example, over whether one should repent of one's sins and follow Jesus Christ as Lord and Savior or should follow the Noble Eightfold Path—reflect not so much diverse *means* toward a common goal but rather very different *ends* that are to be pursued. These differences grow out of more basic disagreements over what is religiously ultimate, the nature of the problem plaguing the universe, and the proper remedy for this predicament.

Some religious teachings that are different might actually be compatible with each other; others, however, seem not to be mutually compatible. Here it is important to distinguish two kinds of incompatible teachings.[6] Two religious claims are *contradictory* if each makes a claim to truth, and both cannot be true, but one claim must be true. The statements "There is an eternal creator God" and "There is not an eternal creator God" are contradictories. On the other hand, two religious claims are *contraries* if each makes a claim to truth, and both cannot be true, but neither claim need be true. The statements "The ultimate reality is sunyata [emptiness]" and "The ultimate reality is Allah" are contraries. They cannot both be true, although they might both be false. Most religious disagreements that seem incompatible are contraries, not contradictories.

What are we to make of conflicting truth claims? There are at least six basic approaches one might adopt with respect to religious disagreement and truth among the religions:

1. There is sufficient reason to conclude that all religions are false; there is no religion whose central claims are true.
2. One particular religion (e.g., Christianity) can be shown to be true or rationally preferable to others.
3. Although it is not possible to show that one religion is true or rationally preferable to others, it nevertheless can be reasonable for a religious believer (e.g., Christian) to regard one's own religion as true.

6. See Paul J. Griffiths, *Problems of Religious Diversity*, 31–37. On conflicting claims in the religions, see William A. Christian, *Oppositions of Religious Doctrines: A Study in the Logic of Dialogue among Religions* (London: Macmillan, 1972); idem, *Doctrines of Religious Communities: A Philosophical Study* (New Haven: Yale University Press, 1987); Ninian Smart, *A Dialogue of Religions* (London: SCM, 1960).

4. Disagreement between religions undermines the claims of any single religion to distinctive truth; the most reasonable perspective is to suspend judgment and remain agnostic.

5. Each religion can be regarded as "true" and "effective" for its own adherents, but there is no objective or tradition-transcending sense in which we can speak of religious truth.

6. There are strong reasons for believing that, in spite of clear disagreements among them, the major religions are all "in touch" with the same ultimate divine reality. No single religion can legitimately claim to be superior to others in terms of truth or soteriological effectiveness.

Atheism, reflected in approach 1, is increasing today, although it remains a minority perspective. Many Christians would accept position 2, with others perhaps more comfortable with 3. Agnosticism, reflected in stance 4, is attractive to many today and can be compatible with religious practice. Some of the issues involved in positions 2, 3, and 4 will be explored in the next two chapters. Option 5 expresses religious relativism,[7] and religious pluralism—which is distinct from relativism—is found in 6.

In this chapter we will examine the perspective in 6, which I will refer to with the term "religious pluralism."[8] The following statements by Mahatma Gandhi express a popular form of pluralism: "The different religions are beautiful flowers from the same garden, or they are branches of the same majestic tree. . . . The root of all religions is one and is pure and all of them have sprung from the same source, hence all are equal."[9] In this sense religious pluralism is the perspective that all of the major religions are (roughly) equally true and provide equally legitimate or effective ways in which to respond to the divine reality. No single religion can legitimately claim to be distinctively true and normative for all people in all cultures at all times. We will use John Hick's theory of religious pluralism as the focus of our attention, although we will also draw upon perspectives from other pluralists. I will argue that pluralism faces insurmountable problems and thus is an untenable option.

7. See Joseph Runzo, "Pluralism and Relativism," in Meister, *Oxford Handbook of Religious Diversity*, 61–76; idem, *Reason, Relativism, and God* (London: Macmillan, 1986).
8. The term "religious pluralism" is employed in different ways. Sociologists often use it in a descriptive sense as a synonym for religious diversity. Others take it to mean a more or less positive attitude toward religious diversity, without carefully defining what this includes. I use it to refer to the view that the major religions are all valid religions in that they are roughly equally true and equally effective as appropriate responses to the one religious ultimate.
9. M. Gandhi, as cited in *Gandhi on Christianity*, ed. Robert Ellsberg (Maryknoll, NY: Orbis Books, 1991), 65; and in *Mahatma Gandhi: Essential Writings*, ed. Judith M. Brown (New York: Oxford University Press, 2008), 50–51.

Religious Pluralism: The Theory

According to Peter Byrne, religious pluralism maintains that "the world's religions do provide good reasons to suppose that humanity is in touch with a sacred, transcendent reality, even while no particular stream of human experience has exclusive contact with that entity or a definitive, reliable account of it."[10] Byrne concisely states three assertions that are at the heart of religious pluralism:

> Pluralism as a theoretical response to religious diversity can now be summarily defined by three propositions. (1) All major forms of religion are equal in respect of making common reference to a single, transcendent sacred reality. (2) All major forms of religion are likewise equal in respect of offering some means or other to human salvation. (3) All religious traditions are to be seen as containing revisable, limited accounts of the nature of the sacred: none is certain enough in its particular dogmatic formulations to provide the norm for interpreting the others.[11]

The first claim provides the necessary unity in a model of pluralism; despite differences among the religions, they have a common ontological referent. Furthermore, regardless how one might construe the soteriological goal of religions, they are equally efficacious in achieving the desired goal. By minimizing the significance of religious teachings or doctrines, the third proposition tries to modify the force of the problem of conflicting truth claims.

To these I would add a necessary condition for a genuinely pluralistic understanding of the religions: A viable model of religious pluralism cannot privilege the perspectives of any single religion or of theistic, pantheistic, or nontheistic forms of religion. The pluralistic views of Swami Vivekananda or Radhakrishnan in chapter 4, for example, accept other religions as viable options, but they do so within a broad Vedanta Hindu framework; thus the highest form of religious truth is that of Vedanta Hinduism, and theistic traditions are granted a lower status. But this is not really pluralism; it is simply a generous form of Vedanta Hinduism.[12] Similarly, there are very accommodating

10. Peter Byrne, "It Is Not Reasonable to Believe That Only One Religion Is True," in *Contemporary Debates in Philosophy of Religion*, ed. Michael L. Peterson and Raymond J. VanArragon (Oxford: Blackwell, 2004), 215.

11. Ibid., 204. See also Peter Byrne's *Prolegomena to Religious Pluralism: Reference and Realism in Religion* (New York: St. Martin's Press, 1995), 12.

12. For a helpful analysis of the ways in which the "pluralism" of Hinduism can be construed, see Arvind Sharma, "All Religions Are—Equal? One? True? Same? A Critical Examination of Some Formulations of the Neo-Hindu Position," *Philosophy East and West* 29.1 (January 1979): 59–72.

forms of theism that regard all religions—including Buddhism and Jainism, which explicitly reject the idea of God—as more or less acceptable religious responses to God. Yet these paradigms too are not genuinely pluralistic but rather are very inclusive forms of theism. A truly pluralistic understanding of the religions will not privilege either theistic or nontheistic religious traditions. As we shall see, this is a very difficult condition to meet.

The most influential model of religious pluralism has come from theologian and philosopher John Hick, whose views are set out most completely in *An Interpretation of Religion*.[13] Hick's theory is a sophisticated and attractive expression of a perspective widely accepted in popular culture. His proposal fits the three propositions stated by Byrne and attempts to meet the condition about not privileging any particular religious tradition. At the heart of Hick's model is this claim:

> The great world faiths embody different perceptions and conceptions of, and correspondingly different responses to, the Real from within the variant ways of being human; and that within each of them the transformation of human existence from self-centredness to reality-centredness is taking place. These traditions are accordingly to be regarded as alternative soteriological "spaces" within which, or "ways" along which, men and women find salvation/liberation/enlightenment.[14]

Elsewhere he puts it thus: "The different world religions—each with its own sacred scriptures, spiritual practices, forms of religious experience, belief systems, founder or great exemplars, communal memories, cultural expressions in ways of life, laws and customs, art forms and so on—taken together as complex historical totalities, constitute different human responses to the ultimate transcendent reality to which they all, in their different ways, bear witness."[15]

Religious pluralism should be understood in terms of ontological religious realism. It holds that there actually is a religious ultimate "out there" to whom (or which) the various religions can be said to be in proper relationship. Byrne states, "The doctrine that all major religious traditions refer to a common sacred, transcendent reality is at the heart of pluralism. To distinguish itself

---

13. John Hick, *An Interpretation of Religion*, 2nd ed. (New Haven: Yale University Press, 2004 [1989]). Other works in which Hick develops his thesis include *Disputed Questions in Theology and the Philosophy of Religion* (New Haven: Yale University Press, 1993); *A Christian Theology of Religions: The Rainbow of Faiths* (Louisville: Westminster John Knox, 1995); *The Fifth Dimension: An Exploration of the Spiritual Realm* (Oxford: Oneworld, 1999); and *Dialogues in the Philosophy of Religion* (New York: Palgrave, 2001).

14. John Hick, *Interpretation of Religion*, 240.

15. John Hick, *Fifth Dimension*, 77.

from naturalism, it must affirm that some sacred, non-human reality informs the religions even though no religion ever describes that reality adequately."[16] This transcendent reality, to which the various religions in their own ways point, is what Hick calls the Real. Hick maintains that, despite the clear differences among religions, there is "an ultimate ineffable Reality which is the source and ground of everything," and that the religions "involve different human conceptions of the Real, with correspondingly different forms of experience of the Real, and correspondingly different forms of life in response to the Real."[17]

But if the religions all are responding to the same divine reality, why is there not greater agreement among them? Why the great diversity in their teachings? Some religions portray the ultimate as a personal Being—as Yahweh, God the Holy Trinity, Allah, or Krishna; others reject theism and regard the ultimate as a nonpersonal reality such as the Dao, Nirguna Brahman, sunyata, or the dharmakaya. When these conceptions are understood within their own respective religious contexts, it is clear that these are not just minor variations of a common theme. What the Muslim means by "Allah" is not the same as what the Advaita Vedantin means by "Brahman"; what the Buddhist means by "sunyata" (emptiness) is usually understood to be incompatible with both the Christian and Islamic concepts of God the creator. How can pluralists maintain that such different perspectives are all properly related to the same religious ultimate?

Hick responds by adapting Immanuel Kant's famous distinction between the noumenon and the phenomenon in the epistemology of perception. Hick distinguishes between what he calls the religious ultimate as it is in itself, and the religious ultimate as it is experienced by historically and culturally conditioned persons. While the Real itself is never the direct object of religious experience, human beings can experience any of a number of symbolic "manifestations" or conceptual images of the Real. Thus those in some religious traditions characteristically experience and think of the Real in personal terms as Yahweh, Allah, Krishna, or Jesus Christ; people in other traditions experience the Real in nonpersonal terms as the Dao, Nirguna Brahman, sunyata, or the dharmakaya. The personal manifestations of the Real are called divine personae, and the nonpersonal manifestations are divine impersonae of the Real. Whereas the particular religions regard the relevant personae or impersonae as the religious ultimate, Hick maintains that they actually are

---

16. Peter Byrne, *Prolegomena*, 31. See also Peter Byrne, *God and Realism* (Burlington, VT: Ashgate, 2003). In *Interpretation of Religion*, chaps. 11–12, Hick argues against religious nonrealism.
    17. Hick, *Christian Theology of Religions*, 27.

penultimate conceptual symbols through which people in various religions think about and respond to what is truly ultimate: the Real.

Now if one is to have a genuinely pluralistic model of the religions, then neither the personae nor the impersonae can be given preferential treatment. Accordingly, Hick insists that the Real itself transcends both personal and nonpersonal characterizations so that none of our concepts or linguistic terms can be applied to the Real itself.

> The distinction between the Real as it is in itself and as it is thought and experienced through our human religious concepts entails . . . that we cannot apply to the Real *an sich* the characteristics encountered in its *personae* and *impersonae*. Thus it cannot be said to be one or many, person or thing, conscious or unconscious, purposive or non-purposive, substance or process, good or evil, loving or hating. None of the descriptive terms that apply within the realm of human experience can apply literally to the unexperienceable reality that underlies that realm.[18]

Thus Hick claims that nothing substantive can be said about the Real in itself: the Real is ineffable.

A common objection to ineffability is that a statement of the form "*x* is ineffable" is self-referentially incoherent: to say that *x* is ineffable is to say *something* about *x*, namely, that *x* has the property of ineffability. In order to avoid this absurdity, Hick distinguishes between purely formal properties (such as the property of being a possible object of reference) and substantial properties, which tell us something significant about what the Real is like. And he insists that no substantial properties can be applied to the Real.[19] "By 'ineffable' . . . I mean having a nature that is beyond the scope of our networks of human concepts. Thus the Real in itself cannot properly be said to be personal or impersonal, purposive or non-purposive, good or evil, substance or process, even one or many."[20]

How does Hick deal with the problem of conflicting truth claims among religions? A viable model of religious pluralism must be able to defuse the problem by doing two things. First, the pluralist must acknowledge the very real differences in teachings across the religions. Second, the pluralist must also be able to show either how these apparently incompatible claims are actually

---

18. John Hick, *Interpretation of Religion*, 350; see also 246–47, 349.
19. See John Hick, "Ineffability," *Religious Studies* 36 (March 2000): 35–46; idem, "Introduction to the Second Edition," in *Interpretation of Religion*, xix–xx; idem, "Religious Pluralism," in *The Routledge Companion to Philosophy of Religion*, ed. Chad V. Meister and Paul Copan (London: Routledge, 2007), 220–23.
20. Hick, *Christian Theology of Religions*, 27.

mutually compatible (a daunting challenge indeed) or provide an alternative understanding of religious teachings and truth such that these conflicts are unimportant. Hick, along with most pluralists, adopts the latter option by downplaying the significance of doctrinal disputes and reinterpreting the notion of religious truth.

Before looking at Hick's views on religious doctrines and truth, we should first notice the critique of propositional truth in religion offered by Wilfred Cantwell Smith, a pluralist who had significant influence on Hick's own views. The problem of conflicting truth claims is said to depend on acceptance of propositional truth in religion; if this view of truth is inapplicable, then the problem can be set aside.

The notion of propositional truth holds that truth is a property of propositions[21] or statements and that, in the words of William Alston, "a statement (proposition, belief . . .) is true if and only if what the statement says to be the case actually is the case."[22] This is closely related to what is often referred to as the correspondence theory of truth, which maintains that "for a statement to be true, there must be some appropriate *correspondence* between true statements and actual features of the world."[23] To say that truth is propositional, then, is to maintain that, in the logically basic sense, truth is a property of propositions such that a proposition is true if and only if the state of affairs to which it refers obtains. Otherwise it is false. Thus, "The heavy rainfall last night resulted in the basement flooding" is true if and only if the heavy rainfall last night did indeed result in the basement flooding. "On the third day Jesus of Nazareth was raised from the dead" is true if and only if on the third day Jesus of Nazareth was raised from the dead. "Muhammad received the revelation constituting the Qur'an from the angel Gabriel" is true if and only if Muhammad actually did receive the revelation constituting the Qur'an from the angel Gabriel. The propositional notion of truth underlies our ordinary commonsense understanding of truth, and it is taken for granted by most religious believers in their acceptance of the claims at the heart of their traditions.

A propositional understanding of truth must be distinguished from epistemic conceptions of truth, which hold that truth is a function of evidence in

21. For our purposes, we can regard "statement" and "proposition" as virtually synonymous. A proposition, then, is the meaning expressed by a declarative sentence or what is conveyed by a sentence that makes an implicit or explicit assertion. By extension, we can also speak of beliefs or teachings as true in a propositional sense.

22. See William P. Alston, *A Realist Conception of Truth* (Ithaca, NY: Cornell University Press, 1996), 5.

23. Paul K. Moser, Dwayne H. Mulder, and J. D. Trout, *The Theory of Knowledge: A Thematic Introduction* (New York: Oxford University Press, 1998), 65, with original emphasis.

favor of a statement or belief.[24] In a true statement, it is the particular relation between what the statement asserts and the way reality actually is that makes the statement true. The question of whether one knows that the statement is true or is justified in believing it is distinct from whether the statement is in fact true.

In some influential writings, however, Wilfred Cantwell Smith argues that religious truth should not be understood as propositional truth but rather as "personal truth." Smith states, "Truth, I submit, is a humane, not an objective, concept. It does not lie in propositions. . . . Truth and falsity are often felt in modern times to be properties or functions of statements or propositions; whereas the present proposal is that much is to be gained by seeing them rather, or anyway seeing them also, and primarily, as properties or functions of persons."[25] Personal truth is a property not of propositions or statements but rather of persons and is a function of one's inner life. "Human behavior, in word or deed, is the nexus between man's inner life and the surrounding world. Truth at the personalistic level is that quality by which both halves of that relationship are chaste, are appropriate, are true."[26] In other words, personal truth does not signify objective correspondence with reality but rather personal integrity, sincerity, faithfulness, and the existential appropriation of particular beliefs in the believer's conduct. "No statement might be accepted as true that has not been inwardly appropriated by its author."[27] Personal truth is changing and person-relative so that statements, beliefs, and even religious traditions can be said to become true or might be true for me but not for you. A religious tradition "becomes more or less true in the case of particular persons as it informs their lives and their groups and shapes and nurtures their faith."[28] No longer should one think of Christianity, for example, as simply being true or false. "Christianity, I would suggest, is not true absolutely, impersonally, statically; rather, it can become true, if and as you or I appropriate it to ourselves and interiorize it, insofar as we live it out from day to day. It becomes true as we take it off the shelf and personalize it, in actual existence."[29]

John Hick was significantly influenced by Wilfred Cantwell Smith, and he also tries to defuse the problem of conflicting truth claims by reinterpreting the

24. Alston, *Realist Conception of Truth*, 7.

25. Wilfred Cantwell Smith, *Towards a World Theology: Faith and the Comparative History of Religion* (Maryknoll, NY: Orbis Books, 1989), 190; idem, "A Human View of Truth," in *Truth and Dialogue in World Religions: Conflicting Truth Claims*, ed. John Hick (Philadelphia: Westminster, 1974), 20.

26. W. C. Smith, "Human View of Truth," 26.

27. Ibid., 35.

28. W. C. Smith, *Towards a World Theology*, 187.

29. Wilfred Cantwell Smith, *Questions of Religious Truth* (London: Gollancz, 1967), 67–68.

notion of truth in religion. Hick distinguishes three levels of conflicting truth claims in religion.[30] First, there are disagreements over matters of historical fact: Did Jesus die on the cross or not? Christians say yes; Muslims typically deny this. Second, a different kind of disagreement concerns matters of transhistorical fact. Is reincarnation true? Is there a soul that survives death, and if so, what happens to the soul? Third, there are disagreements over ultimate ways of thinking about the cosmos and the religious ultimate: Is the religious ultimate personal or nonpersonal? What is the relation between the religious ultimate and the universe? Hick holds that questions in the first two categories can in principle be answered by us, although in practice there is usually little consensus on these matters. But questions of the third kind cannot be settled with our present understanding and categories.

According to Hick, the problem of conflicting truth claims arises when we treat disagreements as matters of "literal truth" (for our purposes, equivalent to propositional truth). But Hick argues that we should understand religious truth not as literal truth but rather as mythological truth, and that when we do so, the problem of conflicting truth claims disappears. The mythological truth of a statement is not a matter of the relation between what a statement asserts and an objective state of affairs; it is a dynamic function of the effect the statement has upon an individual or community. As such, it resembles Smith's notion of personal truth.

> The literal truth or falsity of a factual assertion (as distinguished from the truth or falsity of an analytic proposition) consists in its conformity or lack of conformity to fact: "it is raining here and now" is literally true if and only if it is raining here and now. But in addition to literal truth there is also mythological truth. A statement or set of propositions about x is mythologically true if it is not literally true but nevertheless tends to evoke an appropriate dispositional attitude toward x. Thus mythological truth is practical, or in one sense of this much abused word, existential. For the conformity of myth to reality does not consist in a literal conformity of what is said to the facts but in the appropriateness to the myth's referent of the behavioural dispositions that it tends to evoke in the hearer.[31]

Hence "true religious myths are accordingly those that evoke in us attitudes and modes of behaviour which are appropriate to our situation in relation to the Real."[32]

30. Hick, *Interpretation of Religion*, 362–76.
31. Ibid., 348.
32. Ibid., 248.

The doctrines from the religions concerning Yahweh, the Trinity, Allah, Nirguna Brahman, sunyata, and the Dao are not literally true or false, but they can be said to be mythologically true insofar as they evoke in the believers appropriate dispositional responses to the Real.[33] Central beliefs—such as the Islamic claim that the Qur'an was dictated to Muhammad by the angel Gabriel, or the Advaita Vedantin assertion about our ultimate identity with Nirguna Brahman, or the claim of Zen about enlightenment providing direct and unmediated access to the ultimacy of emptiness—can thus be mythologically true, although they are not literally true. On either Smith's or Hick's understanding of religious truth, the problem of conflicting truth claims vanishes, for truth becomes a property not of beliefs or statements themselves but of the believer's relationship to particular beliefs, and this varies with believers.

Why Postulate the Real?

Why postulate the Real as the religious ultimate toward which the religions are all pointing? A complete answer would involve discussion of Hick's general religious epistemology, including his well-known treatments of religious ambiguity, cognitive freedom, "experiencing-as," and the implications of religious experiences.[34] Although we cannot provide full discussion here, we will briefly notice three claims that are central to Hick's case for religious pluralism: religious ambiguity, religious experience, and moral transformation within the religions.

A crucial assumption behind Hick's model is the claim that the universe is religiously ambiguous on two levels. First, he maintains that there is religious ambiguity in that it can be reasonable to interpret the universe in either religious or nonreligious (naturalistic) terms. Rational considerations alone cannot determine which interpretation is preferable; there are some reasons to believe in a creator God, but there are also good reasons not to do so.[35] There is also ambiguity in the fact that careful analysis of the universe and experience alone cannot settle the question: Which religious perspective is most likely to be

33. Hick, *Disputed Questions*, 116–17.

34. See John Hick, *Faith and Knowledge*, 2nd ed. (Ithaca, NY: Cornell University Press, 1966); idem, *Arguments for the Existence of God* (London: Macmillan, 1970); idem, *Interpretation of Religion*, chaps. 5–13; idem, *Between Faith and Doubt: Dialogues on Religion and Reason* (New York: Palgrave, 2010).

35. Hick, *Interpretation of Religion*, 124. Robert McKim also develops the notion of religious ambiguity in support of a form of religious pluralism. See Robert McKim, *Religious Ambiguity and Religious Diversity* (New York: Oxford University Press, 2001); idem, *On Religious Diversity* (New York: Oxford University Press, 2012).

true? Rational analysis alone cannot determine whether the religious ultimate is a personal creator God or the sunyata (emptiness) of Mahayana Buddhism.

Although the universe is religiously ambiguous, Hick regards religious experience as the decisive element in the epistemological equation. He claims that naturalistic explanations entailing that religious experiences are not veridical are unpersuasive, and thus we cannot simply rule out religious experiences as delusory. But given the highly interpretative nature of such experiences, neither can we look to them to settle the chief question: Which religious tradition is true? Nevertheless, for those who have religious experiences in appropriate circumstances, it can be reasonable for them to treat such experiences as veridical and to interpret reality accordingly. "It is as reasonable for those who experience their lives as being lived in the presence of God, to believe in the reality of God, as for all of us to form beliefs about our environment on the basis of our experience of it."[36] This is based upon what Hick calls the "critical trust" principle, which maintains, "It is rational to believe that what seems to be so is indeed so, except when we have reason to think otherwise."[37] Hick contends that this principle, which entails a general presumption of the veridicality of religious experiences, applies not only to Christian experiences but likewise to experiences within other religious traditions.[38] And this, he maintains, suggests a common ultimate reality "behind" the various religious experiences.

Another significant assumption justifying postulation of the Real is Hick's appeal to what he perceives as a common moral transformation among adherents of the religions. Hick states, "My reason to assume that the different world religions are referring, through their specific concepts of the Gods and Absolutes, to the same ultimate Reality is the striking similarity of the transformed human state described within the different traditions as saved, redeemed, enlightened, wise, awakened, liberated. This similarity strongly suggests a common source of salvific transformation."[39] Hick claims that the religions exhibit a common soteriological structure consisting of a moral transformation from "self-centredness" to "Reality-centredness." The religions constitute

variations within different conceptual schemes on a single fundamental theme: the sudden or gradual change of the individual from an absorbing self-concern

36. Hick, *Interpretation of Religion*, 210.
37. Hick, "Religious Pluralism," 220.
38. The general presumption of veridicality can, of course, be overruled by factors that call into question an experience or one's interpretation of an experience.
39. Hick, *Christian Theology of Religions*, 69.

to a new centring in the supposed unity-of-reality-and-value that is thought of as God, Brahman, the Dharma, Sunyata, or the Tao. Thus the generic concept of salvation/liberation, which takes a different specific form in each of the great traditions, is that of the transformation of human existence from self-centredness to Reality-centredness.[40]

Hick holds that this moral transformation is occurring roughly to the same extent across the major religions. "So far as we can tell, [the religions] are equally productive of the transition from self to Reality which we see in the saints of all traditions."[41]

Similarities in the ethical ideals of the religions, the moral values exemplified in the lives of saints of the religions, and the degree to which moral transformation occurs among adherents of the religions all suggest a common source behind the religions. "The production of saints, both contemplative and practical, individualistic and political, is thus one valid criterion by which to identify a religious tradition as a salvific response to the Real. In light of this criterion we can readily see that each of the great world faiths constitutes a context for salvation/liberation: for each has produced its own harvest of saints."[42] This provides a moral criterion that serves two functions in Hick's model: First, it allegedly provides a positive reason for concluding that the religions are not entirely mistaken in their claims but rather are somehow "grounded" in the same religious ultimate. Second, moral transformation provides a criterion for discriminating between what are and are not authentic responses to the Real. Not all religious traditions are to be accepted; only those that exhibit moral transformation are to be regarded as appropriate responses to the Real.

Hick's model of pluralism has stimulated an enormous body of literature, and the model has been subjected to some strong criticisms.[43] His proposal can be challenged on a variety of grounds. For example, Hick's model depends on his claims concerning religious ambiguity, but it is not at all obvious that the universe is as ambiguous as he maintains. If in fact the universe is not so ambiguous—if, that is, there are compelling reasons for accepting naturalism

40. Hick, *Interpretation of Religion*, 36.

41. John Hick, *Problems of Religious Pluralism* (New York: St. Martin's Press, 1985), 86–87.

42. Hick, *Interpretation of Religion*, 307.

43. See Paul Rhodes Eddy, *John Hick's Pluralist Philosophy of World Religions* (Burlington, VT: Ashgate, 2002); *Problems in the Philosophy of Religion: Critical Studies of the Work of John Hick*, ed. Harold Hewitt (New York: St. Martin's Press, 1991); Harold A. Netland, "Religious Pluralism as an Explanation for Religious Diversity," in *Philosophy and the Christian Worldview*, ed. David Werther and Mark D. Linville (New York: Continuum, 2012), 25–49; Philip L. Quinn and Kevin Meeker, eds., *The Philosophical Challenge of Religious Diversity* (New York: Oxford University Press, 2000).

rather than any religious perspective, or for accepting theism rather than nontheistic or naturalistic alternatives—then religious pluralism becomes epistemically untenable. We will return to this issue in the next two chapters. Critics have also pointed out that the ontological status of the personae and impersonae and their relation to the Real within Hick's system is problematic. Are they merely concepts, with no extramental referent, through which different groups think about the Real? Or do they have some kind of extramental reality? Exactly how are they related to the Real?[44] He has also been criticized for being reductionistic in his treatment of the common soteriological structure to the religions. While it is true that in a very formal sense the religions do manifest a common structure—a transformation from an undesirable state to a much better state—the religions provide very different ways of understanding the undesirable state, the preferred state, and the means for attaining the desired state. In what follows, however, we will focus upon problems in three areas: Hick's reinterpretation of religious truth, his appeal to culture to explain religious differences, and the ineffability of the Real.[45]

Reinterpreting Religious Truth

Both Smith's notion of personal truth and Hick's proposal concerning mythological truth, if intended to replace propositional truth in religion, are problematic. The first thing to recognize about both views is that they do not fit the way that most religious believers think about religious assertions. When a Christian affirms, "Because of Jesus's sacrificial death on the cross, I can be reconciled to God," she intends to be making a statement that accurately reflects reality—that she can be reconciled to God because of Jesus's sacrificial death on the cross. She does not regard the statement as true only in the sense

44. For a penetrating critique of the ontological issues concerning the personae/impersonae in Hick's model, see George Mavrodes, "Polytheism," in *The Rationality of Belief and the Plurality of Faith*, ed. Thomas D. Senor (Ithaca, NY: Cornell University Press, 1995), 261–86. A helpful analysis of the dispute between Hick and Mavrodes is found in William Hasker, "The Many Gods of Hick and Mavrodes," in *Evidence and Religious Belief*, ed. Kelly James Clark and Raymond J. VanArragon (New York: Oxford University Press, 2011), 186–99. Elsewhere, Mavrodes examines Paul Tillich and John Hick, both of whom postulate a religious ultimate beyond the God of theism, and shows how this move vacillates between being so abstract that it is meaningless and being "absorbed" by the lower deities. George I. Mavrodes, "The Gods above the Gods: Can the High Gods Survive?," in *Reasoned Faith: Essays in Philosophical Theology in Honor of Norman Kretzman*, ed. Eleonore Stump (Ithaca, NY: Cornell University Press, 1993), 179–203.

45. The latter two issues were explored in an earlier essay: Netland, "Religious Pluralism as an Explanation for Religious Diversity."

that if she acts appropriately on it and orders her life in accordance with it, then the statement can become true for her. Similarly, when a Hindu claims, "Only when a person recognizes his own essential identity with Brahman can he attain liberation from rebirth," he intends to be making a statement that depicts reality accurately, regardless of whether one happens to accept it and allows it to shape one's dispositions and conduct. Religious believers would be surprised to learn that their assertions are not true in the sense that they reflect reality but that they can become true to the extent that they enable believers to adopt appropriate dispositional responses to the Real. Regardless of whether the claims of Hindus or Christians do in fact reflect reality accurately, any theory about religious truth that ignores the intention of believers and reinterprets truth in a way that is alien to the discourse of believers is unacceptable unless there are compelling reasons for such reinterpretation. I see no reason for reinterpretation apart from a desire to avoid the problem of conflicting truth claims.

Furthermore, neither personal truth nor mythological truth can be an alternative to propositional truth because the former logically depend upon the latter. One cannot have personal truth in religion unless particular beliefs are true in a propositional—not personal—sense. Existentially appropriating a belief does not occur in a cognitive vacuum. Roger Trigg correctly observes, "In any sphere the fact of commitment logically entails certain beliefs and precludes certain others. One must believe in the truth of what one is committed to."[46] Take, for example, the statement "Allah is a righteous judge."[47] On Smith's proposal, this statement is not in itself either true or false, but it can become true if Muslims accept it and shape their life in accordance with it in an appropriate manner. Doing so would presumably mean that a Muslim lives a life of sincerity, ethical integrity, and faithfulness to the teachings of the Qur'an, so that there is no glaring gap between what one professes and how one lives. On this understanding, to say "Allah is a righteous judge" is true means to affirm that this particular person's life is congruous with belief that Allah is a righteous judge.

But notice that "Allah is a righteous judge" can be true in this personal sense only if it, and other related beliefs, are taken as true in a nonpersonal or propositional sense. The statement "Allah is a righteous judge" will be appropriated personally only if the Muslim believer is first convinced that statements 1 and 2 below are true in a nonpersonal or propositional sense:

46. Roger Trigg, *Reason and Commitment* (London: Cambridge University Press, 1973), 44.
47. Here I am indebted to the fine discussion by William J. Wainwright, "Wilfred Cantwell Smith on Faith and Belief," *Religious Studies* 20 (September 1984): 353–66.

1. Allah exists.
2. Allah is righteous and will judge those who do wickedness.

It is because declarations 1 and 2 are understood as accurately reflecting the way reality is, regardless of one's personal feelings about the matter, that the Muslim will respond appropriately to "Allah is a righteous judge." But if so, then personal truth cannot be an alternative to propositional truth since it presupposes propositional truth. Smith confuses the issue of truth with that of the believer's response to the truth.

Similarly, Hick's notion of mythological truth is also logically dependent upon nonmythological, or propositional, understandings of truth. What does it mean to adopt an appropriate dispositional response to the Real? Answering this question requires our knowing something about the Real so that we can distinguish appropriate responses from inappropriate ones. Having such knowledge about the Real involves being able to identify statements about the Real that are true—not in a metaphorical but in a propositional sense—as accurately portraying what the Real is like and what an appropriate response to the Real involves.

On Hick's proposal, for example, the statement "God is loving and is pleased when people treat others in loving ways" is not literally true, but it can become metaphorically true for Christians if accepting it produces an appropriate dispositional response to the Real. What would such a response look like? Presumably it would involve Christians acting toward others in loving ways. If so, this is because the nature of the Real is such that treating others in loving ways is an appropriate response, and acting selfishly toward others is not. But notice that this makes sense only if the statement "The nature of the Real is such that treating others in loving ways is an appropriate response and acting selfishly toward others is not" is true in a propositional, not metaphorical, sense.

Thus the problem of conflicting truth claims cannot be eliminated so easily. What makes religious pluralism so attractive for many today is the assumption that only pluralism enables us to accept all the major religions as they are, without rejecting the central teachings of some religions as false. An implication of the problem of conflicting truth claims seems to be that millions of sincere, morally respectable, and intelligent religious believers are mistaken in their basic religious commitments, but pluralism seems to offer a way of avoiding this conclusion. Ironically, however, even with pluralism one cannot escape the conclusion that large numbers of religious believers are wrong about their beliefs. On Hick's model, the Christian who believes that Jesus Christ is actually God incarnate, fully God and fully man, is mistaken because, strictly speaking, that statement is false, even if it can be considered metaphorically true. Similarly with the Buddhist claim that the experience of satori (enlightenment) provides direct, unmediated access to what is religiously ultimate. Although possibly metaphorically true, this claim too is literally false. And similar reasoning applies to core claims in the various religions. Thus, even if we accept Hick's proposal on religious pluralism, we cannot escape the conclusion that large numbers of sincere, intelligent, and morally good people are mistaken in their religious beliefs.

Pluralism on Culture and Religion

As we have seen, pluralists appeal to contingent historical and cultural influences in order to explain the enormous diversity in religious belief and practice. As Hick explains,

> We always perceive the transcendent through the lens of *a particular religious culture* with its distinctive set of concepts, myths, historical exemplars and devotional or meditational techniques. And it is this inexpungible human contribution to religious awareness that accounts for the fascinating variations of religious thought, experience, and practice around the globe and down through the centuries, in all their rational and irrational, profound and shallow, impressive and absurd, morally admirable and morally reprehensible features.[48]

Elsewhere he states, "The ultimate transcategorial Real affects humanity in ways made possible by our human conceptualities and spiritual practices. These differ among *the different ways of being human which are the great cultures of the world.*"[49] In *Problems of Religious Pluralism*, Hick says,

> And if we next ask why a variety of religious conceptions and visions have become plausible within different streams of human life, we have I think to draw upon the fact that the main cultures of the world have been sufficiently different to constitute different ways of being human—including the Chinese, the Indian, the African, the Semitic, and the Graeco-Semitic ways. These different ways of being human have involved different ways of being religious.[50]

Differences in religious beliefs and practices are due to the different historical and cultural contexts in which believers find themselves.

48. Hick, *Interpretation of Religion*, 8, with added emphasis.
49. Hick, "Religious Pluralism," 221, with added emphasis.
50. Hick, *Problems of Religious Pluralism*, 74.

Peter Byrne also speaks of "the influence of *cultural forms and contingencies* on the religious imagination" in explaining religious diversity.

> Diversity and disagreement suggest the following interpretation of it: religious
> diversity is explained by the setting of religious life in *the concretely different
> forms of human culture*. It has a natural, ready anthropological explanation:
> the influence of cultural forms and contingencies on the religious imagination.
> In this respect, both naturalist and pluralist favor a certain deconstruction of
> religious traditions. These traditions are, in at least some very large measure, the
> product of the same anthropological forces which shape other facets of culture.
> There is no need to think that their symbols or beliefs derive from knowledge
> of a divine being outside human life.[51]

Religious beliefs and practices are thus the product of the interrelationship
between the Real and various historical, social, and cultural factors. Similarities
across religions are explained by a common relation to the Real; differences are
said to be due to contingent historical and cultural factors. Although people
in the religions (indirectly) encounter the same divine reality, contingent historical and cultural factors provide a kind of filter or grid that shapes both
the awareness of and response to this reality.

But just how does culture account for the diversity and disagreement among
the religions? Pluralists give no explanation for how this works, and their rather
scattered references to culture seem to presuppose some problematic assumptions. For example, pluralists sometimes speak as if the influences of culture and
history are determinative, so that given one's social location, it is almost inevitable
that one is a Christian or a Hindu or a Buddhist. Consider Hick's statement:

> It is evident that in some ninety-nine per cent of cases the religion which an
> individual professes and to which he or she adheres depends upon the accidents
> of birth. Someone born to Buddhist parents in Thailand is very likely to be a
> Buddhist, someone born to Muslim parents in Saudi Arabia to be a Muslim,
> someone born to Christian parents in Mexico to be a Christian, and so on. There
> are of course conversions from one faith to another, but in the case of the great
> world religions these are peripheral to the massive transmission of each from
> one generation to the next within its own population.[52]

Similarly, Joseph Runzo asserts, "One's religious beliefs seem largely to be
an accident of birth. . . . The religious tradition that one follows is largely

---

51. Byrne, "It Is Not Reasonable to Believe That Only One Religion Is True," 205, with
added emphasis.
52. Hick, *Interpretation of Religion*, 2.

determined by such factors as where and when one was born, one's ethnic background, and past colonial influences on one's culture."[53] This is certainly an important point: the time and place of one's birth does affect all kinds of things, including one's worldview and religious commitments, if any. But Hick's and Runzo's comments give the impression that religious commitments are almost entirely a matter of family and cultural influences. There are at least two problems with this.

First, there is much more movement and change when it comes to worldview commitments than these statements suggest. One wonders where Hick got his figure of 99 percent, but surely this is a wild exaggeration. The amazing growth of Christianity throughout Asia, Africa, and Latin America in the past six decades; the significant increase in the numbers of nonreligious people worldwide; the numbers of Westerners converting to Islam or Buddhism; and the growth of new religious movements and hybrid forms of spirituality all demonstrate that religious identities are much more fluid than Hick and Runzo suggest. Religious commitments are not simply static products of one's environment. With migration, globalization, and evangelizing efforts on many fronts, religion and place cannot be so neatly aligned. Places that once were animistic or polytheistic now are Christian, while places that once were Christian now are Muslim.

Furthermore, as Alvin Plantinga points out in his response to Hick, the appeal to historical and cultural determinism has self-referential consequences: Hick's commitment to pluralism can also be attributed to the fact that he was born in a twentieth-century Western society.

> Suppose that we concede that if I had been born in Madagascar rather than Michigan, my beliefs would have been quite different. . . . But of course, the same goes for the pluralist. Pluralism isn't and hasn't been widely popular in the world at large; if the pluralist had been born in Madagascar, or medieval France, he probably wouldn't have been a pluralist. Does it follow that he shouldn't be a pluralist or that his pluralistic beliefs are produced in him by an unreliable belief-producing process? I doubt it.[54]

Although social location clearly does influence religious commitments, this should not be exaggerated.

More broadly, we can observe two problems with the pluralist appeal to culture to explain religious differences. First, if culture is to serve this explanatory

53. Runzo, "Pluralism and Relativism," 61–62.

54. Alvin Plantinga, "A Defense of Religious Exclusivism," in *The Rationality of Belief and the Plurality of Faith*, ed. Thomas D. Senor (Ithaca, NY: Cornell University Press, 1995), 211–12.

function, then there should be clearly identifiable and distinct cultures that can be mapped onto similarly identifiable and distinct religious beliefs and practices, which in turn define the various religions. In other words, historical and phenomenological investigation of religions should reveal a neat correlation between particular cultures and religious traditions, such that culture A is correlated with religious tradition A^*, culture B with religious tradition B^*, and so on. Belief in an eternal creator, for example, should be clearly linked to particular cultures, thus resulting in monotheistic traditions; and belief in sunyata (emptiness) linked to other cultures, resulting in Buddhist traditions; and belief in the Dao linked to yet other cultures, producing Daoist traditions; and so on. To the extent that differences in belief clearly correlate with distinct cultures, without significant overlap between different cultures and religions, then it could be promising to look at culture as a key variable in shaping religious disagreements. But if there is not such a neat correlation, then this becomes less plausible as an explanation for such differences.

The pluralist proposal, then, seems to presuppose that cultures are clearly identifiable and distinct entities, with clear boundaries that can be correlated in a one-to-one manner with distinct religious traditions. But, as we saw in chapter 1, this is a simplistic and misleading understanding of both cultures and religions. Cultures are fluid, with imprecise boundaries, so that it is often unclear where one culture begins and another ends. While some religious traditions are more closely linked to particular people and cultures than others (such as Shinto and the Japanese people), in general there is no clear alignment between particular cultures and religions. Buddhist beliefs and practices emerged in the same linguistic, social, and cultural setting of northern India that already included many varieties of Hinduism and Jainism. Many assumptions and practices were shared by Hindus, Jains, and Buddhists. And yet the teachings of the Buddha were quickly recognized as being sufficiently different in certain respects that bitter disputes arose between Brahmins, Buddhists, and Jains, with Buddhists being rejected by Brahmins as heretics. It is difficult to see how such disagreements in belief can be explained on the basis of historical and cultural variables when, apart from the controversial beliefs themselves, Hindus, Buddhists, and Jains shared many assumptions and practices. Much about the early history of religions is unclear and controversial; yet instead of a neat correlation between particular religious perspectives and particular cultures, what we see are diverse forms of theism, polytheism, pantheism, and animism scattered across geographical locations and cultures.

Furthermore, in appealing to cultural and historical factors to explain religious phenomena, pluralists can appear reductionistic. Peter Byrne acknowledges this problem and says that religious pluralism must define its commitment to the cultural basis of religious thought very carefully. It cannot, on pain of incoherence, ally itself to any doctrine affirming that all thought, or all religious thought, is through and through culturally relative or determined. It needs instead an account of how religious thought is culturally *limited* and hence relative *to a degree*. A more thoroughgoing relativism is out for two reasons. First, pluralism says of the major traditions that they make reference to a sacred, transcendent focus. They could not do that if human thought is too radically determined by its cultural background. The notions of reference and cognitive contact required to make sense of this affirmation demand an ability in human cognition to rise to some degree above its cultural background. Second, pluralism is a theory about the religions which itself claims to rise above the culturally set bounds of human thought. It would be unstatable and insupportable unless human thinking were capable of being detached to some degree from the restraints of cultural background.[55]

Both Hick and Byrne wish to maintain ontological realism, and thus religious beliefs and practices cannot be reduced merely to social or cultural factors. The religions are all, in their own ways, supposed to "point toward" or be "in touch with" an actual transcendent reality. Thus historical or cultural factors, while having some explanatory force, can never be sufficient to explain the particularities of religious phenomena. On a realist account, there will always be *something more* that transcends cultural influences and provides the "stuff" for the content of religious experience and belief.

What is the source of this "something more" that forms the content of religious belief and practice and is "filtered" through the contingencies of history and culture? Theistic religions appeal to divine revelation for this; nontheistic religious traditions typically locate it in the access to ultimate reality provided by mystical experience. In both cases there is said to be access to that which lies beyond cultural and historical influences. But Hick has ruled out both these options, since adopting either would privilege certain traditions over others.[56] There is no direct revelation from the Real to humankind, nor do mystical experiences provide direct access to the Real. What then, in his model, provides the "something more" that, when combined with local cultural and historical factors, results in the diverse beliefs of the religions? Hick provides no answer, apart from vague statements about the "universal presence" of the Real being "experienced in the various forms made possible by our conceptual-linguistic systems and spiritual practices" or the various religions embodying "different perceptions and conceptions of, and correspondingly different responses to,

55. Byrne, *Prolegomena to Religious Pluralism*, 22, with original emphasis.
56. See Hick, *Interpretation of Religion*, chap. 10.

the Real from within the variant ways of being human."⁵⁷ If the Real were
the God of theism, then it might make sense to think of the Real as revealing
himself to human beings in their historical and cultural contexts and to count
the differences in religions as being partially explained by historical and cultural contingencies. But if Hick made such a move, he would be abandoning
genuine pluralism and working within a broadly theistic framework. With
Hick's position, it is hard to see how culture can bear the explanatory burden
that his pluralist model demands.

Incoherence of Ineffability

In order not to privilege either personal or nonpersonal conceptions of the
religious ultimate, Hick insists that the Real transcends all concepts with which
we are familiar. But the appeal to ineffability vitiates the attempt to use the
Real as part of an explanation for religious phenomena; it is not surprising
that this aspect of Hick's model has been the subject of more criticism than
anything else.⁵⁸ Yet despite the criticism, in the introduction to the second edition
of *An Interpretation of Religion*, Hick continues to insist upon a strong sense
of ineffability with respect to the Real. The Real is "beyond the range of our
human conceptual systems" so that "we cannot apply [to the Real] literally the
attributes that we apply to its humanly thought and experienced forms, such
as being good, loving, powerful, just, etc."⁵⁹ Although Hick claims that "love
of one's fellow humans is, and hatred of them is not, an appropriate response
to the Real," nevertheless "it does not follow from this that the Real in itself
loves or is loving." Why not? "For love and hate, knowledge and ignorance,
wisdom and folly, being just and being unjust, etc., are attributes of persons,
and it is only by identifying the Real with a God made in our own image as a
person, but magnified to infinity, that we can attribute such qualities to it."⁶⁰
No substantial properties, positive or negative, can be applied to the Real.

Here are at least two significant problems. First, despite his claims about
ineffability, Hick repeatedly uses language presupposing that we *do* have some
positive understanding of the Real and that at least *some* concepts do apply

57. Ibid., xix, 240.

58. For criticism of Hick's notion of ineffability, see Keith Yandell, *Philosophy of Religion:
A Contemporary Introduction* (London: Routledge, 1999), 65–80; Alvin Plantinga, *Warranted
Christian Belief* (New York: Oxford University Press, 2000), 43–63; William Rowe, "Religious
Pluralism," *Religious Studies*, 35.2 (1999): 139–50; Keith Ward, "Truth and the Diversity of
Religions," *Religious Studies* 26.1 (March 1990): 2–11.

59. Hick, "Introduction to the Second Edition," *Interpretation of Religion*, xix–xx.
60. Ibid., xxiv.

meaningfully to the Real. For the Real is said to be the "source and ground of everything," a "transcendent reality," "the necessary condition of our existence and highest good," and "that to which religion is a response." It is also said to "affect humanity," to have a "universal presence," and so forth.[61] Such language clearly implies causality of some sort, but in using language suggesting that the Real is causally responsible for certain states of affairs, Hick is going well beyond what ineffability allows.[62] Despite efforts to depict the Real in terms that do not privilege any particular religious tradition, Hick tacitly assumes certain theistic characteristics of the Real (intentional action, creation, revelation) even as he states that no such attributes can apply to the Real.

Second, there is a fundamental inconsistency at the heart of Hick's model. Repeatedly Hick tells us that the Real itself is beyond moral categories such as good and evil.

> "Good" and "benign"—together with our other value terms—are human conceptions. They apply within human life, and they apply to the range of divine phenomena which we have ourselves partially constructed; but not to the ultimate noumenal reality in itself. Our human nature, with its range of concepts and languages, is such that *from our point of view* the Real, experienced in a variety of divine phenomena, is benign and good.[63]

And yet, as we have seen, Hick makes use of a moral criterion both as a reason for postulating the existence of the Real and for discriminating between authentic and inauthentic responses to the Real. But if the Real in itself is beyond moral categories so that it is neither good nor evil, how can moral transformation serve as a criterion for an appropriate relationship to the Real? Why suppose that the moral transformation of religious believers indicates that they are manifesting an appropriate dispositional response to the Real? Why presume that loving others is appropriate with respect to the Real but hating others is not? If the moral criterion is to be used in this manner, then the Real must itself be a moral Being characterized by moral properties such as love, goodness, justice, benevolence, and mercy. But characterizing the Real in this manner is to favor theistic over nontheistic understandings of the religious ultimate.

Does it make any sense to claim that there is a Real, but that no substantial properties with which we are familiar can apply to the Real? What would it mean for an entity to exist without it having *any* substantial properties? Why

61. See Hick, *Christian Theology of Religions*, 27, 60, 63, 67; idem, "Religious Pluralism," 221.
62. See Yandell, *Philosophy of Religion*, 71–72.
63. Hick, "Ineffability," 44, with original emphasis.

postulate such an entity in the first place? How does "There is an x, but x is such that no concepts of substantial properties can be ascribed to it" differ from "x does not exist"?

Postulation of an ineffable Real provides no help in providing an explanation of religious diversity. On Hick's terms, no causal properties can be ascribed to the Real. But if that is the case, then the existence of the Real cannot be used as part of a causal explanation for religious phenomena being what they are; and the Real cannot be causally responsible for religious experiences being what they are or for the moral transformation of religious believers. As Keith Yandell observes, "If one cannot in principle ascribe any property to x by virtue of which x can explain y, then positing x as an explanation of y is entirely vacuous—it offers a sham explanation." Religious pluralism "cannot ascribe to the Real any property by virtue of which positing it might explain anything whatever."[64]

Not surprisingly, then, some religious pluralists reject Hick's strict ineffability of the Real and contend that the religious ultimate must have a particular character such that at least some affirmations can be made of it and some religious interpretations accepted while others are rejected. Pluralists influenced by Christian theism apply attributes associated with God to the Real. Thus Robert McKim modifies Hick's proposal by suggesting that at least some substantive properties can be ascribed to the Real. McKim argues that we should think of the Real as a "morally positive" or "good Real," which can be characterized as "favourably disposed to altruism, or compassion or goodness."[65]

Keith Ward rejects the pluralistic model of Hick, with its insistence upon the ineffability of the Real. But he advocates what he calls "soft pluralism," the view that "the Real can manifest in many traditions, and humans can respond to it appropriately in them." Ward claims, "It is coherent to hold that there is a God who is infinite and beyond human comprehension in his essential nature, who discloses something of that nature, as it stands in relation to us, in many religious traditions."[66] Ward's pluralism has God, a Being with personal attributes and capable of revealing himself to humankind, as the religious ultimate to whom the various religions are responses. In *Concepts of God*, Ward looks at Hinduism, Buddhism, Judaism, Islam, and Christianity and argues for a "similarity in the basic structure of faith" in each. He calls this structural similarity "the iconic vision," central to which is "a dual aspect

64. Keith Yandell, *Philosophy of Religion*, 79. See also idem, "How to Sink in Cognitive Quicksand: Nuancing Religious Pluralism," in Peterson and VanArragon, *Contemporary Debates in Philosophy of Religion*, 197.
65. McKim, *On Religious Diversity*, 113–14.
66. Ward, "Truth and the Diversity of Religions," 16.

theism."[67] In light of this, he states, "It makes sense to say that the same God is worshiped in many diverse faiths."[68]

Some also propose that God or the religious ultimate might be understood as having many natures, or at least a complex nature, so that it might be experienced and described in both personal and nonpersonal categories. Robert McKim suggests that the Real might have many natures or a complex nature.[69] Similarly, Peter Byrne holds that the religious ultimate might be understood as "multiaspectual," so that "the Ultimate might be one while manifesting itself to human beings now as personal God or now as an impersonal absolute. This is the notion that the one transcendent, sacred reality is one but has many aspects."[70] The critical issue, however, is not simply whether the Ultimate can be described in personal and nonpersonal terms but whether its nature is such that both sets of properties can apply to the actual nature of the Real—such that it actually is both a personal Being and a nonpersonal entity or state. Although I cannot pursue this issue further here, it is far from clear that this is a coherent notion.

Two brief comments are in order with respect to theistic forms of pluralism. First, Ward's "iconic vision," which supposedly includes a rudimentary theism in Advaita Vedanta Hinduism and Shankara's teachings and in Buddhism as well, is certainly open to question. There are many theistic traditions that do have much in common. But it is problematic to maintain that Advaita Vedanta Hinduism and most forms of Buddhism are theistic since that is not how these religious traditions have been traditionally understood. And this leads to the second issue.

Theistic pluralism has abandoned the requirement that a genuinely pluralistic model not privilege any particular religious traditions. Ward's soft pluralism and McKim's "good Real" are both forms of theism maintaining that some personal attributes and agency apply to the religious ultimate: God. If one is to avoid the incoherence of Hick's proposal, something like this seems unavoidable. But this is not strict pluralism, as Buddhists, among others, will be quick to point out. It is a very open and generous form of theism. Hence the implication is that theistic forms of religion are more correct than nontheistic forms of religion, and while that is welcome news for theists, it is no longer genuine religious pluralism.

67. Keith Ward, *Concepts of God: Images of the Divine in Five Religious Traditions* (Oxford: Oneworld, 1998), vii–viii.

68. Ibid., 2. See also Keith Ward, "Pluralism Revisited," in *Religious Pluralism and the Modern World: An Ongoing Engagement with John Hick*, ed. Sharada Sugirtharajah (New York: Palgrave Macmillan, 2012), 58–67.

69. Robert McKim, *On Religious Diversity*, 120–23; idem, "Could God Have More Than One Nature?," *Faith and Philosophy* 5.4 (October 1988): 378–98.

70. Byrne, "Philosophical Approach," 38.

$$=== 6 ===$$

On the Idea of Christianity
as the One True Religion

The relation between the Christian faith and other religious traditions is often portrayed in terms of a competition in which Christianity, at least according to Christians, eventually supersedes other religions. The following statement made in 1896 by Judson Smith, a member of the American Board of Commissioners for Foreign Missions, expresses the perspective of many Christians on other religions:

> Missionaries do not aim to Americanize or Europeanize the people of the Orient, or to bring them under the political control of the great powers of the West or to impose our type of civilization upon them. . . . They have a deeper aim and address a more vital need; they seek to Christianize these peoples, to penetrate their hearts and lives with the truth and spirit of the Gospel, to enthrone Jesus Christ in their souls. . . . There is no faith which Christianity is not worthy to replace, which it is not destined to replace. It is not to share the world *with* Islam, or *with* Buddhism, or *with* any other religious system. It is the one true religion for man as man in the Orient and in the Occident, in the first century and in the twentieth century and as long as time shall last.[1]

1. Judson Smith, "Foreign Missions in the Light of Fact," *North American Review* (January 1896): 25; as quoted in Robert E. Speer, *The Finality of Jesus Christ* (New York: Revell, 1933), 161–62.

Although an important point is made here, I suggest that this is not the most helpful way to think about the matter.

The problem lies in a certain tension within Smith's statement between two different ways of thinking about Christianity. On the one hand, Judson Smith rightly acknowledges that the Christian gospel is a universal message, intended for all people at all times. Thus Christianity, along with Islam and Buddhism, is what Mark Juergensmeyer calls a transnational religion, which holds at its core the idea that it "is greater than any local group and cannot be confined to the cultural boundaries of any particular region." Christianity, Islam, and Buddhism have "universal pretensions and global ambitions," and "followers of each of these competitive global ideologies often regard their faith as intellectually superior to the others."[2] Furthermore, although written during the heyday of Western imperialism, Smith's comments are careful to distinguish the gospel of Jesus Christ from American and European cultures and to repudiate, at least in principle, the imposition of Western civilization upon other peoples. The common critique is that Christian missions is just another dimension of Western imperialism, and Smith rightly distinguishes Christian witness from "Americanizing" or "Europeanizing" other peoples.

At the same time, however, Judson Smith speaks not simply of the gospel but also of *Christianity* and other religions, and he sees the relation between them as one of competition and conflict. There is no room for accommodation between Christianity and Islam or Buddhism, for Christianity is to replace other religions. The reason for this is the fact that Christianity "is the one true religion" for all people at all times. The tension in Smith's statement is produced by the ambiguity in his use of the words "Christianity" and "Christianize." He disavows any intention of imposing European or American civilization upon others; so when he speaks of Christianity as the true religion that replaces other religions, he seems to be using "Christianity" as a synonym for the gospel of Jesus Christ. But religion includes the social, cultural, and historical patterns of religious communities so that in speaking of Christianity we cannot entirely separate the gospel from the lived realities of actual Christian communities in particular times and places. Thus, in speaking of Christianity as the one true religion, it is not clear whether Smith is referring to the core teachings of the Christian faith or to empirical Christianity, with all of its social and cultural accoutrements. This ambiguity makes talk of Christianity as the one true religion susceptible to unfortunate misunderstandings.

2. Mark Juergensmeyer, "Thinking Globally about Religion," in *Global Religions: An Introduction*, ed. Mark Juergensmeyer (New York: Oxford University Press, 2003), 7.

Most Christians assume that Christianity is the true religion, just as most Muslims consider Islam to be the true religion, and most Buddhists regard Buddhism as true. In so doing, they adopt what Peter Byrne calls a "confessionalist" approach to religions.[3] Confessionalists believe that with respect to truth, their own religion is superior to other religions. But just what does it mean to assert that a particular religion is true? In this chapter I will explore this question with reference to Christianity. Although I do think that, properly qualified, Christianity is the true religion, I will not be arguing for that here. My concern is with clarifying what is involved and what is not involved in making that claim.

We will begin by identifying two objections to the idea that there is one true religion. Some object to the belief that there is one true religion as a kind of absolutism that should be rejected because it leads to mistreatment of religious others and religious violence. The second objection comes from the fact that in speaking of one religion as true, we are ascribing superiority to that religion in terms of rationality, truth, goodness, or pragmatic effects. But, it is said, we cannot grade or evaluate religions in these ways, and thus it makes no sense to claim that one religion is true. After responding to these objections, we will examine Hans Küng's proposed criteria for determining truth in religion. The chapter will conclude with a discussion of the sense in which we might speak of Christianity as the true religion.

Religious Absolutism and Violence

Today it is widely assumed that one should reject the idea of one's own religion as true and others as false because such "exclusivism"[4] or "absolutism" (inevitably?) leads to terrible consequences. We are told that what fans the flames of religious tensions and violence is the mind-set that regards one's own religion as true and all others false and thus restricts salvation only to members of one's own religious group. Only if we get rid of this exclusivism and accept all religions (or at least all the "good" ones) as equally true can adherents of diverse religions live together peaceably, we hear. Atheist critics of religion such as Sam Harris, Christopher Hitchens, and Richard Dawkins

3. Peter Byrne, "A Philosophical Approach to Questions about Religious Diversity," in *The Oxford Handbook of Religious Diversity*, ed. Chad V. Meister (New York: Oxford University Press, 2010), 36.

4. The terms "exclusivism" and "exclusivistic," unless carefully defined, are problematic because they are used in such different ways. See Harold A. Netland, "Religious Exclusivism," in *Philosophy of Religion: Classic and Contemporary Issues*, ed. Paul Copan and Chad V. Meister (Oxford: Blackwell, 2008), 67–80.

routinely castigate religions for supposedly causing wars and conflicts around the globe.[5] But even those sympathetic to religion often blame the belief that there is only one true religion as promoting tensions and violence. Charles Kimball, for example, attributes part of the cause for religious violence today to the exclusivistic and absolutist mind-set that regards its own perspective as true and all others to be false.[6] John Hick states, "The Catholic theologian Hans Küng has said that there will never be peace between the nations until there is peace between the religions. And I would add that there will never be genuine peace between the religions until each comes to recognize the equal validity of the others."[7] We will examine both Hick's and Küng's views more fully below.

But consider also the words of the Tenzin Gyatso, the fourteenth Dalai Lama, as he eloquently pleads for religious unity in *Toward a True Kinship of Faiths*.[8] In 1959 the Dalai Lama was exiled from Tibet because of Chinese persecution and since then has been based in Dharamsala, India, traveling worldwide as a spokesperson for the Tibetan people and advocate of religious harmony.[9] He speaks passionately of "the challenge of peaceful coexistence" among religions, which "will define the task of humanity in the twenty-first century." Although past history is littered with "conflicts generated by religious differences," in our globalized world "harmony between the world's religions is one of the essential preconditions for genuine world peace."[10] Therefore "the challenge before religious believers is to genuinely accept the full worth of faith traditions other than one's own. This is to embrace the spirit of pluralism." According to the Dalai Lama, exclusivistic mind-sets, assuming that "one's own religion [is] the only legitimate faith" and that other religions are evil and false, are obstacles to peaceful coexistence with religious others.[11]

---

5. Sam Harris, *The End of Faith: Religion, Terror, and the Future of Reason* (New York: Norton, 2004); idem, *Letter to a Christian Nation* (New York: Knopf, 2006); Christopher Hitchens, *God Is Not Great: How Religion Poisons Everything* (New York: Twelve Books, 2007); Richard Dawkins, *The God Delusion* (New York: Houghton Mifflin, 2006).

6. Charles Kimball, *When Religion Becomes Evil: Five Warning Signs* (New York: HarperCollins, 2002), chap. 2.

7. John Hick, *Who or What Is God?* (London: Seabury, 2009), 74.

8. His Holiness the Dalai Lama, *Toward a True Kinship of Faiths: How the World's Religions Can Come Together* (New York: Doubleday Religion, 2010).

9. See The Dalai Lama, *Freedom in Exile: The Autobiography of the Dalai Lama* (New York: HarperCollins, 1990).

10. The Dalai Lama, *Toward a True Kinship of Faiths*, x.

11. Ibid., ix. In the case of the Dalai Lama, we see once again how contact with Theosophists influenced a prominent modern religious leader. The Dalai Lama credits an early encounter with the Theosophical Society in 1956 in Chennai (then Madras) with helping him move away from an exclusivistic attitude and toward a more pluralistic perspective on other religions:

Christian theologian Miroslav Volf also emphasizes the importance of religious harmony and links agreement with religious others to peaceful co-existence:

> Muslims and Christians will be able to live in peace with one another only if (1) the identities of each religious group are respected and given room for free expression, and (2) there are significant overlaps in the ultimate values that orient the lives of people in these communities. These two conditions will be met only if the God of the Bible and the God of the Qur'an turn out to embody overlapping ultimate values, that is, if Muslims and Christians, both monotheists, turn out to have a "common God."[12]

Volf's comments are made in the context of an important discussion of similarities and differences between the Islamic and Christian concepts of God. His concern is to find common ground with Muslim understandings and thereby overcome the legacy of animosity and antagonism between Muslims and Christians. This is clearly an important objective, and there is much that is laudable in Volf's discussion, although his conclusions are problematic in some respects.[13] The crucial point for our purposes is Volf's claim that Christians and Muslims can only live together peacefully if they have a "common God," that is, if they can be said to worship the same God. The implication

---

There I was first directly exposed to people, and to a movement, that attempted to bring together the wisdom of the world's spiritual traditions as well as science. I felt among the members a sense of tremendous openness to the world's great religions and a genuine embracing of pluralism. When I returned to Tibet in 1957, after more than three months in what was a most amazing country for a young Tibetan monk, I was a changed man. I could no longer live in the comfort of an exclusivist standpoint that takes Buddhism to be the only true religion. (ibid., 6)

12. Miroslav Volf, *Allah: A Christian Response* (New York: HarperCollins, 2011), 8–9.

13. For a critical assessment, see Gerald McDermott and Harold A. Netland, *A Trinitarian Theology of Religions: An Evangelical Proposal* (New York: Oxford University Press, 2014), chap. 2. The question whether Muslims and Christians worship the same God is complicated and must be unpacked carefully. Since there can be only one eternal creator God who has created everything apart from God, both Christians and Muslims can be said to denote the same Being when they speak of God. But Muslims and Christians have quite different views on the nature of God, and thus their concepts of God are not the same. See Lamin Sanneh, "Do Christians and Muslims Worship the Same God?," *Christian Century* 121.9 (May 4, 2004): 35–36; J. Dudley Woodberry, "Do Christians and Muslims Worship the Same God?," *Christian Century* 121.9 (May 4, 2004): 36–37; Jacob Neusner, Baruch A. Levine, Bruce D. Chilton, and Vincent J. Cornell, *Do Jews, Christians and Muslims Worship the Same God?* (Nashville: Abingdon, 2012); Miroslav Volf, ed., *Do We Worship the Same God? Jews, Christians, and Muslims in Dialogue* (Grand Rapids: Eerdmans, 2012); Timothy C. Tennent, *Theology in the Context of World Christianity: How the Global Church Is Influencing the Way We Think about and Discuss Theology* (Grand Rapids: Zondervan, 2007), 25–51.

is that if the concepts of God in Islam and Christianity turn out to be irreconcilable, then peaceful relations are impossible.

This is a strong assertion, but why assume it is true? Is it really the case that we can only get along with those with whom we agree? What then are the prospects for irenic relations between Christians and Buddhists or secular atheists, both of whom deny the reality of a creator God? Is it not rather a mark of maturity to be able to live harmoniously with those with whom we have deep disagreements? Surely a more realistic and responsible approach is to learn to respect deep differences where they occur and to live together in peace despite these disagreements. A strong commitment to respecting religious others and to working together with those from other religions for the common good does not require minimizing or ignoring the very real differences in the basic teachings of the religions.

Moreover, the relation between religious belief and violence is considerably more complicated than these critiques suggest. Let us focus on the claim that one's own religion is correct, and since this perspective is often labeled "exclusivism," let us have E stand for the following:

E = My own religion is true and all others are false.

The critic asserts that acceptance of E by religious believers leads to religious bigotry, tensions among religious communities, and religious violence, and that therefore E should be rejected. Several comments are relevant here.

First, suppose that the critic is correct and there is a clear, demonstrable link between religious communities maintaining E and these communities then treating religious others in inappropriate ways, including violence and even wars. This would indeed be a sad state of affairs and would reflect badly on religious believers who think their own religious views are correct and others are not. But undesirable as this might be, it does not necessarily follow that there is no one true religion or that religious believers are mistaken or epistemically unjustified in maintaining E. Deplorable as it may be, this would be another case in which true beliefs have highly negative consequences. (The belief that if I refuse to eat anything, I will eventually die, is both true and has unfortunate consequences.) Unless one adopts a pragmatic definition of truth, the truth of a belief must be distinguished from the consequences of the belief.

But why should we accept the critics' assertion that affirming E results in religious violence? To be sure, there is plenty of evidence that religious believers have engaged in violence against others and that religious commitments played some role in this. History is replete with tragic examples of brutal wars between religious communities, and religious institutions have persecuted those who do not submit to their authority. Sadly, the cynical quip is only too apt: "Oh, how we hate one another for the love of God!" Religious violence runs across most religious traditions. Christians slaughtered Jews and Muslims; Muslims in turn massacred Christians and Jews. Muslims and Hindus have fought bitterly in the Indian subcontinent. Baha'is have faced systematic persecution from Muslims. Buddhists attack Hindus and Muslims in Southeast Asia. As Os Guinness wryly observes, "Much of the world can agree on this with no further argument: bad religion is very bad indeed."[14]

While it is clear that religion often has been involved in violence, what is less apparent is the nature of such involvement and the degree to which distinctively religious factors are responsible for the violence. Several complicated questions need to be sorted out. As we have seen, religion is a multifaceted phenomenon, and religious elements are often intertwined with social, economic, political, and ethnic considerations so that identifying the cause of a particular instance of violence as distinctively religious can be a daunting task.[15] What is required to sustain the critics' thesis is identifying causal factors as distinctively religious—and not social, ethnic, political, or economic—and establishing a clear link between these religious factors and acceptance of E.[16] We must also remember that much violence is not linked to religion, so for religious "absolutists" to be picked out as especially problematic, it also must be established that religious communities accepting E engage in violence to a significantly greater degree than do other religious and nonreligious communities. This empirical question would be very difficult to answer definitively. But it is worth observing that in the twentieth century it was not religious regimes but rather atheistic or nonreligious totalitarian regimes that were responsible for the tragic genocides. While religious violence is an urgent issue that demands the attention of leaders from all religions, I am not persuaded that claiming there is a true religion should be abandoned because of the dire consequences that supposedly flow from it.

14. Os Guinness, *The Global Public Square: Religious Freedom and the Making of a World Safe for Diversity* (Downers Grove, IL: InterVarsity, 2013), 23.

15. See Joshua C. Thurow, "Religion, 'Religion,' and Tolerance," in *Religion, Intolerance, and Conflict*, ed. Steve Clarke, Russell Powell, and Julian Savulescu (New York: Oxford University Press, 2013), 146–62.

16. The amount of literature on religious violence is enormous, but helpful discussions include Mark Juergensmeyer, *Terror in the Mind of God*, 3rd ed. (Berkeley: University of California Press, 2003); idem, *Global Rebellion: Religious Challenges to the Secular State, from Christian Militias to Al Qaeda* (Berkeley: University of California Press, 2008); William T. Cavanaugh, *The Myth of Religious Violence* (New York: Oxford University Press, 2009); Bryan Rennie and Philip L. Tite, eds., *Religion, Terror and Violence* (London: Routledge, 2008); Keith Ward, *Is Religion Dangerous?* (Grand Rapids: Eerdmans, 2006).

John Hick on Grading Religions

In asserting that there is one true religion, we are making a comparative judgment about religions. We are claiming that one religion is clearly superior to the rest with respect to truth. But can we do so? We examined John Hick's views on religious pluralism in chapter 5, but here we will focus on how he discusses the possibility of "grading" or evaluating religions.

Hick acknowledges that it makes no sense to regard all religious teachings and practices as equally valuable or respectable. In ordinary life we make distinctions between what is morally repugnant (human sacrifice, child prostitution in temples) and what is praiseworthy (humility, compassion, caring for the poor and vulnerable) in the religions. Great religious leaders typically are reformers, rejecting immoral or evil practices. Hick observes that "some kind of assessing of religious phenomena seems to be a corollary of deep religious seriousness and openness to the divine."[17]

But how should we assess religions? Religions are vast, complex systems of intellectual, social, and religious traditions. How can we take Christianity as a whole and compare it with Hinduism? Hick proposes two criteria for such evaluation: reason applied to the teachings of particular religions, and moral judgment applied to the historical outworking of those teachings.[18] But while rational assessment of the teachings of the religions is possible, Hick maintains that this is inconclusive. Each major religion has its own impressive intellectual system, and it does not seem possible to demonstrate that one is clearly superior to the rest. "I doubt whether the great enduring systems of Thomas Aquinas, al-Ghazali, Shankara, and Buddhaghosa can realistically be graded in respect of their intellectual quality. They seem, broadly speaking, to be equally massive and powerful systematisations of different basic visions."[19] Hick maintains that pervasive religious ambiguity prevents us from showing one religion as more likely to be true than the others on the basis of rational considerations.

What about the moral criterion? Here again, Hick claims that although in principle it is possible to grade religions on moral grounds, in practice this becomes problematic. Drawing upon observations from his own experience, Hick states, "Coming to know both ordinary families, and some extraordinary individuals, whose spirituality has been formed by these different traditions and whose lives are lived within them, I have not found that the people of the world religions are, in general, on a different moral or spiritual level

17. John Hick, *Problems of Religious Pluralism* (New York: St. Martin's Press, 1985), 67.
18. Ibid., 79.
19. Ibid., 81.

from Christians. They seem on average to be neither better nor worse than the Christians."[20] Hick acknowledges that this judgment is personal and anecdotal. "We can only go on personal observation and the reports of others, both contemporary and historical, and on this basis form a global impression, though one that we cannot claim to prove." Indeed, how could one possibly assess the moral quality of believers in all the major religious traditions over the past centuries, compare them objectively, and determine which tradition, if any, produces a greater number of saints?

> My own global impression, based inevitably on having known a limited number of families and individuals and having read a limited amount of history and travelers' accounts, is that the virtues and vices seem to be spread more or less evenly among human beings, regardless of whether they are Christians or—to confine ourselves for the moment to the "great world religions"—Jews, Muslims, Hindus (including Sikhs), or Buddhists.[21]

What about evaluating the cultures and civilizations associated with particular religions? Hick admits that in principle we should be able to rank religions on the basis of their moral contribution to society, but in practice an objective assessment along these lines proves to be impossible.

> How are we to weigh the lethargy of many Eastern countries in relation to social and economic problems, so that they suffer from endemic poverty, against the West's ruthlessly competitive greed in the exploitation of the earth's resources— the Western capitalist rape of the planet at the expense of half the world and of all future generations? How are we to weigh the effect of Hindu and Buddhist "otherworldliness" in retarding social, economic and technological progress against the use of the Christian Gospel to validate unjust social systems in Europe and South America, and to justify and perpetuate massive racial exploitation in South Africa? How are we to weigh the unjust caste-system of India against the unjust class-system and pervasive racism of much of the Christian West? How do we weigh the use of the sword in building great Muslim, Hindu and Buddhist empires against the use of the gun in building great Christian empires? How do we weigh the aggressive Muslim incursion into Europe in the fourteenth century against the previous Christian incursion into the Middle East known as the Crusades? How do we weigh the hideous custom of the "voluntary" burning of widows (suttee) in India against the equally hideous burning of "witches" in Christian Europe and North America? How do we weigh the savage aspects

---

20. John Hick, "A Pluralist View," in *Four Views on Salvation in a Pluralistic World*, ed. Dennis L. Okholm and Timothy R. Phillips (Grand Rapids: Zondervan, 1996), 39.
21. Ibid., 40–41.

of life in some Eastern and Middle Eastern countries—the bloody massacres at the time of the partition of India, the cutting off of a thief's hands under Islamic law—against the Christian persecution of the Jews throughout the ages and above all in our own century?[22]

Hick concludes, "Whilst we can to some extent assess and grade religious phenomena, we cannot realistically assess and grade the great world religions as totalities. For each of these long traditions is so internally diverse, containing so many different kinds of both good and evil, that it is impossible for human judgment to weigh up and compare their merits as systems of salvation."[23] Nevertheless, Hick maintains that, as far as we can tell, the great religions "are equally productive of that transition from self to Reality which we see in the saints of all traditions."[24]

Hick raises important points. One need not accept his pluralistic assumptions in order to agree that many adherents of other religious traditions (as well as explicit atheists) lead morally exemplary lives, and surely we must rejoice whenever and wherever we find examples of moral virtue. Hick is also correct in recognizing the difficulty of evaluating the complex historical legacies of religious civilizations, including the Christian-influenced societies of the West. Sadly, the empirical record of Christians throughout the past two millennia is mixed, with Christians being responsible for not only much good but also much evil and suffering.

Nevertheless, several points should be registered. Hick readily admits the impressionistic and anecdotal nature of his judgment about the rough parity of moral virtue among the religions. Others might have quite different impressions based on *their* experiences, with one or another religion seeming to exemplify significantly higher instances of saintliness. Impressionistic observations from one's own experience are inherently limited, subjective, and unreliable, thus providing an insufficient basis for sweeping generalizations.

Furthermore, is it really the case that empirical evidence does not support the claim that some religious traditions have been more beneficial to human flourishing than others? It is one thing to maintain that the empirical track record of all religions is mixed, containing both good and evil. But it is something else again to insist that no meaningful comparisons across religious traditions can be made.

Notice that Hick's contention actually presupposes that responsible assessment across religions is possible and that we can conclude on the evidence that

22. Hick, *Problems of Religious Pluralism*, 84–85.
23. Ibid., 86.
24. Ibid., 87.

the religions are roughly equal in their historical record. But how does Hick know this? If grading of religions is indeed as inconclusive as he claims, then we should remain agnostic and not assert that the religions are all basically equal in this regard. While doing so is difficult and controversial, it seems that *some* comparative assessment of the historical impact of the religions is possible and that this might well result in one or more religions having a stronger record than others.

Finally, why should we accept Hick's claim that rational considerations leave the major religions in basically the same position with respect to truth? As we saw in the previous chapter, a crucial part of Hick's model of religious pluralism is his notion of religious ambiguity. If Hick is correct, then no particular religious worldview can be judged more reasonable or more likely to be true than any other. But if a strong version of religious ambiguity is rejected, as I believe it should be, then it is possible that one religious worldview can be shown to be rationally superior to others. We will revisit this issue in chapter 7.

Hans Küng on True Religion

The Roman Catholic theologian Hans Küng (b. 1928) has also addressed the question of evaluating religions in terms of truth. Küng's commitment to ecumenical relations and interreligious dialogue is well known. Yet he also sees clearly that we cannot ignore the thorny issue of truth in religions.

> The confrontation between the world religions goes beyond the issue of peace. It calls decisively for a clarification of the *question of truth*. Much as the material analysis of the various religions, much as comparison of religions can make convergencies and divergencies apparent, the question of the truth must still be raised continually and inexorably. Is there one true religion or are there several? Is there a system of criteria for justifying the claims to truth of the individual religions?[25]

If we are to take the religions seriously, we cannot avoid the question of truth.

Küng rejects both an arrogant absolutism claiming "Only my religion is true and all others are false" and a simplistic pluralism insisting "All religions are equally true." While he is uncomfortable with a strictly pragmatic criterion

25. Hans Küng, "Is There One True Religion? An Essay in Establishing Ecumenical Criteria," in *Christianity and Other Religions: Selected Readings*, ed. John Hick and Brian Hebblethwaite, rev. ed. (Oxford: Oneworld, 2001), 119. See also idem, "What Is True Religion? Toward an Ecumenical Criteriology," in *Toward a Universal Theology of Religion*, ed. Leonard Swidler (Maryknoll, NY: Orbis Books, 1987), 237–50.

for evaluating the religions, he proposes that we link the idea of the truth with that of the goodness of a religion.

> The question of the truth of any religion aims at more than pure theory. The nature of truth is never established only in systems of true statements about God, man and the world, never only in a series of propositional truths, as opposed to which all others are false. Truth is always at the same time also a *praxis*, a way of experience, enlightenment and proven worth, as well as of illumination, redemption and liberation. If, accordingly, religion promises an ultimate, all-encompassing sense of our living and dying, if it proclaims supreme, indestructible values, sets up unconditionally binding standards for our acting and suffering and provides a spiritual home, then this means: The dimensions of the *True* (*verum*) and the *Good* (*bonum*), of the meaningful and the valuable, overflow into one another in religion; and the question of the truth (understood more theoretically) or meaningfulness of religion is at the same time the question of its goodness (understood more practically) or valuableness. A "true" Christian or Buddhist is the "good" Christian or Buddhist. To that extent the question "What is true and false in religion?" is identical with the other, "What is good and what is bad in religion?"[26]

For Küng, then, the question of the truth of a religion is inseparable from the sense of meaning that a religious community derives from the religion, the goodness and value in the religion, or the degree to which religious adherents embody and live out the positive elements of the religion in real life.

Küng suggests three criteria that can be applied in assessing religions for truth. The first is a general ethical norm based on our common humanity, which stipulates, "Man should live in a human, not an inhuman, fashion; he should realize his humanness in all his relationships." According to Küng, this criterion has both a positive and a negative expression. Positively, "Insofar as a religion serves the virtue of humanity, insofar as its teachings on faith and morals, its rites and institutions *support* human beings in their human identity, and allows them to gain a meaningful and fruitful existence, it is a *true* and *good* religion." Put negatively, "Insofar as a religion *spreads inhumanity*, insofar as its teachings on faith and morals, its rites and institutions hinder human beings in their human identity, meaningfulness, and valuableness, insofar as it *helps to make them fail to achieve* a meaningful and fruitful existence, it is a *false* and *bad* religion."[27]

Küng also offers a general religious criterion: "A religion is measured . . . by its *normative doctrine or practice* (Torah, New Testament, Qur'an, Vedas) and

26. Küng, "Is There One True Religion?," 129.
27. Ibid., 134, with original emphasis.

sometimes too by its normative *figure* (Christ, Muhammad, the Buddha)."[28] Each religion has a set of normative standards by which the teachings and practices of the religious community are to be evaluated. This criterion assesses the degree to which adherents of a religion are faithful to their own internal normative ideals. According to this criterion, "a religion is true and good if and insofar as it remains true to its own *origin* or *canon*; its authentic 'essence,' its normative scripture or figure, which it continually invokes."[29]

Finally, Küng proposes a specifically Christian criterion, which maintains that "a religion is true and good if and insofar as it allows us to perceive the spirit of Jesus Christ in its theory and practice." This criterion is first applied directly to Christianity, "posing the self-critical question whether and to what degree the Christian religion is at all Christian." Küng suggests that this criterion can also be applied indirectly to other religions, as we try to discern "whether and to what degree one also finds in other religions (especially Judaism and Islam) something that we would label Christian."[30] In speaking of the truth of Christianity, Christians must speak from within the perspective of their existential commitment to Jesus Christ as their Lord.

> Thus I profess my faith in my historically conditioned standpoint; this one religion is *for me the true religion* for whose truth I can cite good reasons, that may possibly convince others. For me Christianity is the path that I take, the religion in which I believe I have found the truth for my living and dying. Still at the same time it is true that *other* religions (which for hundreds of millions of persons are the *true* religion) are for that reason *still in no way untrue religions*, are by no means simply untruth.[31]

Jesus Christ is an appropriate criterion for Christians to use in assessing other religions because "Jesus Christ is for Christians the *deciding regulative factor*."[32]

So we have three criteria: (1) A general ethical criterion: Does the religion enhance human flourishing? (2) a general religious criterion: Is the religion consistent with its own internal normative ideals? and (3) a religion-specific criterion, as for Christians: Does the religious tradition enable us to perceive the "spirit of Jesus Christ"?

Where does this leave us? Küng distinguishes an "outer" perspective on the question of truth from an "inner" perspective. "Seen from *without*, viewed by the history of religion, there are *various true religions*: religions that, with all

28. Ibid., 136, with original emphasis.
29. Ibid., 138, with original emphasis.
30. Ibid.
31. Ibid., 139–40, with original emphasis.
32. Ibid., 139, with original emphasis.

their ambivalence, at least fundamentally meet the governing criteria (ethical and religious)." Many religions can be true to the extent that they meet the first two criteria. But, "seen from *within*, from the standpoint of a believing Christian oriented on the New Testament, *the true religion for me*, inasmuch as it is impossible for me to follow all ways at the same time, is the way I attempt to go: Christianity, insofar as it bears witness in Jesus to the one true God."[33] The third criterion is necessarily person-relative and determines a religion to be true for the believer from the perspective of the believer.

Religions can be evaluated in many ways, and Küng's criteria are helpful for certain purposes. For example, there can be value in asking whether a given religion, either in its ideals or its practice, promotes our common humanity or our "humanness." Or again, there can be value in asking whether a particular religious tradition is indeed faithful to its normative origin or canon. And certainly each religious tradition has its own internal criteria for authenticity or faithfulness, so that as a Christian I can ask whether I am living in accordance with "the spirit of Christ."

But do these criteria really help us to determine whether a religion is true? Küng's general ethical criterion, which stipulates that religions are "true" to the extent that they promote and foster our basic humanness, is too vague to be helpful. What does it mean to "live in a human fashion" and to "support human beings in their human identity"? What constitutes "fruitful and meaningful existence"? The meaning of these phrases is spelled out somewhat in Küng's other writings, where prominence is given to modern liberal values concerning individual liberties and basic human rights.[34] Küng might well be correct in emphasizing these values and criticizing religions that fail to support them, but using this as a criterion for assessing religions in terms of truth requires further justification. Why these values and not others? Not all religions share Küng's commitments to individual liberty and human rights. Moreover, religions such as Christianity, Hinduism, and Buddhism have fundamentally different ways of understanding what it means to be authentically human, with their perspectives being rooted in the particular religion's understanding of the nature of the human person, the person's relation to what is religiously ultimate, and the ensuing implications for how we are to live in relation to others. On those issues the religions provide quite different perspectives. So as it stands, the general criterion is of little use in determining which religion, if any, is true.

33. Ibid., 138–40, with original emphasis.
34. See, e.g., Hans Küng, *A Global Ethic for Global Politics and Economics* (New York: Oxford University Press, 1998); idem, ed., *A Global Ethic* (New York: Continuum, 2006).

Moreover, by linking the question of truth with the question of the goodness or utility of a religion, Küng conflates issues that are best kept separate. Whether the teachings of a religion are true is distinct from whether there is goodness or moral value in the religion, and both of these issues should be distinguished from the question of whether a religion has existential meaning or practical benefits for its adherents. Even if the central teachings of a religion are false, there might still be goodness and moral value in some of its teachings, practices, and institutions. A religion that provides no benefits for its adherents, that does not give any sense of meaning or purpose, will not long survive. But a religion can provide practical benefits or exhibit goodness and beauty even if its central claims about humankind and the religious ultimate are false.

Küng's second and third criteria are also not particularly helpful when it comes to determining whether a given religion is true. The second criterion merely assesses the degree to which a religious community is living out the ideals of its own religion, which by itself tells us nothing about the truth or falsity of those normative ideals. And while there might indeed be value, from a Christian perspective, for a criterion that considers the extent to which "the spirit of Jesus Christ" is manifest in the lives of Christians, it is hard to see how this helps resolve the question of whether there is one true religion. This is a criterion for evaluating the lives of Christians and the degree to which they reflect Christ's teachings and model, but it does not by itself inform us of the truth or falsity of these teachings.

Can there be one true religion? Two objections to answering this in the affirmative have been considered and found problematic. We also examined Küng's proposed criteria for identifying a religion as true and found them to be unhelpful. Yet I see no reason to conclude that there cannot be one true religion. In what follows, I will focus on Christianity and ask what is involved in the claim that Christianity is the true religion. While this might seem like a simple and straightforward question, it is more complex than might be assumed. It will be helpful to begin by clarifying what is *not* included in the assertion that Christianity is the one true religion.

What Is *Not* Involved in Making the Claim

First, the question of whether Christianity is the one true religion must be distinguished from the question of whether there is truth or goodness in other religions. Some Christians believe that if they hold that Christianity is the one true religion, then it follows that there cannot be *any* truth or goodness in other religions, that other religions are nothing but falsehood and evil.

But there is no reason to adopt such an extreme position. Nothing in the Christian Scriptures demands such a position; one can be entirely faithful to the biblical witness and still acknowledge that there is some truth, beauty, and goodness in other religions. To deny this is to commit oneself to the view that *all* of the claims of all other religions are false. But this is hardly defensible. A religion teaching that the universe was created by God is teaching the truth, even if there might be significant differences between that religion and Christianity on their respective understandings of the nature of God. Similarly, if a religion teaches that there is life after physical death and the destruction of the body, it is teaching truth, although the particular manner in which such life after death is construed (e.g., realization of unity with Brahman) may not be true. If the Christian faith is indeed true, then any teachings from other religions that are incompatible with essential teachings of Christianity will be false or incomplete. But this does not mean that there are *no* truths embraced by other religions. The Christian faith actually shares some significant common beliefs with other religions, though more so with some religions than others. Similarities with other religious teachings are perhaps most apparent in basic moral principles. Ronald Green states,

> One of the most striking impressions produced by comparative study of religious ethics is the similarity in basic moral codes and teachings. The Ten Commandments of Hebrew faith, the teachings of Jesus in the Sermon on the Mount and of Paul in his epistles, the requirements of *sadharana*, or universal dharma, in Hinduism (*Laws of Manu* 10.63), Buddhism's Five Precepts, and Islam's Decalogue in the Qur'an (17:22–39) constitute a very common set of normative requirements. These prohibit killing, injury, deception, or the violation of sacred oaths. C. S. Lewis has called basic moral rules like these "the ultimate platitudes of practical reason," and their presence and givenness in such diverse traditions supports his characterization.[35]

Moreover, maintaining that some of the central beliefs of other religions are false and that other religions sometimes manifest terrible evils is compatible with acknowledging that there is also goodness in the lives of religious others and that there is beauty in other religious traditions. Religions, including

35. Ronald Green, "Morality and Religion," in *The Encyclopedia of Religion*, ed. Mircea Eliade (New York: Macmillan, 1987), 10:99. The reference to C. S. Lewis is to his *Abolition of Man* (New York: Macmillan, 1947), 56–57. Lewis provides examples of moral injunctions from Hinduism, Jainism, Buddhism, and Zoroastrianism (95–121).

empirical Christianity as it has been lived out throughout history, manifest both goodness and evil.

Nor, in claiming that the Christian faith is true, am I suggesting that Christians are necessarily morally better people than Muslims or Hindus or Sikhs. By simply observing the lives of religious believers on an empirical level, surely we must admit that there are good and evil persons in all religions, including among those who claim to be Christian. John Hick rightly reminds us of the tragic blemishes in the Christian record and the moral ambiguities in the lives of Christians. The claim that Christianity is the true religion does not commit one to defending everything that the institutional Christian church has done or advocated over the past two millennia. Sadly, much in the history of the Christian church betrays the teachings of Jesus Christ, and there is no reason for Christians to pretend otherwise. On occasion the institutional church has taught what is false and done what is immoral. Although Christians have been responsible for much good and for powerful movements of social reform throughout the world, they have also badly mistreated others, engaged in shameful and evil behavior, and misused Scripture to justify such abuses.[36]

The claim that Christianity is the true religion should not result in religious elitism or in withdrawing from pursuit of the common good for all. Nor does it imply that Christians should not cooperate with other religious communities in working to eradicate the many problems plaguing our world. To the contrary, leaders of the major religions, especially Christians, must work together to reduce conflict between religious communities, promote justice for all, and enable all to have at least the minimal requirements for sustainable life. Nothing in this chapter should be taken as detracting from the urgency of such interreligious cooperation.

Finally, in speaking of the truth of Christianity, one must also distinguish the issue of truth from the question of salvation. Some Christians are hesitant to speak of truth in other religions for fear that this will lead either to the view that salvation is equally available in all religions or to the conclusion that all people will ultimately be saved. While the concern is legitimate, one must treat each issue responsibly on its own terms and not conflate questions. To affirm that Christianity is the true religion does not, by itself, commit one to any

36. What is needed here is a candid and fair assessment of the complex legacy of institutional Christianity and individual Christians throughout history. An interesting area of recent research is the effect of Protestant missionary efforts on the worldwide development and spread of democratic values and practices, including religious liberty and social reforms. See Robert D. Woodberry, "The Missionary Roots of Liberal Democracy," *American Political Science Review* 106.2 (May 2012): 244–74. For a perceptive analysis of the relation between democracy and religion in different religious and cultural settings, see Ian Buruma, *Taming the Gods: Religion and Democracy on Three Continents* (Princeton: Princeton University Press, 2010).

particular view about the extent of salvation—an issue over which Christians, including evangelicals, disagree.[37] But this question is distinct from that of the truth of central Christian claims. There is no logical connection between the assertion that Christianity is the true religion and any particular view of the extent of salvation.

For example, no doubt most who believe that Christianity is the true religion also believe that ultimately not everyone will be saved. This has historically been the dominant position among Christians. Yet some believe that Christianity is true but also embrace soteriological universalism. Conversely, while it might well be true that most religious pluralists are also universalists, since they hold that ultimately all people will attain the desired soteriological state, there is nothing about religious pluralism as such that requires universalism. Religious pluralism maintains that the major religions are roughly equal with respect to truth and soteriological efficacy, and thus it affirms equal soteriological access among the religions. But it is compatible with this to maintain that, despite such equality of access, relatively few people will actually attain the desired soteriological goal. Thus questions about the extent of salvation must be addressed separately from the issue of the truth of Christian theism itself.

What Does It Mean for a Religion to Be "True"?

What then do we mean when we say that a religion is true? In chapter 5 I argued that religious truth must include the notion of propositional truth, so that truth in religion, as in other domains, is a property of propositions or beliefs or statements. In other words, truth and falsity in religion are properties of religious claims or teachings. A religious claim is true if the state of affairs to which it refers is as the claim asserts it to be. If the state of affairs is as the teaching asserts, then it is true; if not, it is false. Whether we know the truth or falsity of the claim is a separate matter. Thus, "God created the universe" is true if and only if God created the universe. "The Buddha

---

37. See, e.g., Clark Pinnock, *A Wideness in God's Mercy: The Finality of Jesus Christ in a World of Religions* (Grand Rapids: Zondervan, 1992); John Sanders, *No Other Name: An Investigation into the Destiny of the Unevangelized* (Grand Rapids: Eerdmans, 1992); Millard Erickson, *How Shall They Be Saved? The Destiny of Those Who Do Not Hear of Jesus* (Grand Rapids: Baker, 1996); John Sanders, ed., *What about Those Who Have Never Heard? Three Views on the Destiny of the Unevangelized* (Downers Grove, IL: InterVarsity, 1995); Christopher W. Morgan and Robert A. Peterson, ed., *Faith Comes by Hearing: A Response to Inclusivism* (Downers Grove, IL: InterVarsity, 2008); McDermott and H. Netland, *Trinitarian Theology of Religions*, chap. 4.

attained enlightenment under the Bodhi tree" is true if and only if the Buddha attained enlightenment under the Bodhi tree. "Muhammad is the final
prophet" is true if and only if Muhammad is the final prophet.

Truth or falsity applies to particular religious claims or teachings. But what
does it mean for a *religion* to be true? Throughout this book we have emphasized the multidimensional nature of religion, as religions include much more
than simply religious teachings or beliefs. Religions are complex systems,
including not only teachings or doctrines but also institutions, social patterns
of behavior, ethical norms, rituals, physical objects, stories or narratives, experiences, saints or religious exemplars, and so on. Moreover, the major world
religions are vast systems that include within them many diverse traditions
or schools, not all of which are even mutually compatible. Consider, for example, the enormous variety of traditions that fall under the general category
of Hinduism or Christianity. Religions also change in important respects over
time, so that in some cases it is difficult to see how a later tradition is at all in
continuity with earlier ones. All of this makes it difficult or even misleading
to speak of the truth or falsity of a particular religion.

Theologian and philosopher Keith Ward suggests that given the diverse and
multidimensional nature of religions, we should avoid speaking about whether
a religious tradition as a whole is true and focus instead on the truth or falsity
of particular truth claims advanced by a religion. Use of the term "religious
tradition," with its close cultural and social affiliations, is especially problematic since it does not seem like the kind of thing that can be true or false.

> Viewed as social phenomena, religious traditions are forms of life which are
> culturally and ethnically differentiated. Since they contain many possibilities of
> diverse interpretation, and many dimensions of significance, it becomes appar-
> ent that a person will usually belong to such a tradition by birth, and can find
> within it many resources of meaning and moral teaching. As it seems absurd
> to say that one culture is "true" and all others "false," so the use of the expres-
> sion "religious tradition" subtly leads one to say that one cannot compare such
> traditions for truth; and that therefore one is not to be preferred to the others,
> except as an expression of cultural imperialism.[38]

Ward observes that we can, however, inquire about the truth of particular
religious teachings or claims. Thus he urges that when we consider questions
of truth in religion, we "refrain from speaking of religio-cultural traditions,
with all the problems of boundary-definition that brings with it, and to insist
on focusing on particular truth-claims, and on particular interpretations of

38. Keith Ward, "Truth and the Diversity of Religions," *Religious Studies* 26.1 (March 1990): 4.

them, which can be properly assessed for truth and falsity."[39] Instead of asking about the truth of Hinduism or Islam, then, we should consider the truth of religious assertions such as "This life is one of a long series of past and future lives" or "Allah revealed the contents of the Qur'an to Muhammad."

Ward is onto something significant here. Speaking of the truth of a religious tradition is problematic since the term "religious tradition" draws upon the multidimensional nature of religions and their close relationship with broader social and cultural phenomena. It is important to keep the sociocultural dimensions in mind, since religions involve more than just systems of doctrines. But to the extent that we think of religions in these multidimensional terms, it becomes difficult to speak of truth in religion since truth does not apply to social institutions or cultural patterns of behavior as such. It does not make sense to speak of the truth or falsity of a particular culture or ritual, whereas we can and do speak of the truth or falsity of religious claims.

Furthermore, religious traditions are part of much larger systems or collectives, so we can speak of a variety of religious traditions within a larger religion. Religions such as Hinduism, Buddhism, Islam, and Christianity are large families, including many distinct and diverse traditions. When the differences among these internal traditions become sufficiently pronounced, questions about the legitimate boundaries of a religion arise, with ongoing disputes among insiders over what is acceptable and what is unacceptable. This, then, makes talk of *the* truth of Christianity or Islam, without qualification, problematic: Whose version of Christianity? Which kind of Islam?

Thus Ward's suggestion is helpful and important. In asking about truth in religion, we should focus primarily upon the truth value of particular religious claims or teachings. While I agree with this, I do not see how we can completely avoid assessing religions in terms of truth. Here it is helpful to recall Keith Yandell's characterization of religions and religious truth in terms of the medical analogy of diagnosis and cure. "A religion proposes a diagnosis of a deep, crippling spiritual disease universal to non-divine sentience and offers a cure. A particular religion is true if its diagnosis is correct and its cure efficacious. The diagnosis and cure occur in the setting of an account of what there is—an account whose truth is assumed by the content of the diagnosis and cure."[40] Religious claims about diagnosis and cure do not appear in isolation; they are part of a broader interconnected web of beliefs that form a particular way of understanding ourselves, the world, and what is religiously

39. Ibid.
40. Keith Yandell, "How to Sink in Cognitive Quicksand: Nuancing Religious Pluralism," in *Contemporary Debates in Philosophy of Religion*, ed. Michael L. Peterson and Raymond J. VanArragon (Oxford: Blackwell, 2004), 191.

ultimate. Believers are expected to accept these teachings as true and to live in accordance with them in ordinary life.

Religious communities advance certain claims and reject others. Buddhists, for example, assert that there is no enduring substantial soul, but Hindus and Jains insist that there are souls. While we can consider the truth of the Buddhist claim about no souls by itself for certain purposes, the teaching on anatman (no self) is part of a larger metaphysical set of issues that bear directly upon how a Buddhist is to live in this life and (hopefully) eventually attain nirvana. Disagreements over the nature of the soul are embedded within other issues; so a Buddhist, who denies the reality of the soul, is not merely disagreeing with Hindus on that particular question but also embracing a different vision of reality and consequently adopting a different way of living. If, by contrast, the Advaita Vedantin Hindu is correct about the essential identity between the soul and Brahman, then the Buddhist is mistaken on a number of interrelated issues, and following the Noble Eightfold Path is pointless. In other words, core religious claims do not stand in isolation but are related to other beliefs that, when taken together, entail certain ways of understanding reality and patterns of living as desirable. When these beliefs and normative expectations are acted upon by particular communities of believers, the various dimensions of religion cohere in the more or less integrated systems that we refer to as the religions. To the extent that certain claims are essential to a particular religious system, we, in affirming the truth of these claims, are also by implication identifying the accompanying way of understanding reality and pattern of living as correct and appropriate. In this sense we can speak of the religion as true. So although in a basic sense particular religious claims or teachings are true or false, there is also a derivative sense in which we can speak of a religion as true. A religion is true to the extent that its core claims are true.

Does this mean that *every* claim made by a religion must be true if the religion is true? Different sects or traditions within a major religion disagree over some teachings, so presumably not all claims made by adherents of a particular religion can be true. Here we must distinguish between beliefs or teachings that are essential to a religion and those that are not. Not all teachings are equally important within a religion. Some are relatively insignificant, and adherents of a religion might disagree among themselves over the truth of such beliefs. Protestant Christians, for example, disagree over the proper form of baptism, and Buddhist traditions disagree over whether monks should be celibate. But in neither case are these disagreements over what would be regarded as core or essential beliefs.

Other beliefs, however, are much more significant, and some beliefs are so important that one cannot be an adherent of that religion in good standing

while rejecting them. William Christian speaks of these as *primary beliefs*.[41]
We might also think of them as *defining beliefs* since they define what is regarded as essential to the worldview of the religion in question. Let us think of a defining belief as follows:

Defining beliefs: *p* is a defining belief of a given religion *R* if and only if being an active participant in good standing within *R* entails acceptance of *p*.

Determining just which beliefs are defining beliefs is often a controversial matter: adherents of a religion sometimes disagree sharply among themselves over the question. That religious insiders do regard some beliefs as defining beliefs for their religion seems clear, even if they might disagree with other insiders over precisely what is to be included in this set. Furthermore, in many cases we can identify at least *some* defining beliefs even if we cannot provide an exhaustive list of such beliefs. For example, belief that Allah has revealed his will for humankind in the Qur'an would seem to be a defining belief of Islam. It is hard to imagine someone who explicitly denies this claim being acknowledged as a Muslim. Similarly, belief in an eternal God who created the universe is generally accepted as a defining belief of Christianity. Belief that the Buddha attained enlightenment and thereby became aware of the causes of suffering is usually taken as a defining belief of Buddhism. What matters here is not unanimity among *all* Muslims or Christians or Buddhists on these examples (Is there complete agreement on any really significant issue?) but rather that most who are regarded as mainstream Muslims, Christians, or Buddhists would accept them.

I suggest that we speak of a religion as true if and only if its defining beliefs are true. For Christianity to be true, then, the defining beliefs of Christianity must be true. If they are true, then Christianity is true; if they are false, then Christianity is false. There is an important ambiguity in the term "Christianity" as used in the above sentences. In speaking of the defining beliefs of Christianity, I am using "Christianity" in both a descriptive and a normative or ideal sense. On the one hand, I am speaking of the empirical tradition stemming from Jesus Christ and the early disciples in Jerusalem around AD 30 and then expanding globally to include diverse communities of Jesus's followers over the past twenty centuries around the world. Here the concern is with what mainstream Christians throughout the centuries have regarded as essential to the Christian faith. But I am also using "Christianity" in a

41. William A. Christian Sr., *Doctrines of Religious Communities: A Philosophical Study* (New Haven: Yale University Press, 1987), 1–2, 5–11.

normative or ideal sense to indicate what communities of Christians *should* be like—in particular, what beliefs about God and Jesus should shape Christians' thinking and conduct. The history of Christianity can be seen as the story of the ongoing tension between what is taken as normative, the gospel of Jesus Christ as revealed in the Scriptures, and the actual positive and negative realities of Christian communities in particular places and times, living out the ideals of the gospel.

Defining Beliefs of Christianity

Are there defining beliefs of Christianity? Is there a set of beliefs that all, or at least most, Christians would, or should, acknowledge as essential to authentic Christianity? An enormous diversity of perspectives fall under the rubric of Christianity. In addition to the general divisions into Roman Catholic, Eastern Orthodox, and Protestant streams—and the many variations within each—there are the new expressions of Christianity in Asia and Africa not directly connected with the traditional divisions. There is also the significant divide that runs across the major divisions, separating theologically liberal from theologically traditional or conservative understandings of Christian teachings. What beliefs, if any, do all these groups have in common?

Given such diversity, one option is to abandon talk of the truth of Christianity as such and speak rather of the truth or falsity of particular kinds of Christianity: Vatican II Roman Catholicism, liberal Protestantism, evangelical Christianity, and so forth. The defining beliefs of a particular form of Christianity would then need to be identified, and the question becomes whether these particular beliefs are true or false. Some forms of Christianity might be true but others not.

Another option is to acknowledge the enormous variety on many issues among Christians throughout the past twenty centuries, while seeking to identify some core affirmations that most, if not necessarily all, Christians accept. This is a minimalist approach that is concerned with what is at the heart of the Christian faith and not with secondary or tertiary issues over which Christians often disagree. In broad terms I will suggest how this second approach might proceed.

The heart of the Christian faith is the gospel or good news of Jesus Christ. The term "gospel" has become a shorthand way of referring to the total redemptive work of Jesus Christ. Thus The Cape Town Commitment from the Third Lausanne Congress on World Evangelization in Cape Town, South Africa, October 2010, states, "The gospel announces as good news the historical events of the life, death and resurrection of Jesus of Nazareth. As the Son of David, the promised Messiah King, Jesus is the one through whom alone God has established his kingdom and acted for the salvation of the world, enabling all nations on earth to be blessed, as he promised Abraham."[42]

We might also think of the apostle Paul's statement in 2 Corinthians 5:19 that "God was reconciling the world to himself in Christ" as an expression of the heart of the Christian message. Here we have a concise statement of a dominant theme throughout the New Testament, and it is difficult to imagine a tradition that is identifiably Christian while also flatly rejecting this theme. Paul's statement must be understood within the broader context of biblical thought and presupposes certain beliefs about a holy and righteous God; human sin and the need for reconciliation with God; the life, death, and resurrection of Jesus of Nazareth; and Jesus's relationship with God. So while "God was reconciling the world to himself in Christ" can be taken as a concise statement of the central message of Christianity, it must be understood within a broader set of beliefs that provide its meaning and significance. Moreover, the statement itself has certain entailments, such as "God exists" and "Reconciliation with God comes through Jesus Christ." If Paul's statement is accepted as a partial expression of what is at the heart of the Christian faith, then some of the beliefs that inform his statement or are entailed by it can be considered essential or defining beliefs of Christianity.

Let us assume, then, that 2 Corinthians 5:19 expresses a basic Christian theme that must be reflected in any set of defining beliefs of Christianity. The following statements are derived from the broader biblical themes that inform the meaning of Paul's statement, and thus they can be understood as being among the defining beliefs of Christianity:

1. God the creator, who created everything apart from God and is morally pure and righteous, exists.
2. Human beings and the world have become alienated from God through sin.
3. It is through Jesus Christ that the world, including sinful humanity, can be reconciled to God.

Although beliefs 1–3 are not explicitly stated in 2 Corinthians 5:19, when this text is taken within the broader context of the Second Letter to the Corinthians and of the canonical Scriptures as a whole, it is clear that these

42. *The Cape Town Commitment: A Confession of Faith and a Call to Action; The Third Lausanne Congress*, Didasko Files (Peabody, MA: Hendrickson, 2011), I.8.B, p. 23, http://www.lausanne.org/en/documents/ctcommitment.html.

statements (or something like them) are presupposed. It makes sense, then, to treat these as among the defining beliefs of Christianity. If they and any other defining beliefs are true, then Christianity is true. If they are false, then Christianity is false.

Can there be more than one true religion? Even if the defining beliefs of Christianity are true, is it possible that the defining beliefs of another religion are also true? The answer depends in part upon how broadly or narrowly we understand "religion." If, for example, we adopt the first option above and think in terms of multiple Christianities, then the question is whether there can be more than one version of Christianity with true defining beliefs. If, for example, Protestant Methodism and Greek Orthodoxy are regarded as different religions, and not simply as distinct Christian traditions, then the issue is whether they have mutually compatible and true defining beliefs. If so, then it makes sense to speak of them both as true religions.

Yet in speaking of religions, we usually do not have in mind particular traditions such as Methodism or Greek Orthodoxy but rather world religions such as Hinduism or Buddhism or Islam. Can any of these religions be true if Christianity is true? The issue here is whether it is plausible to hold that the defining beliefs of Christianity and Hinduism, Buddhism, or Islam are all compatible. I think not. If the core teachings of these religions are taken as they are understood within their own traditions—and given the diversity within Hinduism, it is difficult to identify a set of core claims that all Hindu traditions embrace—then it is implausible to maintain that there are two or more religions with true defining beliefs. For at crucial points each religion affirms what others deny and denies what others affirm. Some religions teach the existence of an eternal creator God, while others deny this; and none of the other religions accepts the central Christian teachings concerning Jesus Christ, which have traditionally been at the heart of the Christian faith. Although some other religions might affirm defining beliefs 1 and 2, only Christianity accepts 3 as a core belief.

Jesus

To say that Jesus Christ is central to the Christian faith is to state the obvious. Paul's statement in 2 Corinthians 5:19 points to the centrality of Jesus Christ for Christianity. Christians have traditionally maintained that God was present and active in Jesus of Nazareth in a way in which God is not present in anyone else. The early Christian community regarded Jesus not just as a great teacher and leader but also, in a mysterious sense, as one who is somehow to be identified with God. This was eventually clarified in creedal statements as Jesus being God incarnate, fully God and fully man. Belief in Jesus as Lord and Savior, fully God and fully man, has thus been regarded by Christians as an essential tenet of orthodox Christianity.

But although all Christians today would surely agree that Jesus Christ is central to the Christian faith, not all accept the teaching that Jesus was in fact God incarnate, fully God and fully man. Nor do all Christians accept the idea that Jesus is the only Lord and Savior for all people. Christology is in ferment today, with widely divergent perspectives about the nature and significance of Jesus being bandied about. Speaking of the many revision-ist Christologies and the implications of these debates for the theology of religions, theologian Carl Braaten observes, "We are facing a conflict in Christology as great as the ancient controversies over the three persons of the Godhead (Nicaea) and the two natures of Christ (Chalcedon)." The critical issue is this: "Does Jesus model the salvation that God is working universally through all the religions? Or is what happens in Jesus the sole constitutive cause of the salvation that God delivers to the world?"[43] The mainstream, orthodox Christian tradition has consistently maintained the latter, although during the twentieth century the former interpretation became increasingly accepted in theologically liberal circles. However, the debate over Christol-ogy among Christian theologians today should not be allowed to obscure the fact that for centuries there has been remarkable consensus concerning the deity and humanity of Jesus Christ.

The significance of the issue was acknowledged by the pluralist John Hick, who admits that if the traditional understanding of Jesus as God incarnate, fully God and fully man, is correct, then Christianity is the one true religion.

Traditional orthodoxy says that Jesus of Nazareth was God incarnate—that is, God the Son, the Second Person of a divine Trinity, incarnate—who became man to die for the sins of the world and who founded the church to proclaim this to the ends of the earth, so that all who sincerely take Jesus as their Lord and Savior are justified by his atoning death and will inherit eternal life. It fol-lows from this that Christianity, alone among the world religions, was founded by God in person. God came down from heaven to earth and launched the salvific movement that came to be known as Christianity. From this premise it seems obvious that God must wish all human beings to enter this new stream of saved life, so that Christianity shall supersede all the world faiths. . . . [Since] Christianity alone is God's own religion, offering a fullness of life that no other

---

43. Carl Braaten, *No Other Gospel! Christianity among World Religions* (Minneapolis: Fortress, 1992), 8.

tradition can provide, it is therefore divinely intended for all men and women without exception.[44]

As we have seen, Hick rejects the orthodox understanding of the incarnation and deity of Jesus Christ in favor of a metaphorical view that regards Jesus as one among many great religious leaders. But Hick correctly sees that if the traditional, orthodox view is correct, then Jesus cannot be regarded as just one great religious leader among many others: God was present and active in Jesus of Nazareth in an utterly unique way.

Although we cannot discuss the biblical material here in any depth, I think it is clear that the New Testament consistently presents Jesus Christ as the unique incarnation of God, the only Lord and Savior for all humankind. Jesus is not portrayed as simply one among other great religious figures. The Gospel of John identifies Jesus with the preexistent Word (the Logos), who "was with God and . . . was God" and through whom "all things were made," and then asserts that "the Word became flesh and made his dwelling among us" (John 1:1–4, 14). The Letter to the Hebrews states, "In the past God spoke to our ancestors through the prophets at many times and in various ways, but in these last days he has spoken to us by his Son, whom he appointed heir of all things, and through whom also he made the universe" (Heb. 1:1–2). The incarnation forms the apex of God's self-revelation to humankind.[45]

Throughout the New Testament writings, sometimes explicitly and often implicitly, the human person Jesus is placed in an unprecedented relationship of identity with Yahweh, the everlasting creator God who revealed himself to the patriarchs and prophets of the Hebrew Scriptures. Jesus is presented as claiming the authority to do things that only God can do, such as forgive sins (Mark 2:5–11); judge the world (Matt. 19:28; 25:31–46); give life, even to the dead (John 5:21, 25–29; 11:17–44); and speak authoritatively for God in interpreting the purposes of the Sabbath (Mark 2:23–27). Jesus states that anyone who has seen him "has seen the Father" (John 14:9)—a remarkable claim in the context of Jewish monotheism. Jesus identifies himself with the "I AM" of Exodus 3:14 and in so doing is understood to be identifying himself with God (John 8:58). The apostle Paul asserts that all of the "fullness" (*plērōma*)

44. John Hick, "A Pluralist View," in *Four Views on Salvation in a Pluralistic World*, ed. Dennis L. Okholm and Timothy R. Phillips (Grand Rapids: Zondervan, 1996), 51–52.

45. For helpful discussions on the incarnation, see *The Incarnation*, ed. Stephen T. Davis, Daniel Kendall, and Gerald O'Collins (New York: Oxford University Press, 2002); Oliver D. Crisp, *Divinity and Humanity: The Incarnation Reconsidered* (Cambridge: Cambridge University Press, 2007); T. V. Morris, *The Logic of God Incarnate* (Ithaca, NY: Cornell University Press, 1986); Simon Gathercole, *The Preexistent Son: Recovering the Christologies of Matthew, Mark, and Luke* (Grand Rapids: Eerdmans, 2006).

of God is present in the human person of Jesus: "In Christ all the fullness of the Deity lives in bodily form" (Col. 1:19; 2:9).

Appealing to biblical texts in this manner presupposes, of course, that the New Testament writings are reliable in their portrayal of the life and teachings of Jesus of Nazareth. Questions concerning the historical Jesus and the reliability of the biblical accounts are complex; while I am fully aware of the critical issues involved, I am also convinced that there are good reasons to accept the reliability of the New Testament portrayal of Jesus and the early Christian community.[46]

It is sometimes said that Jesus himself never taught anything like the orthodox Christian teaching on the incarnation and that this was a later doctrinal innovation of the Christian church. Sometimes a parallel with developments in Buddhism is affirmed. For example, many maintain that although Gautama was originally regarded by his followers merely as an extraordinary human being who attained enlightenment, over several centuries he gradually came to be understood within Mahayana traditions as an almost deified figure, part of the Trikaya (Three Bodies of the Buddha), the human manifestation of the dharmakaya (Buddha essence). So too, we are told, although Jesus was originally understood by his followers to be just a good teacher and perhaps even the Messiah, over time he became revered as more than merely a man. Under the influence of Greek metaphysics, Christians came to think of him as Son of God, then as God the Son, and finally in terms of the sophisticated trinitarian formula as the Second Person of the Holy Trinity. This parallel is suggested by John Hick:

> Gautama was a human teacher, though one who had attained perfect enlightenment and who accordingly spoke with the authority of firsthand knowledge. After his death he was spoken about in the developing Buddhist literature in exalted terms, frequently as the Blessed One and the Exalted One. Stories of his many previous lives became popular, and legend attributed to him a supernatural conception, birth and childhood. . . . The later Mahayana doctrine of the Trikaya is comparable with the Johannine doctrine of the Logos and its

46. For helpful discussion, see N. T. Wright, *The New Testament and the People of God*, vol. 1 of *Christian Origins and the Question of God* (Minneapolis: Fortress, 1992); idem, *Jesus and the Victory of God*, vol. 2 of *Christian Origins and the Question of God* (Minneapolis: Fortress, 1996); Richard Bauckham, *Jesus and the Eyewitnesses: The Gospels as Eyewitness Testimony* (Grand Rapids: Eerdmans, 2006); Larry Hurtado, *Lord Jesus Christ: Devotion to Jesus in Earliest Christianity* (Grand Rapids: Eerdmans, 2003); Paul Rhodes Eddy and Gregory A. Boyd, *The Jesus Legend: A Case for the Historical Reliability of the Synoptic Jesus Tradition* (Grand Rapids: Baker Academic, 2007); Mark Allan Powell, *Jesus as a Figure in History*, 2nd ed. (Louisville: Westminster John Knox, 2013).

development of the incarnation idea. As Jesus was the incarnation of the pre-existent Word/Son, who was of one substance with the Father in the eternal Trinity, so Gautama was the earthly manifestation of a heavenly Buddha, and all the Buddhas are one in the ultimate reality of the eternal Dharmakaya. Thus, the developed Buddhology of the Mahayana, some five centuries after the death of Gautama, parallels the developed Christology that reached its completion at the fifth-century Council of Chalcedon.[47]

According to Hick, the Christian teaching on the deity of Jesus Christ is the product of a long evolutionary process similar to the process in Buddhism that produced the view of the exalted Buddha in Mahayana.

There is much that should be said in response to this claim, but we will limit ourselves to just one major point distinguishing Jesus from Gautama. Given the significant time gap between the life of Gautama and the earliest Pali writings, and the gap between the earlier Theravada traditions and the later Mahayana teachings on the Trikaya, it does make sense to think in terms of gradual progression within Buddhist traditions on the nature and significance of Gautama. Depending on the dates accepted for his death, there is a gap of some 300 to 400 years between the death of Gautama and the writing of the earliest Pali texts, and the Mahayana texts with the exalted views of the Trikaya come even later.[48]

But the case of Jesus and the New Testament is quite different. While some development in christological understanding within the New Testament writings themselves can be discerned, the "high Christology" that identifies Jesus with God the creator is actually found in the earliest evidence we have of Christian belief and practice. It cannot be explained as an innovation by the Christian church several centuries later.

All the writings of the New Testament were completed by about AD 90 (many of them considerably earlier); thus at most there is a gap of some sixty years between the death of Jesus in AD 30 or 33 and the completion of the New Testament. This is insufficient time for a radical evolution from the view of Jesus as just a great leader to that of his being God the creator become man. New Testament scholar C. F. D. Moule insists that the claim that such "high" Christology evolved from a primitive "low" Christology by a gradual process over time does not fit the data. To the contrary, he argues, the transition from invoking Jesus as revered Master to the acclamation of him

47. John Hick, *Disputed Questions in Theology and the Philosophy of Religion* (New Haven: Yale University Press, 1993), 47.

48. See Keith Yandell and Harold A. Netland, *Buddhism: A Christian Exploration and Appraisal* (Downers Grove, IL: InterVarsity, 2009), 10–15, 200–201, 206–9.

as divine Lord is best understood as a development in understanding according to which "the various estimates of Jesus reflected in the New Testament [are], in essence, only attempts to describe what was already there from the beginning. They are not successive additions of something new, but only the drawing out and articulating of what is there." As Moule claims, "Jesus was, *from the beginning*, such a one as appropriately to be described in the ways in which, sooner or later, he did come to be described in the New Testament period—for instance, as 'Lord' and even, in some sense, as 'God.'"[49] Some of the most elevated Christology and clearest affirmations of the deity of Christ are in the Pauline Epistles, widely accepted as the earliest documents in the New Testament (cf. Rom. 9:5; Phil. 2:5–11; Col. 1:15–17, 19; 2:9). Similarly, Martin Hengel argues that the title Son of God is not a late accretion to Christology but rather was already applied to Jesus before AD 50.[50]

In this connection it is especially helpful to consider the devotional practices of the early Christians, which were already in place when the New Testament was being written. Larry Hurtado demonstrates that worship of Jesus is presupposed by the earliest New Testament writings; thus the practice of early followers (most of whom were Jewish) worshiping Jesus as divine must be even earlier than these writings.[51] Hurtado shows that within the first couple of decades of the Christian movement, between roughly AD 30–50, "Jesus was treated as a recipient of religious devotion and was associated with God in striking ways."[52] He emphasizes the fact that "the origins of the worship of Jesus are so early that practically any evolutionary approach is rendered invalid as historical explanation. Our earliest Christian writings, from approximately 50–60 CE, already presuppose cultic devotion to Jesus as a familiar and defining feature of Christian circles wherever they were found (1 Cor. 1:2)."[53]

Not only was this devotion to Jesus very early, and thus not a product of extraneous influences in a later stage of development, but it also "was exhibited in an unparalleled intensity and diversity of expression, for which we have no true analogy in the religious environment of the time." Furthermore, Hurtado maintains, "This intense devotion to Jesus, which includes reverencing him as

49. C. F. D. Moule, *The Origin of Christology* (Cambridge: Cambridge University Press, 1977), 2–4, with original emphasis.
50. Martin Hengel, *The Son of God: The Origin of Christology and the History of the Jewish-Hellenistic Religion* (Philadelphia: Fortress, 1976), 2, 10.
51. Larry W. Hurtado, *One God, One Lord: Early Christian Devotion and Ancient Jewish Monotheism* (Philadelphia: Fortress, 1988); idem, *Lord Jesus Christ: Devotion to Jesus in Earliest Christianity* (Grand Rapids: Eerdmans, 2003); idem, *How on Earth Did Jesus Become a God? Historical Questions about Earliest Devotion to Jesus* (Grand Rapids: Eerdmans, 2005).
52. Hurtado, *Lord Jesus Christ*, 2.
53. Hurtado, *How on Earth Did Jesus Become a God?*, 25.

divine, was offered and articulated characteristically within a firm stance of exclusivist monotheism, particularly in the circles of early Christians that anticipated and helped to establish what became mainstream (and subsequently, familiar) Christianity."[54] Significantly, the ascription of deity to Jesus did not include a modification of Jewish monotheism. As Richard Bauckham argues, it involved "identifying Jesus directly with the one God of Israel, including Jesus in the unique identity of this one God."[55] So the claim that the belief in Jesus as God incarnate is a later development—akin to the exaltation of Buddha found in Mahayana Buddhism—is untenable given the high Christology evident in the earliest strands of the New Testament writings.

54. Hurtado, *Lord Jesus Christ*, 2–3.
55. Richard Bauckham, *Jesus and the God of Israel* (Grand Rapids: Eerdmans, 2008), 3.

7

Religious Diversity
and Reasons for Belief

I t is easy to assume that awareness of religious diversity is a new phenomenon and that, before the late twentieth century, people in Europe and
North America were not bothered by the encounter with religious others.
In fact, however, the European voyages of discovery in the sixteenth and seventeenth centuries stimulated enormous interest in the peoples of the New
World, and reports about the different beliefs and customs of those in Asia,
the Americas, and Africa fostered relativism and skepticism concerning the
truth of the Christian religion.

Among those troubled by these issues was the great chemist and philosopher
Robert Boyle (1627–91). A devout Christian, Boyle wrote an essay in which he
addresses a concern expressed by a friend: given the many different religions in
the world with their competing claims, is not the wisest course to refrain from
embracing any particular religion as true? In "De diversitate Religionum" (On
the diversity of religions), Boyle responds by arguing that "a wise Christian
should not be disturbed by the number and diversity of religions."[1] But Boyle
was well aware of the force of the skeptical challenge presented by religious
diversity, which he expresses as follows:

1. Robert Boyle, "De diversitate Religionum," in *The Works of Robert Boyle*, ed. Michael
Hunter and Edward B. Davis (London: Pickering & Chatto, 2000), 14:237.

In other words, if we observe how many nations there are in the world, with so many millions of men in them divided into the four great sects, namely Christians, Jews, Mohammedans and pagans, each of which is subdivided into several different systems of belief, and if we now further consider with what assurance each one puts faith in its own religion and cause—if, says [the critic], we bear these things in mind, then no man of prudence or moderation will imagine that, surrounded by such a variety of opinions and warring sects, each with learned men amongst its followers, he is at all likely to embrace the one and only true religion, especially when everyone maintains that his religion is true, and all acknowledge that there is only one true one while some suspect that none is wholly true.[2]

Boyle lived at a time and place in which most people accepted Christianity as the true religion. But religious skepticism and relativism were increasingly attractive options for many, and Boyle clearly sensed the plausibility of the challenge posed by religious disagreement. Travis Dumsday explains the quandary:

At the root of the question is how one can rationally affirm the Christian faith in the midst of skeptical worry arising from diversity. Boyle's concern lies not in why God would allow diversity, or in how exactly salvation is played out in such a world, but rather in how anyone could rationally believe himself correct in choosing a particular religion—in Boyle's case Christianity—when faced with such a vast throng of competitors.[3]

This is an issue that resonates with many today. In light of religious disagreement, can one have confidence that one's own religious convictions are true and that beliefs incompatible with them are false? How does one determine which religion, if any, is true? For his part, Boyle responds by arguing that, in Dumsday's words, "despite all of these difficulties, it is both possible and a moral necessity to conduct a proper, objective enquiry into religious truth. And if one does so, the result will be that Christianity emerges as the most plausible faith."[4] Boyle contends that Christians can have confidence that the Christian faith is true despite awareness of rival claims, appealing to the

2. Ibid., 237–38.

3. Travis Dumsday, "Robert Boyle on the Diversity of Religions," *Religious Studies* 44 (2008): 318.

4. Ibid., 320. Not all were as confident as Boyle. Jean Bodin (1530–96) was deeply troubled by religious conflict in Europe and well aware of the different religious traditions outside Europe. In his *Colloquium of the Seven about Secrets of the Sublime* (1593, but not published until 1857), seven men—a Catholic, a Calvinist, a Lutheran, a Muslim, a Jew, and two persons not identified with any religion—engage in a vigorous dialogue over religious disagreement and truth. When a Christian participant asks, "Who can doubt that the Christian religion is the true religion or rather the only one?" the answer from another (no doubt representing Bodin) exposes the

sublime nature of Christian ethical teachings ("the holiness of the doctrine itself") and the evidence of biblical miracles to show the superiority of Christianity to other religions.

Today we are even more aware than Boyle of the bewildering variety of religious claims; the pervasive contemporary skepticism about religion is due in no small measure to such disagreement. In chapter 6 I argued that, properly qualified, we can think in terms of there being one true religion and that, if the defining beliefs of Christianity are true, then Christianity is the true religion. But given religious diversity and disagreement, is it reasonable to believe that Christian theism is true?

Epistemological questions concerning religious diversity can be framed in various ways. Our concern is with a particular question: *Given the many religious and nonreligious worldviews available today, why should one accept the central claims of Christian theism as true?* To be sure, this is not the only question worth addressing, nor is it even the most significant one. But it is an increasingly pressing issue, both for Christian believers and for those considering whether to become Christian. The question can be asked from the perspective of either a committed Christian or someone who is not a believer. For the Christian, the issues concern whether awareness of religious diversity and disagreement call into question epistemic justification for the Christian's beliefs about the unique truth of Christian claims. Does the Christian need to provide appropriate evidence to support core Christian beliefs, justifying their acceptance in spite of religious disagreement?

What about the person who has no religious commitments at this point but is considering whether to embrace Christian claims? Should awareness of religious disagreement be factored into that decision-making process? Or consider the committed Muslim who hears a carefully reasoned presentation of the Christian gospel, including evidence in support of the deity of Jesus Christ. Should such awareness of disagreement and new evidence challenging Islamic commitments affect the justification of the Muslim's beliefs?

These are not merely academic questions. Ordinary people regularly evaluate alternative perspectives and make choices. Baptists become Buddhists, atheists convert to Baha'i, Hindus become Roman Catholics, and Mormons turn into agnostics. People do make judgments about whether it is reasonable to accept the teachings of one or another religion. Some conclude that the claims in question "make sense," and they become committed believers; others regard the claims as fantastic or lacking in rational support and reject religious

problem: "Almost the whole world." As quoted in J. Samuel Preus, *Explaining Religion: Criticism and Theory from Bodin to Freud* (New Haven: Yale University Press, 1987), 3.

beliefs. Some committed believers lose confidence in the truth of what they profess and either abandon their commitments or continue to participate in religious activities while no longer believing the religious teachings. There is much religious mobility in many directions; although rational consideration of religious claims is not always a factor in such decisions, in many cases it is.

Religious disagreement produces what Peter Byrne calls "peer conflict."[5] But it is not just disagreement by itself that causes the problem. As Robert McKim observes,

> It is not just the fact that there are diverse beliefs that is striking: it is the fact that wise people who think carefully and judiciously, who are intelligent, clever, honest, reflective, and serious, who avoid distortion, exaggeration, and confabulation, who admit ignorance when appropriate, and who have relied on what have seemed to them to be the relevant considerations in the course of acquiring their beliefs, hold these beliefs.[6]

Similarly, Paul Griffiths observes that loss of confidence in one's own beliefs increases when those making rival claims are perceived to be trustworthy and authoritative.[7] He is right. Although there are scoundrels and hypocrites in all religions, many Christians, Hindus, Buddhists, and Muslims are intelligent, conscientious, and morally respectable—in short, apparently trustworthy.

Peer conflict, especially when it involves morally respectable and intelligent participants, raises questions about whether one can be justified in believing in the truth of one's own religious claims, with the implication that others are mistaken in their beliefs. Byrne brings us to the heart of the issue:

> Given peer conflict, then, we have a serious problem about judging which, if any, religion possesses true theories about the Ultimate and which, if any, religious believers have warrant for their beliefs about the Ultimate. By warrant I mean substantive truth-indicative grounds for religious beliefs. Warrant is important because the fact of peer conflict seems too easy to reconcile with the concession that epistemic peers across different religions are all entitled to their religious convictions, where entitlement is a matter of having broken no epistemic obligations in the forming and maintaining of one's beliefs. In this minimal sense, atheists might indeed concede that many religious believers are entitled to their beliefs even though they are false—just as pre-Copernican astronomers in Europe

5. Peter Byrne, "A Philosophical Approach to Questions about Religious Diversity," in *The Oxford Handbook of Religious Diversity*, ed. Chad V. Meister (New York: Oxford University Press, 2010), 30.

6. Robert McKim, *Religious Ambiguity and Religious Diversity* (New York: Oxford University Press, 2001), 129.

7. Paul Griffiths, *Problems of Religious Diversity* (Oxford: Blackwell, 2001), 75.

were entitled to believe that the earth was the stationary center of a concentric universe. But warrant, as defined, is a different matter. If "substantive truth-indicative grounds" means "grounds that make a belief more probable than not," then it is flatly impossible for two incompatible beliefs to be both warranted.[8]

Issues in epistemic justification (or warrant, in Byrne's terms) are highly controversial, and there is little consensus on the meaning of the concept or the conditions for its obtaining.[9] There is an important distinction between *knowing* that a belief p is true and *being justified in believing* that p is true. Knowledge and justification of belief are different concepts. It is widely accepted, for example, that truth is among the necessary conditions for knowledge, so that one is entitled to claim to know that p only if p in fact is true. If p is false, then one cannot know that p.

Justification, by contrast, is not necessarily linked to truth in the way that knowledge is. Under appropriate circumstances one can be justified in believing p even if in fact p is false. Justification is person-relative and context-relative, so that given certain background beliefs and relevant conditions, one person might be justified in believing p, whereas another, with different background beliefs and conditions, might not. Although it is difficult to spell out precisely, justification has a normative element: to be justified in believing p means that one is in an epistemically appropriate or desirable state; to lack justification for belief is usually an indication of an epistemic deficiency.

Since there are degrees of justification, we can picture a continuum with a weak sense of justification on one end and a strong sense of justification on the other. With a weak sense of justification, it can be rational for two or more people to believe incompatible things. Here justification has a weak, permissive sense: it can be reasonable for one person to believe p, but it can also be reasonable for another person not to believe p or to believe some other proposition q that is incompatible with p. But there are also stronger or normative notions of justification. For example, for adults in the United States with normally functioning cognitive faculties, acceptance of the belief "The

8. Byrne, "Philosophical Approach," 30.
9. Helpful introductory works in epistemology include Richard Fumerton, *Epistemology* (Oxford: Blackwell, 2006); Noah Lemos, *An Introduction to the Theory of Knowledge* (New York: Cambridge University Press, 2007); Matthias Steup, *An Introduction to Contemporary Epistemology* (Upper Saddle River, NJ: Prentice-Hall, 1996); and Paul K. Moser, Dwayne H. Mulder, and J. D. Trout, *The Theory of Knowledge: A Thematic Introduction* (New York: Oxford University Press, 1998). For religious epistemology, see Michael Peterson, William Hasker, Bruce Reichenbach, and David Basinger, *Reason and Religious Belief*, 5th ed. (New York: Oxford University Press, 2013); William J. Wainwright, ed., *The Oxford Handbook of Philosophy of Religion* (New York: Oxford University Press, 2005).

earth is flat" is not justified. For someone to believe that the earth is flat is to fail in some way in meeting one's epistemic obligation.

Responding to peer conflict in the minimalist or weak justification sense that Byrne speaks of in the quotation above—so that Christians (and others) can be within their epistemic rights in believing as they do despite religious disagreement—is popular today. But, as we shall see, it comes at some cost since the same move is open to those advancing very different religious claims.

In this chapter we will consider first the question of whether, given religious diversity, a Christian must have sufficient reasons for belief in order to be rational, considering in particular Alvin Plantinga's response to the issue. I will argue that minimalist perspectives, which hold that the Christian is fully entitled to accept Christian beliefs apart from providing evidence or reasons for belief, are inadequate. While not every Christian can be expected to provide good reasons for their beliefs, in certain circumstances it is important for believers to have appropriate reasons for belief, and a special burden falls on leaders in the Christian community to provide such reasons. Although I will not argue for the truth of Christian claims here, I will conclude by sketching in broad terms how a comprehensive case for Christian theism might proceed.

Plantinga, Religious Disagreement, and Evidence

In the seventeenth century, Robert Boyle responded to the challenge of religious diversity by providing what he regarded as cogent reasons for continuing to accept Christian theism. Regardless of whether they find Boyle's arguments persuasive, many Christians today would agree with his conviction that religious diversity does raise a serious challenge; in response, Christians should provide adequate reasons for belief. But this perspective has been rejected in recent decades by some influential philosophers who insist that Christians can be perfectly reasonable in believing as they do without having sufficient evidence for their beliefs and that awareness of religious diversity does not alter this fact.

Since the time of John Locke, David Hume, and Immanuel Kant, it has been widely accepted that in order to be rational in holding Christian beliefs, one should provide sufficient evidence for the beliefs. This assumption is part of a broader perspective often called "evidentialism," which maintains that, with the exception of a small special class of beliefs, the strength of one's commitment to a belief should always be proportional to the evidence for that belief. Religious skeptics insist that Christian beliefs are insufficiently supported by the available evidence and therefore that believing in Christian theism is not rational. Many Christian apologists have accepted the terms set by evidentialism and have tried to show that the evidence for Christian claims actually is compelling and therefore that belief is justified.

But since the 1980s, Alvin Plantinga and others have championed what is called Reformed epistemology, a unique perspective that includes a trenchant critique of evidentialism and the evidentialist challenge to Christian faith. Plantinga is one of the most influential philosophers of religion of the past half century, and he has almost single-handedly changed the nature of debate in religious epistemology.[10] Although his work has implications for many issues, here we are primarily interested in the relation between religious diversity and Plantinga's claims that (1) belief in God can be "properly basic" and that (2) Christian beliefs can be "warranted" apart from appeal to arguments or evidence. Although the two claims are distinct, they both reflect Plantinga's conviction that there is no need for the Christian to provide "sufficient reasons" for central Christian claims and that it can be "entirely right, rational, reasonable, and proper to believe in God without any evidence or argument at all."[11]

In his seminal essay "Reason and Belief in God" (1983), Plantinga analyzes the criticism that belief in Christian theism is irrational because it is not supported by sufficient evidence and places that criticism within the context of "classical foundationalism," which, according to Plantinga, has been dominant in Anglo-American philosophy in the modern era. Foundationalism is a theory of epistemic justification holding that the set of justified beliefs "consists of *basic beliefs*—beliefs that a subject is justified in holding even in the absence of any justifying reason for them—and [that] all other justified beliefs derive their justification at least in part from such basic beliefs."[12] A basic belief is

10. Among Alvin Plantinga's many significant works are *Faith and Rationality: Reason and Belief in God*, ed. Alvin Plantinga and Nicholas Wolterstorff (Notre Dame, IN: University of Notre Dame Press, 1983); *The Nature of Necessity* (Oxford: Clarendon, 1974); *God, Freedom, and Evil* (Grand Rapids: Eerdmans, 1974); *Warrant: The Current Debate* (New York: Oxford University Press, 1993); *Warrant and Proper Function* (New York: Oxford University Press, 1993); *Warranted Christian Belief* (New York: Oxford University Press, 2000); and *Where the Conflict Really Lies: Science, Religion, and Naturalism* (New York: Oxford University Press, 2011).

11. Alvin Plantinga, "Reason and Belief in God," in *Faith and Rationality: Reason and Belief in God*, 17. For a helpful overview and sympathetic critique of Plantinga's project, see James Beilby, "Plantinga's Model of Warranted Christian Belief," in *Alvin Plantinga*, ed. Deane-Peter Baker (Cambridge: Cambridge University Press, 2007), 125–65; James Beilby, *Epistemology as Theology: An Evaluation of Alvin Plantinga's Religious Epistemology* (Aldershot, UK: Ashgate, 2006).

12. James van Cleve, "Why Coherence Is Not Enough: A Defense of Moderate Foundationalism," in *Contemporary Debates in Epistemology*, ed. Matthias Steup and Ernest Sosa (Oxford: Blackwell, 2005), 168, with original emphasis. See also Laurence Bonjour, *The Structure of Empirical Knowledge* (Cambridge, MA: Harvard University Press, 1985), 26–28; Noah Lemos, *An Introduction to the Theory of Knowledge*, chap. 3. For a helpful discussion of moderate forms

a belief that one accepts without it being supported by or derived from other beliefs one holds; in a foundationalist model, basic beliefs form the foundation upon which other beliefs are established. With basic beliefs, a person who is in the proper conditions simply finds oneself having the appropriate beliefs. Basic beliefs that are epistemically appropriate are called properly basic beliefs.

Classical foundationalism, as defined by Plantinga, holds that a belief p is rational if and only if p is a properly basic belief or can be inferred from one or more properly basic beliefs. It has a very restricted class of properly basic beliefs, so that *only* beliefs that are *evident to the senses*, *self-evident*, or *incorrigible* can properly be basic beliefs. Beliefs that are evident to the senses include beliefs constituting reports of sense experience ("I hear a loud noise"). Self-evident beliefs are such that upon understanding the meanings of the terms, one can immediately see the truth (or falsity) of the statement ("2 + 2 = 4" or "Bachelors are unmarried males"). Incorrigible beliefs are beliefs about which one cannot be wrong, if uttered sincerely ("I feel pain"). Classical foundationalism holds that belief in p is rational if and only if p is a belief that is evident to the senses, self-evident, incorrigible, or can be inferred from one or more such beliefs through proper inference procedures.

Plantinga launches a devastating critique of classical foundationalism that rests on two issues.[13] First, he explains that the statement of classical foundationalism itself is self-referentially incoherent since it does not meet the conditions that it stipulates for all rational belief. It is neither a properly basic belief, nor can it be derived from such beliefs. On its own terms, then, it should be rejected as irrational. Second, he points out that classical foundationalism is far too restrictive in its criteria for properly basic beliefs, for it rules out many beliefs that we normally accept as perfectly reasonable. For example, beliefs about the reality of other minds, an external world, the general reliability of memory, or that the universe did not simply pop into existence five minutes ago would all need to be rejected since they are neither properly basic on classical foundationalism's criteria nor has anyone shown how they can be inferred from such beliefs. Although Plantinga demonstrates the inadequacy of classical foundationalism, his critique should not be understood as refuting all forms of foundationalism. There are other more moderate forms that are not susceptible to his criticisms.

The set of properly basic beliefs that classical foundationalism allows is far too restrictive, and thus any acceptable form of foundationalism must enlarge

---

of foundationalism by two evangelical philosophers, see J. P. Moreland and Garrett DeWeese, "The Premature Report of Foundationalism's Demise," *Reclaiming the Center: Confronting Evangelical Accommodation in Postmodern Times*, ed. Millard Erickson, Paul Kjoss Helseth, and Justin Taylor (Wheaton, IL: Crossway, 2004), 81–108.

13. Plantinga, "Reason and Belief in God," 59–63; idem, *Warranted Christian Belief*, 94–99.

this set. But how inclusive should we be? Plantinga goes well beyond other foundationalists in claiming that for the Christian in appropriate circumstances, belief in God can be properly basic and thus be epistemically appropriate apart from any appeal to supporting evidence. "There is no reason at all to think that Christian belief requires argument or propositional evidence, if it is to be justified. Christians—indeed, well-educated, contemporary, and culturally aware Christians—can be justified . . . even if they don't hold their beliefs on the basis of arguments or evidence, even if they aren't aware of any good arguments for their beliefs, and even if, indeed, there aren't any."[14]

In appropriate circumstances, beliefs such as "This vast and intricate universe was created by God" can be properly basic for Christians; and since the existence of God is entailed by such a belief, we can say that belief in God's existence can thus be properly basic. Such beliefs are not inferred from other beliefs, nor do they need to be supported by evidence or arguments. But, according to Plantinga, holding these beliefs in a basic way is not arbitrary, for there are appropriate grounds (as distinct from evidence) for them. The grounds for belief in God are the conditions or circumstances that give rise to belief in God when the relevant noetic faculties are functioning properly and one is in the appropriate circumstances. It is, for example, the experience of sensing God's reality as one gazes at the heavens above that provides the grounds for the belief "This vast and intricate universe was created by God."

In *Warranted Christian Belief*, Plantinga addresses the question of whether Christians can be said to know certain truths about God when these beliefs are for them properly basic. Plantinga frames the issues in terms of whether Christian beliefs can be warranted, where warrant is understood as the property that, when combined with true belief, results in knowledge. "Warrant" is "a name for that property—or better, *quantity*—enough of which is what makes the difference between knowledge and mere true belief." Warrant is connected with proper function so that, in addition to its being true, "a belief has warrant just if it is produced by cognitive processes or faculties that are functioning properly, in a cognitive environment that is propitious for the exercise of cognitive powers, according to a design plan that is successfully aimed at the production of true belief."[15] In other words, a belief is warranted only if it is produced by our epistemic faculties (noetic structure and epistemic inclinations) when they are functioning properly in accordance with their design plan in appropriate circumstances. Plantinga understands the design plan in accordance with Christian teaching about God and creation, and he makes

14. Plantinga, *Warranted Christian Belief*, 93.
15. Ibid., xi, with original emphasis.

special reference to John Calvin's notion of the *sensus divinitatis* (sense of the divine). God has created us in such a way that in appropriate circumstances, when our epistemic faculties are functioning as designed, the *sensus divinitatis* produces within us belief in God. Moreover, according to Plantinga these beliefs are typically not the product of appeal to evidence or argument. Thus, if we grant that the relevant beliefs are also true, a Christian can be warranted in believing some of the claims of Christian theism apart from any appeal to evidence or argument. If the beliefs are held with sufficient firmness to yield a degree of warrant sufficient for knowledge, then the Christian can be said to know that these beliefs are true.[16]

The notions of proper basicality and warrant are defeasible, so that changing epistemic circumstances—including the introduction of new evidence or arguments—can result in a belief being no longer properly basic for a person or no longer warranted. Plantinga acknowledges that there can be potential defeaters for proper basicality or warrant so that objections to Christian belief cannot simply be ignored.[17] Proper basicality and warrant are relative to a person's noetic structure, background beliefs, and circumstances, and if there are successful defeaters for a belief, then it can no longer be properly basic. Thus objections such as the problem of evil or the claims of biblical higher criticism or the projection theories of Freud and Feuerbach need to be responded to and shown to be untenable. But Plantinga claims that objections to the rationality or justification of Christian beliefs (what he calls the de jure question) are not independent of the question of the truth of core Christian claims (the de facto question), and thus "a successful atheological objection will have to be to the *truth* of theism, not to its rationality, justification, intellectual respectability, rational justification, or whatever."[18] Thus the critic must somehow show that Christian theism is false, not simply argue that it is irrational or intellectually deficient in some manner. So long as Christian theism is not shown to be false, however, a Christian can be fully justified in accepting some beliefs about God as properly basic, and these beliefs can also be warranted.

Plantinga is not claiming to have demonstrated that God exists or that central Christian claims are in fact true. His contention rather is that *if* God, as Christians understand him, exists, and if a Christian's belief in God meets

16. Beilby, "Plantinga's Model of Warranted Christian Belief," 127.
17. A defeater is a condition or reason that removes epistemic justification or warrant for holding a belief. A rebutting defeater for a belief p is a reason that attacks p directly; it provides reason for believing -p. An undercutting defeater undermines the justification of believing that p by providing grounds for questioning the reasons for p or the reliability of the belief-forming mechanism that produced p.
18. Plantinga, *Warranted Christian Belief*, 191.

the other requirements for warrant stipulated above, then the Christian's belief is probably warranted and constitutes knowledge. But the skeptic wants to know whether Christian theism is *true*. At the end of his massive *Warranted Christian Belief*, Plantinga addresses this question: "But *is* it true? This is the really important question. And here we pass beyond the competence of philosophy, whose main competence, in this area, is to clear away certain objections, impedances, and obstacles to Christian belief. Speaking for myself, and of course not in the name of philosophy, I can say only that it does, indeed, seem to me to be true, and to be the maximally important truth."[19]

Does awareness of religious diversity alter the epistemic calculus? Even if we grant that there are circumstances in which a Christian can be entitled to treat belief in God as properly basic, does not exposure to religious diversity change the conditions so that belief in God in these circumstances requires some evidential support? Given the competing claims to exclusive truth among the religions, shouldn't anyone who insists "*My* religion is true" be expected to produce supporting evidence?

In an important essay that is later expanded and included in *Warranted Christian Belief*, Plantinga maintains that even when confronted by radical religious disagreement, Christians need not defend their beliefs by appealing to reasons or evidence.[20] He acknowledges that for some people, awareness of diversity does sometimes undermine confidence in one's own beliefs. "For at least some Christian believers, an awareness of the enormous variety of human religious responses does seem to reduce the level of confidence in their own Christian belief."[21] But this is merely a sociological or psychological fact about how some people respond to diversity, and it has no implications for what is required in order to be rational in believing. Plantinga acknowledges that having reasons for belief can be helpful for those who do find their confidence in Christian beliefs diminishing. While this may be psychologically reassuring, it is not required in order to be rational in accepting core Christian claims.

Not surprisingly, Plantinga's Reformed epistemology has elicited a vigorous debate, with Christian philosophers disagreeing over its merits.[22] As a corrective to an excessive form of evidentialism, it makes an important contribution. Reformed epistemologists rightly point out that we cannot be expected

---

19. Ibid., 499.

20. See Alvin Plantinga, "Pluralism: A Defense of Religious Exclusivism," in *The Rationality of Belief and the Plurality of Faith*, ed. Thomas D. Senor (Ithaca, NY: Cornell University Press, 1995), 191–215; idem, *Warranted Christian Belief*, 422–57.

21. Plantinga, *Warranted Christian Belief*, 456.

22. See the symposium discussion on *Warranted Christian Belief* by Douglas Geivett, Greg Jesson, Richard Fumerton, Keith Yandell, and Paul Moser, along with a response by Alvin Plantinga, in *Philosophia Christi* 3.2 (2001): 327–400.

to produce "sufficient evidence" for many of the common beliefs we accept. Many of our convictions are basic beliefs, and many of these no doubt are also properly basic. And we must acknowledge that not everyone must be able to provide sufficient evidence for one's own belief in God in order to be rational in so believing. Many ordinary Christians would be unable to provide any significant evidence for their beliefs, and surely it would be implausible to insist that they are all irrational unless they can do so. So let us assume that Plantinga is correct in saying that it can be entirely reasonable for belief in God to be properly basic for some people in appropriate circumstances. It does not follow that belief in God is properly basic for all Christians in all circumstances. Specifying the necessary and sufficient conditions for proper basicality is both difficult and controversial.

It is important to distinguish empirical questions from epistemic questions. Whether awareness of religious diversity *does* reduce confidence in one's own beliefs is an empirical matter; whether it *should* do so is an epistemic issue. Empirical research by Robert Wuthnow and others indicates that sustained exposure to religious diversity can have a destabilizing effect upon one's own beliefs.[23] But people respond to diversity in different ways, with some people deeply bothered by it and others not. Clearly a variety of factors are involved in one's response. Those with an initial high degree of confidence in their own beliefs will likely be less bothered than those with less confidence.

With respect to the empirical issue of how Christians do respond to religious diversity, Plantinga seems to have an idealized and monolithic view of Christian believers as characteristically accepting Christian beliefs in a basic (noninferential) manner and not being particularly bothered by diversity or disagreement. He states, "In the typical case, Christian belief is immediate; it is formed in the basic way. It doesn't proceed by way of an argument from, for example, the reliability of Scripture or the church."[24] We are led to believe that it is the typical believer, not the unusual Christian, who has properly basic beliefs about God. Although Plantinga does concede that religious diversity might undermine confidence in beliefs for some people, the impression given is that this is not the norm for genuine, mature believers.

But is this really how it works for most Christians? There is greater variety in responses to religious disagreement than Plantinga suggests. Kelly James Clark states, "There is a variety of Christian believers affected in a variety of ways by awareness of religious diversity, eliciting a variety of equally valid responses.

23. See Robert Wuthnow, *America and the Challenges of Religious Diversity* (Princeton: Princeton University Press, 2005); Wade Clark Roof, *Spiritual Marketplace: Baby Boomers and the Remaking of American Religion* (Princeton: Princeton University Press, 2005).
24. Plantinga, *Warranted Christian Belief*, 259.

Plantinga has set up one situation that provides a model of what a Christian could or even must think if her belief is to be warranted in the face of religious diversity. But how many Christians are in that epistemic situation?"[25] For many believers, the process of coming to embrace Christian commitments is complex and messy, involving a wide variety of factors. As Beilby observes, "The religious beliefs of the typical Christian are more likely based on a complex mixture of personal, social, and evidential factors in addition to pneumatological factors such as the internal instigation of the Holy Spirit."[26] The internal instigation of the Spirit can work along with or through a wide variety of factors in producing confidence in the truths of the gospel. In many cases some consideration of the evidence for Christian claims does play a significant role in Christian commitments, and there is no reason to think this is at odds with the work of the Holy Spirit. While some may fit Plantinga's profile of basic belief in God even in the face of religious diversity, it seems that many more struggle with whether their beliefs are still acceptable and attempt to resolve the cognitive dissonance by considering reasons for their commitments.

Regardless of the empirical question, should awareness of religious disagreement have any effect upon the requirement to have evidence for one's beliefs? Even if we grant that in certain circumstances it can be entirely appropriate for someone to believe in God without being able to provide reasons for such belief, does religious diversity change the epistemic expectations? Gary Gutting expresses the view of many: "How can a believer just blithely claim that it's utterly obvious that he's entitled to believe without having any reasons for his belief? What of the fact that there are all sorts of honest and intelligent people who've thought a lot about religious belief and simply don't see belief in God as properly basic?"[27] Beliefs about the reality of the external world or the general reliability of memory are widely accepted as properly basic in part because there is little serious dispute about their truth, but this is not the case with belief in God. Many intelligent and morally respectable people sharply disagree about the reality of God. As Gutting puts it, "Isn't it just common sense to admit that, when there is widespread [disagreement] about a claim, with apparently competent judges on both sides, those who assert or deny the claim need to justify their positions?"[28]

25. Kelly James Clark, "Pluralism and Proper Function," in Baker, *Alvin Plantinga*, 177.
26. Beilby, "Plantinga's Model of Warranted Christian Belief," 148.
27. Gary Gutting, "The Catholic and the Calvinist: A Dialogue on Faith and Reason," *Faith and Philosophy* 2 (1985): 241.
28. Gary Gutting, *Religious Belief and Religious Skepticism* (Notre Dame, IN: University of Notre Dame Press, 1982), 83. I have substituted "disagreement" for "agreement" in the original text since the latter is evidently a misprint.

Here the problem concerns what Beilby calls Plantinga's "minimalist approach to religious epistemology."[29] We should acknowledge that Plantinga's primary interest is with the question of how, given their metaphysical commitments, Christians should think about the epistemic status of their own beliefs; he is not trying to argue for the truth of Christian theism or even to show the skeptic that there is good reason for accepting Christian claims.[30] Consequently, his conclusion is fairly modest: it is possible for Christians in appropriate circumstances to maintain some of their Christian beliefs in a properly basic manner; and if the claims of Christian theism are true, then such beliefs can also be warranted, resulting in knowledge about God. Although helpful as far as it goes, Plantinga's discussion leaves many unsatisfied. In contexts of competing religious truth claims, many are seeking reasons for accepting any particular perspective—including Christian theism—as true, or at least as more likely to be true than other alternatives.

Furthermore, Plantinga's minimalism results in a situation in which adherents of other religions can also, in principle, defend the propriety of their respective beliefs in a manner parallel to Plantinga's defense of Christian beliefs. The appeal to proper basicality for one's religious beliefs is also open to sincere believers from other religions. Philip Quinn, for example, observes that "this is a game any number can play. Followers of Muhammad, followers of Buddha, and even followers of the Reverend Moon can join the fun."[31] It is difficult to see why belief in God can be properly basic for Christians but fundamental beliefs in other religions cannot also, in principle, be properly basic for their adherents.[32] For example, the central insights of Zen Buddhism—including the belief that ultimate reality is sunyata, or emptiness—are said to be perceived directly in the experience of enlightenment. They are not the product of rational argument; indeed, evidence and argument are counterproductive in attaining enlightenment. Moreover, the experience of enlightenment grounds the relevant claims. Thus belief in emptiness as the ultimate reality can be a

29. Beilby, "Plantinga's Model of Warranted Christian Belief," 145.

30. See ibid., 129, 133, 139–40.

31. Philip Quinn, "In Search of the Foundations of Theism," *Faith and Philosophy* 2.4 (1985): 473. See also Beilby, "Plantinga's Model of Warranted Christian Belief," 143–44; William Wainwright, *Philosophy of Religion*, 2nd ed. (Belmont, CA: Wadsworth, 1999), 167–70; Robert McKim, *Religious Ambiguity and Religious Diversity*, 182.

32. This point is nicely made with reference to Advaita Vedanta Hinduism by Rose Ann Christian, "Plantinga, Epistemic Permissiveness, and Metaphysical Pluralism," *Religious Studies* 28 (December 1992): 568–69. David Tien argues that according to Plantinga's proposal, the Neo-Confucian philosopher Wang Yangming's religious beliefs can be properly basic and warranted: David Tien, "Warranted Neo-Confucian Belief: Religious Pluralism and the Affections in the Epistemologies of Wang Yangming (1472–1529) and Alvin Plantinga," *International Journal for Philosophy of Religion* 55 (2004): 31–55.

basic belief for Zen Buddhists. Is it also properly basic for Zen Buddhists? There is nothing in Reformed epistemology to show why this could not be the case. While Reformed epistemology might provide a mechanism for a Christian to be within one's own epistemic rights in maintaining that Christian theism is true, there does not seem to be anything preventing adherents of other religions from making the same move within their own respective religious traditions.

Nor will it help matters to appeal to Plantinga's discussion of warrant and proper function at this point, for the dispute then simply shifts to the question of what constitutes proper function or what is a reliable belief-forming mechanism. In responding to Plantinga's claims, William Hasker states, "The religious believer is rational in affirming that experientially grounded beliefs are warranted if and only if she is rational in affirming a *reliability thesis* to the effect that the processes generating such beliefs are epistemically reliable."[33] But Hasker points out that religious disagreement undermines any particular religion's claims about reliability in belief-forming mechanisms. Buddhists, for example, maintain that belief in a personal creator God is both false and the product of malfunctioning cognitive faculties, so the mechanism producing such belief is not reliable. The dispute, then, between the Christian and Buddhist is not merely a disagreement over what beliefs can be properly basic. It also concerns what constitutes proper function of the cognitive faculties, and settling *that* question requires determining the truth value of some central metaphysical claims of the Christian or Buddhist traditions.

There is a further consequence of Plantinga's minimalist approach: it provides no guidance for someone who is not a Christian but is trying to determine whether Christian theism is true or rationally preferable to other alternatives.[34] Many people considering religious questions do examine, as best they can, whether the basic teachings of a religion "make sense" or whether there are good reasons to accept them as true. The sincere inquirer who asks for reasons to believe the core teachings of Christian theism deserves a thoughtful answer that includes, as appropriate, good reasons for belief.

The attempt to provide reasons for preferring Christian theism over other alternatives is typically identified with natural theology or positive apologetics, and Plantinga is ambivalent at best on natural theology. On the one hand, he clearly rejects the idea that natural theology is necessary for rational belief in God, even in cases of religious diversity. Nor is he optimistic about the prospects of natural theology settling basic issues of religious disagreement.

---

33. William Hasker, "Proper Function, Reliabilism, and Religious Knowledge: A Critique of Plantinga's Epistemology," in *Christian Perspectives on Religious Knowledge*, ed. C. Stephen Evans and Merold Westphal (Grand Rapids: Eerdmans, 1993), 82–83, with original emphasis.
34. See Richard Swinburne, "Plantinga on Warrant," *Religious Studies* 37 (2001): 206–7.

Nevertheless, he does think that there are some good theistic arguments, and he acknowledges that natural theology might have some benefit for some people.[35]

Alston and Religious Disagreement

William Alston's *Perceiving God*[36] is an influential attempt to ground the rationality of religious belief in religious experience. Alston examines "doxastic practices," or belief-forming practices, that give rise to beliefs. He draws a crucial analogy between (1) practices relying on sense perception, which provide access to the physical world around us, resulting in beliefs about the physical world; and (2) religious practices that provide the believer with experiences or "perceptions" of God, thereby producing beliefs about God. In both sense perception and perception of God, beliefs are formed by engaging in certain doxastic practices, or socially established practices resulting in formation of appropriate beliefs. In neither case is it possible to justify the reliability of the doxastic practices in a strictly noncircular manner. Yet in both cases we have established procedures for distinguishing appropriate from inappropriate beliefs. Thus, Alston argues, beliefs formed through the relevant doxastic practices can be granted prima facie justification; if there are no sufficient "overriders" (factors that would rebut or undermine the beliefs), then they can be considered "unqualifiedly justified" as well. So the Christian can be rationally justified in believing in God based upon the individual's experience or perception of God.

Now, as Alston himself recognizes, religious diversity presents a twofold challenge to this thesis. First, while Alston's argument supports the rationality of Christian beliefs, based upon Christian experiences of God, it also in principle supports the rationality of the beliefs of practitioners of other religions, based upon *their* respective religious experiences. At best, then, Alston's argument supports a weaker notion of rationality of religious belief, such that divergent religious communities all can be rational in holding their respective beliefs even if these beliefs are in fact mutually incompatible. But, more significantly, religious diversity actually seems to undermine Alston's thesis about the general reliability of religious doxastic practices for religious

35. See Alvin Plantinga, "The Reformed Objection to Natural Theology," in *Proceedings of the American Catholic Philosophical Association* 54 (1980): 49–62; idem, "The Prospects for Natural Theology," in *Philosophy of Religion, 1991*, ed. James E. Tomberlin, Philosophical Perspectives 5 (Atascadero, CA: Ridgeview, 1991), 287–315; idem, "Two Dozen (or So) Theistic Arguments," in *Alvin Plantinga*, 203–27.

36. William P. Alston, *Perceiving God: The Epistemology of Religious Experience* (Ithaca, NY: Cornell University Press, 1991).

belief formation. Here the differences between sense perception and religious perception are important. While the doxastic practices for sense perception produce similar beliefs about the external world among diverse peoples (water is wet for Buddhists and Christians alike), the doxastic practices of different religious communities result in strikingly different, even incompatible, beliefs. Thus religious diversity seems to call into question the reliability of any single doxastic practice, including that of the Christian community. For even if one form of practice is uniquely reliable in religious belief formation, we have no non-question-begging way of determining which one that is. While acknowledging the force of this objection, Alston concludes that it still can be rational for the Christian to "sit tight with the practice of which I am a master and which serves me so well in guiding my activity in the world" and to continue to hold Christian beliefs on the basis of experiences of God.[37]

In responding to Alston, John Hick argues that if a Christian is in this manner justified in believing that Christianity is uniquely true, then it follows that the Christian should conclude that most of the beliefs of adherents of other religions, based upon their respective experiences, are actually false. But if so, then it also follows that most of the religious beliefs based upon religious experience worldwide are in fact false. And thus, for members of one particular religious community to assume that *their* doxastic practices are reliable and that *their* beliefs are justified, when those of the other religious communities are not, is simply arbitrary unless this assumption can be justified on independent grounds.[38] William Wainwright similarly concludes that if the rationality of Christian beliefs is to be established, then the acceptability of Christian doxastic practices for Christian belief formation will need to be supported by "introducing empirical and metaphysical arguments that establish the superiority of (e.g.) the Christian worldview"—a task normally associated with natural theology.[39] Significantly, Alston is open to natural theology assuming some role in establishing the epistemic superiority (to some degree) of Christian theism over other alternatives, although he does not pursue this possibility. Toward the end of *Perceiving God*, he states, "The attempt to argue from neutral starting points for the truth of Christian beliefs deserves much more serious consideration than is commonly accorded it today in philosophical

37. Ibid., 274.

38. John Hick, "The Epistemological Challenge of Religious Pluralism," *Faith and Philosophy* 14.3 (1997): 278. Hick's essay is reprinted in John Hick, *Dialogues in the Philosophy of Religion* (New York: Palgrave, 2001), 25–36, and is followed in the same volume (37–52) by Alston's response to Hick's critique.

39. William J. Wainwright, "Religious Language, Religious Experience, and Religious Pluralism," in Senor, *Rationality of Belief and the Plurality of Faith*, 187.

and (liberal) theological circles. I believe that much can be done to support a theistic metaphysics, and that something can be done by way of recommending the 'evidences of Christianity.'"[40]

Providing Reasons for Belief

Taking a different approach from Reformed epistemologists such as Alvin Plantinga, David Basinger maintains that in circumstances in which there is religious disagreement, Christians should be prepared to provide some positive reasons for their beliefs. He recognizes the force of the objection that bothered Robert Boyle four hundred years ago: "If it is in fact the case that seemingly sincere, knowledgeable individuals differ on the nature of the divine, can the proponent of any specific perspective justifiably claim that she alone has the truth, or is at least closer to truth than all others"?[41] Basinger asserts that sustained exposure to religious disagreement can, and often does, result in "epistemic peer conflict," something we face "in those contexts in which we have no objective reason to doubt that those with whom we disagree are (1) equally knowledgeable, that is, have access to as much relevant information as we do; and (2) equally sincere, that is, desire as much as we do to affirm what is true."[42]

How should the Christian believer respond to epistemic peer conflict? Basinger admits that it can be epistemically appropriate, as Plantinga argues, for a believer to remain within one's "epistemic rights" and continue to believe without providing reasons for belief. But any believer who wants to maximize truth and minimize error has an epistemic obligation to reexamine one's own beliefs to see if there are good reasons for accepting them. What he calls "Basinger's Rule" stipulates, "If a religious exclusivist wants to maximize truth and avoid error, she is under a prima facie obligation to attempt to resolve significant epistemic peer conflict."[43] In other words, in appropriate circumstances a religious believer who undergoes epistemic peer conflict as a result of awareness of religious diversity has an obligation to reassess his or her own beliefs, as well as the relevant beliefs of others, in an effort to determine whether "those beliefs that form the core of [one's own] exclusivity really are beliefs worthy of continued acceptance."[44] A person cannot legitimately

40. Alston, *Perceiving God*, 270.
41. David Basinger, *Religious Diversity: A Philosophical Assessment* (Burlington, VT: Ashgate, 2002), vii.
42. Ibid., 11.
43. Ibid.
44. Ibid., 27.

claim that one's own religion is true and others not true and then refuse to submit one's own beliefs to reassessment. It is not necessary to come up with compelling reasons for belief that any rational person would accept: that is an impossible ideal. But the believer should make an effort to determine which beliefs are supported by the strongest reasons. Insofar as the Christian makes a responsible effort to reassess one's beliefs in light of competing claims and finds no compelling reasons to reject those views, that Christian can be reasonable in maintaining those beliefs.

Given the many religious and nonreligious worldviews available today, why should one accept the central claims of Christian theism as true? Basinger's Rule maintains that a Christian believer experiencing epistemic peer conflict should reexamine the reasons for maintaining one's own beliefs to see whether doing so is justified. But Basinger has fairly modest expectations on what such rational assessment can produce. Rational considerations might allow continued belief for the Christian but may not be sufficient to require change of perspective on the part of a religious skeptic or Buddhist. Fulfilling the requirements of Basinger's Rule might mean, for example, that in some circumstances adherents of two or more mutually incompatible religious worldviews can be justified in holding their respective beliefs. Although "only one set of incompatible exclusivistic perspectives on a given religious issue can in fact be correct, proponents of each perspective can, in principle, justifiably continue to maintain that they alone have the truth."[45]

There is a tension between (1) Basinger's call for believers in conditions of epistemic peer conflict to reexamine their beliefs to see whether there are good reasons for maintaining them, and (2) his low expectations for what rational assessment of rival claims can produce. In discussing competing religious perspectives, Basinger repeatedly asserts, "There exists no objective, non-question-begging way of demonstrating that one perspective [rather than another] is actually correct."[46] There is no "objective," non-question-begging way rationally to settle basic disputes between religious systems. Nowhere does Basinger give readers a definition of "objective," although at times he equates "[a] set of objective criteria" with "criteria accepted by all parties in the dispute."[47] If this is the meaning of "objective," then his claim is hardly surprising, for few issues of any significance enjoy criteria that are objective in that sense. But why should we suppose that objective criteria are criteria that all relevant parties will accept? A more natural and helpful meaning would

45. Ibid., 7.
46. Ibid., 65; see also 12–13, 31, 38–40, 44, 61, 65, 104.
47. Ibid., 13; see also 34, 38, 62, 65.

be criteria that are not question-begging or arbitrary since they are logically and ontologically independent of individual or collective human states of consciousness; thus they are not merely the products of, nor can they be reduced to, what any group happens to accept at a given time. Understood in this way, it is not at all obvious that there are no objective criteria for resolving disputes between religious systems.

Possibly what Basinger means here is that, although there may well be *some* nonarbitrary criteria that can be used in such assessment, the application of these criteria to particular claims is not very helpful in determining which religious system is more likely to be true. Thus he states, "While the consideration of criteria such as self-consistency and comprehensiveness can rule out certain options, there exists no set of criteria that will allow us to resolve most cases of epistemic disputes in a neutral, non-question-begging manner."[48] But the tension with Basinger's Rule remains: if indeed we do not have access to nonarbitrary criteria that enable us to adjudicate basic religious disputes, what does it mean to say that the religious believer has an epistemic obligation to reassess one's own beliefs to be sure of having adequate "reasons for continuing to consider her perspective superior to that of her epistemic competitors"?[49] It is not clear whether these reasons are to be understood as being merely persuasive to the believer or are such that anyone, including a religious skeptic or adherent of another religion, ought to find them compelling.

Paul Griffiths, like Basinger, holds that in cases of epistemic peer conflict, it is important to provide reasons for one's own commitments. Griffiths is a Christian theologian and philosopher yet also an authority on Buddhism. He argues that in cases where there are conflicting truth claims advanced by diverse religious communities, there is an obligation on the part of the intellectual leaders of the religious communities to respond to the rival claims. If intellectual leaders of a specific religious community come to believe that some or all of their own core doctrines are incompatible with some claims made by representatives of another religious community, then they have an obligation to respond to the rival claims by trying to show that those claims are unjustified or that one's own beliefs are not threatened by such claims.[50]

Griffiths rightly maintains that there is both an epistemic and a moral component to this obligation.[51] Religious communities regard their own

48. Ibid., 31.
49. Ibid., 99.
50. Paul Griffiths, *An Apology for Apologetics: A Study in the Logic of Interreligious Dialogue* (Maryknoll, NY: Orbis Books, 1991), 3.
51. Ibid., 15–16.

teachings as true; thus when a community is confronted by other claims challenging these beliefs, it has an epistemic duty to consider whether the challenge makes it epistemically improper for members to continue believing as they do. Moreover, most religions also insist that there is significant salvific value in accepting and acting on their teachings as true. If a religious community believes that humankind suffers from a general malady (sin, ignorance), that its central religious claims are true, and that accepting and acting appropriately upon these beliefs can bring about deliverance from the problem, then the community has an ethical obligation to share this good news with those outside the tradition, trying in suitable ways to persuade them of the truth of the community's beliefs. This will, in appropriate circumstances, involve providing reasons for accepting its claims as true. It is significant that Griffiths construes these obligations in terms of the intellectual leaders of the religious community and not something that falls to all members equally. We will return to this point in chapter 8, as we discuss the place of apologetics in interreligious contexts.

Religious Ambiguity

Let us assume that in appropriate circumstances of religious disagreement, religious believers do have some sort of obligation to provide reasons justifying their beliefs. Should we expect that rational consideration of rival religious teachings can result in one claim or set of claims clearly having greater support than others? Or should we be content with, at best, a weak sense of rationality such that members of different religious communities can be equally justified in their respective beliefs, even if all of these beliefs cannot be true? A popular response to these questions appeals to the idea of religious ambiguity, or what is sometimes called the epistemic parity thesis. This is the view that evidential or rational considerations relevant to religious belief are such that no particular religious tradition can be shown to be rationally superior to others: the data are sufficiently ambiguous that the major religions enjoy more or less epistemic parity in their basic claims. If this thesis is sound, then there is no point in trying to show that any particular religious perspective has greater evidential support or is more likely to be true than others. At best, we could conclude that members of diverse religious communities are all rational in believing as they do, even if not all of their respective claims can be true.

Religious ambiguity is a crucial element in John Hick's model of religious pluralism, examined in chapter 5. Hick insists that all experience involves interpretation ("experiencing-as"), with interpretation playing a greater role in religious matters than in sense perception or moral judgments.[52] Having rejected the classical theistic arguments as inconclusive, Hick insists that we are left with inescapable ambiguity on religious questions.

> It seems, then, that the universe retains its inscrutable ambiguity. In some respects it invites whilst in others it repels a religious response. It permits both a religious and a naturalistic faith, but haunted in each case by a contrary possibility that can never be exorcised. Any realistic analysis of religious belief and experience, and any realistic defence of the rationality of religious conviction, must therefore start from this situation of systematic ambiguity.[53]

Religious ambiguity extends to the religions as well, so that no single religion can be shown to be rationally superior to the others.

The decisive factor that makes it reasonable for religious believers to believe as they do is religious experience. "It is as reasonable for those who experience their lives as being lived in the presence of God, to believe in the reality of God, as for all of us to form beliefs about our environment on the basis of our experience of it."[54] But Hick acknowledges that this principle applies to believers in other religions as well, and thus it does not provide a basis for demonstrating the rational superiority of Christian theism. Christians can be entitled to believe as they do based upon their experiences, but so too can Muslims or Hindus or Buddhists.

Robert McKim appeals to religious disagreement in support of religious ambiguity:

> To say that the world is religiously ambiguous is to say that it is open to being read in various ways, both religious and secular, by intelligent, honest people. . . . The presence of disagreement suggests that the matters about which there is disagreement are ambiguous. In particular, disagreement in the area of religion suggests that this is an area in which the available evidence does not point clearly in one direction rather than another, and it suggests that the matters about which religions purport to speak are matters about which it is unclear what we ought to believe."[55]

52. John Hick, *An Interpretation of Religion: Human Responses to the Transcendent*, 2nd ed. (New Haven: Yale University Press, 2004), chaps. 8–10.

53. Ibid., 124. Hick's discussion of the theistic arguments can be found in John Hick, *Arguments for the Existence of God* (London: Macmillan, 1970); and idem, *Interpretation of Religion*, chaps. 5–6.

54. Hick, *Interpretation of Religion*, 210.

55. Robert McKim, *Religious Ambiguity and Religious Diversity* (New York: Oxford University Press, 2001), 25, 181–82.

In a later work McKim argues for what he calls "extremely rich ambiguity" when it comes to the religions. This is a condition that obtains when (1) there is an abundance of relevant evidence for various religious claims; (2) this evidence is diverse, multifaceted, and complicated; (3) there are elements of evidence that are especially congenial to advocates of particular interpretations of the evidence; (4) advocates of different interpretations disagree about the status of much of the evidence; (5) because of the above, it is very difficult to tell whether the evidence supports one side over others; and (6) the relevant evidence is "superabundant" so that no single person can have access to more than a small portion of the evidence.[56]

Given such ambiguity, the proper response for believers is to adopt a moderate skepticism and tentativeness in their beliefs. "It is unlikely that certainty about the details of the doctrine of any particular religion about God is either obligatory or appropriate, and it is likely that tentative belief, at most, is appropriate." A suitably tentative approach "will view different accounts of the nature or purposes of God, especially the details of those accounts, as equally likely to be true, as stabs in the right direction of something about which it is difficult to be certain. The implication is that theists ought to be skeptical of many of the claims about God that are made by the dominant theistic traditions, including their own."[57]

Hick's and McKim's positions on religious ambiguity have considerable appeal today and fit what sociologists of religion such as Robert Wuthnow have termed the spirituality of seeking or journey.[58] Reflecting on his study of American baby boomers, Wade Clark Roof observes, "Doubt is now more openly acknowledged and perhaps even assumes a more significant religious role" than with previous generations. "It is not that the world has gone secular, lost all its scripts embedding the sacred; instead, the world has become a gigantic maze of alternative paths requiring of individuals a level of decision-making and accountability on a scale unlike anything previous Americans have known—and involving in a most fundamental way, things of the spirit."[59] There can be little question that many people today agree with Hick and McKim that we live in a religiously ambiguous world, and thus we should be suspicious of any claims about one religious perspective being more likely to be true than the others.

56. Robert McKim, *On Religious Diversity* (New York: Oxford University Press, 2012), 137–39.

57. McKim, *Religious Ambiguity and Religious Diversity*, 123–24.

58. See Robert Wuthnow, *After Heaven: Spirituality in America since the 1950s* (Berkeley: University of California Press, 1998).

59. Wade Clark Roof, *Spiritual Marketplace*, 47, 313.

But while we can acknowledge the sociological realities, we cannot ignore the epistemic or normative issues. That there is widespread religious disagreement on some issues is clear, but it does not necessarily follow that there is no correct position or that the available evidence does not favor one position over others. Is it really the case that the proposition "God exists" has no greater evidential or rational support than its denial? Or is it really true that the central claims of Theravada Buddhism or Jainism or Shinto have the same degree of rational support as those of orthodox Christianity? I think not.

The expectations for successful resolution of the problem of conflicting truth claims are often set impossibly high. It is often assumed that if the claims of Christianity are to be judged as rationally superior to those of Buddhism, for example, then the evidence in favor of Christianity should be such that all rational persons examining the evidence will agree that Christianity is rationally superior to Buddhism. If this is the standard that must be met, then it is hardly surprising that the default position is skepticism or religious ambiguity. But why expect that all reasonable persons must agree? Few disputes of real significance in the physical sciences, history, politics, economics, or philosophy meet this standard. Despite lack of complete unanimity in these areas, we regularly engage in vigorous debate, seek, to the best of our ability, to determine which perspective has the greatest evidential support, and conclude that it is rationally superior to others. The issue, then, is not whether we can present arguments for the Christian faith that will convince every reasonable person but whether there are stronger reasons for accepting the claims of Christian theism than those of alternative perspectives.

Natural Theology

I have argued that in many contexts of religious disagreement, it is not sufficient for Christians merely to maintain that belief in God is for them properly basic and they are not violating any epistemic norms in believing as they do. In contexts of religious diversity, it is important for Christians to provide appropriate reasons for accepting their own claims rather than those of other religious traditions. The attempt to provide such reasons is often called natural theology, which can be broadly understood as the attempt to establish claims about God's existence and/or nature on the basis of arguments whose premises do not depend upon the authority of sacred Scripture or what is accepted as special revelation.[60] Often

60. See Eugene Thomas Long, ed., *Prospects for Natural Theology*, Studies in Philosophy and the History of Philosophy 25 (Washington, DC: Catholic University of America Press, 1992);

natural theology is identified with the attempt to conclusively "prove" God's existence through sound deductive arguments. A dominant tradition, stemming from some medieval theologians and philosophers, does try to definitively demonstrate God's existence. Scott MacDonald characterizes this tradition as "a kind of demonstrative science," consisting of "truths about God that are either (1) self-evident or evident to sense perception, or (2) derived by deductively valid proofs the (ultimate) premises of which are self-evident or evident to sense perception."[61] This approach has exerted enormous influence upon philosophy and theology from the thirteenth through the early nineteenth centuries and still has highly capable advocates today.

One can readily see the attraction of this approach. If one can formulate a deductive argument for God's existence that successfully accomplishes what it sets out to do, the issue is settled. It would definitively establish that God does exist and thereby falsify atheistic worldviews as well as religious worldviews that deny the reality of God. With one argument, then, one could eliminate many alternative perspectives and establish the truth of one of the defining beliefs of Christian theism.

But it is extremely difficult to formulate a deductive argument for God's existence that does everything it is supposed to do. Deductive arguments are intended to establish conclusively or to entail the truth of the conclusion. Minimally, the argument must be valid and the premises all true. An argument is valid if its form is such that it is logically impossible for the premises all to be true and the conclusion false. An example of a valid argument form is modus ponens:

If A then B

A

Therefore, B

Any argument of this form will be valid. But validity alone is insufficient; it is also necessary that the premises all be true. An argument whose form is valid and all the premises true is a sound argument.

But if a deductive argument is to be used to settle a dispute, such as the question of God's existence, then more than mere soundness is required; the argument also needs to extend knowledge and be persuasive to the skeptic. Thus successful deductive theistic arguments are not only objective in the sense that

---

Charles Taliaferro, "The Project of Natural Theology," in *The Blackwell Companion to Natural Theology*, ed. William Lane Craig and J. P. Moreland (Oxford: Wiley-Blackwell, 2012), 1–23.

61. Scott MacDonald, "Natural Theology," in *Routledge Encyclopedia of Philosophy*, ed. Edward Craig (London: Routledge, 1998), 6:708.

they are sound, but they are also person-relative in that they are intended to persuade a particular audience. In an important discussion, George Mavrodes distinguishes between an argument's "cogency" and its "convincingness." An argument is cogent if and only if it is sound, whereas an argument is convincing for some person N if and only if it is cogent and "N knows that each of its premises is true, without having to infer any of them from its conclusion or from any other . . . statements that he knows only by an inference from that conclusion."[62] In other words, what is desired is an argument in which the argument form is valid, the premises are all true, the premises are known (or can be shown) to be true, and we (including the skeptic) initially have greater confidence in the truth of the premises than in the truth of the conclusion. If there is reasonable doubt about the truth of one of the premises, there will be reasonable doubt about the conclusion.

It is extremely difficult to come up with a deductive argument that meets all of these conditions when the conclusion is controversial and contested. The most popular forms of deductive theistic arguments are cosmological arguments, and many philosophers are convinced that one or another version of the cosmological argument is sound. Consider, for example, the following argument:[63]

1. A contingent being exists.
2. This contingent being has a cause or explanation for its existence.
3. The cause or explanation of its existence is something other than the contingent being itself.
4. What causes or explains the existence of this contingent being must be either other contingent beings or include a noncontingent (necessary) being.
5. Contingent beings alone cannot cause or explain the existence of a contingent being.
6. Therefore, what causes or explains the existence of this contingent being must include a noncontingent being.
7. Therefore, a necessary being exists.

62. George Mavrodes, *Belief in God: A Study in the Epistemology of Religion* (New York: Random House, 1970), 34. See also Keith Yandell, *Philosophy of Religion: A Contemporary Introduction* (London: Routledge, 1999), 169–70; William J. Wainwright, "Theistic Proofs, Person Relativity, and the Rationality of Religious Belief," in *Evidence and Religious Belief*, ed. Kelly James Clark and Raymond J. VanArragon (New York: Oxford University Press, 2011), 82–88.
63. This argument is in Michael Peterson et al., *Reason and Religious Belief*, 90. For helpful discussion of theistic arguments, see Keith Yandell, *Philosophy of Religion: A Contemporary Introduction* (London: Routledge, 1999), 167–211; Craig and Moreland, *Blackwell Companion to Natural Theology*; and J. P. Moreland, Chad V. Meister, and Khaldoun A. Sweis, eds., *Debating Christian Theism* (New York: Oxford University Press, 2013).

A contingent being is one that, although it does exist, might not have existed. The universe as a whole is contingent, as are human beings and mountains. It is logically possible that none of these would exist. But they do. Why? The argument claims that only a noncontingent being can explain or account for the fact that any contingent entities exist. Many people, including many philosophers, find the argument convincing. Although the conclusion does not speak of God, it is not implausible to suppose that the noncontingent being causally responsible for bringing into being contingent entities is the same reality that theists refer to as God.

However, two of the premises are controversial.[64] Premise 2 depends upon the principle of sufficient reason, which holds that every contingent entity has a reason or explanation for why it exists, and critics of the argument question whether we know that this is true for all contingent things. Some also question whether premise 5 is true: why should we believe that contingent realities cannot provide adequate explanations for contingent entities? Both premises strike me as eminently plausible, but there are those who question whether we really do know that they are true. My point here is simply that if the argument is to be convincing to someone who does not already believe that God exists, then the skeptic will need to be persuaded to accept premises 2 and 5. To the extent that the skeptic is unconvinced about either premise, the conclusion will also be problematic. This is simply the nature of deductive arguments.

But we should not think of natural theology merely in terms of deductive theistic arguments. In the early modern period, for example, John Locke, Joseph Butler, and William Paley advanced inductive and probabilistic arguments for Christian theism. In a much more general sense, then, we might think of natural theology as any attempt to offer arguments in support of Christian theism from premises that are not themselves derived from the authority of divine special revelation. Undoubtedly one of the most impressive recent examples of natural theology is the sustained probabilistic argument of Richard Swinburne. After rich and rigorous discussion of the evidence, Swinburne concludes that "on our total evidence theism is more probable than not. . . . The experience of so many people in their moments of religious vision corroborates what nature and history show to be quite likely—that there is a God who made and sustains man and the universe."[65] If Swinburne

---

64. See Peterson et al., *Reason and Religious Belief*, 90–93, for discussion of the critical premises.

65. Richard Swinburne, *The Existence of God*, 2nd ed. (Oxford: Clarendon, 2004), 342; see also by idem, *The Coherence of Theism* (Oxford: Clarendon, 1977; rev. ed., 1993); *Faith and Reason* (Oxford: Clarendon, 1981); *Responsibility and Atonement* (Oxford: Clarendon, 1989); *Revelation* (Oxford: Clarendon, 1992); *The Christian God* (Oxford: Clarendon, 1994); and *Providence and the Problem of Evil* (Oxford: Clarendon, 1998).

is correct, and I think he is, then strong views on religious ambiguity should be abandoned, for there actually are good reasons for preferring Christian theism over denying it.

Natural theology today must take into account not only the challenges from secular atheism but also issues prompted by religious disagreement. As early as 1960, Ninian Smart, an authority on Hindu and Buddhist thought as well as a Christian analytic philosopher, challenged Christians to address the question "Why be a Christian rather than a Buddhist?"[66] In a 1961 essay Smart states,

> Any appeal to religious experience (whether intuitive or otherwise) must inevitably lead to a consideration of the experience not merely of Christians but of Buddhists and others, and thereby to an examination of the way experience is linked to different sorts of doctrines. Through this investigation one is bound to ask what the criteria are for choosing between different formulations of religious belief. And from the apologetic point of view it is necessary to give reasons for accepting one's own faith rather than some other.[67]

Smart advocates a fresh kind of natural theology that takes seriously the issues of competing truth claims across religions. As we saw in chapter 1, Smart understands religions as complex, multidimensional phenomena, with each religious tradition manifesting a particular worldview or set of core beliefs in terms of which it interprets humanity, the cosmos, and the religious ultimate. Smart calls for a kind of "worldview analysis," which includes assessment of the truth or rationality of different worldviews. Thus a primary task for "cross-cultural philosophy of religion" is "to clarify the criteria for determining the truth as between worldviews."[68] Smart speaks of this project as "soft natural theology." While recognizing that there are nonarbitrary criteria that can be applied in evaluating worldviews, Smart does not think that we have demonstrative knockdown arguments that resolve the issues conclusively.

There are, of course, degrees of softness. While Smart correctly recognized that with respect to religious diversity, natural theology is not likely to be conclusive, he was perhaps excessively modest in his expectations for what can be

66. See Ninian Smart, *A Dialogue of Religions* (London: SCM, 1960), 11.

67. Ninian Smart, "Revelation, Reason and Religions," in *Prospect for Metaphysics: Essays of Metaphysical Exploration*, ed. Ian Ramsey (London: Allen & Unwin, 1961), 92.

68. Ninian Smart, "The Philosophy of Worldviews, or the Philosophy of Religion Transformed," in *Religious Pluralism and Truth: Essays on Cross-Cultural Philosophy of Religion*, ed. Thomas Dean (Albany: State University of New York Press, 1995), 24. See also by idem, *Reasons and Faiths: An Investigation of Religious Discourse; Christian and Non-Christian* (London: Routledge and Kegan Paul, 1958); "Soft Natural Theology," in *Prospects for Natural Theology*, 198–206; *Worldviews: Crosscultural Explorations of Human Beliefs*, 2nd ed. (Englewood Cliffs, NJ: Prentice-Hall, 1995).

accomplished through worldview analysis. To be sure, the complexity of the issues should not be minimized, but neither should they be exaggerated. We have already considered the possibility of there being one or more versions of a sound, persuasive deductive argument for God's existence. If there is such an argument, as many believe, then there is compelling reason for accepting a defining belief of Christian theism and for rejecting some defining beliefs of nontheistic religious worldviews.

Careful rational analysis can also call into question certain assertions made by some religious traditions. We might, for example, consider the epistemology of religious experience and the claims based upon certain kinds of introspective experiences in Hinduism, Buddhism, or Jainism. Is it really just as rational to accept as veridical purported experiences of Nirguna Brahman among Hindus or of emptiness among Buddhists as it is to accept purported experiences of the personal God of Christian theism? Keith Yandell, among others, has persuasively argued that certain introspective enlightenment experiences at the heart of some forms of Hinduism or Buddhism *cannot* be veridical because, as presented, they are incoherent.[69] If he is correct, and I think he is, this has significant implications for religious claims based upon such experiences. Similarly, if the notion of anattta (no self) in classical Buddhism is indeed incoherent, as many argue, then this provides positive reason for rejecting a central tenet of many Buddhist traditions.[70] And so on.

Even if there are sound and persuasive deductive theistic arguments, providing good reasons for accepting the defining beliefs of Christian theism will involve more than simply arguing for God's existence. Other central Christian claims concerning God's revelation in Scripture and the person and work of Jesus Christ will also need to be established. Deductive arguments may play a role in this, but they cannot do everything required in establishing the case for Christian theism. More promising here is a cumulative-case approach, or argument by inference to the best explanation, which maintains that a strong case for Christian theism can be established through the careful accumulation and analysis of a wide variety of evidential data from various dimensions of our experience and the world.[71] The cumulative case approach begins by identifying a variety of factors in the world that need some explanation.

69. See Keith Yandell, *Philosophy of Religion*, chaps. 12–13; idem, *The Epistemology of Religious Experience* (New York: Cambridge University Press, 1993), chaps. 8–9, 13–14.

70. See Yandell, *Philosophy of Religion*, chap. 12; Keith Yandell and Harold A. Netland, *Buddhism: A Christian Exploration and Appraisal* (Downers Grove, IL: InterVarsity, 2009).

71. On cumulative case arguments, see Basil Mitchell, *The Justification of Religious Belief* (Oxford: Oxford University Press, 1981); and William J. Abraham, "Cumulative Case Arguments for Christian Theism," in *The Rationality of Religious Belief: Essays in Honour of Basil Mitchell*, ed. William J. Abraham and Steven W. Holtzer (Oxford: Clarendon, 1989), 17–37.

These factors are diverse and might include the fine-tuning and contingency of the universe; human consciousness and intentionality; the objectivity of moral values and principles and our awareness of such principles; goodness and beauty in the world and the human capacity to appreciate it; the widespread belief across cultures and historical eras that there is more to reality than simply this life and the physical world; and experiences across time and cultures that are taken to be encounters with God. A cumulative-case argument for Christian theism would also include factors concerning the extraordinary composition of the Bible over a period of roughly 1,500 years; the life, teachings, death, and apparent resurrection of Jesus of Nazareth; and the rapid growth of the early Christian community. While none of these phenomena, either individually or collectively, entail the truth of Christian theism, the argument claims that Christian theism provides a more plausible explanation for these factors than other alternatives. That is, if Christian theism is false, then it is difficult to account for these things. But if, on the other hand, Christian theism is true, then we have a satisfactory explanation for these realities. Furthermore, if Christian theism is true, then (at least some of) these are precisely the kinds of phenomena we would expect to encounter in our world. For example, given the reality of a morally good and holy creator God, it is not surprising that reality includes moral values and that human beings are capable of moral awareness.

There is an inescapable measure of personal judgment in such an argument, but this does not mean that such judgments are necessarily arbitrary. As William Abraham puts it, "Personal judgment simply means the ability to weigh evidence without using some sort of formal calculus."[72] There is no reason to expect that an appropriate natural theology will produce a simple algorithmic procedure for testing worldviews or even that it will provide a definitive knockdown argument for Christian theism.

A creative and helpful approach conducive to a cumulative case argument for Christian theism has been suggested by C. Stephen Evans, who argues that classical theistic arguments should be understood as being grounded in "natural signs" that point to God's reality.[73] Although these natural signs can be used to develop deductive or inductive arguments, they can also "point to God's reality with no argument or conscious inference being part of the process." In other words, they can provide "non-inferential knowledge of God."[74] Thus they provide a kind of direct, noninferential evidence for God's reality.

72. Abraham, "Cumulative Case Arguments," 34.
73. C. Stephen Evans, *Natural Signs and Knowledge of God: A New Look at Theistic Arguments* (New York: Oxford University Press, 2010).
74. Ibid., 45, 154.

Theistic arguments typically pick up on aspects of the natural signs, developing them into formal arguments. But in so doing, they usually include at least one premise that is debatable. Yet even if a formal argument is inconclusive, the basic insight at its heart, what Evans calls the natural sign, can still have evidential value. "Even if an argument developed from a sign fails as a coercive argument, the sign may still point to God and make knowledge of God possible for those who have the ability and will to read the sign properly."[75] Theistic natural signs "can reasonably be viewed as providing prima facie evidence for belief in God."[76]

Evans argues that the natural sign at the heart of the cosmological argument is the experience of the world as "mysterious and puzzling," or a sense of "cosmic wonder." Cosmological arguments are "reflective attempts" to pick out those characteristics that cry out for explanation, such as the contingency of the universe. Why is there something rather than nothing? "The experience of cosmic wonder, when we encounter objects in the universe or the universe as a whole and see this natural order as 'contingent,' might simply be a perception of the createdness of the natural world."[77]

Teleological arguments are grounded in the natural sign of "beneficial order." Evans states that "the natural world contains many examples of orderly, complex structures where the order seems to be in the service of some good. This order is the result of an intelligent designer, a Mind that is powerful and cares about those good ends."[78] An example of such beneficial order is the fine-tuning of the universe, or the intricate set of conditions that must obtain for carbon-based life either to emerge or be sustained.[79]

Evans sees two natural signs embedded in moral arguments: (1) our experience of ourselves as responsible and accountable moral beings, and (2) our perception of the special value and dignity of the human person.[80] Evans states that even the atheist feels the force of moral obligation and the dignity of human persons. "The fact that people continue to affirm the value of humans even when they lack any plausible account of why humans have such value shows the force of the sign."[81]

Finally, Evans summarizes the natural signs at the heart of the cosmological, teleological, and moral arguments as follows:

75. Ibid., 3.
76. Ibid., 184.
77. Ibid., 63.
78. Ibid., 90.
79. See Robin Collins, "The Teleological Argument: An Exploration of the Fine-Tuning of the Universe," in *Blackwell Companion to Natural Theology*, 202–81.
80. Evans, *Natural Signs and Knowledge of God*, 132.
81. Ibid., 147.

Cosmic wonder suggests that whatever lies behind the natural universe exists in some deeper, more secure way than the contingent things that cry out for explanation. It has a firmer grip on reality than the transient realities we encounter in our world. Beneficial order suggests that what lies behind the universe is intelligent because purposive. Moral obligation suggests that whatever lies behind the universe is personal and cares about moral goodness; the reality must be a being capable of creating an obligation.[82]

What Evans identifies as natural signs can be used in constructing a comprehensive cumulative case argument for Christian theism, thus showing that there are strong reasons for adopting Christian theism rather than other religious or nonreligious alternatives.

82. Ibid., 185.

=== 8 ===

Living with Religious Diversity
as Jesus's Disciples

During the week before the ninth anniversary of the terrible attacks on the World Trade Center and Pentagon on September 11, 2001, the pastor of a small church in Florida suddenly became the center of international attention. People from around the world watched with both fascination and horror as Terry Jones solemnly announced that God had instructed him to burn copies of the Qur'an on September 11, 2010. An obscure and peculiar pastor was suddenly the focus of intense media scrutiny.

Public sentiment was largely negative. Not only did the idea of burning the Qur'an strike many as being in particularly bad taste, but there was also widespread apprehension about the anticipated violent response from radical Muslims. As the day approached, there was a flurry of activity as General David Petraeus, Secretary of State Hillary Clinton, and even President Obama publicly called for Jones to abandon his plans. Secretary of Defense Robert Gates spoke directly with the pastor on the phone. Just before September 11, Jones reconsidered, claiming that God now was instructing him not to burn the Qur'an. Despite some public demonstrations in Pakistan and Afghanistan, there was a global collective sigh of relief when September 11 came and went without the much-publicized desecration of the Muslim holy book.

But the relief was temporary: on March 21, 2011, Jones held a mock trial of the Qur'an and publicly set a copy on fire. Incited by the burning of their sacred text, mobs in Mazar-e Sharif and Kandahar, Afghanistan, attacked a United Nations compound and other Western targets, killing sixteen and wounding over ninety.[1]

This tragic and instructive episode serves as a window into the volatile and complex world of the early twenty-first century. It is yet another reminder that religion plays a very real and important public role in our world today. Those working in international relations, the military, public policy, or business and marketing are all acutely aware of the importance of understanding the religious dynamics in various societies. Yet this sad affair also demonstrates how important it is for Christian leaders, especially American evangelicals, to understand these dynamics.

Such events illustrate for us the challenges of living in a global world, connected by telecommunications technologies that transmit images and messages around the world in a matter of seconds. Fifty years ago the threat to burn the Qur'an would have prompted little interest by the media, and it would have taken days for visual images of the burning to be transferred worldwide. Globalization has produced a complex interconnectedness that is redefining our understanding of the local and its relation to the world. The actions of a pastor in Gainesville, Florida, now have instantaneous repercussions in Kandahar. Christian leaders today must assume that what is said to a small group in the basement of a church might be available globally through the internet within minutes.

One is also struck by the deep emotions evoked by the threat to burn the Qur'an. Religion is a potent, volatile social and political force, and social observers today are increasingly alarmed by the deep tensions and acts of violence that have religious roots. While violence by Islamist radicals receives the most attention, Mark Juergensmeyer and others remind us that in the past century all the major religious traditions have had their own problems with religiously sanctioned violence.[2]

Most significantly, however, this incident raises questions for those in Christian ministry. The man who burned the Qur'an was a Christian minister. While he was hardly a mainstream Christian leader—he had a record of extreme views placing him on the fringe of traditional Christianity—he was a Christian

1. Kevin Sieff, "Florida Pastor Terry Jones's Koran Burning Has Far-Reaching Effect," *Washington Post*, April 2, 2011, http://www.washingtonpost.com/local/education/florida-pastor-terry-joness-koran-burning-has-far-reaching-effect/2011/04/02/AFpiFoQC_story.html.

2. Mark Juergensmeyer, *Global Rebellion: Religious Challenges to the Secular State, from Christian Militias to Al Qaeda* (Berkeley: University of California Press, 2008).

pastor. Why would a Christian minister think that God had directed him to do such a thing? How should other Christians respond?

The facts that the pastor was an American and the sacred text he burned was the Qur'an also have symbolic significance. Why did Terry Jones burn the Qur'an and not other sacred texts, such as the popular Hindu scripture Bhagavad Gita, the Confucian Analects, or the Lotus Sutra of Buddhism? The idea that one might burn any of *these* texts seems ludicrous, and this surely suggests something about both the fascination and revulsion American Christians have with Islam. In American Christians' eyes, especially after September 11, 2001, Islam is not simply another religion: it is the Diabolical Other. Images of Muslims provoke intense passions among many American Christians that are absent when considering Buddhists, Hindus, or Mormons. Thomas Kidd's superb study of the issue, *American Christians and Islam*,[3] reminds us that there is a long history of American Christians vilifying Islam and Muslims, going back to the seventeenth century.

Burning the Qur'an was certainly a symbolic act, but Jones was not simply making a religious or theological statement, a public demonstration of his commitment to Christ and rejection of Islam as an idolatrous religion. In the context of post-9/11 American nationalism, Jones's action takes on powerful social and political significance as well. Although Jones's theological convictions were undoubtedly important, by desecrating the Qur'an he was also reasserting his understanding of American/Christian identity and exceptionalism in the face of perceived threats. Jones's act is another example of ways in which religion today can be closely linked to issues of ethnicity, nationalism, and politics, usually with unhappy results.

But the issues here are broader and deeper than whether it is appropriate to burn the Qur'an. The United States is rapidly becoming a very religiously diverse place.[4] What is appropriate behavior with respect to religious others? There is nothing particularly problematic about Jones disagreeing with Muslims over whether the Qur'an really is the Word of God. People disagree over religious matters all the time, and one of the distinctives of the American system is the freedom of religious conscience: people are free to believe or not to believe what they wish. But why did he think that burning the Qur'an was something that a good Christian and American citizen *should* do? This is yet another illustration of the ambiguities and complexities of living in a free society characterized by religious diversity and disagreement. Legal observers

3. Thomas S. Kidd, *American Christians and Islam: Evangelical Culture and Muslims from the Colonial Period to the Age of Terrorism* (Princeton: Princeton University Press, 2009).

4. See Charles L. Cohen and Ronald L. Numbers, eds., *Gods in America: Religious Pluralism in the United States* (New York: Oxford University Press, 2013).

agree that Jones had the legal right to burn the Qur'an. But *should* he have done so? Here, as in so many cases, the rights of free speech and freedom of religious expression clash with what seem to be common sense and simple decency. There is an important distinction between what one is legally permitted to do in a free and diverse society and what one ought, as a good citizen, to do. Being a good citizen involves cultivating civic virtue, a moral quality that takes one beyond simply being scrupulous not to break any laws and maintaining one's rights. Civic virtue sometimes means resisting what one has the right to do for the sake of a common higher good.

How should followers of Jesus Christ respond to the religiously diverse and pluralistic world of the early twenty-first century? A host of fresh questions demand attention, and Christian leaders are only beginning to think through the knotty issues they raise. Although consulting enduring principles from the past is important, new ways of thinking must also be crafted since the religious, cultural, and political landscape of many nations in the twenty-first century is uncharted territory. Simply repeating what has been done in the past is insufficient. Moreover, Christian leaders should seize the initiative and not simply react to patterns set by others. Christians should lead by example, showing others how to be both firmly committed to Jesus Christ as Lord and also good citizens, embracing in appropriate ways the rich diversity of our societies.

In this concluding chapter my focus is upon issues confronting Christians in the United States, although the general principles will apply to Christians elsewhere as well. Today many nations are democratic in political structure, committed to freedom of religious expression, and they also have diverse religious populations. Although local contexts will vary in the particulars, many of the larger issues are similar, regardless of the local religious traditions or cultural distinctives. Christian leaders around the world need to think carefully and creatively about what it means to be both disciples of Jesus Christ and good citizens amid the changing global realities. In general terms I will highlight some principles here that should guide Christian deliberation on these issues. The discussion is suggestive, certainly not exhaustive.

Disciples of Jesus and Good Citizens

Christians have two sets of obligations, both of which need to be taken seriously and navigated carefully. Scripture makes it clear that while God remains sovereign over all affairs and Christ's lordship covers all of life, Christians have legitimate obligations to non-Christian civil authorities. When he was questioned by the Pharisees about whether Jews should pay taxes to Caesar—implicitly acknowledging the legitimacy of Roman rule—Jesus responded by distinguishing obligations to God from obligations to the Roman authorities. "Give back to Caesar what is Caesar's, and to God what is God's" (Matt. 22:21). Biblical writers elsewhere not only affirm the legitimacy of pagan governing authorities but also call upon Christ's followers to live in an exemplary manner that honors the ruling authorities (Rom. 13:1–7; 1 Pet. 2:13–17).

To be sure, where obligations as citizens clearly violate obligations as followers of Jesus, Christians are to obey God rather than human authorities (Dan. 3:16–18; 6:10, 21–22; Acts 4:19–20; 5:29). Certainly in many places in the world today, following Jesus entails taking a stand against certain demands of the state, often at considerable personal cost. Most of the issues Christians confront with the religious diversity in the United States, however, do not involve irreconcilable conflicts between obligations as citizens and obligations as Christians.

Politically, the United States is a republic with a constitution that explicitly rules out the establishment of a state religion and guarantees the free exercise of religion. The relevant phrase in the First Amendment of the US Constitution states, "Congress shall make no law respecting an establishment of religion, or prohibiting the free exercise thereof." It is easy to forget how radical this statement was when adopted in 1791. Throughout history, in most societies the religion of the ruler was the religion of the people, and there was little interest on the part of rulers in the freedom of religious conscience. For that matter, freedom of religious expression was not highly valued during the centuries of European Christendom. Things changed, however, with the American experiment, and today American Christians are the beneficiaries of a system that champions freedom of religious expression.

There have been lengthy debates over the extent of Christian influence upon the founders of the American Republic and whether the United States is a Christian nation.[5] Historically, the nation has been influenced by Christian values and principles, along with other significant influences from the Enlightenment, and the majority of citizens today still claim to be Christian. But the United States cannot be called a Christian nation in anything but a demographic sense, since there is no state religion. Although the influence of Christian values and principles upon American society is evident in some areas, many other aspects of American life reflect profoundly non-Christian values and principles. Even where American society explicitly acknowledges

---

5. The literature is vast, but helpful discussions can be found in Edwin S. Gaustad, *Proclaim Liberty throughout All the Land: A History of Church and State in America* (New York: Oxford University Press, 1999); and idem, *Faith of the Founders: Religion and the New Nation, 1776–1826* (Waco: Baylor University Press, 2011).

Christian ideals, it often fails to live up to these principles. Moreover, American society today includes many different religious traditions as well as a growing population that is explicitly nonreligious. Such diversity can be expected to be even more pronounced in the years ahead.

For American Christians, being a disciple of Jesus Christ means being a good and responsible citizen of the United States, honoring the legal and social expectations of the land unless it becomes clear that doing so is incompatible with one's responsibilities as Christ's disciples. The dual obligations of being Christ's disciples and good citizens should be considered on at least three distinct levels. First is the dimension of interpersonal relationships with religious others, how Christians interact with neighbors and colleagues at work or school who follow other religious paths. Second is the domain involving Christian presence and conduct in the broader society, or what is often referred to as "the public square." Finally, given our globalizing world, Christians must also consider the implications of Christian public presence and conduct in the world at large. What is needed here is a comprehensive, fresh framework that enables us to deal with the range of issues on all three levels. But rather than propose such a framework here, I will suggest some general principles in several areas that can guide Christians as they struggle with these issues.

Christian Witness amid Religious Diversity

The Christian faith is not a local, tribal religion restricted to a particular people or place. Along with Buddhism and Islam, Christianity is a transnational or missionary religion. The Christian gospel is inherently missionary, pushing followers of Jesus to cross boundaries of geography, class, ethnicity, and religious affiliation in calling all peoples to repentance and commitment to Jesus as Savior and Lord. The gospel is good news of redemption and reconciliation with God that must be shared with a world ravaged by sin and evil. Thus witness and evangelism are not optional for the Christian church; Christ's followers are to be his witnesses, beginning locally and moving progressively across geographic, ethnic, and cultural boundaries "to the ends of the earth" (Acts 1:8).

Evangelism, from the Greek *euangelizomai*, means to bring or announce the good news, the *euangelion*, the gospel. The apostle Paul identifies the gospel with the death of Jesus Christ for our sins, his burial, and his resurrection from the dead on the third day (1 Cor. 15:1–4). The gospel is "the power of God that brings salvation to everyone who believes: first to the Jew, then to the

Gentile" (Rom. 1:16). The good news that Christians proclaim in evangelism, then, is that Jesus is Savior and Lord, and that in his name people can have forgiveness and redemption from sin, new life through the indwelling power of the Holy Spirit, and ultimately everlasting fellowship with God.

During the twentieth century the necessity of evangelism was often based upon the so-called Great Commission of Matthew 28. This was especially the case with evangelicals, who have given this text prominence in their theologies of mission. But evangelicals often treat Matthew 28:18–20 as a text that is detached from the rest of the Gospel of Matthew. This results in a superficial understanding of the text as commanding Christians simply to transmit to "all nations" some basic information about Jesus Christ and the possibility of forgiveness of sins, resulting in eternal life with God in heaven. Once this information transfer has encompassed sufficient groups of people, Christians can conclude that the Great Commission has been fulfilled.

But Matthew 28:18–20 is not an isolated text. David Bosch states, "It is inadmissible to lift these words out of Matthew's gospel, as it were, allow them a life of their own, and understand them without any reference to the context in which they first appeared."[6] This passage must be understood within the broader context of the entire Gospel of Matthew; when this is done, it becomes clear that Jesus gives a much richer and more challenging command than is often assumed. The text itself states,

> Then Jesus came to them and said, "All authority in heaven and on earth has been given to me. Therefore go and make disciples of all nations, baptizing them in the name of the Father and of the Son and of the Holy Spirit, and teaching them to obey everything I have commanded you. And surely I am with you always, to the very end of the age."

The primary emphasis in the text is upon "mak[ing] disciples" (*mathēteusate*) of all peoples.[7]

Two observations are appropriate here. First, Christ's followers are to make disciples of all peoples, without exception, and this includes sincere adherents of other religions. The command is not to make disciples simply of the nonreligious or atheists, but rather of all peoples. So if they are to be faithful to their Lord, Christians cannot abandon witness among devoted followers of other religious paths.

6. David Bosch, *Transforming Mission* (Maryknoll, NY: Orbis Books, 1991), 57.
7. See D. A. Carson, "Matthew," in *The Expositor's Bible Commentary*, ed. Frank E. Gabelein (Grand Rapids: Zondervan, 1984), 8:595–96; R. T. France, *The Gospel of Matthew* (Grand Rapids: Eerdmans, 2007), 1115.

Second, the command is to make disciples, not to make Christians or to convert people to the religion of Christianity. In Christian witness, the most important thing is not the religious labels or categories that one adopts but rather becoming an authentic disciple of Jesus Christ. Andrew Walls draws a helpful contrast between a proselyte and a convert. Becoming a proselyte is a matter of accepting labels and adopting external behavioral changes without having one's inner disposition—one's values, commitments, and ways of thinking—transformed. The converts, on the other hand, are transformed in their commitments, values, and beliefs, with changes in behavior flowing from a new way of understanding reality. The converts not only have a transformed understanding but also live out gospel principles within their linguistic and cultural frame of reference.[8] In making disciples, Christians are to cultivate converts, not proselytes.

What does it mean to "make disciples"? Bosch notes that the term "disciple" (*mathētēs*) occurs seventy-three times in Matthew. "The theme of discipleship is central to Matthew's gospel and to Matthew's understanding of the church and mission."[9] Clearly "making disciples" involves much more than simply passing on some information about Jesus to others. In making disciples, we are to shape others, through the power of the Holy Spirit, so that they live in conformity with all that Jesus instructed his followers. Jesus's teachings throughout the Gospel of Matthew, in the great discourses such as the Sermon on the Mount and the parables, provide a good picture of what a disciple looks like. One of Jesus's most significant teachings is in Matthew 22, where a religious leader questions him about the greatest commandment: Of all the commandments in the Hebrew Scriptures, which is most important? Jesus's answer has implications for how Christians are to carry out the Great Commission.

> One of them, an expert in the law, tested him with this question: "Teacher, which is the greatest commandment in the Law?" Jesus replied, "'Love the Lord your God with all your heart and with all your soul and with all your mind.' This is the first and greatest commandment. And the second is like it: 'Love your neighbor as yourself.' All the Law and the Prophets hang on these two commandments." (Matt. 22:35–40; cf. Deut. 6:4–5; Mark 12:28–34; Luke 10:25–37)

8. Andrew Walls, "Culture and Conversion in Christian History," in *The Missionary Movement in Christian History* (Maryknoll, NY: Orbis Books, 1996), 51–53.
9. David Bosch, *Transforming Mission*, 73. On discipleship in Matthew, see Michael J. Wilkins, *Discipleship in the Ancient World and Matthew's Gospel*, 2nd ed. (Grand Rapids: Baker, 1995).

Jesus's disciples love God with their entire beings and love their neighbors as they love themselves. One's neighbors in America today include devout adherents of many religions as well as those who are nonreligious.

Another significant command of Jesus is the so-called Golden Rule in Matthew 7:12: "So in everything, do to others what you would have them do to you, for this sums up the Law and the Prophets."[10] The ethical principle behind Jesus's statement has enormous ramifications for how Jesus's disciples are to treat others, including how Christians should engage in evangelism and witness among religious others. The Great Commission, the Great Commandment, and the Golden Rule are all at the heart of Jesus's teaching and help to define what a disciple of Jesus Christ is to be like. In carrying out the Great Commission, then, Christians are to follow the Great Commandment and the Golden Rule. Thus Christians have at least three obligations with respect to adherents of other religions: (1) to make disciples of religious others; (2) to love religious others; and (3) to treat religious others the way Christians would want to be treated by them.

Given the many tensions in today's world, it is critical that Christians bear witness to the gospel of Jesus Christ in fresh ways that are not only faithful to the biblical message but also respectful and sensitive to others. In suggesting some principles for Christian witness in our pluralistic world, I will draw on two very significant recent documents, one from evangelicals and one more ecumenical in nature, which nicely reflect themes from the texts noted above.

In 2011, after a five-year period of study, reflection, and dialogue, the Roman Catholic Pontifical Council for Interreligious Dialogue, the World Council of Churches, and the World Evangelical Alliance jointly put forward a short document titled "Christian Witness in a Multi-religious World: Recommendations for Conduct." Despite its nature as a consensus document, this provides an excellent guide for winsome witness in multireligious contexts. Christian Witness echoes themes that are also found in The Cape Town Commitment, a theologically and missiologically rich statement produced by the Third Lausanne Congress on World Evangelization, held at Cape Town, South Africa, in October 2010. The Cape Town Commitment builds upon earlier documents from the Lausanne Movement, especially The Lausanne Covenant (1974) and The Manila Manifesto (1989). In what follows I will mention several themes

10. The Golden Rule articulates a basic moral principle that is embraced by many ethical systems and is reflected in the moral codes of many cultures. It finds clear expression, e.g., in the Analects of Confucius. See *Confucius: The Analects*, trans. D. C. Lau (London: Penguin Books, 1979), 112 (12.2), 135 (15.24). See Harry J. Gensler, *Ethics and the Golden Rule: Do unto Others* (New York: Routledge, 2013); Jeffrey Wattles, *The Golden Rule* (New York: Oxford University Press, 1996).

from both Christian Witness in a Multi-religious World and The Cape Town Commitment that are especially significant for Christian witness today.

1. *Bearing witness to the gospel of Jesus Christ among religious others is not optional, but rather is obligatory for the Christian church.* Thus The Cape Town Commitment begins by stating, "We remain committed to the task of bearing worldwide witness to Jesus Christ and all his teachings."[11] It then reaffirms traditional doctrines on the lostness of humankind due to sin, Jesus Christ as the one Lord and Savior for all people, and the need for Christians "to be the whole Church, to believe, obey, and share the whole gospel, and to go to the whole world to make disciples of all nations."[12] Similarly, Christian Witness in a Multi-religious World declares, "Mission belongs to the very heart of the church. Proclaiming the word of God and witnessing to the world is essential for every Christian. At the same time, it is necessary to do so according to gospel principles, with full respect and love for all human beings."[13] The issue is not whether Christians should bear witness to Jesus Christ as Lord but rather how they should do so.

2. *Christians are to bear witness to the gospel in accordance with God's love.* Significantly, Christian Witness in a Multi-religious World links witness to the Great Commandment: "Christians believe that God is the source of all love and, accordingly, in their witness they are called to live lives of love and to love their neighbors as themselves (cf. Matt. 22:34–40; John 14:15)."[14] Similarly, The Cape Town Commitment gives eloquent expression to the importance of love in Christian mission: "The mission of God flows from the love of God. The mission of God's people flows from our love for God and for all that God loves."[15] The Cape Town Commitment also acknowledges the centrality of the Great Commandment for mission, observing, "'Love your neighbour as yourself' includes persons of other faiths."[16] Witness grows out of and reflects love—love for God and love of others.

3. *Christian witness must be respectful of others and be conducted with humility and moral integrity.* The call for moral integrity and humility in the lives of Christians is foundational to Christian Witness in a Multi-religious

---

11. *The Cape Town Commitment: A Confession of Faith and a Call to Action; The Third Lausanne Congress*, Didasko Files (Peabody, MA: Hendrickson, 2011), preamble, p. 6, http://www.lausanne.org/en/documents/ctcommitment.html.

12. Ibid., 8.

13. Christian Witness in a Multi-religious World, http://www.oikoumene.org/en/resources/documents/wcc-programmes/interreligious-dialogue-and-cooperation/christian-identity-ins-pluralistic-societies/christian-witness-in-a-multi-religious-world. Preamble.

14. Ibid., "Principles," 1.

15. *Cape Town Commitment*, I.1, p. 9.

16. Ibid., II.C.1, p. 47.

World: "Christians are called to conduct themselves with integrity, charity, compassion and humility, and to overcome all arrogance, condescension and disparagement (cf. Gal. 5:22)."[17] Christ's witnesses are to be men and women of moral integrity, humble, honest in speech, compassionate and generous with those in need, and gracious in demeanor.

Similarly, The Cape Town Commitment distinguishes evangelism from proselytizing and calls for humble and respectful witness that is "scrupulously ethical."

> We are called to share good news in evangelism, but not to engage in unworthy proselytizing. *Evangelism*, while it includes persuasive rational argument following the example of the Apostle Paul, is "to make an honest and open statement of the gospel which leaves the hearers entirely free to make up their own minds about it. We wish to be sensitive to those of other faiths, and we reject any approach that seeks to force conversion on them." *Proselytizing*, by contrast, is the attempt to compel others to become "one of us," to "accept our religion," or indeed to "join our denomination."[18]

The Commitment calls upon Christians to "reject any form of witness that is coercive, unethical, deceptive, or disrespectful."[19] The Commitment candidly acknowledges past failures in Christian witness. "In the name of the God of love, we repent of our failure to seek friendships with people of Muslim, Hindu, Buddhist and other religious backgrounds. In the spirit of Jesus we will take initiatives to show love, goodwill and hospitality to them."[20]

Christian Witness in a Multi-religious World states, "Christians are to speak sincerely and respectfully; they are to listen in order to learn about and understand others' beliefs and practices, and are encouraged to acknowledge and appreciate what is true and good in them. Any comment or critical approach should be made in a spirit of mutual respect, making sure not to bear false witness concerning other religions."[21] Among other things, this means that in depictions of religious others, Christians are to be fair and honest, refusing to promote misleading characterizations or caricatures and resisting language that incites fear or hatred. The command in the Decalogue not to bear false witness against one's neighbor applies to religious others as well (Exod. 20:16). The Cape Town Commitment also reminds us that the

---

17. Christian Witness in a Multi-religious World, "Principles," 3.
18. *Cape Town Commitment*, II.C.1, p. 47. The embedded citation is from The Manila Manifesto, section 12, http://www.lausanne.org/en/documents/manila-manifesto.html.
19. *Cape Town Commitment*, II.C.1.A, p. 48.
20. Ibid., II.C.1.B, p. 48.
21. Christian Witness in a Multi-religious World, "Principles," 10.

plausibility of interreligious witness is directly related to the moral integrity and Christlikeness manifest in Christians. "The evangelization of the world and the recognition of Christ's deity are helped or hindered by whether or not we obey him in practice."[22] Sadly, Christian witness is often undermined by the lack of Christlikeness in how Christians live and treat others.

The Cape Town Commitment also refers to another biblical theme that should inform our interactions with religious others. "We respond to our high calling as disciples of Jesus Christ to see people of other faiths as neighbours in the biblical sense. They are human beings created in God's image, whom God loved and for whose sins Christ died."[23] The fact that all people, including sincere adherents of other religions, are created in the image of God (Gen. 1:26–27; 5:1–3; 9:6; 1 Cor. 11:7; James 3:9) has significant implications for how we understand and relate to religious others. Despite the many differences between disciples of Jesus and religious others, there is a basic unity among all as fellow creatures created by God.

One of the many implications of this concerns the fundamental categories Christians use in thinking about religious others. If the primary category for identification is Hindu or Buddhist or Muslim, then the differences between them and Christians are accentuated along with the barriers that need to be overcome. On the other hand, if religious others are understood primarily as fellow human beings created by God and loved by God, then this acknowledges a fundamental commonality that is more basic than any differences. All human beings share commonality in being creatures created by God in his image, sinners in rebellion against God, and beggars in need of God's redeeming grace. The differences between Christians and Muslims or Hindus remain real, but they are secondary to this fundamental commonality.

4. *Christian witness should include appropriate forms of interreligious dialogue.* Thus The Cape Town Commitment calls for "the proper place of dialogue with people of other faiths," a dialogue that "combines confidence in the uniqueness of Christ and in the truth of the gospel with respectful listening to others."[24] Christian Witness in a Multi-religious World states, "Christian witness in a pluralistic world includes engaging in dialogue with people of different religions and cultures."[25] Many evangelicals are suspicious of interreligious dialogue because the agenda of some persons most prominently involved in dialogue seems to be incompatible with evangelism and witness. Much, of course, depends upon how dialogue is understood and practiced,

22. *Cape Town Commitment*, "Conclusion," 71.
23. Ibid., II.C.1, p. 47.
24. Ibid., II.C.1, c and e, p. 72.
25. Christian Witness in a Multi-religious World, "A Basis for Christian Witness," 4.

but properly construed, there is nothing in dialogue itself that is incompat-ible with evangelical commitments. Indeed, given global religious realities, it is difficult to see how Christian leaders in the coming decades can engage responsibly in mission without participating at some level in dialogue with those from other religions.[26]

5. *Christians are to reject violence and the abuse of power in witness.* Christians must give careful attention to the perceived and real relationship between witness and power. Physical violence is surely unacceptable, yet the abuse of power can also include psychological, social, economic, or political forms of manipulation or coercion. Christian Witness in a Multi-religious World states, "Christians are called to reject all forms of violence, even psy-chological or social, including the abuse of power in their witness. They also reject violence, unjust discrimination or repression by any religious or secular authority, including the violation or destruction of places of worship, sacred symbols or texts."[27] Religious violence and the abuse of power often are found in cases of ethnic conflict, when religious identity becomes enmeshed with ethnicity. The Cape Town Commitment confesses past Christian involvement in such conflicts:

> We acknowledge with grief and shame the complicity of Christians in some of the most destructive contexts of ethnic violence and oppression, and the lam-entable silence of large parts of the Church when such conflicts take place. . . . For the sake of the gospel, we lament, and call for repentance where Christians have participated in ethnic violence, injustice or oppression. . . . We long for the day when the Church will be the world's most visibly shining model of ethnic reconciliation and its most active advocate for conflict resolution.[28]

In setting out the qualities that are to be found in his disciples, Jesus said, "Blessed are the peacemakers, for they will be called children of God" (Matt. 5:9). When Jesus's disciples respond to violence and persecution, not with further violence but rather by working sacrificially for reconciliation, it is a powerful witness to the transformative power of God's grace.[29]

---

26. See Terry C. Muck, "Interreligious Dialogue: Conversations That Enable Christian Witness," *International Bulletin of Missionary Research* 35.4 (October 2011): 187–92; Gerald McDermott and Harold A. Netland, *A Trinitarian Theology of Religions* (New York: Oxford University Press, 2014), 277–83; Douglas McConnell, "Missional Principles and Guidelines for Interfaith Dialogue," *Evangelical Interfaith Dialogue* 1 (Winter 2010): 3–6.

27. Christian Witness in a Multi-religious World, "Principles," point 6.

28. *Cape Town Commitment*, II.B.2, p. 40.

29. See David W. Shenk, "The Gospel of Reconciliation within the Wrath of Nations," *International Bulletin of Missionary Research* 32.1 (January 2008): 3–9; Miroslav Volf, *Exclusion*

Each of these principles has rich implications for Christian witness in our multireligious world, but if we were to reduce matters to just one general principle, it would be difficult to improve upon Jesus's teaching in Matthew 7:12: "So in everything, do to others what you would have them do to you, for this sums up the Law and the Prophets." How should Christians engage in evangelism among religious others? Well, how would Christians like to be treated by someone from another religion eager to convert them to the other faith? In witness, Christians should treat religious others the way they would wish to be treated in return.

Apologetics and Religious Diversity

Christian witness today takes place in a world with many conflicting and competing perspectives.[30] Many believers face a crucial question: *Given the many religious and nonreligious worldviews available today, why should anyone accept the central claims of Christian theism as true?* This is a natural and reasonable question, and it deserves a responsible answer. In many contexts this will involve providing appropriate and persuasive reasons for accepting the truth of the Christian gospel, an activity usually identified with Christian apologetics. The Christian faith includes some audacious and controversial claims, and it is not surprising that many people treat them with incredulity. Christian apologetics is the attempt to respond to critiques of Christian claims in a biblically faithful, intellectually sound, and culturally appropriate manner. It actively seeks to persuade those who are skeptical to accept Christian beliefs.

But apologetics has always been somewhat controversial within the Christian community.[31] Properly construed, however, apologetics has an important role to play in the church today, and the use of reason in defending Christian claims need not be antithetical to faith or reliance upon the work of the Holy Spirit. There is nothing about the human capacity to use reason (which is a

---

and Embrace: A Theological Exploration of Identity, Otherness, and Reconciliation (Nashville: Abingdon, 1996).

30. Earlier versions of this section are found in Gerald McDermott and Harold A. Netland, *A Trinitarian Theology of Religions: An Evangelical Proposal* (New York: Oxford University Press, 2014), 283–92; and Harold Netland, "Interreligious Apologetics," in *Christian Apologetics: An Anthology of Primary Sources*, ed. Khaldoun A. Sweis and Chad V. Meister (Grand Rapids: Zondervan, 2012), 39–45.

31. For discussion of various approaches to apologetics, see Steven B. Cowan, ed., *Five Views on Apologetics* (Grand Rapids: Zondervan, 2000); James K. Beilby, *Thinking about Christian Apologetics: What It Is and Why We Do It* (Downers Grove, IL: InterVarsity, 2011); and John S. Feinberg, *Can You Believe It's True? Christian Apologetics in a Modern and Postmodern Era* (Wheaton, IL: Crossway, 2013).

gift from God in creation) that is inimical to the exercise of faith, and acting responsibly as disciples of Jesus Christ requires the appropriate use of reason in distinguishing what is epistemically acceptable from what is not.

Apologetics should be part of a comprehensive Christian witness today. When John Stott reflected back upon the twenty years since the first Congress on World Evangelization at Lausanne in 1974 and The Lausanne Covenant it produced, he made a clear link between apologetics and effective evangelism:

> We evangelical people need to repent of every occasion on which we have divorced evangelism from apologetics, as the apostles never did. We have to argue the Gospel we proclaim. We need to be able to say confidently to our hearers what Paul said to Festus: "What I am saying is true and reasonable" (Acts 26:25). We cannot possibly surrender to the current understanding of "pluralism" as an ideology that affirms the independent validity of every religion. Our task, rather, is to establish the criteria by which truth claims can be evaluated and then to demonstrate the uniqueness and finality of Jesus Christ.[32]

It is significant that The Cape Town Commitment calls for a renewed emphasis on apologetics in Christian witness in a pluralistic world. The Commitment rightly sees skepticism about religious truth as a central issue for witness today. "We long to see greater commitment to the hard work of robust apologetics." Responsible apologetics must involve both "those who can engage at the highest intellectual and public level in arguing for and defending biblical truth in the public arena" and pastors and other Christian leaders who can equip ordinary believers so that they are confident in their faith.[33] For too long evangelical approaches to Christian witness—especially in multireligious contexts—have been dominated by a pervasive pragmatism and anti-intellectualism that ignores difficult issues about the plausibility of the Christian faith. Apologetics can take various forms and degrees of sophistication, and it should be adapted to fit varying cultural contexts. But whatever its form, it should always be faithful to the biblical witness, intellectually responsible, and culturally sensitive.

The obligation to provide reasons for belief does not fall equally on every believer. Some obligations might fall on the church as a whole, or on certain intellectual leaders within the church, without necessarily applying to every Christian. Although not every believer can be expected to be able to provide adequate reasons for accepting Christian claims, many lay Christians will find themselves in contexts in which they should reflect critically upon their

---

32. John Stott, "Twenty Years after Lausanne: Some Personal Reflections," *International Bulletin of Missionary Research* 19.2 (April 1995): 54.
   33. *Cape Town Commitment*, II.A.2.A, p. 34.

commitments to determine whether they can responsibly conclude that their beliefs are justified. For most ordinary lay Christians who encounter conflicting claims, it is sufficient if the following conditions are met: (1) they give the relevant issues some careful thought; (2) upon careful reflection, they see no decisive reasons not to believe as they do; and (3) they know that other Christians who are more competent than they are have examined the issues carefully and assure them that belief is justified. For some—those with greater intellectual curiosity or specialized education in an area directly relevant to contested issues—a greater degree of investigation might be necessary. The third condition places a special burden upon Christian leaders for investigating intellectual challenges to the faith. These leaders—pastors, denominational leaders, seminary professors, Christian intellectuals in various academic disciplines—have a greater obligation to clarify and defend Christian beliefs than ordinary lay Christians.

Apologetics has a vital role to play in witness among those who are not yet followers of Jesus Christ. Christians do not simply accept any religious claim without considering the reasons for doing so, and they should not expect others to approach Christian claims any differently. Much of apologetics in the West has focused on questions prompted by nonreligious atheists or agnostics. It is important that those who are not yet disciples of Jesus become aware of good reasons for accepting the claims of the Christian faith rather than simply remaining agnostic or atheist. What things count as "good reasons" will vary somewhat with the individual, the relevant circumstances, and the broader cultural context.

Yet is there a place for apologetics when interacting with followers of other religions? Many today think of Christian apologetics as a modern Western response to the challenges posed by the European Enlightenment. Thus, while there may be a place for apologetics in the modern West, some claim it has no place in interreligious encounters. Religions of Asia, it is said, are not concerned with demonstrating the truth or rationality of their own views; apologetics is at best a Western, theistic concern that is not shared by Asian religious traditions.

This conclusion, however, is seriously misleading. Apologetics, understood as providing reasons for one's own religious commitments and raising questions about the beliefs of religious others, is not a modern, post-Enlightenment innovation but can be traced back to the early church itself. During the second and third centuries, Christian apologists—such as Justin Martyr, Claudius Apollinaris, Athenagoras, Tatian, Theophilus of Antioch, Clement of Alexandria, Tertullian, and Origen—responded to critics with important defenses of Christian belief and practice. Some addressed attacks from pagan

Greco-Roman thinkers; others tried to persuade Jews to accept the claims of the New Testament.[34] Throughout the history of the church, Christian thinkers have defended the claims of Christian theism in intellectual engagement with Muslims, Hindus, Buddhists, Confucians, and Daoists, as well as secular agnostics and atheists.[35]

Furthermore, the attempt to defend the truth of one's own religious beliefs through appeal to reason and argument and to persuade others to accept them has a long history among Asian religious traditions. While it is true that some traditions within Hinduism, Buddhism, and Daoism minimize the role of reason in favor of direct, intuitive experiences of the religious ultimate that allegedly transcend reason, many other traditions within these religions historically have made use of rigorous rational analysis in supporting their claims. There were vigorous debates among competing schools within Hinduism and Buddhism as well as between adherents of religions such as Jainism, Hinduism, Buddhism, Daoism, and Confucianism. Speaking of Hinduism, for example, Richard Fox Young observes,

> Proponents of the great *darsanas*, philosophical views or systems, endeavored to brace their own ideas or doctrines by exposing the fallacies of others. To cite only one instance, Sankara's commentary on the Brahmasutras refuted, in turn, each of the major theories, cosmological, metaphysical, soteriological, etc., to which other Hindu thinkers, Buddhists, Jains, and materialists subscribed. Apologetics was so much a part of classical works on religion and philosophy that a text without at least an adumbration of the standard criticisms of its rivals would surely seem incomplete.[36]

There were rigorous debates among Hindus, Buddhists, and Jains over whether there are enduring substantial souls (Hindus and Jains say yes; Buddhists deny this) or whether a creator God exists (some Hindus say yes; Jains and Buddhists deny this).[37] The introduction of Christianity to Asian cultures was regarded

---

34. See Robert M. Grant, *Greek Apologists of the Second Century* (Philadelphia: Westminster, 1988); Mark Edwards, Martin Goodman, and Simon Price, eds. *Apologetics in the Roman Empire* (Oxford: Oxford University Press, 1999); Avery Dulles, *A History of Apologetics* (Philadelphia: Westminster, 1971), chap. 2.

35. Harold Netland, "Interreligious Apologetics," in Sweis and Meister, *Christian Apologetics*, 39–45.

36. Richard Fox Young, *Resistant Hinduism: Sanskrit Sources on Anti-Christian Apologetics in Early Nineteenth Century India* (Vienna: Institut für Indologie der Universität Wien, 1981), 13.

37. For Buddhist critiques of the existence of God, see Parimal G. Patil, *Against a Hindu God: Buddhist Philosophy of Religion in India* (New York: Columbia University Press, 2009); Arvind Sharma, *The Philosophy of Religion: A Buddhist Perspective* (Delhi: Oxford University Press, 1995); and Gunapala Dharmasiri, *A Buddhist Critique of the Christian Concept of God*

by Hindus, Muslims, and Buddhists as a direct threat to their teachings and ways of life. Proclamation of the Christian gospel was often met with vigorous intellectual critiques by Hindus, Muslims, and Buddhists, who tried to demonstrate the falsity or irrationality of Christian claims.[38]

But interreligious apologetics strikes many today as distasteful and inappropriate. Thus Paul Griffiths speaks of "an underlying scholarly orthodoxy on the goals and functions of interreligious dialogue," an orthodoxy maintaining that "understanding is the only legitimate goal; that judgment and criticism of religious beliefs and practices other than those of one's own community is always inappropriate; and that an active defense of the truth of those beliefs and practices to which one's community appears committed is always to be shunned."[39] In *An Apology for Apologetics*, Griffiths provides a trenchant critique of this view, arguing persuasively that in certain circumstances religious communities have an obligation to engage in interreligious apologetics (see chap. 7 above).

Awareness of religious diversity and disagreement can result in Christians questioning their own religious commitments; in such cases apologetics can have an effective role in a response to challenges from religious disagreement. Another part of an effective response is having an adequate theology of religions that enables one to understand religious diversity in light of Christian principles. Griffiths explains that loss of confidence in one's own beliefs can be in part a function of the degree to which one's own theological commitments fail to provide a plausible explanation for diversity and disagreement.[40] If a Christian is aware of a plausible theological explanation for why there is so much religious disagreement, then the epistemic challenge can be mitigated to some extent. But if there is no such explanatory framework available, then awareness of diversity is more problematic. For Christians, this indicates the

---

(Antioch, CA: Golden Leaves, 1988). For analysis of such critiques, see Paul Williams, "Aquinas Meets the Buddhists: Prolegomena to an Authentically Thomas-ist Basis for Dialogue," in *Aquinas in Dialogue: Thomas for the Twenty-First Century*, ed. Jim Fodor and Christian Bauerschmidt (Oxford: Blackwell, 2004), 87–117; Yandell and H. Netland, *Buddhism: A Christian Exploration and Appraisal*, 180–92.

38. See Richard Fox Young, *Resistant Hinduism: Sanskrit Sources on Anti-Christian Apologetics in Early Nineteenth Century India*; R. F. Young and S. Jebanesan, *The Bible Trembled: The Hindu-Christian Controversies of Nineteenth-Century Ceylon* (Vienna: Institut für Indologie der Universität Wien, 1995); Kenneth W. Jones, ed., *Religious Controversy in British India* (Albany: State University of New York Press, 1992); Harold Coward, ed., *Hindu-Christian Dialogue: Perspectives and Encounters* (Maryknoll, NY: Orbis Books, 1989); Paul J. Griffiths, ed., *Christianity through Non-Christian Eyes* (Maryknoll, NY: Orbis Books, 1990).

39. Paul Griffiths, *An Apology for Apologetics: A Study in the Logic of Interreligious Dialogue* (Maryknoll, NY: Orbis Books, 1991), xi.

40. Paul Griffiths, *Problems of Religious Diversity* (Oxford: Blackwell, 2001), 73–75.

importance of a responsible theology of religions that, among other things, provides a broader theological framework for explaining religious diversity.

In concluding the discussion of interreligious apologetics, we will briefly identify three issues. First, the kind of issues dealt with in interreligious apologetics differ somewhat from those addressed in contexts of secular agnosticism or atheism. Some questions will be similar. The question of God's existence and the problem of evil, for example, will be central with Buddhists and Jains as well as with secular agnostics and atheists. Questions about the deity of Jesus Christ are relevant for Muslims, Hindus, and Buddhists as well as atheists.

But other issues are especially significant in an interreligious context. How is one to know which, if any, sacred scriptures are indeed divinely inspired? Why accept the Bible as God's Word but not the Qur'an? Many religions include claims of miracles. Are they all to be accepted as true? If not, why should we accept the miracle claims in the Bible but not those in other religious texts? Do certain mystical states provide direct access to ultimate reality? If not, why not? How should we assess reports of religious experiences in the many religions? And so on.

As with Christian apologetics generally, the two most significant issues are the question of God's existence and that of the identity of Jesus of Nazareth. If there are good reasons for believing that an eternal creator God exists, then there are good reasons for rejecting religious worldviews, such as those of classical Buddhism or Jainism, that deny God's existence. If there are good reasons for accepting the New Testament picture of Jesus as fully God and fully man, the one Lord and Savior for all humankind, then there are good reasons for rejecting religious worldviews that deny this.

Second, those engaging in interreligious apologetics must study other religious traditions carefully, making sure that they understand other religious worldviews accurately and are not merely addressing simplistic caricatures. This requires much time and intellectual discipline, mastering the requisite languages and literature and engaging intellectuals from these traditions in serious dialogue. Responsible interreligious apologetics must be fair in its treatment of other perspectives, willingly acknowledging what is true and good in them even as it points out what is false or otherwise problematic.

Interreligious apologists need to be especially sensitive to the importance of culturally appropriate means of persuasion. They must recognize that interreligious encounters do not occur in a historical or cultural vacuum; both sides of the encounter bring with them the legacies of past relations as well as the real potential for misunderstandings in the present. Effective use of morally acceptable and culturally appropriate means of persuasion requires dealing with the legacy from the past as well as with the present realities within which the encounter takes place.

Third, Christian apologists must be sensitive to the place of symbolic power within interreligious encounters. The attempt to persuade religious others to change their fundamental beliefs and accept core Christian claims as true can easily be perceived as an inappropriate exercise of power, especially if the Christian is associated with significant cultural, economic, political, or military frameworks of power. Any activity that is manipulative or coercive, or otherwise infringes upon the dignity of the other, must be rejected. In certain contexts historical factors make interreligious apologetics especially sensitive. Contexts in which Christianity has been closely associated with cultural superiority, racism, persecution, or economic exploitation make interreligious apologetics particularly problematic. Christians should be especially careful about apologetics encounters with religious communities, such as Jewish and Muslim communities, which have suffered greatly in the past at the hands of Christendom. Apologists in interreligious contexts must not only be skilled at defending the truth of the Christian message; they must also be winsome and gracious, responding to critics with gentleness and respect (1 Pet. 3:15–16).

Christ's Disciples and Civic Virtue

Christians are not only disciples of Jesus Christ; they are also members of local communities, citizens of nations, and participants in a globalizing world. Bearing witness to Jesus Christ in appropriate ways in our multireligious world involves civic virtue, or being good and responsible citizens both locally and in the broader global community.[41] Robert Audi, a Christian philosopher, defines civic virtue as "the trait that underlies good citizenship when the conduct in question is grounded in the character of the citizen and not, for instance, a manifestation of merely self-interested cooperation."[42] It is "that virtue whose

41. An issue arising from the dual obligations Christians have as disciples of Jesus and citizens is the proper perspective on nationalism. While this is an issue for all Christians, regardless of nationality, it has become an especially significant issue for American Christians in the aftermath of the terrorist attacks of Sept. 11, 2001. Many Christians, including many Christian leaders, became caught up in a jingoistic nationalism that equated being Christian with being American and identified a belligerent response to the "war on terror" with God's will. See Wes Avram, ed., *Anxious about Empire: Theological Essays on the New Global Realities* (Grand Rapids: Brazos, 2004).

42. See Robert Audi, *Democratic Authority and the Separation of Church and State* (New York: Oxford University Press, 2011), 136.

possession makes one a good citizen."[43] Acting in accordance with civic virtue involves more than merely obeying the laws and refraining from evil. It calls for "a measure of supererogation, in the sense of good conduct not morally or (properly) legally required," but which contributes to the common good. Civic virtue takes one beyond concern solely with one's rights to consideration of the public welfare. "There is a sense in which citizens in a liberal democracy *ought* to meet standards of, for instance, mutual concern and mutual respect, even if they have a right not to."[44] Audi challenges American Christians to model civic virtue in an increasingly pluralistic society, arguing that, for Christians, civic virtue includes acting in accordance with Jesus's command to love others and to treat others as Christians would wish to be treated by them.[45]

What does it mean, then, for American Christians to be both disciples of Jesus and good citizens? Politically, the United States is a republic with a constitution that explicitly rules out the establishment of a state religion and that guarantees the free exercise of religion.[46] American society is also becoming remarkably diverse, with an astonishing variety of religious traditions.[47] Historically, America has been influenced by Christian values and principles, and it retains a dominant Christian population today. But now American society includes many different religious traditions, as well as growing numbers of those who are explicitly nonreligious, and it is expected to become even more diverse in the decades ahead.

Christian conduct in the public sector should be marked by the moral qualities Jesus Christ expects from his followers and by the civic virtue expected of good citizens. Indeed, living in accordance with Jesus's moral expectations will result in Christ's disciples manifesting civic virtue. Earlier we noted a distinction between what is legally permitted and what people ought to do as good citizens. A good citizen is someone who exemplifies moral qualities in public conduct by advancing the common good in ways that go beyond one's own immediate interests. I will conclude by identifying three areas in which exemplifying civic virtue can make a significant difference in the public conduct of American Christians. In doing so, I will make reference

43. Robert Audi, *Religious Commitment and Secular Reason* (Cambridge: Cambridge University Press, 2000), 150.
44. Ibid., 155, 85, with original emphasis.
45. Audi, *Democratic Authority*, 136–38.
46. The meaning and implications of the First Amendment of the US Constitution have been the subject of endless debate and litigation. For a helpful survey of relevant issues and a defense of the notion of "religious neutrality," see Andrew Koppelman, *Defending American Religious Neutrality* (Cambridge, MA: Harvard University Press, 2013).
47. See Cohen and Numbers, *Gods in America*; Robert Wuthnow, *America and the Challenge of Religious Diversity* (Princeton: Princeton University Press, 2005).

to The Williamsburg Charter, a document drafted by Os Guinness in 1988.[48] Guinness, an evangelical Christian, produced The Williamsburg Charter as a celebration of the First Amendment religious liberty clauses. The document sets out some principles by which people with very different values and worldviews can contend in a robust but civil manner in the public sector. It provides "a call to a vision of public life that will allow conflict to lead to consensus, religious commitment to reinforce political civility. In this way, diversity is not a point of weakness but a source of strength."[49] This Charter was signed by over a hundred prominent leaders in government, academics, business, law, and public policy, as well as religious leaders from a variety of religious traditions.

First, Christians should move beyond a concern merely for protecting their own religious rights and commit to preserving religious liberties for all. It is easy to take for granted the rights to freedom of religious belief and practice in the United States, and American Christians must be vigilant in making sure that the right to the free exercise of religion is not eroded. Both as disciples of Jesus and as good citizens, Christians also have obligations that go beyond merely preserving the rights of Christians. The right to free exercise of belief applies to followers of other religions as well as Christians.

Evangelical Christian discussions about religion in the public square in the United States have focused largely upon protecting the rights of Christians against the alleged agenda of secularists. Little attention has been given, however, to the host of complex questions about how Christians should live as good citizens in a religiously diverse society, promoting justice and fairness for all. The issues are complex, and they directly affect areas such as military, prison, and hospital chaplaincy; instruction in public schools; employment and housing policies; building permits for centers of worship; appropriateness of religious symbols and dress in public settings; public observance of religious holidays; the use of religious symbolism in governmental institutions and activities; and so on. The First Amendment grants freedom of religious expression to all, not just to Christians. As a matter of both justice and prudence, the religious majority should intentionally champion the rights of religious minorities; this is a matter of simple justice.

At the same time, however, it is in the interests of the majority to safeguard the rights of religious minorities. The Williamsburg Charter explicitly connects protection of religious liberty for the dominant religious group—Christians—with

---

48. The Williamsburg Charter is included in Os Guinness, *The Case for Civility: And Why Our Future Depends on It* (New York: HarperCollins, 2008), 177–98; also available at http://www.religioustolerance.org/wil_burg.htm.

49. Guinness, *The Case for Civility*, 178–79.

protection of the religious liberties of religious minorities and links this mutual compact with the Golden Rule.

> We affirm that a right for one is a right for another and a responsibility for all. A right for a Protestant is a right for an Orthodox is a right for a Catholic is a right for a Jew is a right for a Humanist is a right for a Mormon is a right for a Muslim is a right for a Buddhist—and for the followers of any other faith within the wide bounds of the republic.
>
> That rights are universal and responsibilities mutual is both the premise and the promise of democratic pluralism. The First Amendment, in this sense, is the epitome of public justice and serves as the Golden Rule for civic life. Rights are best guarded and responsibilities best exercised when each person and group guards for all others those rights they wish [to be] guarded for themselves.[50]

Thus Christians should be concerned with protecting the religious liberties of religious minorities, including Muslims. Commitment to basic Christian principles of justice and the dignity of others as created in God's image should motivate Christians to defend the legal and social rights even of those with whom they profoundly disagree.

A second implication of civic virtue has to do with the nature of public discourse in debates over public policy issues. The so-called culture wars that have ravaged American society since the 1960s have produced vitriolic and caustic public denunciations of the other by both the left and the right. Especially when religious or moral issues in public policy are concerned, disagreement quickly degenerates into demonization, distortion, and ridicule of the other. Sadly, all too often Christians are among the worst offenders. But participating in such poisonous public discourse is inconsistent with the qualities expected of Jesus's disciples and with civic virtue. Jesus's followers are to be men and women of the truth, and this includes not misrepresenting or distorting the positions of others. The Letter to the Colossians says, "Let your conversation always be full of grace, seasoned with salt, so that you may know how to answer everyone" (4:6).

The Williamsburg Charter rightly emphasizes the importance of speaking carefully in the public domain, so as not to misrepresent others or become unnecessarily inflammatory. "Civility obliges citizens in a pluralistic society to take great care in using words and casting issues."[51] Genuine disagreements must, of course, be acknowledged and debated vigorously, but the discourse used to address these differences must be respectful, sensitive, and

---

50. Ibid., 193.
51. Ibid., 188.

true. The Charter proposes four helpful principles that should govern public disagreements.[52] (1) "Those who claim the right to dissent should assume the responsibility to debate." It is not sufficient simply to disagree or reject the position of the other; significant public disagreements affecting large numbers of people should be the subject of serious public debate. (2) "Those who claim the right to criticize should assume the responsibility to comprehend." Too often public criticism of another position is offered without the critic having taken the time to understand the relevant issues. (3) "Those who claim the right to influence should accept the responsibility not to inflame." This is not a call to abandon controversy. Public disputes involving religious matters are often highly controversial, but vigorous debate over contested issues need not be inflammatory. (4) "Those who claim the right to participate should accept the responsibility to persuade." Persuasion is more than simply securing enough votes to pass a particular piece of legislation; it also involves providing convincing reasons for adopting a position so that minds are changed. On a large social or cultural scale, it also involves bringing about significant change in the centers of cultural power, transforming the plausibility structures of society.

A third area in which acting in accordance with civic virtue can make a difference is the question of the degree to which one's religious commitments should shape decisions on public policy matters. This is a complex and controversial set of issues, with few easy, clear-cut answers. There is no reason to suppose that religious values or beliefs should *not* have any impact on how Christians and others approach public policy. Not only is such a restriction not what the First Amendment has in mind, but also it is impossible for religious people not to act somewhat out of their core commitments.

It is tempting to maintain that Christians should always determine public policy on the basis of Christian commitments. In a democracy, the majority rules; so one might assume that if Christians compose a majority and they can secure 51 percent of the vote, then they should legislate according to Christian values and principles. Minority perspectives are defeated at the ballot box. There is much to be said for this perspective. Yet it turns public policy making into an exercise in power politics, so that the group with the most votes on any occasion controls the outcome. Public policy then is at the mercy of ongoing struggles for power by various interest groups. This might seem desirable so long as Christians are in the solid majority, but it is much less attractive when Christians constitute a tiny minority—as in Japan. An acceptable general framework for addressing religion and public policy should apply not just to

52. Ibid., 194–97.

cases in which Christians are the majority but also to settings in which they are a small minority. Moreover, not all Christians agree on the implications of biblical teachings for public policy, so the struggle for political power will be not only between Christians and others but also among various Christian subgroups. Is raw power politics really the best way?

A more principled approach to the question of religious commitments in determining public policy is to return to the Golden Rule and use this as a guide for Christians in policy disputes. The principle embedded in the Golden Rule is relevant not only for questions about relations between individuals but also in working through broader social and political issues in religiously diverse societies. It applies both to contexts in which Christians compose the majority and in which they are the minority, yet it has special relevance for the former. Should the religious majority—Christians in the United States—determine public policy based *simply* upon their own religious commitments? What if the situation were reversed, and Christians were the minority in a society dominated by atheists or Hindus or Muslims? At the heart of the Golden Rule is a thought experiment: If conditions were reversed and I found myself in the position of the other, would I want to be treated in the manner in which I am considering treating the other? If not, then I should reconsider my proposed course of action. Robert Audi draws upon the idea of reciprocity in the Golden Rule in developing his principles for the place of religious reasons and motivations in public policy decision making. Audi asks,

> What should conscientious and morally upright religious citizens in a pluralistic society want in the way of protection of their own freedom and promotion of standards that express respect for citizens regardless of their religious position? . . . One answer that may occur to me if I am aware of religious diversity in my society is that I should limit my zeal because I would like people in other faiths, with different socio-political ideals, to limit theirs.[53]

One need not agree with all of Audi's specific proposals to see the wisdom of his application of the Golden Rule to questions about religious grounds for public policy decisions.

As disciples of Jesus exhibit moral integrity and civic virtue in the way they treat others, living out the values expressed by Jesus and echoed throughout the rest of the New Testament (Matt. 5–7; 22:37–40; see also Rom. 12:9–21; James 2:8–26; 1 Pet. 2:11–25), they will be powerful witnesses to the grace and mercy of God available in Jesus Christ. The Cape Town Commitment provides

53. Audi, *Religious Commitment and Secular Reason*, 84–85.

a concise summary of what Christ's disciples are to be like in a religiously diverse and pluralistic world: "Loving God in the midst of a world that rejects or distorts him, calls for bold but humble witness to our God; robust but gracious defence of the truth of the gospel of Christ, God's Son; and a prayerful trust in the convicting and convincing work of his Holy Spirit."[54]

54. *Cape Town Commitment*, I.2.B, p. 12.

Bibliography

Abraham, William J. "Cumulative Case Arguments for Christian Theism." In *The Rationality of Religious Belief: Essays in Honour of Basil Mitchell*, edited by William J. Abraham and Steven W. Holtzer, 17–37. Oxford: Clarendon, 1989.

Aldridge, Alan. *Religion in the Contemporary World: A Sociological Introduction.* Cambridge: Polity, 2000.

Almond, Philip C. *The British Discovery of Buddhism.* Cambridge: Cambridge University Press, 1988.

Alston, William P. *Perceiving God: The Epistemology of Religious Experience.* Ithaca, NY: Cornell University Press, 1991.

———. *A Realist Conception of Truth.* Ithaca, NY: Cornell University Press, 1996.

Annas, Julia, and Jonathan Barnes. *The Modes of Skepticism: Ancient Texts and Modern Interpretations.* Cambridge: Cambridge University Press, 1985.

Asad, Talal. *Genealogies of Religion: Discipline and Reasons of Power in Christianity and Islam.* Baltimore: Johns Hopkins University Press, 1993.

Audi, Robert. *Democratic Authority and the Separation of Church and State.* New York: Oxford University Press, 2011.

———. *Religious Commitment and Secular Reason.* New York: Oxford University Press, 2000.

Balagangadhara, S. N. *"The Heathen in His Blindness . . .": Asia, the West and the Dynamic of Religion.* Leiden: Brill, 1994.

Barker, Gregory A., and Stephen E. Gregg, eds. *Jesus beyond Christianity: The Classic Texts.* New York: Oxford University Press, 2010.

Barth, Karl. *The Doctrine of Reconciliation.* Vol. IV/3 of *Church Dogmatics.* Translated by G. W. Bromiley. Edited by G. W. Bromiley and T. F. Torrance. Edinburgh: T&T Clark, 1961.

———. *The Doctrine of the Word of God.* Vol. I/2 of *Church Dogmatics.* Edited by G. W. Bromiley and T. F. Torrance. New York: Charles Scribner's Sons, 1956.

Basinger, David. *Religious Diversity: A Philosophical Assessment*. Burlington, VT: Ashgate, 2002.

Batchelor, Stephen. *Buddhism without Beliefs: A Contemporary Guide to Awakening*. New York: Riverhead Books, 1997.

———. "Life as a Question, Not a Fact." In *Why Buddhism? Westerners in Search of Wisdom*, edited by Vickie Mackenzie, 142–62. London: Element, 2002.

Bauckham, Richard. *Jesus and the Eyewitnesses: The Gospels as Eyewitness Testimony*. Grand Rapids: Eerdmans, 2006.

———. *Jesus and the God of Israel*. Grand Rapids: Eerdmans, 2008.

Bavinck, J. H. *The Church between Temple and Mosque: A Study of the Relationship between the Christian Faith and Other Religions*. Grand Rapids: Eerdmans, 1966.

Beattie, John. *Other Cultures: Aims, Methods, and Achievements in Social Anthropology*. New York: Free Press, 1964.

Beilby, James. "Plantinga's Model of Warranted Christian Belief." In *Alvin Plantinga*, edited by Deane-Peter Baker, 125–65. Cambridge: Cambridge University Press, 2007.

Bellah, Robert. "Civil Religion in America." *Daedalus* 96 (1967): 1–21.

Berger, Peter, ed. *The Desecularization of the World*. Grand Rapids: Eerdmans, 1999.

———. "Epistemological Modesty: An Interview with Peter Berger." *Christian Century* 114.30 (October 29, 1997): 972–78.

———. *A Far Glory: The Quest for Faith in an Age of Credulity*. New York: Anchor Books, 1992.

———. "Four Faces of Global Culture." *National Interest* 49 (Fall 1997): 23–29.

———. *Questions of Faith: A Skeptical Affirmation of Christianity*. Oxford: Blackwell, 2004.

———. "Reflections on the Sociology of Religion Today." In *Sociology of Religion* 62 (2001): 443–54.

———. *The Sacred Canopy: The Social Construction of Reality*. New York: Anchor Books, 1967.

———. "Secularization and De-secularization." In *Religions in the Modern World*, edited by Linda Woodhead, Paul Fletcher, Hiroko Kawanami, and David Smith, 291–98. London: Routledge, 2002.

Berger, Peter, Grace Davie, and Effie Kokas. *Religious America, Secular Europe? A Theme and Variations*. Burlington, VT: Ashgate, 2008.

Bhargava, Rajeev, ed. *Secularism and Its Critics*. Delhi: Oxford University Press, 1998.

Bilgrami, Akeel. "Gandhi's Religion and Its Relation to His Politics." In *The Cambridge Companion to Gandhi*, edited by Judith M. Brown and Anthony Parel, 93–116. Cambridge: Cambridge University Press, 2011.

Blauw, Johannes. "The Biblical View of Man in His Religion." In *The Theology of the Christian Mission*, edited by Gerald H. Anderson, 31–41. New York: McGraw-Hill, 1961.

Bloom, Alfred. *Shinran's Gospel of Pure Grace*. Tucson: University of Arizona Press, 1965.

Bosch, David. *Transforming Mission*. Maryknoll, NY: Orbis Books, 1991.

Boyle, Robert. "De diversitate Religionum." In *The Works of Robert Boyle*, edited by Michael Hunter and Edward B. Davis, 14:237–64. London: Pickering & Chatto, 2000.

Braaten, Carl. *No Other Gospel! Christianity among World Religions*. Minneapolis: Fortress, 1992.

Bragt, Jan van. "Buddhism—Jodo Shinshu—Christianity: Does Jodo Shinshu Form a Bridge between Buddhism and Christianity?" *Japanese Religions* 18 (January 1993): 47–75.

———. "Multiple Religious Belonging of the Japanese People." In *Many Mansions? Multiple Religious Belonging and Christian Identity*, edited by Catherine Cornille, 7–19. Maryknoll, NY: Orbis Books, 2002.

Brannen, Noah S. "Three Japanese Authors Look at Jesus: A Review." *Japan Christian Quarterly* 54.3 (Summer 1988): 132–41.

Brekke, Torkel. *Makers of Modern Indian Religion in the Late Nineteenth Century*. New York: Oxford University Press, 2002.

Brown, Judith M. *Gandhi: Prisoner of Hope*. New Haven: Yale University Press, 1989.

———, ed. *Mahatma Gandhi: Essential Writings*. New York: Oxford University Press, 2008.

Bruce, Steve. *God Is Dead: Secularization in the West*. Oxford: Blackwell, 2002.

———. *Religion in the Modern World: From Cathedrals to Cults*. Oxford: Oxford University Press, 1996.

———. *Secularization*. New York: Oxford University Press, 2011.

Burkett, Delbert. "Images of Jesus: An Overview." In *The Blackwell Companion to Jesus*, edited by Delbert Burkett, 1–9. Oxford: Blackwell, 2011.

Buruma, Ian. *Taming the Gods: Religion and Democracy on Three Continents*. Princeton: Princeton University Press, 2010.

Buruma, Ian, and Avishai Margalit. *Occidentalism: The West in the Eyes of Its Enemies*. New York: Penguin, 2004.

Byrne, Peter. "It Is Not Reasonable to Believe That Only One Religion Is True." In *Contemporary Debates in Philosophy of Religion*, edited by Michael L. Peterson and Raymond J. VanArragon, 201–10. Oxford: Blackwell, 2004.

———. "A Philosophical Approach to Questions about Religious Diversity." In *The Oxford Handbook of Religious Diversity*, edited by Chad V. Meister, 29–41. New York: Oxford University Press, 2010.

———. *Prolegomena to Religious Pluralism: Reference and Realism in Religion*. New York: St. Martin's Press, 1995.

Cape Town Commitment, The: A Confession of Faith and a Call to Action; The Third Lausanne Congress. Didasko Files. Peabody, MA: Hendrickson, 2011. http://www.lausanne.org/en/documents/ctcommitment.html.

Carson, D. A. "Matthew." In *The Expositor's Bible Commentary*, edited by Frank E. Gabelein, 8:3–599. Grand Rapids: Zondervan, 1984.

Casanova, José. *Public Religions in the Modern World*. Chicago: University of Chicago Press, 1994.

———. "The Secular, Secularizations, Secularisms." In *Rethinking Secularism*, edited by Craig Calhoun, Mark Juergensmeyer, and Jonathan VanAntwerpen, 54–74. New York: Oxford University Press, 2011.

Cavanaugh, William T. *The Myth of Religious Violence*. New York: Oxford University Press, 2009.

Chanda, Nayan. *Bound Together: How Traders, Preachers, Adventurers, and Warriors Shaped Globalization*. New Haven: Yale University Press, 2007.

Chatterjee, Margaret. *Gandhi and the Challenge of Religious Diversity*. New Delhi: Promilla, 2005.

———. *Gandhi's Religious Thought*. London: Macmillan, 1983.

Ch'en, Kenneth K. S. *Buddhism in China: A Historical Survey*. Princeton: Princeton University Press, 1964.

———. *The Chinese Transformation of Buddhism*. Princeton: Princeton University Press, 1973.

Christian, Rose Ann. "Plantinga, Epistemic Permissiveness, and Metaphysical Pluralism." *Religious Studies* 28 (December 1992): 568–69.

Christian, William A. *Doctrines of Religious Communities: A Philosophical Study*. New Haven: Yale University Press, 1987.

———. *Oppositions of Religious Doctrines: A Study in the Logic of Dialogue among Religions*. London: Macmillan, 1972.

Christian Witness in a Multi-religious World. http://www.oikoumene.org/en/resources /documents/wcc-programmes/interreligious-dialogue-and-cooperation/christian -identity-in-pluralistic-societies/christian-witness-in-a-multi-religious-world.

Chua, How Chuang. "Japanese Perspectives on the Death of Christ: A Study in Contextualized Christology." PhD diss., Trinity Evangelical Divinity School, 2007.

Clark, Kelly James. "Pluralism and Proper Function." In *Alvin Plantinga*, edited by Deane-Peter Baker, 166–87. Cambridge: Cambridge University Press, 2007.

Clarke, J. J. *Oriental Enlightenment: The Encounter between Asian and Western Thought*. London: Routledge, 1997.

Cohen, Charles L., and Ronald L. Numbers, eds. *Gods in America: Religious Pluralism in the United States*. New York: Oxford University Press, 2013.

Coleman, James William. *The New Buddhism: The Western Transformation of an Ancient Tradition*. New York: Oxford University Press, 2001.

Coward, Harold, ed. *Hindu-Christian Dialogue: Perspectives and Encounters*. Maryknoll, NY: Orbis Books, 1989.

Crisp, Oliver D. *Divinity and Humanity: The Incarnation Reconsidered*. Cambridge: Cambridge University Press, 2007.

Dalai Lama, The 14th (Tenzin Gyatso). "Buddhism and Other Religions." In *Philosophy of Religion: Selected Readings*, edited by Michael Peterson et al., 577–80, 4th ed. New York: Oxford University Press, 2010.

———. *Freedom in Exile: The Autobiography of the Dalai Lama*. New York: Harper-Collins, 1990.

———. *The Good Heart: A Buddhist Perspective on the Teachings of Jesus*. Edited by Robert Kiely. Boston: Wisdom, 1996.

———. *Toward a True Kinship of Faiths: How the World's Religions Can Come Together*. New York: Doubleday, 2010.

Davie, Grace. *Europe: The Exceptional Case; Parameters of Faith in the Modern World*. London: Darton, Longman & Todd, 2002.

———. *Religion in Britain since 1945: Believing without Belonging*. Oxford: Blackwell, 2004.

Davis, Stephen T. "Faith, Evidence, and Evidentialism." In *Religious Pluralism in the Modern World: An Ongoing Engagement with John Hick*, edited by Sharada Sugirtharajah, 190–203. New York: Palgrave Macmillan, 2012.

Davis, Stephen T., Daniel Kendall, and Gerald O'Collins, eds. *The Incarnation*. New York: Oxford University Press, 2002.

Dawkins, Richard. *The God Delusion*. New York: Houghton Mifflin, 2006.

Di Noia, J. A. "Religion and the Religions." In *The Cambridge Companion to Karl Barth*, edited by John Webster, 243–57. Cambridge: Cambridge University Press, 2000.

Dubuisson, Daniel. *The Western Construction of Religion: Myths, Knowledge, and Reality*. Baltimore: Johns Hopkins University Press, 2003.

Dulles, Avery. *A History of Apologetics*. Philadelphia: Westminster, 1971.

Dumoulin, Heinrich. *India and China*. Vol. 1 of *Zen Buddhism: A History*. Translated by James W. Heisig and Paul Knitter. New York: Macmillan, 1988.

———. *Japan*. Vol. 2 of *Zen Buddhism: A History*. Translated by James W. Heisig and Paul Knitter. New York: Macmillan, 1990.

———. *Zen Enlightenment: Origin and Meaning*. New York: Weatherhill, 1979.

Dumsday, Travis, "Robert Boyle on the Diversity of Religions." *Religious Studies* 44 (2008): 315–32.

Dupré, Luis. *The Enlightenment and the Intellectual Foundations of Modern Culture*. New Haven: Yale University Press, 2004.

Eddy, Paul Rhodes. *John Hick's Pluralist Philosophy of World Religions*. Burlington, VT: Ashgate, 2002.

Eddy, Paul Rhodes, and Gregory A. Boyd. *The Jesus Legend: A Case for the Historical Reliability of the Synoptic Jesus Tradition*. Grand Rapids: Baker Academic, 2007.

Ellsberg, Robert, ed. *Gandhi on Christianity*. Maryknoll, NY: Orbis Books, 1991.

Endo, Shusaku. *Deep River*. Translated by Van C. Gessel. New York: New Directions, 1994.

————. *A Life of Jesus*. Translated by Richard A. Schuchert. Tokyo: Tuttle, 1978 [1973].

————. *The Samurai*. Translated by Van C. Gessel. New York: Harper & Row, 1982.

————. *Silence*. Translated by William Johnston. New York: Taplinger, 1969.

Evans, C. Stephen. *Natural Signs and Knowledge of God: A New Look at Theistic Arguments*. New York: Oxford University Press, 2010.

Fader, Larry A. "D. T. Suzuki's Contribution to the West." In *A Zen Life: D. T. Suzuki Remembered*, edited by Masao Abe, 95–108. New York: Weatherhill, 1986.

Faure, Bernard. *Chan Insights and Oversights: An Epistemological Critique of the Chan Tradition*. Princeton: Princeton University Press, 1993.

Fischer, Louis, *The Life of Mahatma Gandhi*. New York: Harper & Row, 1950.

Fitzgerald, Timothy. *The Ideology of Religious Studies*. New York: Oxford University Press, 2000.

France, R. T. *The Gospel of Matthew*. Grand Rapids: Eerdmans, 2007.

Franklin, J. Jeffrey. *The Lotus and the Lion: Buddhism and the British Empire*. Ithaca, NY: Cornell University Press, 2008.

French, H. W. "Swami Vivekananda's Experiences and Interpretations of Christianity." In *Neo-Hindu Views of Christianity*, edited by Arvind Sharma, 82–105. Leiden: Brill, 1988.

Frykenberg, Robert Eric. *Christianity in India: From Beginnings to the Present*. New York: Oxford University Press, 2008.

————. "Christian Missions and the Raj." In *Missions and Empire*, edited by Norman Etherington, 107–31. New York: Oxford University Press, 2005.

————. "Constructions of Hinduism at the Nexus of History and Religion." *Journal of Interdisciplinary History* 23.3 (Winter 1993): 523–50.

Frykhom, Amy. "Double Belonging: One Person, Two Faiths." *Christian Century* 128.2 (January 25, 2011): 20–23.

Gandhi, M. K. *An Autobiography: Or, The Story of My Experiments with Truth*. Translated by Mahadev Desai. New York: Viking Penguin, 1982 [1927].

Garfield, Jay L. "Translation as Transmission and Transformation." In *TransBuddhism: Transmission, Translation, Transformation*, edited by Nalini Bhushan, Jay L. Garfield, and Abraham Zablocki, 89–103. Amherst: University of Massachusetts Press, 2009.

Gathercole, Simon. *The Preexistent Son: Recovering the Christologies of Matthew, Mark, and Luke*. Grand Rapids: Eerdmans, 2006.

Gay, Peter. *The Enlightenment: An Interpretation; The Rise of Modern Paganism*. New York: Norton, 1966.

Geertz, Clifford. *The Interpretation of Cultures*. New York: Random House, 1973.

Gensler, Harry J. *Ethics and the Golden Rule: Do unto Others*. New York: Routledge, 2013.

Giddens, Anthony. *The Consequences of Modernity*. Stanford, CA: Stanford University Press, 1990.

Gombrich, Richard. *Theravada Buddhism: A Social History from Ancient Benares to Modern Colombo*. London: Routledge & Kegan Paul, 1988.

Gombrich, Richard, and Gananath Obeyesekere. *Buddhism Transformed: Religious Change in Sri Lanka*. Princeton: Princeton University Press, 1988.

Green, Garrett. "Challenging the Religious Studies Canon: Karl Barth's Theory of Religion." *Journal of Religion* 75 (1995): 473–86.

Green, Ronald. "Morality and Religion." In *The Encyclopedia of Religion*, edited by Mircea Eliade, 10:92–105. New York: Macmillan, 1987.

Grenier, Richard. "The Gandhi Nobody Knows." *Commentary*, March 1983, 59–72.

Griffith, Sidney H. *The Church in the Shadow of the Mosque: Christians and Muslims in the World of Islam*. Princeton: Princeton University Press, 2008.

Griffiths, Paul J. *An Apology for Apologetics: A Study in the Logic of Interreligious Dialogue*. Maryknoll, NY: Orbis Books, 1991.

———, ed. *Christianity through Non-Christian Eyes*. Maryknoll, NY: Orbis Books, 1990.

———. *On Being Buddha: The Classical Doctrine of Buddhahood*. Albany: State University of New York Press, 1994.

———. *Problems of Religious Diversity*. Oxford: Blackwell, 2001.

Guinness, Os. *The Case for Civility: And Why Our Future Depends on It*. New York: HarperCollins, 2008.

———. *The Global Public Square: Religious Freedom and the Making of a World Safe for Diversity*. Downers Grove, IL: InterVarsity, 2013.

Gutting, Gary. "The Catholic and the Calvinist: A Dialogue on Faith and Reason." *Faith and Philosophy* 2 (1985): 236–56.

———. *Religious Belief and Religious Skepticism*. Notre Dame, IN: University of Notre Dame Press, 1982.

Hardacre, Helen. *Shinto and the State: 1868–1988*. Princeton: Princeton University Press, 1989.

Hardiman, David, "Gandhi's Global Legacy." In *The Cambridge Companion to Gandhi*, edited by Judith M. Brown and Anthony Parel, 239–57. Cambridge: Cambridge University Press, 2011.

Harries, Patrick. "Anthropology." In *Missions and Empire*, edited by Norman Etherington, 239–60. New York: Oxford University Press, 2005.

Harris, Ishwar. "S. Radhakrishnan's View of Christianity." In *Neo-Hindu Views of Christianity*, edited by Arvind Sharma, 156–81. Leiden: Brill, 1988.

Harris, Sam. *The End of Faith: Religion, Terror, and the Future of Reason*. New York: Norton, 2004.

———. *Letter to a Christian Nation*. New York: Knopf, 2006.

Harrison, Peter. "Karl Barth and the Non-Christian Religions." *Journal of Ecumenical Studies* 23.2 (Spring 1986): 207–24.

———. *"Religion" and the Religions in the English Enlightenment*. Cambridge: Cambridge University Press, 1990.

Harvey, Peter. "Buddha, Story of." In *Encyclopedia of Buddhism*, edited by Damien Keown and Charles S. Prebish, 137–49. London: Routledge, 2010.

Hasker, William. "The Many Gods of Hick and Mavrodes." In *Evidence and Religious Belief*, edited by Kelly James Clark and Raymond J. VanArragon, 186–99. New York: Oxford University Press, 2011.

———. "Proper Function, Reliabilism, and Religious Knowledge: A Critique of Plantinga's Epistemology." In *Christian Perspectives on Religious Knowledge*, edited by C. Stephen Evans and Merold Westphal, 82–83. Grand Rapids: Eerdmans, 1993.

Hengel, Martin. *The Son of God: The Origin of Christology and the History of the Jewish-Hellenistic Religion*. Philadelphia: Fortress, 1976.

Henrici, Peter. "The Concept of Religion from Cicero to Schleiermacher." In *Catholic Engagement with World Religions: A Comprehensive Study*, edited by Karl J. Becker and Ilaria Morali, 1–20. Maryknoll, NY: Orbis Books, 2010.

Herbert of Cherbury. "Common Notions concerning Religion." In *Christianity and Plurality: Classical and Contemporary Readings*, edited by Richard J. Plantinga, 171–81. Oxford: Blackwell, 1999.

Hick, John. *Arguments for the Existence of God*. London: Macmillan, 1970.

———. *Between Faith and Doubt: Dialogues on Religion and Reason*. New York: Palgrave, 2010.

———. *A Christian Theology of Religions: The Rainbow of Faiths*. Louisville: Westminster John Knox, 1995.

———. "Christology at the Crossroads." In *Prospect for Theology*, edited by F. G. Healey, 137–66. London: Nisbet, 1966.

———. *Dialogues in the Philosophy of Religion*. New York: Palgrave, 2001.

———. *Disputed Questions in Theology and the Philosophy of Religion*. New Haven: Yale University Press, 1993.

———. "The Epistemological Challenge of Religious Pluralism." *Faith and Philosophy* 14.3 (1997): 277–86.

———. *Faith and Knowledge*. 2nd ed. Ithaca, NY: Cornell University Press, 1966.

———. *The Fifth Dimension: An Exploration of the Spiritual Realm*. Oxford: Oneworld, 2004.

———. *God and the Universe of Faiths*. New York: St. Martin's Press, 1973.

———. *God Has Many Names*. Philadelphia: Westminster, 1980.

———. "Ineffability." *Religious Studies* 36 (March 2000): 35–46.

———. *An Interpretation of Religion: Human Responses to the Transcendent*. 2nd ed. New Haven: Yale University Press, 2004.

———. "Jesus and the World Religions." In *The Myth of God Incarnate*, edited by John Hick, 167–85. London: SCM, 1977.

———. *John Hick: An Autobiography*. Oxford: Oneworld, 2002.

———. *The Metaphor of God Incarnate: Christology in a Pluralistic Age*. Louisville: Westminster/John Knox, 1993.

———. "A Pluralist View." In *Four Views on Salvation in a Pluralistic World*, edited by Dennis L. Ockholm and Timothy R. Phillips, 27–59. Grand Rapids: Zondervan, 1995.

———. *Problems of Religious Pluralism*. New York: St. Martin's Press, 1985.

———. "Religious Pluralism." In *The Routledge Companion to Philosophy of Religion*, edited by Chad V. Meister and Paul Copan, 220–23. London: Routledge, 2007.

———. *Who or What Is God?*. London: Seabury, 2009.

Hiebert, Paul. *Cultural Anthropology*. 2nd ed. Grand Rapids: Baker, 1983.

———. *Transforming Worldviews: An Anthropological Understanding of How People Change*. Grand Rapids: Baker Academic, 2008.

Hirakawa, Akira. *A History of Indian Buddhism: From Sakyamuni to Early Mahayana*. Translated and edited by Paul Groner. Honolulu: University of Hawaii Press, 1990.

Hitchens, Christopher. *God Is Not Great: How Religion Poisons Everything*. New York: Twelve Books, 2007.

Homer, Jack, ed. *The Gandhi Reader*. New York: Grove, 1956.

Hopkins, A. G., ed. *Globalization in World History*. New York: Norton, 2002.

Hume, David. *The Natural History of Religion*. Edited by H. E. Root. Stanford, CA: Stanford University Press, 1956.

———. *A Treatise of Human Nature*. New York: Doubleday, 1961.

Hunt, Lynn, Margaret C. Jacob, and Wijnand Mijnhardt. *The Book That Changed Europe: Picart and Bernard's "Religious Ceremonies of the World."* Cambridge, MA: Harvard University Press, 2010.

Hurtado, Larry W. *How on Earth Did Jesus Become a God? Historical Questions about Earliest Devotion to Jesus*. Grand Rapids: Eerdmans, 2005.

———. *Lord Jesus Christ: Devotion to Jesus in Earliest Christianity*. Grand Rapids: Eerdmans, 2003.

———. *One God, One Lord: Early Christian Devotion and Ancient Jewish Monotheism*. Philadelphia: Fortress, 1988.

Isomae, Jun'ichi. "Deconstructing 'Japanese Religion.'" *Japanese Journal of Religious Studies* 32.2 (2005): 235–48.

James, William. *The Varieties of Religious Experience*. New York: Random House, 1936 [1902].

Jayatilleke, K. N. *The Message of the Buddha*. Edited by Ninian Smart. New York: Free Press, 1974.

Johnson, Todd M., and Brian J. Grim. *The World's Religions in Figures: An Introduction to International Religious Demography*. Oxford: Wiley-Blackwell, 2013.

Johnston, William. "Endo and Johnston Talk of Buddhism and Christianity." *America* 171.16 (November 19, 1994): 18–20.

Jones, E. Stanley. *Mahatma Gandhi: An Interpretation*. New York: Abingdon-Cokesbury, 1948.

Jones, Kenneth W. "Swami Dayananda Sarasvati's Critique of Christianity." In *Religious Controversy in British India: Dialogues in South Asian Languages*, edited by Kenneth Jones, 52–74. Albany: State University of New York Press, 1992.

Jordens, J. T. F. "Dayananda Sarasvati's Interpretation of Christianity." In *Neo-Hindu Views of Christianity*, edited by Arvind Sharma, 120–42. Leiden: Brill, 1988.

———. "Gandhi and Religious Pluralism." In *Modern Indian Responses to Religious Pluralism*, edited by Harold G. Coward, 3–38. Albany: State University of New York Press, 1987.

Josephson, Jason Ānanda. *The Invention of Religion in Japan*. Chicago: University of Chicago Press, 2012.

Judd, Denis. *The Lion and the Tiger: The Rise and Fall of the British Raj*. New York: Oxford University Press, 2004.

Juergensmeyer, Mark. *Global Rebellion: Religious Challenges to the Secular State, from Christian Militias to Al Qaeda*. Berkeley: University of California Press, 2008.

———. *Terror in the Mind of God*. 3rd ed. Berkeley: University of California Press, 2003.

———. "Thinking Globally about Religion." In *Global Religions: An Introduction*, edited by Mark Juergensmeyer, 3–13. New York: Oxford University Press, 2003.

———. "Thinking Globally about Religion." In *The Oxford Handbook of Global Religions*, edited by Mark Juergensmeyer, 3–12. New York: Oxford University Press, 2006.

Kalupahana, David. *Buddhist Philosophy: A Historical Analysis*. Honolulu: University of Hawaii Press, 1976.

Kant, Immanuel. *Religion within the Limits of Reason Alone*. Translated by Theodore M. Greene and Hoyt H. Hudson. New York: Harper Torchbooks, 1934.

———. "What Is Enlightenment?" In *The Enlightenment: A Comprehensive Anthology*, edited by Peter Gay, 383–90. New York: Simon & Schuster, 1973.

Kidd, Thomas S. *American Christians and Islam: Evangelical Culture and Muslims from the Colonial Period to the Age of Terrorism*. Princeton: Princeton University Press, 2009.

Kimball, Charles. *When Religion Becomes Evil: Five Warning Signs*. New York: HarperCollins, 2002.

King, Richard. *Orientalism and Religion: Postcolonial Theory, India and "The Mystic East."* London: Routledge, 1999.

Kisala, Robert. "Japanese Religions." In *Nanzan Guide to Japanese Religions*, edited by Paul L. Swanson and Clark Chilson, 3–13. Honolulu: University of Hawaii Press, 2006.

Knott, Kim. "How to Study Religion in the Modern World." In *Religions in the Modern World: Traditions and Transformations*, edited by Linda Woodhead, Hiroko Kawanami, and Christopher Partridge, 13–36. 2nd ed. London: Routledge, 2009.

Koedyker, John. "Another Jesus." *Japan Christian Quarterly* 52.2 (1986): 167–69.

Koppelman, Andrew. *Defending American Religious Neutrality*. Cambridge, MA: Harvard University Press, 2013.

Kroeber, A. L., and Clyde Kluckhohn. *Culture: A Critical Review of Concepts and Definitions*. New York: Vintage Books, 1952.

Küng, Hans, ed. *A Global Ethic*. New York: Continuum, 2006.

———. *A Global Ethic for Global Politics and Economics*. New York: Oxford University Press, 1998.

———. "Is There One True Religion? An Essay in Establishing Ecumenical Criteria." In *Christianity and Other Religions: Selected Readings*, edited by John Hick and Brian Hebblethwaite, 118–45. Rev. ed. Oxford: Oneworld, 2001.

———. "What Is True Religion? Toward an Ecumenical Criteriology." In *Toward a Universal Theology of Religion*, edited by Leonard Swidler, 237–50. Maryknoll, NY: Orbis Books, 1987.

Learman, Linda, ed. *Buddhist Missionaries in the Era of Globalization*. Honolulu: University of Hawaii Press, 2005.

Lechner, Frank, and John Boli, eds. *The Globalization Reader*. 2nd ed. Oxford: Blackwell, 2004.

Lessing, Gotthold Ephraim. "On the Proof of the Spirit and of Power." In *Lessing's Theological Writings*, translated and edited by Henry Chadwick, 51–56. Stanford, CA: Stanford University Press, 1957.

Levine, Alan, ed. *Early Modern Skepticism and the Origins of Toleration*. New York: Lexington, 1999.

Locke, John. *Epistola de Tolerantia: A Letter on Toleration*. Edited by Raymond Klibansky. Translated by J. W. Gough. Oxford: Clarendon, 1968.

———. *Two Treatises of Government*. With Introduction by Peter Laslett. Cambridge: Cambridge University Press, 1966.

Lohmann, Roger Ivar. "Culture." In *Encyclopedia of Religion*, edited by Lindsay Jones, 3:2086–90. 2nd ed. New York: Thomson Gale, 2005.

Lopez, Donald S., Jr. *From Stone to Flesh: A Short History of the Buddha*. Chicago: University of Chicago Press, 2013.

———. *The Scientific Buddha: His Short and Happy Life*. New Haven: Yale University Press, 2012.

———. *The Story of Buddhism: A Concise Guide to Its History and Teachings*. New York: HarperCollins, 2001.

MacDonald, Scott. "Natural Theology." In *Routledge Encyclopedia of Philosophy*, edited by Edward Craig, 6:707–13. London: Routledge, 1998.

Madsen, Richard. "Secularism, Religious Change, and Social Conflict in Asia." In *Rethinking Secularism*, edited by Craig Calhoun, Mark Juergensmeyer, and Jonathan VanAntwerpen, 248–69. New York: Oxford University Press, 2011.

Martin, David. *The Future of Christianity: Reflections on Violence and Democracy, Religion and Secularization*. Burlington, VT: Ashgate, 2011.

———. *A General Theory of Secularization*. Oxford: Blackwell, 1978.

———. *On Secularization: Towards a Revised General Theory*. Burlington, VT: Ashgate, 2005.

———. *Tongues of Fire: The Explosion of Protestantism in Latin America*. Oxford: Blackwell, 1990.

———. "Towards Eliminating the Concept of Secularization." In *Penguin Survey of the Social Sciences*, edited by J. Gould, 169–82. Harmondsworth, UK: Penguin Books, 1965.

Mase, Hiromasa. "The Fall of Christian Imperialism." In *How Wide Is God's Mercy? Christian Perspectives on Religious Pluralism: Hayama Missionary Seminar, 1993*, edited by Dale W. Little, 53–61. Tokyo: Hayama Seminar, 1993.

———. "Religious Pluralism from a Japanese Perspective." *Theology and the Religions: A Dialogue*, edited by Viggo Mortensen, 443–48. Grand Rapids: Eerdmans, 2003.

Masuzawa, Tomoko. "Culture." In *Critical Terms for Religious Studies*, edited by Mark C. Taylor, 70–93. Chicago: University of Chicago Press, 1998.

———. *The Invention of World Religions: Or, How European Universalism Was Preserved in the Language of Pluralism*. Chicago: University of Chicago Press, 2005.

———. "World Religions." In *Encyclopedia of Religion*, edited by Lindsay Jones, 14:9800–9804. 2nd ed. New York: Thomson Gale, 2005.

Mavrodes, George I. *Belief in God: A Study in the Epistemology of Religion*. New York: Random House, 1970.

———. "The Gods above the Gods: Can the High Gods Survive?" In *Reasoned Faith: Essays in Philosophical Theology in Honor of Norman Kretzman*, edited by Eleonore Stump, 179–203. Ithaca, NY: Cornell University Press, 1993.

———. "Polytheism." In *The Rationality of Belief and the Plurality of Faith*, edited by Thomas D. Senor, 261–86. Ithaca, NY: Cornell University Press, 1995.

Maxey, Trent E. *The "Greatest Problem": Religion and State Formation in Meiji Japan*. Cambridge, MA: Harvard University Press, 2014.

McConnell, Douglas, "Missional Principles and Guidelines for Interfaith Dialogue." *Evangelical Interfaith Dialogue* 1 (Winter 2010): 3–6.

McDermott, Gerald R., and Harold A. Netland. *A Trinitarian Theology of Religions: An Evangelical Proposal*. New York: Oxford University Press, 2014.

McKim, Robert. "Could God Have More Than One Nature?" *Faith and Philosophy* 5.4 (October 1988): 378–98.

———. *On Religious Diversity*. New York: Oxford University Press, 2012.

———. *Religious Ambiguity and Religious Diversity*. New York: Oxford University Press, 2001.

McMahan, David L., ed. *Buddhism in the Modern World*. London: Routledge, 2012.

———. *The Making of Buddhist Modernism*. New York: Oxford University Press, 2008.

———. "Repackaging Zen for the West." In *Westward Dharma: Buddhism beyond Asia*, edited by Charles S. Prebish and Martin Baumann, 218–29. Berkeley: University of California Press, 2002.

Mitchell, Basil. *The Justification of Religious Belief*. Oxford: Oxford University Press, 1981.

Mitchell, Donald W. *Buddhism: Introducing the Buddhist Experience*. 2nd ed. New York: Oxford University Press, 2008.

Moffett, Samuel Hugh. *Beginnings to 1500*. Vol. 1 of *A History of Christianity in Asia*. New York: HarperCollins, 1992.

Mohr, Michel. *Buddhism, Unitarianism, and the Meiji Competition for Universality*. Cambridge, MA: Harvard University Press, 2014.

Montaigne, Michel de. *An Apology for Raymond Sebond*. Translated and edited by M. A. Screech. London: Penguin Books, 1987.

Moreland, J. P., and Garrett DeWeese. "The Premature Report of Foundationalism's Demise." In *Reclaiming the Center: Confronting Evangelical Accommodation in Postmodern Times*, edited by Millard Erickson, Paul Kjoss Helseth, and Justin Taylor, 81–108. Wheaton: Crossway, 2004.

Morimoto, Anri. "The (More or Less) Same Light but from Different Lamps: The Post-Pluralist Understanding of Religion from a Japanese Perspective." *International Journal for Philosophy of Religion* 53 (2003): 163–80.

Moule, C. F. D. *The Origin of Christology*. Cambridge: Cambridge University Press, 1977.

Muck, Terry C. "Interreligious Dialogue: Conversations That Enable Christian Witness." *International Bulletin of Missionary Research* 35.4 (October 2011): 187–92.

Murti, T. R. V. "Radhakrishnan and Buddhism." In *The Philosophy of Sarvepalli Radhakrishnan*, edited by Paul Arthur Schilpp, 567–605. New York: Tudor, 1952.

Nagao, Kayako. "Paul Carus' Involvement in the Modernization of Japanese Education and Buddhism." *Japanese Religions* 34.2 (July 2009): 171–85.

Nakamura, Hajime. *Gotama Buddha: A Biography Based upon the Most Reliable Texts*. Vol. 1. Translated by Gaynor Sekimori. Tokyo: Kosei, 2000.

———. "Unity and Diversity in Buddhism." In *The Path of the Buddha: Buddhism Interpreted by Buddhists*, edited by Kenneth W. Morgan, 364–400. New York: Ronald, 1956.

———. *Ways of Thinking of Eastern Peoples: India, China, Tibet, Japan*. Edited by Philip P. Wiener. Honolulu: University of Hawaii Press, 1964.

Nash, Ronald H. *Worldviews in Conflict: Choosing Christianity in a World of Ideas*. Grand Rapids: Zondervan, 1992.

Netland, Harold A. *Encountering Religious Pluralism*. Downers Grove, IL: InterVarsity, 2001.

———. "Interreligious Apologetics." In *Christian Apologetics: An Anthology of Primary Sources*, edited by Khaldoun A. Sweis and Chad V. Meister, 39–45. Grand Rapids: Zondervan, 2012.

———. "Natural Theology and Religious Diversity." *Faith and Philosophy* 21.4 (October 2004): 503–18.

———. "Religious Exclusivism." In *Philosophy of Religion: Classic and Contemporary Issues*, edited by Paul Copan and Chad V. Meister, 67–80. Oxford: Blackwell, 2008.

———. "Religious Pluralism as an Explanation for Religious Diversity." In *Philosophy and the Christian Worldview*, edited by David Werther and Mark D. Linville, 25–49. New York: Continuum, 2012.

Neufeldt, Ronald. "Hindu Views of Christ." In *Hindu-Christian Dialogue: Perspectives and Encounters*, edited by Harold Coward, 28–46. Maryknoll, NY: Orbis Books, 1989.

Neusner, Jacob, Baruch A. Levine, Bruce D. Chilton, and Vincent J. Cornell. *Do Jews, Christians and Muslims Worship the Same God?* Nashville, Abingdon, 2012.

Newbigin, Lesslie. *The Gospel in a Pluralist Society*. Grand Rapids: Eerdmans, 1989.

———. "Truth and Authority in Modernity." In *Faith and Modernity*, edited by Philip Sampson, Vinay Samuel, and Chris Sugden, 60–88. Oxford: Regnum, 1994.

———. *Truth to Tell: The Gospel as Public Truth*. Grand Rapids: Eerdmans, 1991.

Niles, D. T. "Karl Barth—A Personal Memory." *South East Asia Journal of Theology* 11 (Autumn 1969): 10–13.

Nongbri, Brent. *Before Religion: A History of a Modern Concept*. New Haven: Yale University Press, 2013.

Oddie, Geoffrey A. "Constructing 'Hinduism': The Impact of the Protestant Missionary Movement on Hindu Self-Understanding." In *Christians and Missionaries in India: Cross-Cultural Communication since 1500*, edited by Robert Eric Frykenberg, 155–82. Grand Rapids: Eerdmans, 2003.

O'Flaherty, Wendy Doniger. "The Origin of Heresy in Hindu Mythology." *History of Religions* 10.4 (1971): 271–333.

Oldmeadow, Harry. *Journeys East: 20th Century Western Encounters with Eastern Religious Traditions*. Bloomington, IN: World Wisdom, 2004.

Patil, Parimal G. *Against a Hindu God: Buddhist Philosophy of Religion in India*. New York: Columbia University Press, 2009.

Pennington, Adrian. "Yoshimitsu, Benedict, Endō: Guilt, Shame and the Post-war Idea of Japan." *Japan Forum* 13.1 (2001): 91–105.

Pennington, Brian K. *Was Hinduism Invented? Britons, Indians, and the Colonial Construction of Religion*. New York: Oxford University Press, 2005.

Plantinga, Alvin. "Pluralism: A Defense of Religious Exclusivism." In *The Rationality of Belief and the Plurality of Faith*, edited by Thomas D. Senor, 191–215. Ithaca, NY: Cornell University Press, 1995.

———. "Reason and Belief in God." In *Faith and Rationality: Reason and Belief in God*, edited by Alvin Plantinga and Nicholas Wolterstorff, 16–93. Notre Dame, IN: University of Notre Dame Press, 1983.

———. *Warranted Christian Belief*. New York: Oxford University Press, 2000.

Pomplun, Trent. *Jesuit on the Top of the World: Ippolito Desideri's Mission to Tibet.* New York: Oxford University Press, 2010.

Powell, Mark Allan. *Jesus as a Figure in History.* 2nd ed. Louisville: Westminster John Knox, 2013.

Prebish, Charles S., and Kenneth K. Tanaka, eds. *The Faces of Buddhism in America.* Berkeley: University of California Press, 1998.

Preus, J. Samuel. *Explaining Religion.* New Haven: Yale University Press, 1987.

Priest, Robert J. "Anthropology and Missiology: Reflections on the Relationship." In *Paradigm Shifts in Christian Witness*, edited by Charles E. Van Engen, Darrell Whiteman, and J. Dudley Woodberry, 23–28. Maryknoll, NY: Orbis Books, 2008.

———. "'Experience-Near Theologizing' in Diverse Human Contexts." In *Globalizing Theology: Belief and Practice in an Era of World Christianity*, edited by Craig Ott and Harold A. Netland, 180–95. Grand Rapids: Baker Academic, 2006.

Prothero, Stephen. *God Is Not One: The Eight Rival Religions That Run the World—and Why Their Differences Matter.* New York: HarperCollins, 2010.

———. *The White Buddhist: The Asian Odyssey of Henry Steel Olcott.* Bloomington: Indiana University Press, 1996.

Putnam, Robert D., and David E. Campbell. *American Grace: How Religion Divides and Unites Us.* New York: Simon & Schuster, 2010.

Quinn, Philip L. "In Search of the Foundations of Theism." *Faith and Philosophy* 2.4 (1985): 468–86.

Quinn, Philip L., and Kevin Meeker, eds. *The Philosophical Challenge of Religious Diversity.* New York: Oxford University Press, 2000.

Radhakrishnan, Sarvepalli. *Eastern Religions and Western Thought.* 2nd ed. London: Oxford University Press, 1940.

———. *The Hindu View of Life.* London: Allen & Unwin, 1927.

———. *An Idealist View of Life.* London: Allen & Unwin, 1932.

———. *Indian Philosophy.* Rev. ed. 2 vols. London: Allen & Unwin, 1929–31.

———. "My Search for Truth." In *Radhakrishnan: Selected Writings on Philosophy, Religion, and Culture*, edited by Robert A. McDermott, 37–39. New York: Dutton, 1970.

Ramachandra, Vinoth. *Faiths in Conflict? Christian Integrity in a Multicultural World.* Downers Grove, IL: InterVarsity, 1999.

———. *Subverting Global Myths: Theology and the Public Issues Shaping Our World.* Downers Grove, IL: InterVarsity, 2008.

Ram-Prasad, C. "Contemporary Political Hinduism." In *The Blackwell Companion to Hinduism*, edited by Gavin Flood, 526–50. Oxford: Blackwell, 2003.

Rao, K. L. S. "Mahatma Gandhi and Christianity." In *Neo-Hindu Views of Christianity*, edited by Arvind Sharma, 143–55. Leiden: Brill, 1988.

Reader, Ian. "Buddhism in Crisis? Institutional Decline in Modern Japan." *Buddhist Studies Review* 28.2 (2011): 233–63.

———. *Religion in Contemporary Japan*. London: Macmillan, 1991.

———. "Secularisation, R.I.P.? Nonsense! The 'Rush Hour Away from the Gods' and the Decline of Religion in Contemporary Japan." *Journal of Religion in Japan* 1 (2012): 7–36.

Reader, Ian, and George J. Tanabe Jr. *Practically Religious: Worldly Benefits and the Common Religion of Japan*. Honolulu: University of Hawaii Press, 1998.

Rennie, Bryan, and Philip L. Tite, eds. *Religion, Terror and Violence: Religious Studies Perspectives*. London: Routledge, 2008.

Richards, Glyn. "Gandhi's Concept of Truth and the Advaita Tradition." *Religious Studies* 22 (1986): 1–14.

Robinson, Richard H., and Willard L. Johnson. *The Buddhist Religion*. 4th ed. Belmont, CA: Wadsworth, 1997.

Roof, Wade Clark. *Spiritual Marketplace: Baby Boomers and the Remaking of American Religion*. Princeton: Princeton University Press, 1999.

Rowe, William. "Religious Pluralism." *Religious Studies* 35.2 (1999): 139–50.

Runzo, Joseph. "Pluralism and Relativism." *The Oxford Handbook of Religious Diversity*, edited by Chad V. Meister, 61–76. New York: Oxford University Press, 2010.

———. *Reason, Relativism, and God*. London: Macmillan, 1986.

Said, Edward. *Orientalism*. New York: Vintage, 1978.

Sanneh, Lamin. "Do Christians and Muslims Worship the Same God?" *Christian Century* 121.9 (May 4, 2004): 35–36.

Sansom, G. B. *Japan: A Short Cultural History*. Stanford, CA: Stanford University Press, 1952.

Schilbrack, Kevin. *Philosophy and the Study of Religions: A Manifesto*. Oxford: Wiley Blackwell, 2014.

———. "Religions: Are There Any?" *Journal of the American Academy of Religion* 78.4 (December 2010): 1112–38.

———. "What *Isn't* Religion?" *Journal of Religion* 93.3 (July 2013): 291–318.

Schmidt, Roger, Gene C. Sager, Gerald T. Carney, Julius J. Jackson, Albert Charles Muller, and Kenneth J. Zanga. *Patterns of Religion*. Belmont, CA: Wadsworth, 1999.

Schreiner, Susan E. *Are You Alone Wise? The Search for Certainty in the Early Modern Era*. New York: Oxford University Press, 2011.

Seager, Richard Hughes. *Buddhism in America*. New York: Columbia University Press, 1999.

Shaner, David Edward. "Biographies of the Buddha." *Philosophy East and West* 37.3 (July 1987): 306–22.

Sharf, Robert H. "Whose Zen? Zen Nationalism Revisited." In *Rude Awakenings: Zen, the Kyoto School and the Question of Nationalism*, edited by James W. Heisig and John C. Maraldo, 40–51. Honolulu: University of Hawaii Press, 1994.

———. "The Zen of Japanese Nationalism." In *Curators of the Buddha: The Study of Buddhism under Colonialism*, edited by Donald S. Lopez Jr., 107–60. Chicago: University of Chicago Press, 1995.

Sharma, Arvind. "All Religions Are—Equal? One? True? Same? A Critical Examination of Some Formulations of the Neo-Hindu Position." *Philosophy East and West* 29.1 (January 1979): 59–72.

———. *Gandhi: A Spiritual Biography*. New Haven: Yale University Press, 2013.

———. *The Philosophy of Religion: A Buddhist Perspective*. Delhi: Oxford University Press, 1995.

Sharma, Jyotirmaya. *A Restatement of Religion: Swami Vivekananda and the Making of Hindu Nationalism*. New Haven: Yale University Press, 2013.

Sharpe, Eric J. *Comparative Religion: A History*. LaSalle, IL: Open Court, 1986.

———. "Neo-Hindu Images of Christianity." In *Neo-Hindu Views of Christianity*, edited by Arvind Sharma, 1–15. Leiden: Brill, 1988.

———. "The Study of Religion in Historical Perspective." In *The Routledge Companion to the Study of Religion*, edited by John R. Hinnells, 21–45. London: Routledge, 2005.

———. *Understanding Religion*. New York: St. Martin's Press, 1983.

Shenk, David W. "The Gospel of Reconciliation within the Wrath of Nations." *International Bulletin of Missionary Research* 32.1 (January 2008): 3–9.

Shimazono, Susumu. *From Salvation to Spirituality: Popular Religious Movements in Modern Japan*. Melbourne: Trans Pacific Press, 2004.

Smart, Ninian. *Beyond Ideology*. San Francisco: Harper & Row, 1981.

———. *Concept and Empathy: Essays in the Study of Religion*. Edited by Donald Wiebe. New York: New York University Press, 1986.

———. *A Dialogue of Religions*. London: SCM, 1960.

———. *Dimensions of the Sacred: An Anatomy of the World's Beliefs*. London: HarperCollins, 1996.

———. "The Philosophy of Worldviews, or the Philosophy of Religion Transformed." In *Religious Pluralism and Truth: Essays on Cross-Cultural Philosophy of Religion*, edited by Thomas Dean, 17–31. Albany: State University of New York Press, 1995.

———. *The Religious Experience*. 5th ed. Upper Saddle River, NJ: Prentice-Hall, 1996.

———. "Revelation, Reason and Religions." In *Prospect for Metaphysics: Essays of Metaphysical Exploration*, edited by Ian Ramsey, 80–92. London: Allen & Unwin, 1961.

———. "Soft Natural Theology." In *Prospects for Natural Theology*, edited by Eugene Thomas Long, 198–206. Washington, DC: Catholic University of America Press, 1992.

———. *World Philosophies*. Edited by Oliver Leaman. 2nd ed. London: Routledge, 2008 [2000].

———. *The World's Religions*. 2nd ed. Cambridge: Cambridge University Press, 1998.

———. *Worldviews: Crosscultural Explorations of Human Beliefs*. 2nd ed. Englewood Cliffs, NJ: Prentice-Hall, 1995.

Smith, Christian. *American Evangelicalism: Embattled and Thriving*. Chicago: University of Chicago Press, 1998.

Smith, Wilfred Cantwell. *Faith and Belief*. Princeton: Princeton University Press, 1979.

———. "A Human View of Truth." In *Truth and Dialogue in World Religions: Conflicting Truth Claims*, edited by John Hick, 20–44. Philadelphia: Westminster, 1974.

———. *The Meaning and End of Religion*. New York: Harper & Row, 1962.

———. *Questions of Religious Truth*. London: Gollancz, 1967.

———. *Towards a World Theology: Faith and the Comparative History of Religion*. Maryknoll, NY: Orbis Books, 1989.

Snodgrass, Judith. *Presenting Japanese Buddhism to the West: Orientalism, Occidentalism, and the Columbian Exposition*. Chapel Hill: University of North Carolina Press, 2003.

Speer, Robert E. *The Finality of Jesus Christ*. New York: Revell, 1933.

Stark, Rodney. "Secularization, R.I.P." In *Sociology of Religion* 60.3 (1999): 249–73.

Stark, Rodney, and William Sims Bainbridge. *The Future of Religion*. Berkeley: University of California Press, 1985.

———. *A Theory of Religion*. New York: Peter Lang, 1987.

Stark, Rodney, and Roger Finke. *Acts of Faith: Explaining the Human Side of Religion*. Berkeley: University of California Press, 2000.

Stott, John. "Twenty Years after Lausanne: Some Personal Reflections." *International Bulletin of Missionary Research* 19.2 (April 1995): 50–55.

Stroumsa, Guy G. *A New Science: The Discovery of Religion in the Age of Reason*. Cambridge, MA: Harvard University Press, 2010.

Sugirtharajah, Sharada. "The Mahatma and the Philosopher: Mohandas Gandhi and John Hick and Their Search for Truth." In *Religious Pluralism and the Modern World: An Ongoing Engagement with John Hick*, edited by Sharada Sugirtharajah, 121–33. New York: Palgrave Macmillan, 2012.

Sun, Anna. *Confucianism as a World Religion: Contested Histories and Contemporary Realities*. Princeton: Princeton University Press, 2013.

Sutin, Lawrence. *All Is Change: The Two-Thousand-Year Journey of Buddhism to the West*. New York: Little, Brown, 2006.

Suzuki, Daisetz Teitaro. *Essays in Zen: First Series*. New York: Weidenfeld, 1961 [1949].

———. *The Essentials of Zen Buddhism: Selected from the Writings of Daisetz T. Suzuki*. Edited by Bernard Phillips. Westport, CT: Greenwood, 1962.

———. *Zen and Japanese Culture*. Princeton: Princeton University Press, 1959.

Swanson, Paul L. "Why They Say Zen Is Not Buddhism: Recent Japanese Critiques of Buddha-Nature." In *Pruning the Bodhi Tree: The Storm over Critical Buddhism*, edited by Jamie Hubbard and Paul L. Swanson, 3–29. Honolulu: University of Hawaii Press, 1997.

Sweetman, Will. "Unity and Plurality: Hinduism and the Religions of India in Early European Scholarship." *Religion* 31 (2001): 209–24.

Swinburne, Richard. *The Existence of God.* 2nd ed. Oxford: Clarendon, 2004.

———. "Plantinga on Warrant." *Religious Studies* 37 (2001): 206–7.

Taber, Charles R. *The World Is Too Much with Us: "Culture" in Modern Protestant Missions.* Macon, GA: Mercer University Press, 1991.

Taliaferro, Charles. "The Project of Natural Theology." In *The Blackwell Companion to Natural Theology*, edited by William Lane Craig and J. P. Moreland, 1–23. Oxford: Wiley-Blackwell, 2012.

Taylor, Charles. "Afterword: Apologia pro Libro suo." In *Varieties of Secularism in a Secular Age*, edited by Michael Warner, Jonathan VanAntwerpen, and Craig Calhoun, 300–321. Cambridge, MA: Harvard University Press, 2010.

———. *A Secular Age.* Cambridge, MA: Harvard University Press, 2007.

———. "Western Secularity." In *Rethinking Secularism*, edited by Craig Calhoun, Mark Juergensmeyer, and Jonathan VanAntwerpen, 31–53. New York: Oxford University Press, 2011.

Tennent, Timothy C. *Theology in the Context of World Christianity: How the Global Church Is Influencing the Way We Think about and Discuss Theology.* Grand Rapids: Zondervan, 2007.

Thelle, Notto R. *Buddhism and Christianity in Japan: From Conflict to Dialogue, 1854–1899.* Honolulu: University of Hawaii Press, 1987.

———. "Jesus in Japanese Religions." *Japan Christian Quarterly* 49.1 (Winter 1983): 23–30.

Thittila, U. "The Fundamental Principles of Theravada Buddhism." In *The Path of the Buddha: Buddhism Interpreted by Buddhists*, edited by Kenneth W. Morgan, 67–112. New York: Ronald, 1956.

Thomas, M. M. *The Acknowledged Christ of the Indian Renaissance.* London: SCM, 1969.

Thurow, Joshua C. "Religion, 'Religion,' and Tolerance." In *Religion, Intolerance, and Conflict*, edited by Steve Clarke, Russell Powell, and Julian Savulescu, 146–62. New York: Oxford University Press, 2013.

Tien, David. "Warranted Neo-Confucian Belief: Religious Pluralism and the Affections in the Epistemologies of Wang Yangming (1472–1529) and Alvin Plantinga." *International Journal for Philosophy of Religion* 55 (2004): 31–55.

Tillich, Paul. *Christianity and the Encounter of World Religions.* New York: Columbia University Press, 1963.

Toft, Monica Duffy, Daniel Philpott, and Timothy Samuel Shah. *God's Century: Resurgent Religion and Global Politics.* New York: Norton, 2011.

Trigg, Roger. *Reason and Commitment.* London: Cambridge University Press, 1973.

Troeltsch, Ernst. "The Place of Christianity among the World Religions." In *Christianity and Other Religions: Selected Readings*, edited by John Hick and Brian Hebblethwaite, 11–31. Philadelphia: Fortress, 1980.

Tweed, Thomas. "American Occultism and Japanese Buddhism: Albert J. Edmunds, D. T. Suzuki, and Translocative History." *Japanese Journal of Religious Studies* 32.2 (2005): 249–81.

Tylor, Edward Burnett. *The Origins of Culture*. Vol. 1 of *Primitive Culture*. New York: Harper Torchbooks, 1958 [1877].

Van Cleve, James. "Why Coherence Is Not Enough: A Defense of Moderate Foundationalism." In *Contemporary Debates in Epistemology*, edited by Matthias Steup and Ernest Sosa, 168–80. Oxford: Blackwell, 2005.

Veer, Peter van der. *Imperial Encounters: Religion and Modernity in India and Britain*. Princeton: Princeton University Press, 2001.

———. *The Modern Spirit of Asia: The Spiritual and the Secular in China and India*. Princeton: Princeton University Press, 2014.

———. "The Moral State: Religion, Nation, and Empire in Victorian Britain and British India." In *Nation and Religion: Perspectives on Europe and Asia*, edited by Peter van der Veer and Hartmut Lehman, 15–43. Princeton: Princeton University Press, 1999.

———. "Smash Temples, Burn Books: Comparing Secularist Projects in India and China." In *Rethinking Secularism*, edited by Craig Calhoun, Mark Juergensmeyer, and Jonathan VanAntwerpen, 270–81. New York: Oxford University Press, 2011.

Verhoeven, Martin J. "Americanizing the Buddha: Paul Carus and the Transformation of Asian Thought." In *The Faces of Buddhism in America*, edited by Charles S. Prebish and Kenneth K. Tanaka, 207–27. Berkeley: University of California Press, 1998.

Vishanoff, David R. "Boundaries and Encounters." In *Understanding Interreligious Relations*, edited by David Cheetham, Douglas Pratt, and David Thomas, 341–64. New York: Oxford University Press, 2013.

Vivekananda, Swami. "Impromptu Comments." In *Dawn of Religious Pluralism: Voices from the World's Parliament of Religions, 1893*, edited by Richard Hughes Seager, 336–38. LaSalle, IL: Open Court, 1993.

Volf, Miroslav. *Allah: A Christian Response*. New York: HarperCollins, 2011.

———, ed. *Do We Worship the Same God? Jews, Christians, and Muslims in Dialogue*. Grand Rapids: Eerdmans, 2012.

———. *Exclusion and Embrace: A Theological Exploration of Identity, Otherness, and Reconciliation*. Nashville: Abingdon, 1996.

Wainwright, William J. "Religious Language, Religious Experience, and Religious Pluralism." In *The Rationality of Belief and the Plurality of Faith*, edited by Thomas D. Senor, 170–88. Ithaca, NY: Cornell University Press, 1995.

———. "Theistic Proofs, Person Relativity, and the Rationality of Religious Belief." In *Evidence and Religious Belief*, edited by Kelly James Clark and Raymond J. VanArragon, 77–94. New York: Oxford University Press, 2011.

———. "Wilfred Cantwell Smith on Faith and Belief." *Religious Studies* 20 (September 1984): 353–66.

Walls, Andrew F. "Culture and Conversion in Christian History." In *The Mission-ary Movement in Christian History: Studies in the Transmission of Faith*, 43–54. Maryknoll, NY: Orbis Books, 1996.

———. "The Gospel as Prisoner and Liberator of Culture." In *The Missionary Move-ment in Christian History: Studies in the Transmission of Faith*, 3–15. Maryknoll, NY: Orbis Books, 1996.

Ward, Keith. *Concepts of God: Images of the Divine in Five Religious Traditions*. Oxford: Oneworld, 1998.

———. *Is Religion Dangerous?* Grand Rapids: Eerdmans, 2006.

———. "Pluralism Revisited." In *Religious Pluralism and the Modern World: An Ongoing Engagement with John Hick*, edited by Sharada Sugirtharajah, 58–67. New York: Palgrave Macmillan, 2012.

———. "Truth and the Diversity of Religions." *Religious Studies* 26.1 (March 1990): 2–11.

Warner, R. Stephen. "The De-Europeanization of American Christianity." In *A Na-tion of Religions: The Politics of Pluralism in Multireligious America*, edited by Stephen Prothero, 233–55. Chapel Hill: University of North Carolina Press, 2006.

———. "Work in Progress toward a New Paradigm for the Sociological Study of Religion in the United States." *American Journal of Sociology* 98.5 (March 1993): 1044–93.

Warner, Rob. *Secularization and Its Discontents*. New York: Continuum, 2010.

Waters, Malcolm. *Globalization*. 2nd ed. New York: Routledge, 2001.

Wattles, Jeffrey. *The Golden Rule*. New York: Oxford University Press, 1996.

Webster, John C. B. "Gandhi and the Christians." In *Hindu-Christian Dialogue: Per-spectives and Encounters*, edited by Harold Coward, 80–99. Maryknoll, NY: Orbis Books, 1989.

Wilkins, Michael J. *Discipleship in the Ancient World and Matthew's Gospel*. 2nd ed. Grand Rapids: Baker, 1995.

Williams, Mark. "Crossing the Deep River: Endo Shusaku and the Problem of Religious Pluralism." In *Xavier's Legacies: Catholicism in Modern Japanese Culture*, edited by Kevin M. Doak, 115–33. Vancouver: UBC Press, 2011.

Williams, Paul. "Aquinas Meets the Buddhists: Prolegomena to an Authentically Thomas-ist Basis for Dialogue." In *Aquinas in Dialogue: Thomas for the Twenty-First Century*, edited by Jim Fodor and Christian Bauerschmidt, 87–117. Oxford: Blackwell, 2004.

———. *Mahayana Buddhism: The Doctrinal Foundations*. 2nd ed. New York: Rout-ledge, 2009.

Williams, Philip. "Images of Jesus in Japanese Fiction." *Japan Christian Quarterly* 49.1 (Winter 1983): 12–22.

Wilson, Bryan. *Religion in Secular Society*. Harmondsworth, UK: Penguin, 1966.

———. *Religion in Sociological Perspective*. Oxford: Oxford University Press, 1982.

————. "Secularization." In *The Encyclopedia of Religion*, edited by Mircea Eliade, 13:159–65. New York: Macmillan, 1987.

Wittgenstein, Ludwig. *Philosophical Investigations*. Translated by G. E. M. Anscombe. 3rd ed. New York: Macmillan, 1958.

Woodberry, J. Dudley. "Do Christians and Muslims Worship the Same God?" *Christian Century* 121.10 (May 4, 2004): 36–37.

Woodberry, Robert D. "The Missionary Roots of Liberal Democracy." *American Political Science Review* 106.2 (May 2012): 244–74.

Woodhead, Linda. "Modern Contexts of Religion." In *Religions in the Modern World: Traditions and Transformations*, edited by Linda Woodhead, Hiroko Kawanami, and Christopher Partridge, 1–12. 2nd ed. London: Routledge, 2009.

Wright, N. T. *Jesus and the Victory of God*. Vol. 2 of *Christian Origins and the Question of God*. Minneapolis: Fortress, 1996.

————. *The New Testament and the People of God*. Vol. 1 of *Christian Origins and the Question of God*. Minneapolis: Fortress, 1992.

Wuthnow, Robert. *After Heaven: Spirituality in America since the 1950s*. Berkeley: University of California Press, 1998.

————. *America and the Challenges of Religious Diversity*. Princeton: Princeton University Press, 2005.

————. *The God Problem: Expressing Faith and Being Reasonable*. Berkeley: University of California Press, 2012.

————. *The Restructuring of American Religion: Society and Faith since World War II*. Princeton: Princeton University Press, 1988.

Wuthnow, Robert, and Wendy Cage. "Buddhists and Buddhism in the United States: The Scope and the Influence." *Journal for the Scientific Study of Religion* 43.3 (2004): 363–80.

Yandell, Keith. *The Epistemology of Religious Experience*. New York: Cambridge University Press, 1993.

————. "How to Sink in Cognitive Quicksand: Nuancing Religious Pluralism." In *Contemporary Debates in Philosophy of Religion*, edited by Michael L. Peterson and Raymond J. VanArragon, 191–200. Oxford: Blackwell, 2004.

————. *Hume's "Inexplicable Mystery": His Views on Religion*. Philadelphia: Temple University Press, 1990.

————. *Philosophy of Religion: A Contemporary Introduction*. London: Routledge, 1999.

Yandell, Keith, and Harold A. Netland. *Buddhism: A Christian Exploration and Appraisal*. Downers Grove, IL: InterVarsity, 2009.

Yang, Fenggang. *Religion in China: Survival and Revival under Communist Rule*. New York: Oxford University Press, 2012.

Yoshinaga, Shin'ichi. "Theosophy and Buddhist Reformers in the Middle of the Meiji Period." *Japanese Religions* 34.2 (July 2009): 119–31.

Young, Richard Fox. "The 'Christ' of the Japanese New Religions." *Japan Christian Quarterly* 57.1 (Winter 1991): 18–28.

———. "*Deus Unus* or *Dei Plures Sunt?* The Function of Inclusivism in the Buddhist Defense of Mongol Folk Religion against William of Rubruck (1254)." *Journal of Ecumenical Studies* 26.1 (1989): 100–135.

———. *Resistant Hinduism: Sanskrit Sources on Anti-Christian Apologetics in Early Nineteenth-Century India*. Vienna: Institut für Indologie der Universität Wien, 1981.

———. "Some Hindu Perspectives on Christian Missionaries in the Indic World of the Mid Nineteenth Century." In *Christians, Cultural Interactions, and India's Religious Traditions*, edited by Judith M. Brown and Robert Eric Frykenberg, 37–60. Grand Rapids: Eerdmans, 2002.

Young, Richard Fox, and S. Jebanesan. *The Bible Trembled: The Hindu-Christian Controversies of Nineteenth-Century Ceylon*. Vienna: Institut für Indologie der Universität Wien, 1995.

Zagorin, Perez. *How the Idea of Religious Toleration Came to the West*. Princeton: Princeton University Press, 2003.

Zhicheng, Wang. "John Hick and Chinese Religious Studies." In *Religious Pluralism and the Modern World: An Ongoing Engagement with John Hick*, edited by Sharada Sugirtharajah, 241–52. New York: Palgrave Macmillan, 2012.

Index